What do clowns do?

How do they do it?

Why do they do it?

Through this rich collection of short readings, Jon Davison presents a wide-ranging and authoritative survey of clown theory, history and practices. From the coining of the word 'clown' in the sixteenth century through to contemporary clowning, this extraordinary volume explores clowns in the theatre, circus, cinema, television, street and elsewhere. Davison's stimulating narrative guides the reader through this diverse history, challenging common assumptions and often turning orthodoxy on its head.

This book draws together a variety of rare and classic documents, including previously unpublished material, making it a valuable resource for students, academics, practitioners, researchers and anyone else interested in the phenomenon of clowning.

JON DAVISON is a visiting lecturer at Central School of Speech & Drama, London, where he was formerly Creative Fellow, investigating clown/actor training. He is a co-founder of the Escola de Clown de Barcelona in Spain, where he developed the first ever Clown History and Theory Unit.

READINGS IN THEATRE PRACTICE

Series Editor: Simon Shepherd

At the heart of every performance lies a tension, a tension between the material object and the magical transformation of theatre. Taking elements of theatre such as sound, puppetry and directing, the series explores this relationship, offering both the vocabulary and the historical context for critical discussion and creative practice.

Published:

Ross Brown: Sound

Jon Davison: Clown

Penny Francis: Puppetry

Scott Palmer: Light

Simon Shepherd: Direction

Forthcoming:

Jane Boston: Voice

Alison Maclaurin and Aoife Monks: Costume

Joslin McKinney: Construction

Readings in Theatre Practice
Series Standing Order
ISBN 978–0–230–53717–0 hardcover
ISBN 978–0–230–53718–7 paperback
(*outside North America only*)

You can receive future titles in this series as they are published by placing a standing order. Please contact your bookseller or, in case of difficulty, write to us at the address below with your name and address, the title of the series and the ISBN quoted above.

Customer Services Department, Macmillan Distribution Ltd, Houndmills, Basingstoke, Hampshire, RG21 6XS, UK

Clown

Readings in Theatre Practice

Jon Davison

palgrave
macmillan

Compilation, original and editorial material © Jon Davison 2013
For copyright information on individual readings see the acknowledgements
on p. vii and viii

First published 2013 by
PALGRAVE MACMILLAN

Palgrave Macmillan in the UK is an imprint of Macmillan Publishers Limited,
registered in England, company number 785998, of Houndmills, Basingstoke,
Hampshire RG21 6XS.

Palgrave Macmillan in the US is a division of St Martin's Press LLC,
175 Fifth Avenue, New York, NY 10010.

Palgrave Macmillan is the global academic imprint of the above companies
and has companies and representatives throughout the world.

Palgrave® and Macmillan® are registered trademarks in the United States,
the United Kingdom, Europe and other countries.

ISBN 978-0-230-30014-9 hardback
ISBN 978-0-230-30015-6 paperback

This book is printed on paper suitable for recycling and made from fully
managed and sustained forest sources. Logging, pulping and manufacturing
processes are expected to conform to the environmental regulations of the
country of origin.

A catalogue record for this book is available from the British Library.

A catalog record for this book is available from the Library of Congress.

10 9 8 7 6 5 4 3 2 1
22 21 20 19 18 17 16 15 14 13

Printed and bound in Great Britain by
CPI Antony Rowe, Chippenham and Eastbourne

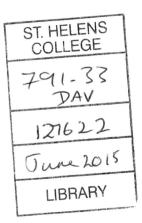

Contents

Illustrations

Acknowledgements

The authors and publishers wish to thank the following for permission to use copyright material:

Alan Clay for excerpts from Clay, Alan: *Angels Can Fly: a Modern Clown User Guide*, © 2005, Artmedia Publishing

Bloomsbury Publishing Plc. for excerpts from Double, Oliver: *Stand-Up: On Being a Comedian*, © 1997, Methuen Drama, an imprint of Bloomsbury Publishing Plc.

Cambridge University Press for excerpts from Bouissac, Paul: *The Profanation of the Sacred in Circus Clown Performances*, in Schechner, Richard and Appel, W. (eds) *By Means of Performance*: *Intercultural Studies of Theatre and Ritual*, © 1990, Wenner-Gren Foundation for Anthropological Research, published by Cambridge University Press

David Wiles and Cambridge University Press for excerpts from Wiles, David: *Shakespeare's Clown* ©1987, Cambridge University Press

Éditions Stock for translated excerpts from Pierron, Agnès: *Dictionnaire de la langue du cirque*, © 2003, Éditions Stock

Faber and Faber, St Martin's Press and David Grossman Literary Agency for excerpts from Louvish, Simon: *Stan and Ollie: The Roots of Comedy*, © 2001, Faber and Faber

International Creative Management, Inc. for excerpts from Mamet, David: *True or False: Heresy and Common Sense for the Actor*, © 1998, David Mamet

Grasset & Fasquelle for translated excerpts from Rémy, Tristan: *Les Clowns*, ©1950, Grasset & Fasquelle, Paris; and for translated excerpts from Fratellini, Albert: *Nous, Les Fratellini*, © 1955, Grasset & Fasquelle, Paris

Joel Schechter for excerpts from Schechter, Joel: *The Congress of Clowns and Other Russian Circus Acts*, © 1998, Kropotkin Club of San Francisco

John Towsen for excerpts from Towsen, John: *Clowns*, © 1976, Hawthorne

L'Arche for translated excerpts from Rémy, Tristan: *Entrées Clownesques*, ©1962, L'Arche Editeur Paris

Nick Hern for excerpts from Wright, John: *Why Is That So Funny?*, © 2006, Nick Herne Books

Northern Arizona University, Cline Library, SCA for the image on p. 253

Pac Holdings SA and Roy Export SAS for excerpts from Chaplin, Charles: *My Autobiography*, © 1964, The Bodley Head

PAJ Publications and Mel Gordon for excerpts from Gordon, Mel: *Lazzi: The Comic Routines of the Commedia Dell'Arte*, © 1983 Performing Arts Journal Publications and Mel Gordon

Philippe Gaulier for excerpts from Gaulier, Philippe: *Le gégéneur/The Tormentor*, ©2007),: Éditions Filmiko

Roy Export SAS for the image from *City Lights* by Charles Chaplin on p. 279

Scott Sedita for excerpts from Sedita, Scott: *The Eight Characters of Comedy*, © 2006, Atides Publishing

Slava Polunin, Julia Shuvalova and Iskander and Bachrom Akramov for excerpts from Polunin, Slava: *Interview with Natalia Kazmina (The Herald of Europe Journal 2001)*, translated by Julia Delvaux (Shuvalova)

The Random House Group Limited, for excerpts from Bellos, David: *Jacques Tati: His Life and Art*, ©1999 Harvill Press

Every effort has been made to trace the copyright holders but, if any have been inadvertently overlooked, the authors and publishers will be pleased to make the necessary arrangements at the first opportunity.

Unless otherwise stated, all citations from works which originally appeared in French, Spanish or Catalan have been translated by the author.

Series Preface

This series aims to gather together both key historical texts and contemporary ways of thinking about the material crafts and practices of theatre.

These crafts work with the physical materials of theatre – sound, objects, light, paint, fabric, and – yes – physical bodies. Out of these materials the theatre event is created.

In gathering the key texts of a craft it becomes very obvious that the craft is not simply a handling of materials, however skilful. It is also a way of thinking about both the materials and their processes of handling. Work with sound and objects, for example, involves – always, at some level – concepts of what sound is and does, what an object is and does . . . what a body is.

For many areas of theatre practice there are the sorts of 'how to do it' books that have been published for at least a century. These range widely in quality and interest but next to none of them is able to, or wants to, position the *doing* in relation to the *thinking about doing* or the thinking about the material being used.

This series of books aims to promote both thinking about doing and thinking about materials. Its authors are specialists in their field of practice and they are charged to reflect on their specialism and its history in order, often for the first time, to model concepts and provide the tools not just for the doing but for thinking about theatre practice.

The series title 'Readings in Theatre Practice' uses the word 'reading' in the sense both of a simple understanding or interpretation and of an authoritative explication, an exegesis as it were. Thus, the books first gather together people's opinions about, their understanding of, what they think they are making. These opinions are then framed within a broader narrative which offers an explanatory overview of the practice under investigation.

So, although the books comprise many different voices, there is a dominant authorial voice organising the material and articulating overarching arguments. By way of promoting a further level of critique and reflection, however, authors are asked to include a few lengthy sections, in the form of interviews or essays or both, in order to make space for other voices to develop their own overviews. These may sit in tension, or indeed in harmony, with the dominant narratives.

Authors are encouraged to be sceptical about normative assumptions and canonical orthodoxy. They are asked not to ignore practices and thinking that might question dominant views; they are invited to speculate as to how canons and norms come into being and what effects they have.

We hope the shape provides a dynamic tension in which the different activities of 'reading' both assist and resist each other. The details of the lived practices refuse to fit tidily into the straitjacket of a general argument, but the dominant overview also refuses to allow itself to fragment into local prejudice and anecdote. And it's that restless play between assistance and resistance that mirrors the character of the practices themselves.

At the heart of each craft is a tense relationship. On the one hand there is the basic raw material that is worked – the wood, the light, the paint, the musculature. These have their own given identity – their weight, mechanical logics, smell, particle formation, feel. In short, the texture of the stuff. And on the other hand there is theatre, wanting its effects and illusions, its distortions and impossibilities. The raw material resists the theatre as much as yields to it, the theatre both develops the material and learns from it. The stuff and the magic. This relationship is perhaps what defines the very activity of theatre itself.

It is this relationship, the thing which defines the practice of theatre, which lies at the heart of each book in this series.

Simon Shepherd

Preface

Comedian Bill Hicks told this story in his show, *Sane Man*:

> I was in Nashville, Tennessee last week and after the show I went to a waffle house, right, and I'm sitting there eating and reading a book, I don't know anybody and I'm eating and I'm reading a book, and this waitress comes over to me and 'tut tut tut tut tut! What you reading for?' I said, 'Wow, I've never been asked that!' Not, "what am I reading?", but "what am I reading *for*?" well, goddammit, you stumped me!' [...] then this trucker in the next booth gets up, stands over me and goes, 'Well, looks like we got ourselves a reader!'
>
> (Hicks 1989)

This book, another kind of reader, has all the makings for being turned into a joke – a book about clown,[1] clowns and clowning, and a serious one at that. Olly Double, the stand-up comedian and academic, begins his second book, *Getting the Joke* (2005), with a section entitled 'I've Got a Degree in Beckhamology' where he tells of the media reaction to his obtaining a full-time academic post at the University of Kent:

> The idea of teaching stand-up comedy at university had all the hallmarks of a silly-season classic, and the press went for the hey-you'll-never-believe-what-these-crazy-academics-are-up-to-now angle. The *Guardian's* piece started: 'I say. I say. Did you hear that they've hired a clown at Kent University? No, really. He's going to be teaching the students stand-up comedy. No. Seriously, laze 'n' gennermen, he's got a Ph.D. in it. Actually, Dr Oliver Double is not a clown, but he is a practising stand-up comedian. And he will be teaching third-year drama students who want it – and ooh, we all want it, don't we, missis! – the art of rambling into a pub microphone and making people choke on their pints with mirth.'
>
> (Double 2005: 1–2)

Of course, the idea of being serious about something which isn't serious, like comedy, or clowning, is funny. In fact, being serious about anything, in the clown's world, is funny. But the idea that we don't, or can't, have ideas about clowns is just plain false. When I was researching this book, I wrote some short reviews of clown performances, books, films and other phenomena, as

---

[1] The last 50 years or so have seen the use of the term 'clown' without an article – 'the' or 'a' – when talking about the genre of clown, in a way which parallels how we speak of 'tragedy', 'melodrama', 'dance' and so on. This usage most probably stems from the description of the programme of studies at Jacques Lecoq's school, and also includes the use of the term *bouffon* (in French), which I have here translated to the English 'buffoon'.

I wanted to find a vocabulary with which to talk about clown on its own terms rather than resort to the terminology of other genres. One clown took offence, not because I had reviewed him negatively (I hadn't) but because he believed that none of us had the knowledge or the licence to be able to criticise others in the profession. Clowns today may on the whole be mutually supportive, as is to be expected given our present low status, both culturally and economically (it was not always thus), but ideas and beliefs – positive and negative, insightful and banal – about clowns are all around us. It might be useful to draw some of them together so that we know what they are and can think about them.

Jon Davison

Introduction: Clown Ideas

I would expect to begin with a clear definition of the field of enquiry, but defining what a clown is is not a straightforward matter. Just about everyone has ideas, preconceptions or opinions about clowns. Clowns themselves certainly do. There is a surprising variety of ideas around about clowns, especially when you start looking beyond your own time and place.

Some define 'clown' in terms of the dynamics of both laughter – 'A clown who doesn't provoke laughter is a shameful mime' (Gaulier 2007a: 289) – and failure – 'this big idiot who regrets not being funny' (Gaulier 2007a: 301). Although others disagree – 'It's okay not to be funny. Clowns do not have to make people laugh' (Simon 2009: 31) – whilst others believe clowns to be sad or to exhibit 'shabby melancholy' (Stott 2009: XVI).

Some define the term in relation to expected behaviour or rules: clowns 'contradict their context' (McManus 2003). 'The key feature uniting all clowns, therefore, is their ability, skill or stupidity, to break the rules' (McManus 2003: 12).

An etymological definition would take us back to the origins of the word clown in 16th-century England, referring to those who do not behave like gentlemen, but in 'clownish or uncivil fashions' (*French Academy*, 1586).

Some identify the clown with the red nose, which they consider to be 'a tiny neutral mask for the clown' (Wright in Chamberlain and Yarrow 2002: 80), which is also 'a quest for liberation from the "social masks" we all wear' (Murray 2003: 79, on Jacques Lecoq).

Some consider that clowning is a route to spirituality and self-knowledge, via 'a great joy, a great confidence, a great acceptance of ourselves, and thus of others too' (Cenoz 2011); 'the main similarity between clown and Zen is that if you are you are thinking, then you are not where you want to be' (Cohen 2005); 'Clowning is about the freedom that comes from a state of total, unconditional acceptance of our most authentic selves' (Henderson 2008).

Some see clowning as a means to relieve suffering, ranging in status from 'respected complementary care providers [and] members of the health care team' (Koller and Gryski 2008) to the more humble friend: 'I would never agree laughter is the best medicine, I've never said it. Friendship is clearly the best medicine' (Adams 2007).

Some believe clowns are responsible for bringing rain to the crops: 'they also fast, mortify themselves, and pray to Those Above that every kind of fruit may ripen in its time, even the fruit in woman's womb' (Bandolier

1890: 34). Some ascribe such powers to their taboo-breaking: 'This "wisdom" magically acquired shows well that this is a question of the breaking of a taboo' (Makarius 1974: 63).

Some think that clowns are a socially useful way to control traffic, since they 'can achieve what traffic police cannot achieve using warning and sanctions [...] by employing artistic and peaceful actions' (Toothaker 2011), but others believe that to be a clown is to sink below human dignity: 'I'm going to earn something, even if it's as a clown' (Partido del Trabajo de México 2009).

At times, some have believed clowns could stop wars: 'The laughter of Bim and Bom almost stopped the Russian Revolution' (Schechter 1998: 33). Alternatively, they might find themselves on the side of governments: 'Nikulin replied: "Who will be the subject of our parody? The government is marvellous"' (Schechter 1998: 15–16). Some think that clowns can teach politicians: 'The World Parliament of Clowns will give scientists, politicians, managers and entrepreneurs, artists and religious leaders [...] immunity to say all their thoughts and ideas and to give all their wisdom to the world without the fear of blame and humiliation. One of the rights of clowns is to fail' (Moshaeva 2006). Others see politicians as clowns: 'In order for the balance to be harmonious, the President must be a whiteface clown and the Prime Minister an auguste, in their nature as much as in their function' (Fallois in Rémy 1945: XIX).

Some see clowns in the street: 'skills that are necessary for clowning, such as [...] street theatre' (Haifa 2006) whilst others do not: 'Dreams of grandeur save the idiot. His ambition isn't to play in the street (not a very comfortable place) but at the Paris Opera' (Gaulier 2007a: 291).

The list is much longer. Clowns have been seen as revolutionary, reactionary, avant-garde, universal, marginal, irrelevant, fundamental, dangerous, harmless, immoral, exemplary, skilled, chaotic, wealthy, poor, innocent, cruel, joyous, melancholic or as fulfilling any number of social, artistic, cultural or political functions as can be imagined.

Today, for some, the clown is a figure that has survived from the past, pre-technological, pre-modern, pre-literate even. For others, the clown has undergone a renewal and has branched out into new and highly contemporary fields: the post-Stanislavskian training of performers; therapy and a means to spiritual self-discovery; or a tool to change politics and decision-making in a world racing towards disaster.

All of these views could be shown to be at least partly true, at least at a particular moment in a particular place. The opposites could also be shown to be true, perhaps in other places and at other times. The point is that clowns, though they may be ubiquitous, are just as varied as any other phenomenon. They have a history, indeed many histories. They occur in different cultural contexts. There are often very precise reasons why they are the way they are. We can usually trace particular characteristics to particular dates, or specific people and places. By looking at a wide range of material on clowns, we can see just how historically and culturally determined they are. If we can see what is specific to times, places and individuals, perhaps we can also see more clearly what clowns have in common, and if there is anything which always holds true for clowns.

Although aiming to be far-ranging, no book can ever be absolutely definitive, so will have to choose not to cover certain ground. In the present case, I have not sought to go more than 500 years back in history, and I mainly focus on the European tradition and its descendents in America, both North and South, together with some incursions into the indigenous clowning of the Americas. The reader searching for information about Asia, Africa and Oceania should look to other sources. For China, see Thorpe (2007); for Iran, see Beeman (1981); as well as more general introductions on Asian clowns in Towsen (1976) and Johnson (2011), or an anthropological perspective in Makarius (1974). On pre-Shakespearean and medieval fools, jesters and clowns there is a considerable literature available to the reader: see, most recently, for example, Hornback (2009).

Containing such an array of perspectives, this book is also bound, at some point or another, to go against the grain of what you think you know about clowns. Whatever one's grain is, it will probably go against it – my own included. And in a way that's what clowns are: they go against the grain. Whenever I see two people in agreement, my instinct is to disagree with them. Maybe that's what led me to be a clown. In any case, it's a useful research tool: a kind of naive scepticism, no malice intended. When two people agree on what clowns are, my ears prick up even more, ready to provide the contrary view if called upon. Or even if not.

So hopefully you will find something in this book that will make you think you might be wrong about clown, which would be no bad thing, since clowns inevitably end up being wrong. I say to clown students that 93 per cent of our lives and actions are failures and only 7 per cent turns out right. That isn't because I or anyone else has done such a scientific experiment; I took to the idea some years ago after reading that 93 per cent of communication is apparently non-verbal. I liked the idea, though for the life of me I couldn't see how you could measure such a thing. So given that the scientist in question was, in my opinion, making it up, I thought I might as well do the same. It feels about right to me, as a clown. When I say 93 per cent of our lives, I mean all human beings, not just clowns. One thing one might say about clowns, though, is that they could be happy with such a statistic. Perhaps that is what marks you out as a clown from the rest. This admission of failure is the bedrock upon which most clown training of the last half-century has been founded (Gaulier, Cenoz, Clay, etc.). The World Parliament of Clowns promotes the use of failure as a form of intelligence, hoping to influence world policy-makers (Moshaeva).

I trust, then, that we will all be happy to give up some of our assumptions about clown throughout the course of this book, and that it will fail to live up to our own prejudices and expectations.

*   *   *

One important practical question in the writing of this book was how to organise such a variety of material covering such a broad field. An additional difficulty is that the relative paucity of general works on clown means that very little groundwork has already been done, upon which it might be possible to overlay an updated view such as this book proposes. For example, mention 'clown history', or 'the evolution of clown costume', and next to nobody will have an idea of what you are referring to. On the other hand, this is also a favourable position to be in because the map is yet to be made and is thus less prone to inherited assumptions about how it should be drawn.

I have elected to take advantage of this and, rather than assuming that each text extract or reference belongs in only one place and that when we find that place we will understand its significance, I have instead sketched out some general themes, corresponding to each chapter, but within which I have felt free to make the connections that seem to illuminate the material on as many different levels as possible. The reader may therefore find themselves asking at times why one reference or text is where it is and not somewhere else. The answer is that it could well be in that other place, and make different connections. This makes for a complex network rather than a neatly organised chronology, which I hope also reflects the fruitfulness of tracing lines of thought which cross the borders of practice, theory and history.

For this reason, each chapter begins with a short introduction summarising the path to be trodden in that chapter, in order to guide the reader through the significance of the text extracts and citations presented.

The book is divided into two parts, the first looking broadly at practice (the 'what' of clowning) and the second at theory (the 'how' of clowning). Chapter 1, 'Grock's Entrée', provides a description of what many have regarded as one of the pinnacles of clowning, as a way of introducing the reader to some of the details of what clowns actually do, and of focusing our attention on the field to be explored. The chapters which follow next all draw in some sense on clown history. In doing so they begin to explain some of the contemporary sorts of clowning and our ideas about clowning today. Chapter 2, 'Clown History', examines the ways in which clowning is moulded by, and moulds its own, history, with a special focus on 'Shakespearean clowns'. Chapter 3, 'Clown and Pierrot', draws on clown history again, but here in order to look at the way in which styles, roles and individual performers evolve, migrate and influence each other. The focus here is on the Italian legacy of the commedia dell'arte and its reinvention in the French and English contexts, leading to an Anglo-French fusion in circus which would lay the foundations for 'classical' clowning at the start of the 20th century. Chapter 4, 'Birth of the Auguste', takes as its starting point the occurrence of the new craze at the end of the 19th century for the auguste clown, later to become the iconic red-nosed clown in the 20th century, and how this new role opened up immense possibilities and permutations for clowns working in duos, trios and solo. Chapter 5, 'Clown Drama', centres on some of the ways in which clown performance is organised, taking as its reference point the mini-dramas of the clown 'entrée', corresponding to the period c.1890–1945. We see how deviations from this 'classical' model give rise to distinct forms of clowning, depending on a range of variables: cultural context, performance spaces and media technology. Chapter 6, 'Death and Rebirth of the Clown', centres on the supposition that post-Second World War clowning was in decline and in need of regeneration, which came in the form of a return to the theatre via the work of Jacques Lecoq and others. I examine here the splits between 'traditional' and 'contemporary', and how this reflects in the work of a variety of clowns today. Chapter 7, 'Clown Women', the last of the first part of the book, takes the growing importance of women in contemporary clowning as its subject, examining the issues this throws up both today and historically.

The second part of the book takes a more clown's-eye view and asks what it is like to clown. Here I ask what performing techniques the clown uses, what their training is and what their way of being in front of an audience is. The questions in this part will be not only 'how do we clown?' but also 'why do we clown?' Chapter 8, 'Clown Theory, Technique and Technology', looks at ways in which clowns and others have thought and theorised about clown practice, as well as the means by which that knowledge is transmitted. I move here from considering some of the 'how' of clowning to addressing the question of the meaning of clowning. Chapter 9, 'Clown Authors', explores clowns as creators and writers, together with the relationship between clowning and text. Chapter 10, 'Clown Training', looks at the huge expansion in clown teaching over the past half-century, examining the key concepts of failure and pleasure, as well as the related but more disputed territory of play, games and rules. I also assess the mutual influences between actor and clown training, and performance, throughout the 20th century. Chapter 11, 'Clown Politics', looks at some of the ways in which clowns have been allied to political demands, whether explicitly or not. Special attention is paid to the development of clowning in the Soviet Union, as well as the ambiguous role of indigenous clowns in the USA, posing the question of whether clowns are a support or a threat to the social order. Chapter 12, 'Clown TV', draws on reflections on how clowning works in the medium of TV, particularly the field of sitcoms, and how clowning is distinguished from other genres of comedy, such as parody and buffoon. Chapter 13, 'Clown Plots', explores a number of means of analysing, understanding and creating clown material, including problem-solving, surprise, and the role of virtuosity. Chapter 14, 'Clown Truth', traces the development of the contemporary concept of the 'personal clown' and its link with the search for authenticity, and asks whether we are now moving into a new phase which reunites tradition with the contemporary. In 'Conclusion: Clown Today', I survey the current state of clowning via some of the ways clown practitioners are using it in a variety of contexts, addressing social, humanitarian, ethical and spiritual issues.

I What Do Clowns Do?

One assumption that grew up in late 20th-century clown training circles and that, despite its age, is still with us today is that contemporary clowning can claim to provide an experience of authenticity. In some cases this claim goes beyond its privileged position and gives rise to the assertion that not only is clowning an authentic experience but this authenticity ousts all other ways of experiencing clowning. In other words, clowning cannot be understood in any other way. For example, John Wright, in his study of comedy entitled *Why Is That So Funny?*, brusquely rejected the notion that we can know what clowns do:

> Asking 'How do clowns walk?' or 'What do clowns wear?' are inane questions. But to ask 'How do clowns make us laugh?' and, more importantly, 'What physical impulses inspire that comedy' will take you to a place where you can find a personal ownership of 'clown' as a level of play.
>
> (Wright 2006: 180)

Wright's policing of this no-go area for contemporary clowns sums up the now rather old-school, post-1968 view that we are all better off since we did away with those nasty texts, authors and anything that admits to being thought out beforehand, and ushered in a new era of spontaneity, improvisation and authenticity:

> Clowning takes us back to basics [...] it's not about routines, or structured material of any kind.
>
> (Wright 2006: 184)

So I would like first to look at some examples of 'what clowns do', because although it has been out of fashion (actually, perhaps *because* it has been out of fashion) for a while, the view of clowning as a highly structured and ordered activity is a very fruitful one. The fruits are 'what clowns do', or 'clown texts'. By 'texts' I don't mean only that which has been written down in words but also whatever is recorded or remembered in some way or another (on film or video, or in the minds of the clown or the spectator). Alongside the post-1960s orthodoxy that clowning is only about play came the belief that, in fact, clown texts don't even exist. Because, apparently, they can't exist. But they *do* exist.

As a clown, I am used to looking out at an audience. Most contemporary clowns, for all their emphasis on the relationship with the audience and their insistence that clowning is a conversation with the audience, tend to be almost exclusively interested in their own inner processes, what it feels like to 'be clown'. But most people are not clowns. It's stating the obvious, but the audience outnumber the performer. The readers of this book will also, I hope, outnumber its author and even the authors cited and extracted here. So the book begins with an audience's-eye view, looking at clowns from the outside, which is what most people do, and first asks the simplest of questions: 'what do clowns do?' I will then branch out into asking 'who clowns?' and 'when, where and for whom have clowns done what they do?'

1 Grock's Entrée

INTRODUCTION

This first chapter presents some extracts from the performances of the clown Grock (1880–1959) at the height of his career between the two world wars. His work is particularly rich in that it includes an unusually large number of examples of different kinds of clown action. It is therefore a useful and efficient way of focusing one's attention on what clowns do, although obviously no single clown will ever encompass all the possibilities.

CLOWN TEXTS

The text of any performance may be written down either before a performance (by either the performer or a writer) or after the performance (either by the performer, a writer, a spectator or another observer). It can be held in the memory, either of the performer or a spectator, to be written out at a later date. It can be recorded on film, video or audio, from which a written version may be extracted. This may sound like an unnecessary statement of the obvious, but a common assumption about clowning is that it is almost always an oral, non-literary form. But the fact is that there are examples of all the above possibilities in the field of clown texts.

Our example, *Grock's Entrée*, is a mixture of several of these. Grock has been judged to be one of the most successful clowns of all time, according to several criteria: international critical acclaim (often referred to as the 'king of clowns'), career longevity (1903–1954), length of solo performance (up to an hour), financial wealth (one of the richest entertainers in the world in the 1930s), fame since his death, skill level (virtuoso musician playing 24 instruments, acrobat and juggler) and loved by audiences worldwide (from monarchs to the masses, in circus and music-hall).

The term 'entrée' refers commonly to a whole clown number in the circus, based on dramatic development, and which has its own place in the programme. In contrast, the 'reprise' is a short sketch designed to fit in between other acts covering the changeover of equipment, according to Agnès Pierron's *Dictionnaire de la langue du cirque* ('Dictionary of Circus

Language'; 2003: 258–259, 486–487). Dominique Jando, circus historian and clown, has a more inclusive definition:

> Clown entrées are the common repertoire of European clowns, short sketches with a precise story and structure around which each clown can improvise according to his/her own personality, and within the context of the story line. Some of these entrées are centuries old, others are more recent (mid-20th century), or have been re-adapted to fit modern tastes. These very same entrées have been used in America by Vaudevillians and Burlesque comedians in the 19th and early 20th centuries, and some of them can pop up from time to time on early television shows and movies performed by these comedians. They are a perfect vehicle for character development and the study of performing discipline and technique.
>
> (Jando 2009)

Although Grock's music-hall act is far longer than a usual 10–20 minute entrée in the circus, it is still referred to as such due to the lack of a contemporary term for such pieces as Grock's.

There are several sources, all containing variants and none definitive. Maurice Willson Disher in *Clowns and Pantomimes* devotes a whole chapter to Grock (1925: 203–220), including part descriptions of his performance, as does Tristan Rémy in *Les Clowns* (1945: 381–412). A script of Grock's performance was published in the journal *Le Cirque dans l'Univers* (1959) by Pierre Paret on the event of his death, and it re-appears translated into English by John Towsen in *Mime, Mask and Marionette* (1978). Laurent Diercksen also includes a full description in *Grock: un destin hors norme* ('Grock: An Exceptional Destiny'; 1999: 206–215), a self-published collection of descriptions, musical compositions, biographical details and photographs, including even the author's oil portrait of Grock. The second half of Carl Boese's film *Grock – La vie d'un grand* artiste ('Grock – The Life of a Great Artist'; 1931), consists entirely of a complete performance by Grock, partnered by Max van Embden. It is not clear how much the later textual publications draw on this audiovisual record, but the similarities and differences will not concern us here. Grock himself also gives isolated details of performances in his two autobiographical works, *Life's a Lark* (1931) and *King of Clowns* (1957).

What follows are some selected parts of the act, taken from my own transcription of Boese's film, together with some details from my translation of Diercksen's version.

THE ENTRÉE

Grock's partner enters playing the saxophone to the final bars of the orchestra's entrance theme. Grock enters, in a huge coat, his head bald, carrying an enormous suitcase in one hand and a chair in the other. Ignoring the partner, he places the suitcase on the chair, opens it and takes out a tiny violin. As Grock is about to mount the chair, the partner touches the violin hanging behind Grock, and Grock gives him a kick backwards. He steps up onto the chair, his huge feet sliding off the chair seat. Using his hand, he places his foot on the seat, slips again but this time mounts the chair, which wobbles crazily. Grock eventually succeeds in balancing and smiles. He rests the violin bow on his foot, where it remains balanced, teasing the partner who thinks it will fall.

Now Grock places the violin under his chin, using it to scrape his chin and neck as if shaving. He is about to play, but the bow slips continuously out of position. Grock returns it. He smiles. He tunes the violin by taking out a balloon, which he inflates and lets deflate to produce a sound, the note of which he tunes the violin to. Grock plays beautifully, the partner approves and, on the final note, Grock sits on the back of the chair. The violin is caught spinning on the end of the bow.

Partner: (*in English*) Very good, bravo, I think you play the little fiddle very well!
Grock: Uh?!
Partner: I said you play the little fiddle very well! You're very clever, indeed . . .
Grock: (*in French*) What's that you say?
Partner: I like your playing. I said you play . . .
Grock: Yes, but I don't understand Spanish.
Partner: (*from now on in French*) Spanish?
Grock: Yes!
Partner: But I'm not speaking Spanish!
Grock: What then?
Partner: I'm speaking English!
Grock: You're speaking English?
Partner: Yes!
Grock: Whyyyy?
Partner: I thought you were English!
Grock: Me English?
Partner: Yes!
Grock: You thought that?
Partner: I did.
Grock: No kidding! But I'm not English!
Partner: You're not English?
Grock: No!
Partner: What are you then?
Grock: Catholic! But I speak English as well, you know.
Partner: You speak English?
Grock: Oh yes.
Partner: Well, say something to me in English!
Grock: Whyyyy? Do you speak English?
Partner: Me?
Grock: Yes.
Partner: But I *am* English!

Grock: Really? No kidding!
Partner: So, say something to me in English.
Grock: In English?
Partner: Yes!
Grock: Now?
Partner: Now! Immediately!
Grock: ... Churchill!
Partner: Is that all you can say?
Grock: Oh, that's quite enough!

(Diercksen 1999: 206–208)

Explaining that he has come in order to play music with the partner, Grock enters a minefield of misunderstandings of whether or not the partner knows him:

Grock: And, so I'm here.
Partner: Yes, it's true, I noticed, you are here.
Grock: You noticed?
Partner: Well, of course!
Grock: No kidding! So you recognised me?
Partner: No, I did not recognise you!
Grock: You didn't recognise me? Whyyyy?
Partner: Because, in order to recognise you, it would first have been necessary that I should have seen you beforehand.
Grock: Say that again...
Partner: I said, it would first have been necessary that I should have seen you beforehand!
Grock: That you should have four hands??
Partner: That I should have *seen* you be ... with my eyes!
Grock: You have eyes in your hands?
Partner: Noooooooo!
Grock: You've never seen me?
Partner: No, this is the first time I've seen you!
Grock: It's the first time you've seen me?
Partner: Yes!
Grock: So you didn't know who it was who was coming back?
Partner: No, I didn't know!
Grock: But it was me!... Do you recognise me now?
Partner: Of course I recognise you!

(Diercksen 1999: 208)

There follows a discussion about which instrument Grock should play, the partner asking if he can play the clarinet, to which he says yes, but he has left his at home. The partner offers his own and Grock is impressed that it is made of silver, asking if the holes are also made of silver.

But what the partner really wants is a pianist. He continues his questioning:

Partner: Tell me your name.
Grock: My name?
Partner: Yes.
Grock: What I'm called?
Partner: Yes.
Grock: Well, my name is the same as my father's.
Partner: And what's your father's name?
Grock: The same as mine!
Partner: Yes, but what are you both called?
Grock: The same!
Partner: Well, what I mean is, what do they call you?
Grock: Ah, you want to know my nickname?
Partner: Please.
Grock: They call me Phili-PPPP (*said with a strange final explosive sound something like a hiccup*)
Partner: What did you say?
Grock: Are you blind?
Partner: I didn't catch it.
Grock: They call me Phili-PPPP!
Partner: But, how do you spell that?
Grock: With a PPPP! You can also use two of them but it's too expensive.
Partner: I'm sorry, it's too difficult for me, I can't say it.
Grock: That's okay, you can just say Phili-, and I'll do the PPPP! Myself.
Partner: Very well, Mr Phili-
Grock: PPPP!
Partner: That won't be necessary.
Grock: Excuse me, I had one stuck.
Partner: In order to play with me . . .
Grock: Without the PPPP!
Partner: Yes, without that, you will need a black suit.

(Diercksen 1999: 211)

Following the discussion about black suits, Grock sings a yodel at the same time as imitating the sound of a double bass, accompanying his eccentric dance. After a quick costume change, he re-appears in an overtight black suit which is far too short on the arms and legs, with a top hat and white gloves. Finding there are no pockets in his trousers, he searches for them but ends up with his hand stuck inside his trousers. The partner leads him behind a screen so he can remove his hand from his trousers in private, but he returns with both of them trapped instead. He again disappears and returns having succeeded. He finally approaches the piano, but finding that it is too far from the stool to reach the keyboard, he rolls up his sleeves and pushes the piano nearer to the stool.

Grock spends a while rolling up his sleeves, discussing with the partner what is most elegant and so on. He removes his hat and falls chin first onto the keys. They discuss what to play, the partner suggesting, 'maybe something classical … Beethoven … Mozart … Wagner … Schumann …' (Diercksen 1999: 212).

Grock scratches his back, using the partner's bow. The partner angrily pulls it out of Grock's shirt, but Grock's reaction is one of pleasure, saying, 'How well you scratch!' They bow politely. Grock plays beautifully, but the keyboard lid closes and he shouts out in pain. The next time he escapes and sticks his tongue out at the piano. He ends up playing with his feet. Grock explains it's because he cannot play properly with his hands with his gloves on. The partner tells him to take them off and Grock asks if he may, although he'd rather not as they look so elegant. He juggles the gloves, rolled up into a ball, as if he were juggling several balls, passing it around his legs.

Back at the piano, Grock plays properly but then makes a clicking sound with his tongue at the end of every musical phrase. The partner hits him and Grock threatens him with the piano lid, which has come unhinged. They return to play.

More chair problems follow, as Grock falls through the seat and the partner helps him out. Back at the piano again, Grock plays delicately and the partner finally plays with him. It works. The music is sentimental. But again Grock falls through the chair seat, and licks the edge of it in order to stick it back. More nice playing follows.

Grock plays the chimes of a clock on the piano, looks at his watch and leaves. The partner drags him back. Now the partner exits the stage. Grock gets his concertina, plays an introduction, slowly steps onto a chair and again falls through it. He is left standing in the hole of the seat, then jumps up and onto the seat back, legs crossed. He wipes his head as if arranging his non-existent hair.

Figure 1 Grock at the piano
Source: Grock (1930) Grock: *Ich lebe gern!* (Munich: Knorr and Hirth), photo by Stone, Berlin

The partner returns and plays, Grock stops him, the partner gets upset and Grock tries to communicate with him by expressing emotions through the sound of his concertina. Finally they are reconciled, but just when the partner is ready, Grock suddenly plays a Russian-style folk tune, dancing at the same time.

Finally, though, the two play together, as virtuosos. We get our concert.

Now Grock is on stage alone. He borrows a violin from the orchestra, a good one. He throws the bow up but fails to catch it and it drops to the ground. He tunes the violin to the piano. The notes are completely different, but it doesn't matter. He throws the bow up again, but he misses it again. In his impatience, he places the violin too hard under his chin and whacks himself. A few moments later he reacts with pain. He throws the bow up again and fails to catch it again. He goes behind the screen to practice, and we see the bow being tossed into the air and when he comes back we know he was successful. But he tries again in full view and fails again. Again behind the screen he succeeds. Now when he comes out he has the violin and bow in the wrong hands. Puzzled, he turns round, and with his back to the audience he places the bow and violin on the floor while he tries to work out what has happened. Then, turning back and picking them up again, he discovers they are now in the correct hands. Shifting his leg position by using his bow, he nearly falls over backwards. His left foot won't budge, so he kicks it with his right foot and falls onto his bottom, crushing the violin beneath him. He returns the crushed violin to the orchestra, saying, 'You know, his one is much better anyway'. Taking the partner's violin, he prepares to play, and without thinking throws the bow into the air and catches it. Realising he has succeeded, he is elated. He is about to try the trick again but thinks better of it and starts to play. The partner returns, takes another bow from his violin case, takes the violin from Grock and plays. Grock approaches and with his own bow plays on the same violin, both of them fingering and bowing the strings simultaneously, Grock smiling out at the audience. The partner leaves and the show ends as Grock marches off.

*   *   *

The 'what' of clowning seems familiar, despite its inherent strangeness. Grock's performance is a catalogue of odd behaviour: accidents, upsets, failures, surprising or unusual uses of objects, verbal misunderstandings, misbehaving bodies, bizarre yet logical thinking, and sudden emotional shifts which project a constant sense that, whilst everything may seem terribly important, it is all just a joke. Despite the recurrence of slips, falls, mistakes, errors and mishaps, the result is not tragedy but joy.

What is not so easy to identify, though, is how it works, where it comes from and what it is for. What does it all mean? Why do we do it? To try to get some answers to such tricky questions, let us move on to looking at the 'when' and the 'who', the history of particular clowns in particular historical contexts. For despite the immediacy of clowning which focuses us on the present moment, its history reveals much of why clowns do what they do. Perhaps then we will be in a better position to say something about its significance and function, and be able to analyse and understand, rather than merely state, what clowns, including Grock, do.

Chapter

2 Clown History

INTRODUCTION

In this chapter I look at clown history from a number of standpoints. The intention is not to produce an exhaustive history of all clowning in all places and at all times but to throw light on just what it might mean merely to consider the existence of clown history, and how that history lies behind many of the ways in which we perceive clowns, their actions and their functions today. History can be used to reveal, to deceive, to inform or to mislead, and clowns have rarely shrunk from the task of encouraging the growth of anecdotes and legends around themselves. In order to unpick these stories, the potted clown histories must be left to one side.

Whilst I am filling in some of the gaps in clown history here, distinct lineages will become apparent, re-occurring in distinct historical periods, whilst responding to the changing performing landscape. The question of whether clowns are omnipresent and unchanging throughout history or are constantly evolving and culturally specific is a complex one. Some clown historians, notably Tristan Rémy, even claim that to speak of 'clown evolution' is impossible.

We begin by looking at William Wallett (1813–1892) and the very particular use of history which was the 19th-century phenomenon of the Shakespearean clown. The relative obscurity of this episode in clowning history has the advantage that we come to it with few prejudices. Hindsight here allows us to untangle with relative ease the construction of this type of clown, and the claims to historical Shakespearean authenticity which were highly resonant of their own era, as well as how it slots into a more general history of speaking, or so-called intellectual, clowns.

We then move on, or back, to the clowns that were actually Shakespeare's contemporaries. Here we have, in contrast, a topic of cultural discussion veritably over-loaded with assumptions, beliefs, opinions, prejudices and knowledge. But we cannot assume that clowns in the time of Shakespeare are necessarily important to the history of clowning simply because Shakespeare's work is important to the history of theatre in general. Side-stepping that question, I therefore take a look at some key clowns of the period on their own terms, privileging 'clown issues' over 'Shakespearean issues' – that is to say, our concern will be more to explore what these performers tell us about clowns rather than what they tell us about Shakespeare.

If nothing else, the second half of the 16th century is important in that it coined the word 'clown' as a term for a new social and stage type, which I examine in the person of Richard Tarlton (died 1588). I then look at Will Kemp (died 1603), examining the relationship between the clown as solo performer and the author, with reference to the sub-literary form of the jig. This contrasts with the onset of a new concept of theatre where the clown's role is brought further under the control of the author, here discussed in the work of Ben Jonson. I conclude with a view of how a new type of clown, or fool, grew to prominence, exemplified in the later plays of Shakespeare by Robert Armin (c.1563–1615), whose performance mode contrasts enormously with his predecessor's.

THE STATE OF CLOWN HISTORY

Although there are relatively few decent books about clowning, which is surprising given its widespread nature, finding summarised histories of clowning is an easy matter, especially since their multiplication in the age of the internet. For some reason a large number of websites and blogs, which on the surface are simply publicity or means of communication for individual performers, companies or other groups of clowns, see the need to include a page on the history of clowning. This seems to indicate an anxiety in the clown world, firstly, that history is important in understanding what clowning is today, secondly, that there isn't enough historical information around, or that we are misinformed and, thirdly (given that these histories generally resemble each other), that almost no-one is doing new research on that history or attempting to update it. One of the better sources of accurate information is Bruce 'Charlie' Johnson, historian of the World Clown Association, who cites Victor Vladimirov, Director of the Moscow State College of Circus and Variety Arts, speaking at the 1993 World Clown Congress:

> In order to have any movement forward in clowning, you have to have a philosophy of clowning. In order to have a philosophy of clowning, you have to have a history of clowning.
>
> (Johnson 2010)

As Johnson points out, 'historical misinformation has led to invalid philosophies' (2010).

Much of the time, though, clown histories tend towards a generic 'potted' version, something like: first came clowns in Ancient Egypt, then in Greece and Rome, then in the Middle Ages we had jesters, the Italians brought commedia dell'arte to the rest of Europe after the Renaissance, there were clowns in Shakespeare, Grimaldi was the greatest English clown ever, clowns had their golden age in the circus at the end of the 19th and the beginning of the 20th centuries, then degenerated post-Second World War, but Lecoq and his followers rescued clowning and turned it into an art-form, and now it's taught in drama schools. Oh, and other cultures have clowns, too.

What this story amounts to is that clowns have existed in all 'important' moments of history– in other words, that clowns are 'important', judged by the criteria established by the ideology of great civilisations. If the Egyptians, Greeks, Romans, Renaissance and Shakespeare had clowns, then we'd better take notice. And, by the way, we've improved on the past and contemporary clowns are better than ever. But such a history makes little attempt to distinguish between historical contexts, nor does it trace how we leap from one great historical moment to another. Historical rigour gives us less reassuring answers, as one of the most respected of clown historians, Tristan Rémy, notes with reference to European clowns of the early 20th century:

> The clown, being of recent tradition, has no ancestors beyond a few generations.
>
> (1945: 14)

Since there is not even enough historical evidence to draw definitive conclusions about the passage from the medieval ancestors of the commedia dell'arte through to the later pantomime,

> it is even more difficult to find the successive transitions that would allow us to state that the actors in medieval theatre are the great grandparents of our circus comics.
>
> (1945: 14)

Rémy suggests that a chronology of clowns, where one leads on to the next one, is misleading. Clowns do not, and cannot, have such an isolated, self-sufficient history. Rather, he proposes that clowns occur in different moments in different societies, being shaped by those moments and societies. In other words, clown history is part of all other histories: cultural, social, political, economic, technological, ideological and so on. If we simply set our sights on what clowns did and how they did it in each historical moment, and how what they did was inter-related to those moments, we might end up with a clown history which is more complex and probably more intriguing than the potted one which re-hashes the march of empires (Egyptians, Greeks, Romans and so on).

WILLIAM WALLET: SHAKESPEAREAN CLOWN

If we consult Agnès Pierron's *Dictionnaire de la langue du cirque* ('Dictionary of Circus Language'; 2003), the entry for 'shakespearean clown' tells us that

> his characteristic is to veer more towards the absurd and the bizarre than to the comic [...] which is why he is also called *jester*.
>
> (2003: 178)

But since Pierron is only concerned with an art-form dating from Astley's first circus at Chelsea in 1768, she is here talking about a kind of clown who appears in 19th-century circus, known as 'shakespearean'. The only other mention the bard gets in Pierron's all-encompassing work of reference is that

> Shakespeare is present in the circus in a parody of *Hamlet* perfected by the comic acrobat Wheal (born 1822).
>
> (Pierron 2003: 178)

John Towsen's *Clowns* (1976) gives more detail about what was an important piece of clown history, today virtually forgotten:

> While some people never tired of Mr. Merryman's old jokes and gagging, there were always those who felt the clown should rise above the level of the buffoon. This demand was answered in the person of William F. Wallett (1808–1892), who helped establish the 'Shakespearean jester' as a part of the circus, supplanting the old-fashioned merryman, Tom Barry, as clown to the ring at Astley's in 1848.
>
> (Towsen 1976: 193)

Whether clowns could, or should, be 'elevated' in this way is a constant theme in clown history, which we shall come across again. Towsen situates the Shakespearean clown in the context of the fashion for a particular kind of speaking clown, dedicating a whole chapter, 'Stand-Up Clowns', to the rise and subsequent influence on clowning of talking clowns in the 19th century (1976: 189–205). His section on 'The Shakespearean Jester' demonstrates both the specificity of the trend and also how it can be seen as part of a longer tradition of comedians with a knack for coming up with a ready witty line even in the most depressing of circumstances:

> Perhaps the best-known European clown-troubadour was the Irish tenor, Johnny Patterson; he was equally popular in the United States, where he performed between 1876 and about 1886. Unlike some vocal humorists, Patterson was known for the spontaneity of his wit. His most quoted remark was also his last. In the summer of 1889, as he lay deathly ill in bed, his doctor optimistically said to him, 'Well, I'll see you in the morning.' Patterson's realistic response was, 'I know, doctor, but will I see you?'
>
> (1976: 193)

William Wallet, broadly part of the lineage of speaking clowns, defined himself in narrower terms, presenting himself most definitely as 'Shakespearean':

> Wallett's erudite humor was popular with his contemporaries, and he spawned a large number of imitators who, like Wallett, capitalized on the British familiarity with Shakespearean quotations.
>
> (1976: 193)

But though he may have been the type's most visible proponent, Wallet is not the originator:

> he personified the nineteenth-century jester-clown. According to his friend Dan Rice, Wallett was tutored in this style of clowning by Joe Blackburn, an American jester-clown who toured England in 1831 as the 'gentleman jester.' It was as a Shakespearean clown with Van Amburgh's circus that Wallett performed before Queen Victoria and Prince Albert in 1844 – after which he capitalized on the publicity to proclaim himself the 'Queen's Jester,' a title he bore throughout his career. To complete the image, he wore a short coat and tights with a matching color design, and on his head an ornamented cap with tassels.
>
> (1976: 193–195)

Wallet's 'authentic' jester was to be superseded by less literary tastes, as the American clown, Dan Rice, who performed with him, recalls:

> Now for the difference between the two clowns. Wallett, when occasion permitted, quoted Shakespeare in an eloquent, impassioned manner that commanded admiration for his ability and scholarly training. I followed with a paraphrase. For instance, once Wallett quoted from *Macbeth* the familiar 'Is this a dagger I see before me,' etc. When I came on with a great flourish I paraphrased it thus:
>
> Is that a beefsteak I see before me
> With the burnt side toward my hand?
> Let me clutch thee! I have thee not,
> And yet I see thee still in form as palpable
> As that I ate for breakfast this morning.
>
> (Brown 1901: 172)

Although his Shakespearean-ness might have failed him at times, Wallet's real technique was based on sharp rejoinders. Once when performing as a monkey-man, a drunken musician played the wrong music for the death scene, which provoked Wallett to quip: 'Do you think any monkey in the world could die to such music as that?' (Towsen 1976: 196). An audience's pleasure in witnessing such a performer is partly in their desire to provoke and test him through heckling:

> At Cambridge, Wallett was a favorite with the undergraduates, who would pay some unsuspecting student to hiss at him on his first appearance in the ring. The clown's verbal retaliation was usually so strong and clever that soon the job of heckler had no takers.
>
> (Towsen 1976: 196)

Nevertheless, he would continue to play the Shakespeare card pedantically until his death:

> My costume, they said, was not correct for a jester, though it was copied from an illuminated drawing in the British Museum.
>
> (Wallett 1870: 152–153)

The pretension to Shakespearean authenticity was not isolated to clowns in the circus. The mid-19th century was thirsty for the supposedly historically authentic, – it was the age of 'archaeological Shakespeare' (Shepherd and Womack 1996: 94).

> The magic which brought some bygone age to life was itself insistently an achievement of the present. It therefore dramatized the remoteness of the past in the same breath as executing its spectacular recovery. Even as these people moved and spoke, you realized that they had been dust for centuries; that was what was exciting. Consequently, the more triumphantly authentic the rendition of the past became, the more conclusively it was objectified, homogenized, resolved into a picture.
>
> (Shepherd and Womack 1996: 94)

What finer example of this could be found than Wallett's museum-piece clown?

Figure 2 William Wallett, Shakespearean clown
Source: Harry Beard Collection, Victoria and Albert Museum, London

Nor could Wheal's circus clown *Hamlet* have had such success in Paris without the renewed fashion across the channel for Shakespeare, which perhaps dates from an 1827 appearance by English actors at the Odéon, a trend upon which the Cirque Olympique capitalised immediately with a three-act pantomime *Hamlet* and *The Scottish Witches* (Rémy 1945: 46). Whether Wallett really did have pretensions to move the clown upmarket intellectually, whereas Wheal may have been more in the business of parody, and whilst the Cirque Olympique cashed in on a new market, all of them played upon the same cultural value ascribed to Shakespeare by their contemporaries.

RICHARD TARLTON AND THE ELIZABETHAN CLOWN: A NEW SOCIAL AND STAGE TYPE

As Pierron observes, the Wallett style was 'nearer to the shakespearean fool […] than to clown' (2003: 178) and, historical authenticity aside, the quip does find a historical echo in Robert Armin's technique, for whom Shakespeare wrote most of the fool roles in his plays. David Wiles, in his hugely detailed study *Shakespeare's Clown* (1987), comments that Armin's publication,

> *Quips upon Questions*, sub-titled *A Clown's Conceit on Occasion Offered*, gives us valuable insight into the Elizabethan sub-culture of clowns and their improvisatory art. We learn that Armin, like Tarlton before him, used to respond to 'themes' flung at him by the audience.
>
> (1987: 138)

But Armin is by no means the whole story as far as clown collaborators with Shakespeare go. Just as Wallett's jester presented his 19th-century audience, accustomed to less intellectual clownery, with a curious novelty, so too Armin, himself an intellectual, provided a glaring contrast with his predecessors at the start of the 17th:

> *Quips upon Questions* makes it clear that the projection of multiple identities is the staple of Armin's clowning. It is this quality which above all else sets him apart from Tarlton's eternal English peasant and Kemp's plain Englishman.
>
> (Wiles 1987: 139)

But although the duality of intellectual/clown is a familiarly trans-historical one, the cultural contexts vary enormously. Wiles tells a number of interlocking stories in order to paint the whole picture at the end of the 16th century. One is of the cultural history of mass immigration to London and the rise of a new social type, 'a clown'. Another presents the evolution of a new stage role, 'the clown'. Further stories tell of the individual clowns, Richard Tarlton, Will Kemp, Robert Armin and others, and how they performed. Wiles shows how all these narratives influence each other, forming a complex picture, which I shall look at now.

'A clown' in the Elizabethan period refers to someone who by virtue of their rustic origins does not understand the ways of the city and who is therefore deemed to be ridiculous and socially inferior. The clown as immigrant to the city is a socio-economic phenomenon:

> The rustic clown was a response to London. London was some twelve to fifteen times bigger than any other city in the country in the 1580s, and was still swelling.
>
> (Wiles 1987: 23)

This clown is also a moral negative, as here in John Northbrooke's puritanical *Treatise against Dicing, Dancing, Plays and Interludes*:

> What is a man nowadays if he know not fashions, and how to wear his apparel after the best fashion? To keep company and to become mummers and dice players? If he cannot thus do, he is called a miser, a wretch, a lob, a clown.
>
> (1577: xvi)

As Wiles notes, the term 'clown' is defined by its opposites:

> No clownish or uncivil fashions are seen in him. (*French Academy*, anon. trans., 1586)
> Both Clowns and Kings one self-same course must run. (Kyd, *Cornelia*, 1594)
> Clean and unclean, the gentle and the clown. (John Davies, *Epigrams*, c.1594)
> In a fool and a wise man; in a clown and a courtier. (Jensen, *Cynthia's Revels*, 1600)
>
> (Wiles 1987: 62)

The word refers, then, not just to a social position but also to that particular behaviour which defines that position – or rather to a lack of a particular behaviour:

> The concept of a 'clown' emerged within a neo-chivalric discourse centred on the notion of 'gentility'. The word 'gentle' has ambiguously genetic and ethical connotations, and to be a 'clown' is the obverse of being 'gentle'.
>
> (Wiles 1987: 62)

The term soon after comes to refer to a stage type. Wiles suggests the first role scripted for a clown might be 'John A-droynes' in George Whetstone's *Promos and Cassandra* (1578), but it is in Richard Tarlton, 'the great comic actor of the 1570s and 1580s, and a seminal influence upon later clowns' (1987: xi), that 'the twin meanings of "comedian" and "rustic" were rendered indisseverable' (1987: 61).

Tarlton's stage-clown fuses two types: the rustic and the medieval comic role of the 'Vice':

> While the Vice exists in a moral/philosophical dimension, the clown exists in a social dimension. While the Vice represents a negative pole in relation to virtue and wisdom, the clown is a negative pole in relation to urbanity and status.
>
> (Wiles 1987: 23)

Not long previously, in Thomas Preston's *Cambises* (1569), these two still have distinct functions:

> Hob and Lob, the 'country patches', are given a risible Mummerset accent, and are the objects of the Vice's mockery.
>
> (Wiles 1987: 12)

But by the time Tarlton is playing 'Derick' in *The Famous Victories of Henry V* (of unknown authorship, probably performed in the 1580s), we have not only 'the fully realized clown type' (Wiles 1987: 12) but also a rustic in London: 'The rustic transposed to an urban setting was the type that Tarlton made his own' (Wiles 1987: 12).

The stage-clown is not just a recognisable type of the times but one of the most important components of Tarlton's audience:

> The majority of Tarlton's London audience must have been visitors or first gener-ation immigrants. Tarlton tapped spectators' anxieties about the rustic boor latent within themselves.
>
> (Wiles 1987: 23)

But as the cultural climate in London moved on, this privileged position of the clown would soon be challenged:

> [Tarlton's] comedy cut across barriers of class, proving acceptable both at court and in the tavern, because most people could accept the proposition that beneath every exterior there lurks a coarse anarchic peasant. By the end of the century, this proposition was less acceptable. Court, theatres, Protestantism and many some-time immigrants had achieved permanence. There was less concern with original sin, more with the innate character of gentility, and with the power of education to change the man. Inversionary anarchy, both at court and in the playhouse, was perceived as a threat to social order. For such reasons as these, stage clowns in the 1590s and 1600s confronted new conditions and adopted new working methods.
>
> (Wiles 1987: 23)

WILL KEMP: SHAKESPEARE'S CLOWN AND THE STAGE JIG

Tarlton's death in 1588 marks a shift in individual clowning styles, as his suc-cessor to the position of most popular clown, Will Kemp, brought different qualities to a new relationship between clown and text:

The charge of improvisation and anarchic up-staging could fairly be levelled at Tarlton, the famous clown of the 70s and 80s, but there is no evidence that Kemp wreaked havoc with writer's scripts.

(Wiles 1987: viii)

Yet it was still not the moment for the clown to be fully incorporated into a closed fictional world of the play under the tight control of the playwright. Kemp was first and foremost a solo comedian, initially loosely associated with the Earl of Leicester's Men, before joining Lord Strange's Men, probably in 1588. In 1592 they produced a new play entitled *A Knack to Know a Knave* in which 'Kemp's section is completely self-contained' (Wiles 1987: 33).

In 1594, Kemp then joined the Lord Chamberlain's men, where he and Burbage 'became the most famous actors of their generation' and where, together with Shakespeare, they were 'the pivotal members of the new company' (Wiles 1987: 34) until Kemp's departure in 1599. The tendency throughout these years was for the clown's presence to be steadily reduced within the play proper and displaced towards the postlude, as a new balance was sought between the demands of clown and writer:

This tension resolved itself in the 1590s. Within the authorial script, the clown was generally given a self-contained sub-plot and a smaller proportion of available stage time than the Vice used to receive. But after the scripted play was over, the clown was allowed the freedom of the stage, freedom for improvisation, rhyming and dancing. The old balance between order and carnivalesque inversion was maintained, but in a new way. As plays grew increasingly orderly, in respect of their writing, performance and reception, the traditional enactment of misrule was displaced onto the postlude. Tarlton had established the custom of taking over the stage at the end in order to sing and exchange extemporal verses with the audience. As the relationship between player and spectator grew more impersonal, as a hunger for narrative was stimulated, Tarlton's techniques were superseded. A contained dramatic action, the jig, became the central event in the postlude.

(Wiles 1987: 43)

The stage jig, as Wiles points out, has received very little critical attention, being a sub-literary form combining farce, song, remnants of folk ritual drama and games, and dance from both folk and courtly traditions. But by all accounts it 'perpetuated the kind of anarchic theatre that flourished under Tarlton' (1987: 47). This fusion reached its height around 1600, according to Baskervill's *The Elizabethan Jig and Related Song Drama*:

There is a bewildering confusion in the use of dance terms around 1600, which points to a lack of distinction in types and the freest transference of features from one type to another.

(Baskervill 1929: 365)

This eclectic creativity would later fall out of favour. Baskervill cites as evidence Richard Brome's later play, *The City Wit*, published in 1653 but the performance of which probably dates from around 1630:

Brome seems to be satirizing the general state of dance when he represents one of the characters of *The City Wit* (IV, i) as saying, 'I can my Cinquepace friend. But I prithee teach me some tricks,' and the friend as replying, 'Ha! Tricks of twenty: Your traverses, Slidings, Falling back, Jumps, Closings, Openings, Shorts, Turns, Pacings, Gracings – As for – Corantoes, Levoltoes, Jigs, Measures, Pavins, Brawls, Galliards, or Canaries.' The best dancers apparently followed their own devices in the interest of variety and novelty.

(Baskervill 1929: 365)

This physicality combines with an elementary plot which typically involves adultery. The connection with folk drama and dance is clear, which by the Elizabethan period had evolved to include

the fool's wooing of the man-woman, the burlesque descendant of the May Queen known as 'Maid Marian'.

(Wiles 1987: 44)

For a contemporary description of this fool's actions, Wiles suggests Thomas Nashe's

the Maid Marian trimly dressed up in a cast gown and a kercher of Dame Lawson's, his face handsomely muffled with a diaper napkin to cover his beard, and a great nosegay in his hand. [... The fool] dances round him in a cotton coat, to court him with a leathern pudding and a wooden ladle.

(McKerrow 1910: I, 83)

It is this wooing which drives the action of the jig. Wife (or husband) feigns death, or disguises her(him)self in order to test the loyalty of the spouse who, believing them dead or absent, seduces another; the trick is revealed and punishment follows. But the morality of the jig is not as simple as this suggests. In *Rowland's Godson*, the servant and the master's wife try to conceal their adultery from the master, who disguises himself as his wife in order to investigate:

There is considerable sexual ambiguity as the triangle is reconstituted, and the husband, still dressed as a woman, sings of his love for his servant.

(Wiles 1987: 51)

Clowning here has far more scope than mere moralising. The question remains, though, why the various elements of the jig, which had existed before Kemp's time and would continue to do so after (the characters survive today as the Tommy and the Betty in English rapper sword-dance, as does the display of elaborate steps and jumps in contemporary morris dance, for example), came together at this particular moment. Was the jig a mere 'fad of the London populace when Elizabethan drama was at its peak' (Baskervill 1929: 6)?

Wiles' detailed analyses of a number of Kemp's clown roles examine how his performing style was a key element in determining the production of the Shakespearean performance text. The clown's performing mode, with its semi-autonomous status with respect to the fictional world of a narrative, opens up new possibilities for the writer. In *The Two Gentlemen of Verona*, Kemp's role of 'Launce'

> marks a transition: in later roles for the Chamberlain's, the clown becomes increasingly integrated with the narrative. From the point of view of Shakespeare, new possibilities are established: Shakespeare is now writing for an actor whose art is rooted in minstrelsy, and who therefore knows how to dominate a stage without support from plot mechanics. This enables Shakespeare to [. . .] create a dramatic structure based on the alternation of different modes of performance.
>
> (Wiles 1987: 73–74)

In other words, as the clown has no need of plot, the plot will have no need of the clown. In *The Two Gentlemen of Verona*,

> For the most part [. . .] Kemp's contact with the main plot remains tangential. While Speed, the proto-clown, is given to bantering with gentry, Launce/Kemp prefers to enjoy his separate merriments.
>
> (Wiles 1987: 102)

If the motor which allows the clown to 'dominate the stage' is not 'plot mechanics' or 'consistent character', then what is it that holds the spectator's interest? In Act II, Scene iii of *The Two Gentlemen of Verona*, Launce attempts to explain his dog's cold-heartedness in not shedding a tear at his departure by using his shoes and other objects to represent his family.

> LAUNCE
> Nay, I'll show you the manner of it. This
> shoe is my father: no, this left shoe is my father:
> no, no, this left shoe is my mother: nay, that
> cannot be so neither: yes, it is so, it is so, it
> hath the worser sole. This shoe, with the hole in
> it, is my mother, and this my father; a vengeance
> on't! there 'tis: now, sit, this staff is my
> sister, for, look you, she is as white as a lily and
> as small as a wand: this hat is Nan, our maid: I
> am the dog: no, the dog is himself, and I am the
> dog – Oh! the dog is me, and I am myself; ay, so,
> so. Now come I to my father; Father, your blessing:
> now should not the shoe speak a word for weeping:
> now should I kiss my father; well, he weeps on. Now
> come I to my mother: O, that she could speak now
> like a wood woman! Well, I kiss her; why, there
> 'tis; here's my mother's breath up and down. Now
> come I to my sister; mark the moan she makes. Now

the dog all this while sheds not a tear nor speaks a
word; but see how I lay the dust with my tears.

All the elements that hold our attention are ridiculous: the idea that a dog
might cry, the emotion of Launce contrasted with the expressionless dog, and
consequently the very idea of sadness; the use of shoes to represent parents,
the confusion as to who is left or right, or the confusion as to whether the dog
represents the dog or not. In fact, nothing escapes ridicule. The clown's freedom from plot mechanics here parallels a freedom at the level of meaning,
where the links between objects, animals and characters and their normal
functions or significance are loosened. This is a clown world, the openly theatrical world of the stage-clown, and not a world of masters and servants,
despite the origin of the role being partly in imitation of a recognisable social
type. The presence of this clown demands a mixed mode of performance in
the play as a whole, and ultimately prohibits the creation of a unified fictional
world:

> Shakespeare constructs character as a set of functions, a set of relationships.
> The dynamics of the stage situation are more important to him than the internal
> consistency of a single character.
>
> (Wiles 1987: 74)

BEN JONSON: THE CLOWN PERFORMANCE MODE

Wiles shows how Jonson's *Every Man in his Humour* illustrates the differences
between this mode, where the clown 'is by definition himself' (Wiles 1987:
79), and the dynamics of a comic character within a world which is fictional
yet is supposed to represent or imitate 'reality'. Jonson's play was probably
first performed in 1598, with the part of Cob written to be played by Will
Kemp. But there is a revised text, published in 1616 and most probably from
a revival some years earlier, where the clown works in a radically different
way. Here are the two versions of the passage which comes just after Cob, the
clown, has claimed that he is descended from a herring:

Matheo: How knowest thou that?
Cob: How know I? Why, his ghost comes to me every night.
Matheo: Oh, unsavoury jest! The ghost of a herring cob!
Cob: Aye, why not the ghost of a herring cob, as well as the ghost of Rashero
   Baccono? They were both broiled on the coals. You are a scholar, upsolve me
   that now.
Matheo: Oh, rude ignorance!

[original version]

Matthew: How know'st thou that?
Cob: How know I? Why I smell his ghost ever and anon.
Matthew: Smell a ghost? Oh unsavoury jest! And the ghost of a herring cob!
Cob: Aye, sir; with favour of your worship's nose, Master Matthew, why not the
   ghost of a herring cob as well as the ghost of rasher bacon?
Matthew: Roger Bacon, thou wouldst say?

Cob: I say 'rasher bacon'. They were both broiled o' the coals. And a man may smell broiled meat, I hope? You are a scholar, upsolve me that, now.
Matthew: Oh raw ignorance.

[revised text]

In the original version, Cob's surrealistic and rapid train of ideas are one step ahead of Matheo. So, despite being absurd and risible, our laughter is with the clown. But in the revised version,

> Jonson establishes reason and plausibility. He expands the jest so that a logical train of thought is laid bare. Cob's fantasy loses conviction when the ghost is no longer said to come to him every night. Instead, the line is turned against Cob and refers to a fish's lingering stench. The introduction of 'sir' and 'Master Matthew' orients the player of Cob towards his interlocutor, and away from the audience. An inaccuracy is then expunged, lest anyone suspect the *author* of thinking that Roger Bacon was really burned at the stake.
>
> (Wiles 1987: 97)

The point may seem an obscure one, and we may ask whether such detailed textual analysis of a 400-year-old text is of relevance to us now. Well, the relevance is that we can still make these same choices, whether we ask, as here, the audience to change sides and now laugh at, rather than with, the clown's stupidity. Furthermore, the author has now taken full responsibility for creating the comedy and all that is to be spoken, and the clown as an autonomous creative artist has disappeared, reduced to being an interpreter only. This is a major step towards the neo-classicism espoused by Jonson, shifting theatre, and the clown with it, towards an imitation of social behaviour. If Jonson's words about the neo-classical perspective on comedy are anything to go by, then the clown has little or no place in the new 'realism':

> Nor is the moving of laughter always the end of comedy; that is rather a fowling for the people's delight, or their fooling. [...] As a [...] rude clown dressed in a lady's habit and using her actions; we dislike and scorn such representations [...] jests that are true and natural seldom raise laughter with the beast, the multitude. They love nothing that is right and proper. The farther it runs from reason or possibility with them, the better it is.
>
> (Jonson 1641: 128–129)

The clown here becomes a device in the author's hands by which a model of behaviour is being promoted.

We can see here two very different ways of seeing the clown's function. On the one hand we have the relative autonomy of Kemp, whose performance mode stands somewhat separate from the creation of a fictional world and is in that way eminently 'theatrical', allowing for tendencies towards the absurd or even the abstract. On the other hand is an author-created role at the service of reflecting society, either as it is or as it should be (in Jonson, what is 'natural' – in other words, decorous and orderly). These two poles are not restricted to this particular period but will re-surface again. The question will be whether clowns are at the service of society's attempts to control behaviour or whether their role is to dissolve order and create chaos. Or both.

The rich clowning possibilities that developed at the end of the 16th century, both within the play and through the jig, recede considerably in the following century. This is in part due to the rise of the 'London realism' of Jonson and others, a world of 'characters' or 'humours' rather than stage functions, or, as Wiles puts it, 'The Shakespearean actor starts with the premise of a situation, the Jonsonian actor with the premise of a character.' When the clown is restricted to a fully drawn character, then 'the ambiguous relationship between actor and role, characteristic of the clown, cannot be maintained' (1987: 70). The clown becomes a mere personality trait rather than a mark of social position or a stage role.

ROBERT ARMIN: SHAKESPEARE'S FOOL

Kemp departed the Chamberlain's Men in 1599. There is no clown part in *Julius Caesar*, performed that autumn, and the following year: 'Shakespeare fails to bring on a clown amongst the "tragedians of the city" in *Hamlet*' (Wiles 1987: 57). Instead it is the tragic hero, Hamlet himself, who now casts himself as the fool:

> It was a significant moment in theatre history when Burbage united within Hamlet the figures of clown and tragic hero.
>
> (Wiles 1987: 59)

According to Wiles, symbolically the multi-modal performance style has been merged into a single individual, through whose consciousness all human experience seems possible, communicated 'through the sophisticated medium of the soliloquy' (Wiles 1987: 60). Although the clown elements within the role of Hamlet are hardly recognisable when compared with the earlier model as personified by Kemp.

The performance style of Kemp's replacement, Robert Armin, pushed the clown as a distinct mode of performance even further into the background, marked by the sudden appearance of 'fools' in Shakespeare's plays, from late 1599. The contrast between Kemp/clown and Armin/fool operates on many levels. As a performer, the soloist Kemp could dominate a stage, as we have seen, so his appearances alternate with scenes that carry forward the main plot, the clown being the leading figure in a sub-plot. Armin, however,

> For a simple physiological reason, [...] could not so easily command the stage in a long monologue. He was of much more use as a foil, or as a distinctive individual who lent visual interest to a group.
>
> (Wiles 1987: 161)

Kemp's clown addresses the audience directly, he is the 'common Englishman'.

The word 'you' as a marker of direct audience address is never found in Armin's speeches. Armin talks to his own alter ego rather than to the audience.

(Wiles 1987: 161)

Kemp's clown was by definition 'not a gentleman'.

Armin belonged to a rising social group. He was an intellectual; a Londoner, and as well attuned to Renaissance notions of folly as to the English folk tradition. As an actor, Armin's skills lay in mime and mimicry, skills which could easily be adapted to a theatre based on satire and the mimesis of manners.

All this pushes the comic roles in Shakespeare towards further integration into the fictional world of the main narrative, and there is no longer 'any necessary tension between the purposes of the dramatist and the purposes of the actor/clown' (Wiles 1987: 136).

So we can see that understanding why certain kinds of clowns occur when and where they do is a complex matter, depending on social, cultural and economic forces in combination with particular individual physical and performance characteristics of specific performers. This dip into clown history from the time of Shakespeare reveals just how interdependent are clowns and their socio-cultural context, despite the fact that one possible characteristic of clowns is to stand outside, to be excluded from or marginalised by that society. The way in which that marginalisation or exclusion manifests will also, of course, be culturally specific. This history suggests that the extent to which the clown is inside or outside the fictional world of the performance is crucial to understanding what clowns are capable, or incapable, of achieving. It also suggests a number of binary terms, which may be useful in understanding the range of modes of clowning, and which will crop up again: realism/theatricality, fiction/fact, character/role, speaking/physical, intellectual/boor, urban/rustic, performer/author, plot/act and soloist/company member.

If we take another glance at Grock's entrée with this in mind, we can see several of these themes at work. His absurd wordplay, most obviously his two catchphrases – 'whyyy?' ('pourquooââ?') and 'no kidding!' ('sans blaaague!') – as well as the non-existent 'PPPP' sound, or the silver holes in the clarinet, reduce the normal logical development of dialogue to dust and surely place him in the same camp as Kemp or Cob. Similarly Grock's whole demeanour, costume and physical actions appear boorish when placed alongside his urbane partner. He is completely out of place in polite society. Yet, as we shall see later, he was acclaimed as the 'philosopher clown' of his time, though not for his witty remarks. He was also very much the soloist, though highly dependent on his partner. I will discuss this further when we come to look at the development of clown duos. From our first look at clown history, then, we can begin to map Grock – and indeed others – into a set of established practices.

Chapter

3   Clown and Pierrot

INTRODUCTION

This chapter is concerned with another part of clown history, and another sort of clown. We begin by picking up the theme of speaking and silent clowns, but our focus will broaden out, via a closer look at the French clown, Pierrot, into considering how variously named clown roles migrate, develop, evolve and occasionally metamorphose into the star attraction in the person of a star performer, the case of Pierrot in France being Jean-Gaspard Deburau (1796–1846). A similar process can be seen in Harlequin in England as incarnated by John Rich (1692–1761) and, more famously, in Joe Grimaldi (1778–1837) as Clown. The specific history here has to do with the significant influence of commedia dell'arte from the 17th century onwards. This becomes important when Pierrot and Clown came to be recruited for the Modernist cause at the end of the 19th century, a move which is fundamental to understanding both the influence of clowning on 20th-century theatre and the way in which our own contemporary perceptions of clowns have been shaped. From here we then move to contemporary reappraisals of historical clowns, specifically the legacy of Grimaldi, and how they tell us as much, if not more, about our own legend-making and what we want to believe about clowns in our own time as about the period under scrutiny. We end the chapter by returning to our chronological story, with a look at the rise of the Hanlon-Lees in the 1870s, the last great development in circus of what the French called the 'English Pierrot', a fashion which exemplifies how clowns often closely reflect the spirit of the times, in this case the harsh aftermath of war, and which next flourished with the invention of cinema.

SPEAKING AND SILENT CLOWNS

Clown speech – what clowns say and how they say it – was touched on in the previous chapter (Armin and Wallett as intellectual quippers, Kemp and Tarlton as plain-speakers, Cob and Grock as absurdists). However, it is noteworthy in general that speaking clowns have been relatively neglected in comparison with what has been written about silent clowns, so much so that in our own time, clowning has been recruited in support of the latest cause, physical theatre. The work of John Towsen exemplifies both sides of the coin. His major work *Clowns* (1976) takes in a wide range of clowning, which is probably partly responsible for it becoming the classic it still is, and it includes much valuable material on speaking clowns. It is principally these passages that I have chosen to draw upon here, but they would probably not be the ones the author would reproduce. Some 35 years on, Towsen has now embarked on an online update in the form of a blog, which includes some of the original chapters, together with material that didn't fit into the book and new posts on a variety of areas of clown research. But what was once called *Clowns* has now become *All Fall Down, the Craft and Art of Physical Comedy* (Towsen 2011).

REVOLUTION, NAPOLEON AND JEAN-GASPARD DEBURAU: THE FRENCH PIERROT

Unravelling the historical shifts between speaking and silent clowning reveals more than clowning styles. The effect of government restrictions on the use of spoken dialogue in certain theatres, circuses and other performing places is well documented, particularly in England and France. The rise of Jean-Gaspard Deburau, who is credited with single-handedly elevating the figure of Pierrot to a dominant role in French pantomime, is usually explained with reference to the effects of such laws on one particular venue, the Théâtre des Funambules (literally, 'The Rope-Walkers' Theatre') in Paris. But just as the histories of talking and silent clowns are in reality one story, so too is the plot of the imposition and lifting of censorship and other restrictions. In fact, as Marvin Carlson explains in 'The Golden Age of the Boulevard', the opening of the Funambules came in the year following the repeal of Napoleon's restrictions:

> but the restored monarchy retained the practice of granting new privileges only with severe limitations on the genre or the method of production. When the Funambules opened in 1816 it was restricted to 'acrobatic displays,' so that when the theatre began to present pantomimes, each actor was still required to make his entrance on a tightrope, which was stretched permanently across the stage. The *Almanach des Spectacles* of 1822 reported that 'The leading man is forbidden to take part in the action and to concern himself with affairs of the heart without having first performed a few leaps and done some cart-wheels.' Even Frédérick Lemaître, greatest of the Boulevard actors, performing at the Funambules early in his career, entered walking on his hands and going into a forward somersault, though his part was a 'Count Adolph' of illustrious lineage. Perhaps the most ingenious director in circumventing such restrictions was Pierre Alaux of the Panorama-Dramatique, who was given permission in 1819 to present dramas, comedies, and vaudevilles on the condition that he never have on stage more than two speaking actors. By hiring a quick-change artist, who could appear as a new character every few minutes, and employing life-size marionettes whose lines

were spoken from the wings, Alaux managed to create the impression of working with a full company.

(2003: 27)

The expansion of popular theatre on the Boulevard du Temple since the 1750s could be seen to be due more to the oscillation between liberalisation and censorship than to one or the other in isolation. The revolution brought expansion:

When all legal restrictions were removed in 1791, Paris already had thirty-five theatres, most of them on, or near, the Boulevard, and in the years that followed, the number rose to nearly one hundred.

(Carlson 2003: 23)

But Napoleon would then bring specialisation. On the one hand, the decree of 1807 reduced Parisian theatres from 33 to 8, each venue having its reper-toire strictly delineated, with rights to their respective genres: new plays, opera, melodrama, ballet, light comedy, pre-revolutionary comedy and so on. On the other hand, this decree did not cover those entertainments considered to be outside the 'legitimate' genres, and so had little effect on the popular offerings of the Boulevard du Temple. And so it was that the turbulent his-tory of political control of theatre meant that '[b]ecause of their diversity, a large number of theatres were able to coexist on the Boulevard without any problems of competition' (Carlson 2003: 29).

But although this very specific political and cultural context may explain the existence of the Funambules, the genre of performances presented there, and even its audience, it is to Deburau that we should turn in order to explain the rise of Pierrot as the icon of French clowning. In his performing career between 1819 and his death in 1846, he transformed the role from the dumb butt of Harlequin's trickery into the star of the show.

PIERROT, PEDROLINO AND THE MIGRATION OF COMMEDIA DELL'ARTE

Tristan Rémy, the mid-20th century French historian of clown and circus, dedicated substantial space to Deburau in *Les Clowns* (1945), a work which, despite being the nearest we have to a definitive history and analysis of clowns, has never been translated into English. Rémy later expanded his analysis into a whole book, *Jean-Gaspard Deburau* (1954).

Pierrot was in one sense a French derivative of the Italian Pedrolino, a minor mask from the commedia dell'arte – basically a simple and credulous peasant – as described by Barry Grantham in *Playing Commedia*:

Pedrolino was one of a number of 'useful' Masks, who could be called upon to ful-fil various requirements of the scenario. These could be anything from the lowest of the Zanni – introduced when Arlecchino's native intelligence took him up a rung or two, leaving a space at the bottom of the ladder – to the role of a respected upper servant and companion to the Innamorato.

(2000: 199)

Giaratoni, variously referred to as Giaraton, Jératon or Jaraton, is credited with being the first Pierrot in 1673 in *La Suite du festin de Pierre,* performing with the Comédie-Italienne, the professional Italian company sponsored by the French king (Campardon 1880: 245). Rémy, drawing on Maurice Sand's *Masques et Bouffons* (1860), traces the lineage of Pierrots appearing at fairs throughout the early 18th century, from Prévot in 1707 to Pietro Sodi in 1749 (Rémy 1945: 34). Deburau, however, did not simply inherit the role handed down to him but added elements from his former experience as a 'paillasse', a ridiculous and clumsy clown which Isabelle Baugé describes as

that type of artist who remained at the theatre entrance and attracted the spectators by their acrobatic or comic displays.

(Baugé 1995: 8)

He also appropriated character traits from other roles:

He gave [to the part] both the faults and the qualities of the heroes of the Italian Comedy, cowardly and reckless like Matamoro, silly like Arlecchino, cunning like Brighella, swindling like Scapin, proud like Pulcinella, miserly like Pantalone. He not only incarnated the known characters of commedia, but he also costumed them in social roles: soldier, coalman, rag-and-bone man, chimney sweep, judge, poet, philosopher, all people of noble status. Thus Deburau's Pierrot heralds the clown who will take its costume from, and personify, according to the scene, such-and-such a representative of the social hierarchy.

(Rémy 1945: 34)

ARLECCHINO, ARLEQUIN AND HARLEQUIN

It is not the first or the last time that a dominant individual performer has taken a role that previously was one amongst many and transformed it into the protagonist. Grimaldi famously put Clown himself centre stage in English pantomime. Before that it was John Rich (1692–1761), director and theatre manager, who not only re-worked Harlequin for the English stage but is generally credited with having transformed the Italian comedy into the English pantomime. The Italian trickster Arlecchino became Rich's mute, dancing Harlequin.

Early in the eighteenth century in London Harlequin took the lead from Mezzetin, Scaramouch and other popular *Commedia* figures, largely because of the personal ascendancy of John Rich, who was not only one of the most powerful men in British show business, as manager of Covent Garden theatre, but was also (as Lun) the star Harlequin of his own pantomimes for some thirty years.

(Findlater 1978: 27)

Les Cosaques (?)

Le Souffre-douleur

Les jolis soldats

Le Billet de mille francs

Figure 3 Four roles of Jean-Gaspard Deburau
Source: Lithographs by Auguste Bouquet in Rémy, Tristan (1954) *Jean-Gaspard Deburau* (Paris: L'Arche)

Maurice Willson Disher considered that Harlequin was highly significant to the history of the English theatre not only because 'No other character has made so many appearances on the stage' (1925: 67) but principally because he represented the re-introduction of the comic who had been marginalised in the 17th century:

[Harlequin's] conquest of the London stage was due to the neglect of the Elizabethan tradition of thrills mingled with laughter. He is the symbol of the drama's failure to fulfil humanity's needs.

(1925: 67)

Those needs were not being met:

The fool of the Restoration was a whipping-stock for the gallants. The poets of the London stage were seeking to emulate French models, but were unable to bring themselves to adopt Moliere's clown. [...] Our notion has ever been that a serving-man may be as outspoken as he will, but not cunning without forfeiting sympathy.

(1925: 72)

This chimes with Wiles' analysis of the decadence of the clown role brought on by the shift towards realism as discussed earlier in relation to Jonson. But, according to Disher, resistance to the Italian invasion was useless. Fiurelli's visit to London in 1673 provoked both emulation and rejection:

Immediately his name became a part of the English language as a term of abuse far more effective than 'Fool' or 'Clown,' and his costume all the rage in masquerades. His success was even more disastrous to the English companies than the competition of the puppets.

(1925: 73)

Disher cites a Dryden epilogue as evidence of English grievances against the Italians:

A French troop first swept all things in its way;
But those hot Monsieurs were too quick to stay:
Yet, to our cost, in that short time, we find
They left their itch of novelty behind.
The Italian merry-andrews took their place,
And quite debauched the stage with lewd grimace:
Instead of wit, and humours, your delight
Was there to see two hobby-horses fight;
Stout Scaramoucha with rush lance rode in,
And ran a tilt at centaur Arlequin.
For love you heard how amorous asses brayed,
And cats in gutters gave their serenade.

(Dryden 1811: 463–464)

The very use here of the term 'merry-andrew' is itself testimony to the comings and goings of clown types associated with particular times and particular nations. As a word meaning 'clown', it was probably coined in early 16th-century England, after the clowns who copied the humour of Andrew Borde, physician to Henry VIII. To refer to an 'Italian merry-andrew', then, is ironic in the context of a complaint about cultural colonisation, but a similar process can be seen at a later date – for example, in the French description of the 'English Pierrot'.

Strangely enough, Fiurelli's reputation in France, where he was a major influence on Molière, was for having introduced a more refined style of performance. And it was supposedly Fiurelli's success in stopping the young French dauphin from crying which led to an increase in value of his role, Scaramouche, and a subsequent higher billing in the cast of commedia dell'arte characters.

The English had some catching up to do, for which imitation and direct copying were the quickest routes:

> Both the London theatres in 1677 prepared translations of *Les Fourberies de Scapin*. Dorset Gardens was first in the field with Otway's version. Drury Lane was therefore unwilling to stage Ravenscroft's.
>
> (1925: 73–74)

Ravenscroft's solution was to present his version as an adaptation, under a different title: *Scaramouche a Philosopher, Harlequin, a Schoolboy, Bravo, Merchant and Magician; a Comedy after the Italian Manner.*

HARLEQUIN AND CLOWN: THE HARLEQUINADE

Some commentators (Smith 1916, Lea 1934) give 1604 as the date for the earliest influence of the commedia dell'arte on English theatre (on the work of Middleton). Disher's opinion, on the other hand, is that the Italian influence steadily made itself felt later, notably with the appearance of Scaramouche and Harlequin in Mountford's 1685 version of Marlowe's *Dr Faustus*:

> The parts of Wagner and Robin are played by Scaramouche, and the Clown and Dick by Harlequin. They meet in a street scene, where Harlequin raps at a door and strikes Scaramouche who opens it. The Pope's feast is changed into a haunted banquet. They conjure up the devil, who sends them 'the giant which St. George destroyed' – since then rotting in the earth – to do their bidding. After Scaramouche has got upon Harlequin's shoulders to salute the ambassador infernal, the giant remarks 'I can divide myself to serve my friends,' breaks in two and commands his breeches to be his page. He conducts them to a feast. Then 'The upper part of the giant flies up, and the under sinks, and discovers a woman in the room.' They kiss her: 'Woman sinks, a flash of lightning.' The table 'removes,' then 'flies up into the air,' they are 'hoisted up to the table,' then the table flies down, and they are let down to the table. When Harlequin takes off the lid of the pasty 'a stag's head peeps out, and out of the pot of fowl flies birds.' Harlequin and Scaramouche fall over their chairs. For want of oil and vinegar Harlequin fetches a lamp and a chamber-pot. The bread 'stirs,' the table sinks amid a flash of lightning, bottles fly up and chairs rise. Harlequin and Scaramouche are caught fast when they sit down. Several Devils black the faces of both, and then squirt milk upon them. Alter a dance they both sink. At the end the Doctor's limbs 'all torn asunder by the hand of hell' come together to provide dance and song.
>
> (Disher 1925: 76–77)

Other imitators and borrowers followed, though the actual extent of that influence is less obvious. Disher includes here Aphra Behn's 1687 *The Emperor of the Moon*, an English version of *Arlequin Empereur dans la Lune* (1684), which is adjudged by Disher as having at once copied and neglected the original:

> The tricks performed in Paris by that most famous of Arlequins, Giuseppe Domenico Biancolelli, are the same as those set down for Jevon. [...] but while the *lazzi* of the original bear on the story the by-play of Aphra Behn's version is inconsequential.
>
> (1925: 77–78)

It is questionable how far we can take Disher's judgement on Aphra Behn's play as being 'an artless imitation of a witty original' (1925: 78) as definitive, as neither he nor we really know how that original might have been performed. What we do know is that Behn's version remained popular until the beginning of the 18th century, 'as letters to *The Spectator* prove' (Disher 1925: 78).

But, according to Disher, England would have to wait a while for its chance of full enjoyment:

> The English Harlequinades of the seventeenth century were but dim shadows, in their byplay as well as in their wit, of the scintillating inventions of the Italian troupe in Paris from 1682 to 1697. Their performances at the Hotel de Bourgogne were inspired by a delight as fresh as that of the nursery in all the objects, common or uncommon, in the world. Most of the tricks of the modern pantomime can be traced to them.
>
> (1925: 80)

Further transformations of Harlequin were to follow:

> Both in France and England he suffered many changes. At the fairs he was long retained as the mountebank's man, but otherwise ceased to be a clown. Marivaux turned him into a pretty simpleton and London pantomimes into a romantic magician. In Italy, however, he remained a comic country servant in the nineteenth century.
>
> (Disher 1925: 82)

Barry Grantham, commedia dell'arte specialist (although these days perhaps better known for his expertise in the genre of eccentric dance), whose career has spanned several decades, has a clear historical perspective in *Commedia Plays – Scenarios, Scripts, Lazzi*, the stated aim of which is to give the reader a collection of texts form different periods that may be of practical use in teaching and performing. His offering from the mid-19th century is *The Haunting of Pantaloon*, which he bases on 'early Victorian "spoken" Harlequinades and a popular theme inspired by Dickens' (2006: 110). Here is Grantham's telling of the history of Pantaloon, Harlequin and Clown:

In the seventeenth century when the *Commedia dell'Arte* eventually succeeded in getting a foothold in England, two traditions were soon established, depending on which actor played the leading role. Performers like John Rich (known as 'Lun'), whose talent was for mime rather than speech, presented a silent Harlequin, but others, like Garrick himself, spoke a scripted version. The source material from this date (complete plays not just scenarios) is plentiful, but piteously infantile. How the mighty Masks of the *Commedia dell'Arte* have fallen! Pantalone has become Pantaloon – a two-dimensional character with hardly a saving grace, inflexible in mind but so weak in body that he must rely on his henchman, Clown, to carry out his tyrannical demands. He is very old, too old one would have thought to have fathered a Columbine, very much younger than her predecessor Colombina, and a creature as simpering as the most feeble of Dickens' heroines. Worst of all, the earthy Arlecchino has become the tiptoeing Harlequin, with the intelligence of a three-year-old. This may be blamed on the fourth character, Clown; or, one should say, on Joseph Grimaldi, creator of the role. In the early years of the nineteenth century Grimaldi presented a character of such comic genius, that it stole from Arlecchino the comic lead, and diminished him to the status of dancing partner and characterless lover.

(2006: 112)

And here a typical scene:

Scene 2
Harlequin, Clown.
Clown laughs at Harlequin for being called a Jackanapes. Although Harlequin has no idea what a Jackanapes is, he doesn't like being called one. Clown teases him, and Harlequin chases him with his slapstick. Clown stops running and asks why he is being hit. Harlequin says his name is 'Harlequin', and he doesn't like to be called other things. They perform several *'Name' Lazzi* including one involving the audience, before leaving the matter and discussing what Harlequin is going to do about his love for Columbine. Clown suggests that he write her a letter, which he, Clown, will deliver. Clown provides paper, pen and ink, and his back as a writing board. They part in opposite directions, Clown promising to put the letter into Columbine's hands.

(2006: 113)

Harlequin here, rather than moving up the social ladder within the pantomime cast-list, has slipped right down to the bottom. In any case, an opening was to be had for whoever could fill the role left vacant.

JOEY GRIMALDI: CLOWN LEGEND

Here is Joey the Clown, the first of 10,000 Joeys who took their name from him; here is the genius of English fun, in the holiday splendour of his reign at Sadler's Wells and Covent Garden: here is Joseph Grimaldi, who during his lifetime (1778 to 1837) was generally acclaimed as the funniest and best-loved man in the British theatre. Look how he strides across the stage, 'some dozen paces to the mile', then vaults and capers in the air, squeaking in a delirium of mischief. See with what joy serene he pockets a pig or steals a string of sausages; watch him nurse a saw-dust baby or serenade a chambermaid; listen to him sing, with changing voices, some rhyming nonsense that sets the theatre in a roar. Now he appears all topsy-turvy, with two odd eyebrows, a pair of left-and-right eyes, a wry nose, a crooked mouth, two left legs and a free and easy body without any bone in it and apparently without any centre of gravity.

(Findlater 1978: 9–10)

This description, taken from Thomas Hood's recollections in 1828 of Grimaldi in his heyday, begins Richard Findlater's 1955 biography, *Joe Grimaldi, His Life and Theatre*. Findlater's work is of considerable rigour, which would be difficult to better, though some have tried. It does not escape entirely, though, from a tendency seemingly common in writings about Grimaldi to meander into whimsical descriptions based on the author's own imaginings of a performer whom it is difficult to imagine. Hence the fantasies.

For our purposes these fantasies around Grimaldi provide a useful introduction to the processes by which clown mythology is constructed. This work of construction of clown images and activities is the main subject of this section on Grimaldi. The man himself is the subject of the following section.

Andrew McConnell Stott's *The Pantomime Life of Joseph Grimaldi* (2009), although containing perhaps just as many facts and figures as Findlater's work, draws its strength more from being written as 'a good read' (evidenced by its swift serialised reading on BBC Radio 4, as well as rave newspaper reviews and the Sheridan Morley Prize for Theatre Biography):

Andrew McConnell Stott's engaging book does not limit itself to the known facts of Grimaldi's life, which are rather skimpy. Instead it presents a fantastic panorama of stage history ... McConnell Stott recounts these wonders with infectious brio.

(John Carey in *The Sunday Times* 11 October 2009)

Curiously, though, such general acceptance with a wider book-reading audience appears to be bought at the risk of alienating clown-lovers. In his prologue, Stott uses a description of his visit to the annual clown service in memory of Grimaldi at a church in Dalston to set a cool and cynical tone:

There's nothing particularly funny about Hackney [... the clowns] stood around drinking tea and being disarmingly normal, a friendly and excited group of children's entertainers and retired circus acts clearly at home with the level of glamour implied by the scuffed-up Scout hall they used as a dressing room. Augustes and Pierrots swapped news with American hobos, while a Coco with a pin head and a tiny bowler hat seemingly reassured his colleague about his prosthetic forehead and mechanical eyebrows. Were it not for the extravagant dress, they could have been any other group of people with a shared enthusiasm. Indeed, I suspected many of membership of the Caravan Club.

(2009: XV–XVI)

Stott's admission of his own cynicism about clowns leads him further into the myth of the clown as melancholy figure:

> The service itself was more disconcerting. I had been a stand-up comic myself and, having twice sought help for depression, was inclined towards the lugubrious in comedy, yet even this left me unprepared for the level of shabby melancholy in which I was about to be immersed. Maybe it was because I was a jet-lagged atheist who was deeply ambivalent about clowns, but I found the experience about as pleasant as a night in a derelict fun park. Presided over by the Vicar of All Saints, and the Clowns' Chaplain, the service began with a clown procession that was followed by prayers, hymns, a sermon, a skit with balloon animals, and Clown Rainbow reading nervously from the Gospel of St Luke; 'Blessed is he, whosoever shall not be offended in me.' There was something intractably laconic about it, especially the sincerity with which they offered worship, like a displaced people pleading to come home.
>
> In a sense, that was what they were, because for decades clowns have occupied an ever-diminishing niche in popular culture, their flapping shoes, hoop-waisted trousers, and streams of multi-coloured handkerchiefs more evocative of forced laughter and jaded memories than genuine fun. Commensurate with their decline is a rise in 'coulrophobia' – the fear of clowns – fuelled by horror flicks and comic-book villains whose particular psychosis troubles the line between laughter and terror. Feeling like an ungrateful guest, I realised it was a prejudice I shared, especially as I caught myself calculating how many diseased minds were lurking behind those blood–red smirks.
>
> Apparently, I was not the only one. The attraction of the abominable draws a big crowd and every year the service is packed with curious onlookers and camera crews who greatly outnumber the dedicated few.
>
> (2009: XVI–XVII)

Indeed, he is not the only one, as the popularity of the book with clown-phobes showed:

> I have a confession. I hate clowns. [...] Nothing in Andrew McConnell Stott's magisterial biography of Grimaldi has altered that opinion.
>
> (*Vulpes Libris* July 29, 2011)

In a sense, Stott's main point is that the life of Grimaldi justifies contemporary popular perceptions influenced by the coulrophobia craze. Such a leap may seem highly debatable, though it is true that the mid-19th century marks the beginning of a trend towards perceiving the clown as split in two, with a mask of joy concealing a dark interior, a process which we shall come to later in this chapter.

But despite the book's success in seeming to explain contemporary myths about clowns, the critics didn't find any new evidence that would explain Grimaldi's success in his own time:

Before 1806, panto was nothing but 'a seasonal afterthought' – a bit of light entertainment to fill in the gaps between more serious pieces of drama. In the wake of Grimaldi's triumph, however, it was transformed into 'the most eagerly anticipated production of the year'. So what was so special about Harlequin and Mother Goose? McConnell Stott doesn't quite seem able to put his finger on the production's X-factor, even though he describes it at great length. He doesn't shed much light on the precise nature of Grimaldi's comic gift, either, although he's very good at tracing its psychological origins, arguing that it was probably a product of a deep-seated eagerness to please (engendered by a violent upbring-ing), and a way of escaping from – or perhaps facing up to – a hugely painful private life.

(Roger Cox in The Scotsman 27 November 2009)

To be fair, explaining just why a clown some two centuries ago was actually funny is a thankless task. Contemporary accounts do not really satisfy our desire to experience that comedy, hence the recourse to psychological spec-ulations which promise an approximation to something more personal and revealing than can be provided by mere historical data alone:

Grimaldi brought into culture the figure of the sad comedian, the solitary being whose disproportionate talent to provoke laughter is born of a troubled soul. With-out Joe, we might not have made martyrs and stoics of those as famous as Tony Hancock, Spike Milligan, Peter Sellers, Lenny Bruce, John Belushi, Richard Pryor, John Cleese, Stephen Fry, Caroline Aherne, Robin Williams and countless others who have wrought their humour through battles with their demons.

(2009: 322)

The consequent temptation, however, is to read such psychologising as more revealing of the author than the subject:

In the second of two rather redundant introductions which create something of a false start to the book, Stott tells us that he himself has endured bouts of depression; it is this, one presumes, that leads him to emphasise the melan-choly in Grimaldi's temperament, seeing him as the prototype of all sad clowns, a proposition not entirely proven in the book.

(Simon Callow in The Guardian 19 December 2009)

Although such a stance might in itself also be guilty of ... psychologising.

The purpose of such a critical reflection is not to invalidate the work but instead to allow us to engage in a double reading of it. In this way, in addi-tion to taking it at face value, we can fruitfully garner insights into how contemporary visions of the clown have been, and are being, constructed. It is then that we can almost see history in the making (or in the writing, if you prefer). We shall look at a more contentious example of this when we come to discuss the dispute over Fellini's pronouncement of the death of the clown. But it is not a simple case of commentators misrepresent-ing clowns. We shall also see later how clowns have often been the first to invent their own myths about themselves (a claim made by Rémy, that most clown-friendly of writers, in discussing the auguste clown, Grock and others).

For example, Stott's recruiting of Dickens to support the view of Grimaldi, or at least his son, 'JS', as an ancestor to today's 'sad' or 'scary' clowns does indeed tell us something about the evolution of these clichés:

> four years after [JS's] death (and two years before he edited Joe's *Memoirs*), Charles Dickens remained sufficiently affected by his fate to grant him a cameo appearance in a story called 'The Stroller's Tale'.
>
> (2009: 304)

The resemblance is apparently enough, bar a few details:

> All the details are consistent with the facts of JS's life – the wasted promise, the intractable alcoholism, the downward mobility and serial expulsions from increasingly depressing venues – although in *Pickwick*, his fictional double, 'John', is embellished with a wife he habitually beats and a child he neglects to the point of starvation.
>
> (2009: 304–305)

Though surely this is just a standard Dickensian part, 'the first of countless images of derelict performers that wend their sorry way through his fiction' (2009: 306):

> I was dressed to leave the house and was crossing the stage on my way out, when he tapped me on the shoulder. Never shall I forget the repulsive sight that met my eye when I turned round. He was dressed for the pantomime, in all the absurdity of a clown's costume. The spectral figures in the Dance of Death, the most frightful shapes that the ablest painter ever portrayed on canvas, never presented an appearance half so ghastly. His bloated body and shrunken legs – their deformity enhanced a hundred fold by the fantastic dress – the glassy eyes, contrasting fearfully with the thick white paint with which the face was besmeared: the grotesquely ornamented head, trembling with paralysis, and the long skinny bands, rubbed with white chalk – all gave him a hideous and unnatural appearance of which no description could convey an adequate idea, and which, to this day, I shudder to think of.
>
> (Dickens 1837: 34)

In a sense, then, Stott is right when he says that 'Dickens invented the scary clown' (2009: 306), although, as we shall see later in this chapter, he would have plenty of help from across the Channel.

The obvious question remains unanswered, however: aside from the fact of JS Grimaldi's life being clearly more of a disaster than his father's, does that really have anything to do with his, or anyone else's, clowning?

JOEY GRIMALDI: THE LEGACY

Leaving psychology aside, what can we say with certainty about Grimaldi? The principal fact is that *Mother Goose* in 1806 was a raging success, despite being a pantomime which Grimaldi himself held in low esteem.

> It is said to have made a profit of over £20,000 for Covent Garden, and although Joe's immediate bonus was somewhat smaller – notably, a gold watch presented by his employer – it made his fortune as a Clown.
>
> (Findlater 1978: 121)

The rest is more speculative:

> What was the secret of its success? One reason seems to be that it broke away from the current vogue of exotic spectacle, and although it had scenes in plenty they were subordinated to the story, which was emphatically English. The austerity of the production has been exaggerated by stage historians, if we are to believe contemporary reports, yet its cost was relatively small, and by reducing display it could afford the time to concentrate on comedy. Moreover, its humours were plainly national, after so many overdressed excursions into foreign and fanciful parts.
>
> (Findlater 1978: 120–121)

Speculative, too, are any pronouncements on the social context of Grimaldi's clowning. D L Murray considered Grimaldi to be in essence a Regency clown:

> his whole conception of the Clown reflects that period of genteel blackguardism, pugilism and practical jokes. The 'grimacing, filching, irresistible Clown', his white face larded with red like a schoolboy's that has been dipped in a surreptitious jam – pot, is a plebeian successor of the mohocks, a companion of Jerry Hawthorn and Corinthian Tom, whose recreations are breaking windows, tripping up old women and assaulting the constables.
>
> (Murray 1930: 125)

And Arthur Bryant thought the violence of the times was reflected in its clowning:

> a heartless disregard for the feelings of others was the hallmark of the 'blood'. It was considered a joke to throw a drunk in a dunghill, drop a live coal on a sleeper's head, rob a blind man of his dog and swear in the presence of ladies and clergymen.
>
> (1952: 123)

The problem with such hypotheses is that they are subjected to the fact that it is difficult for us now to really know the essence of Grimaldi's clowning. This may be true not just of Grimaldi but of any clowning that one does not actually witness. The other trap to avoid is assuming that the qualities of a clown separated from us by time, in this case Grimaldi, are unique to them and not generic:

> In this respect, then, Grimaldi reflected the manners of the Regency; and he himself, in clowning, played havoc with the watch, tripped up old women, assaulted Pantaloon, and committed every kind of felony with infectious zest and perfect licence; yet it must be remembered that, compared with his contemporaries, Grimaldi was a gentle, good-humoured Clown, and that this kind of horseplay was only one facet of his comic genius. The violence that he expressed, moreover, far from being peculiar to the ten years of the Regency, lies at the heart of all clowning, although the forms may change.
>
> (Findlater 1978: 140)

This brings Findlater to spot another trap, the mirror image of the latter one, which is to assume all jokes are universal:

> Said *The Times* in 1823:
>
> A pun tells only once – but it is not so with a poke in the eye. There will always be a certain comicality about a man's breaking his shins, or having his toes trodden upon – or in an old woman's firing off a gun, and being knocked down by the report – and with a fit of the colic, in male or female, we could commune for ever. These things have all been jokes in the last century, and will be so six centuries to come.
>
> That was a dangerous prophecy, for these jokes have long ago lost their savour; nor is a modern audience likely to sympathize with Andrew Halliday's rhetorical question, posed forty years later, 'Where is the witticism that can compete with sitting on a baby, and flattening it to the shape of a pancake?' [*Comical Fellows* 1863: 5]. Yet though manners have become superficially milder (and mime has almost disappeared) the savagery of clowning – and, in particular, its self-punishment – endures in the verbalised buffoonery of many entertainers who thrive on insult and humiliation, in the tradition of cruelty transformed by art.
>
> (1978: 140–141)

Disher's judgements on the legacy of Grimaldi are concerned not with scary clowns, nor even with aesthetics, style or sense of humour, but with fame, reputation and status, which is really all we have left of Grimaldi:

> His ardent passion for his art had invested clownship with the rites and secrets of a religion. It had practices of its own and a language of its own. It had dignity. If his son had proved worthy of the trust it might still be a great English tradition.
>
> (1925: 111)

In the short term, following Grimaldi's death, the traditions of the actors of the harlequinade

> enabled Clowns and Pantaloons, bearing their names but not of their blood, to make fortunes in the next fifty years. After their time motley was a shrivelled relic, and its tricks old customs observed almost religiously like the singing of 'Hot

Codlins' and 'Tippetywichet' which continued to the 'sixties'. Yet the Harlequinade became a deflated wineskin when Grimaldi retired. The strength of his new vintage had stretched it to the uttermost. Once emptied, it could not be completely refilled. The old story of eloping lovers, then the basis of every Harlequinade, had been deranged by the swollen size of this minor character.

(1925: 143)

PIERROT AND MELODRAMA

Fiurelli, Rich, Grimaldi, Deburau – in all these cases there is a simultaneous elevation of both the individual performer's own status as a star and the position of the role within the hierarchy of relationships between roles. As we shall see, in the case of Clown, the promotion would be such that by the last decades of the 19th century, the position of butt had been left so vacant that a new figure was obliged to appear, the Auguste.

Every clown that has basked long enough in the world's love has grown too small for his boots, taken wings and flown into fancy. And at each metamorphosis the world has to hatch another from a clod.

(Disher 1925: 34)

The metamorphosis can work both ways, too. According to Rémy, the new and complex Pierrot of Deburau would soon return to its original simplicity when, in the second half of the 19th century, the French comic performers moved *en masse* from the theatres to the circus. The new performing space found it difficult to tolerate 'a character so complicated as Pierrot was in the hands of Deburau and his colleagues' (1945: 35). The English clown would suffer the same downgrading:

And in parallel the clown from across the channel, since acclimatising himself to France, loses his importance. He becomes a secondary character in the show. His character is eroded. He merges with the French clown into one type.

(1945: 35)

Meanwhile, however, the mutability of the post-Deburau Pierrot lived on, becoming, as the century wore on, ever more mysterious, ever darker. Deburau's early-19th century clown had already held its own in a theatrical culture dominated by melodrama. Clowns continued to play a familiar and important role in those melodramas, cropping up as servants in subplots and semi-autonomous from the main proceedings. In England, for example, John Baldwin Buckstone, leading comedian at the Adelphi from 1827 to 1833 (and later manager of the Haymarket from 1853 to 1878), appeared in his own *Luke the Labourer* (1826/7) as Bobby Trot, clown in all but name.

But in the second half of the century, Pierrot ceased to provide inno-cent contrast to the gruesome goings-on of melodrama, and acquired his own taste for the macabre. The intellectual and literary élite had feted the silent clown during his lifetime, but it was only later that Pierrot would become a purely literary device, a clown icon, and thus the perfect vehicle for Modernism.

Isabelle Baugé, in her introduction to a collection of 19th-century French pantomimes, asks:

> Why were such farces, such slapstick, such harlequinades taken so seriously by personalities as respectable as the great figures of the Romantic generation like Janin, Champfleury, Nodier, Gautier, but also by Nerval, Banville, Sand and later by Baudelaire, Flaubert, Zola?
>
> (1995: 3–4)

In part, their championing of the Théâtre des Funambules should be put down to

> at once an intention to defy the 'classical' actors who triumphed at the Opéra, at the Italiens, at the Comédie-Française, whose gestures they adjudged to be frenetic and their style pretentious, and in the hope of engaging in a new aes-thetic battle: their interest in the art of silence and gesture drove them to activate, starting from the absence of speech, a reflection on their own practice of writing. Deburau the Mime, for his part, remained well outside of the literary theories and intellectual quarrels of which he was the subject.
>
> (Baugé 1995: 4)

But it was not only the formal aspects of Deburau's Pierrot that interested the intellectuals. There were more ways he could be appropriated:

> He composed the figure of Pierrot from contrasting elements: the poetry of this silent, lunar and mysterious character was allied to the grotesque old-fashioned clown with his lewd farces. The stuff of the new Pierrot was thus deliber-ately ambiguous and could henceforth serve as a pretext for comic as well as tragic 'speeches'. That undoubtedly explains the diversity of contemporary accounts – a diversity sometimes bordering on contradiction. Jules Champfleury insisted on the 'social' aspect of the hero, who favoured complicity with his popular audience, drawn from the Parisian working-class suburbs and often illiterate. [...] According to Champfleury, then, Pierrot was 'the ancient slave, the modern proletarian, the pariah, the passive and disinherited being who witnesses, glumly and slyly, the orgies and the follies of his masters' (*Memo-ries of the Funambules*). George Sand, on the other hand, had a more refined vision, closer to that of the dandy (or as they would say at the time, 'fash-ionable') beloved of journalists and writers: 'He is not deceitful, but mocking and amusing; he is not wrathful either; he is just, and when he delivers his admirable kicks, it is with the impartiality of an enlightened judge and the grace of a marquis. He is essentially a gentleman right to the ends of his

long sleeves, of which there is not one flick executed without the manners and ways of the court,' she wrote in *Questions of Art and Literature*, in February 1846.

(Baugé 1995: 8–9)

Wondering how such diverse interpretations could have occurred, Baugé considers that it was the rebellion of the Romantics against Classical models and their

refusal to be inspired by the old forms without any surprise; and so Pierrot served as a pretext for a parody of the traditional hero and allowed for the elaboration of an 'anti-hero', whose actions would always fail, to the great pleasure of the spectators.

(Baugé 1995: 9)

In this sense the clown was, formally speaking, an ideal spokesperson for the Romantic project.

In terms of content rather than form, judging by the title of Jules Champfleury's *Pierrot Pendu* ('Pierrot Hanged'), dating from three months after Deburau's death in 1846, we are already in the realm of macabre clowning, but despite the cast-list including devils, demons and three judges, this mid-century Pierrot still indulges in standard commedia dell'arte or harlequinade antics. Scene iii takes place in a street of shops, first at a bootmaker's:

The bootmaker is mending boots in front of the door. Pierrot appears, and asks to be measured up. The bootmaker consents, and Pierrot says he doesn't have time. So, he tries some boots on. Some are too small, some are too big; however one pair fits him. He walks around with them on to make sure they are alright and won't hurt; then he escapes with them on. Surprise and anger from the bootmaker who takes down his display, fearing more robberies.

(Baugé 1995: 43–44)

Next, Pierrot robs an old woman of her basket whilst feigning an embrace, and sticking his head up her skirt, he runs off with her. Meeting Polichinelle, Pierrot shares the food in the woman's basket with him. The two, having drunk lemonade, then run off without paying the seller. Harlequin and Colombine appear and Harlequin throws a huge rat onto Pierrot's plate. After his initial shock, Pierrot waves the rat at Polichinelle to scare him. Polichinelle 'cries out', after which 'Pierrot eats the rat and declares it to be a great delicacy'. (Although Champfleury uses verbs of speech, the cries and declarations are, of course, played in mime.) To end the scene, Harlequin beats them, the old woman appears, signals to the cobbler. They all kick them. The Captain enters, saying: 'Pierrot, you will hang!' (1995: 44).

Champfleury, a key early proponent of the Realist literary movement, would not remain within the simplicity of the pantomime form, however, with its blank stage directions in the present tense.

> *Polichinelle and the Cat* (December 1863) is another example of the talent deployed by Champfleury in pantomime. The style here is remarkable and, as in *The Kingdom of the Carrots,* the author does not respect the rules of writing that usually guided the practice of mime-composition. They generally wrote in the present indicative tense, their sentences were short and their syntax elementary. Similarly they avoided metaphors, similes and other rhetorical devices, which would be difficult to transpose to the silent stage. But Champfleury was able to give these last two texts a written, literary dimension, which cannot fail to surprise when one considers the genre to which they belong: the use of the past imperfect tense, figures of speech, ironical proverbs, visual images of characters (such as this passage describing the cat: 'The terrors of his hair are replaced by silky roundness, and climbing up on Polichinelle who he now deeply despises, the cat has the calm aspect of his Egyptian brothers wrapped in sacred bandages') cannot fail to pleasantly surprise the reader used to summaries composed too often in haste and without any concern for aesthetic beauty.
>
> (Baugé 1995: 17)

PIERROT AFTER DEBURAU: A MODERNIST HERO

Surely even Deburau would struggle to stage such 'beauty'? This literary boldness in the field of clowning might be seen as a precursor to an even bolder step, taken more than two decades later. Donald McManus in *No Kidding! Clown as Protagonist in Twentieth-Century Theater* (2003) traces the influence of clowning on theatre in the past century. The irresistible conclusion of his book, though not explicitly stated as such, is that the aesthetics and practices of major figures of the period (principally Brecht and Beckett) are not only influenced by, but virtually founded upon, clowning. The story McManus tells is fundamentally the story of Modernism.

He begins with the 1888 performance of Paul Margueritte's 'self-consciously modernist version of clown entitled *Pierrot assassin de sa femme* ["Pierrot Assassin of His Wife"]', which was premiered as part of an evening of performances by authors of the Naturalist literary movement, organized in order to counteract how Émile Zola, its figurehead, had supposedly wandered off into sentimentality. 'All of the pieces were grim, realistic vignettes with the exception of *Pierrot assassin de sa femme,* which was a grim, unrealistic vignette' (McManus 2003: 20).

> *Pierrot assassin* is remarkably similar to the *lazzo* of suicide. Pierrot, like Harlequin, cannot bear to see Columbine, to whom he is married in Margueritte's version, with another man. In both plays, the clown tickles himself to death. Both Pierrot and Harlequin realize that their métier offers them the perfect, ironic

(Harlequinesque) death, but Pierrot decides it is the perfect, ironic (Pierrotesque) murder weapon first. Margueritte has already committed the murder of Columbine before the play begins. During the course of the play he reenacts his crime for the audience. In retelling the earlier event, he passes from the mimetic mode to the diegetic mode. While telling the story he becomes infected with the terrible laughter with which he murdered Columbine and dies himself. He performs in the mimetic, present tense, and diegetic, past tense simultaneously.

(McManus 2003: 21)

McManus cites the following key passage in Margueritte's text, which gives a good idea of the complexity of the layers of thought in the piece:

But how am I going to do it? *(Because Pierrot, as somnambulant, reenacts his crime, and in his hallucination, the past becomes the present.)* Of course there's always the rope you pull it tight, snap it's all over! Yes but the tongue hanging out, the face turned horrible? No. – The knife? Or a sabre, A huge sabre? Slash through the heart,.. Yes! But the blood flows in torrents, it gushed out. – Whew I'll be damned . . . of course there's always the gun, bang! But the bang! Would be heard. Nothing. I come up with nothing. *(He paces about solemnly and meditates. Accidentally he stumbles.)* Ouch that hurts! *(He rubs his foot.)* Ow! That hurts! It won't last long it's better now. *(He keeps rubbing and tickling his foot.)* Ah! Ah! That's funny! No! It makes you laugh. Ah! *(He suddenly lets go of his foot. He strikes his forehead.)* I've got it!. *(Slyly.)* I've got it! I'll tickle my wife to death that's it!

(Margueritte 1886)

As McManus points out, Margueritte's Pierrot 'reads similarly' to the older commedia lazzo performed by Harlequin, but 'they play very differently':

Where Harlequin had used almost the same series of thoughts to arrive at a means of killing himself, Pierrot arrives at a means of committing murder, but which transforms into the means of a self-inflicted death as well.

(2003: 21)

According to McManus, Margueritte's pantomime marks a key point in the rise of Symbolism:

Symbolist poet Stephane Mallarmé [. . .] developed an entire aesthetic treatise 'Sketched at the Theater' based solely on Margueritte's pantomime. Mallarmé suggested that pantomime reflected a greater truth than realist forms.

(2003: 23)

For McManus, the point about Margueritte's take on Pierrot is not its macabre content but its revolutionary form:

The clown techniques, transformation of space and objects, and the use of various levels of representation, (confusion of mimetic and diegetic modes) were more novel, even shocking, than the death and murder of the story.

(2003: 23)

As we have seen, the clown as stand-in for the tragic hero had already pleased the Romantic imagination, but the Modernists took it one step further.

> The popular perception of a clown is synonymous with laughter, but clown as adopted by twentieth-century artists, has more frequently been the means through which the contemporary tragic impulse has been expressed. Clown makes an ideal protagonist of twentieth-century theater because theatrical modernism was preoccupied with breaking the expectations of older genre systems and exposing the mechanism of art-making. If a character in twentieth-century theater looks like a clown and acts like a clown, but does not make us laugh, it is usually because our attention is being channelled in a new direction. What was once a joke has now been presented as an insight, question, or commentary. Clown has become, in contemporary theatre, a character from whom audiences can expect philosophizing, angst, or political criticism as much as physical comedy and fractured language. Clown's historical association as a comic character makes him instantly distinct from the protagonist in tragedies from earlier periods. The contradiction of having a traditionally comic character stand in for the tragic hero is complemented by the clown's inherently contradictory nature as a stage character.
>
> (McManus 2003: 11–12)

MODERNISM AND CLOWN THEORY

If today the echoes of that historical moment of formal shock have faded, the separation between what the clown represents and what we see the clown doing is still with us. What was a formal revolution for the Symbolists has today degenerated into some of our culture's favourite myths about the clown: the tears of the clown and the evil clown are both examples of this displacement of the comic icon of the clown into the place of the tragic hero or, rather, the place of the sentimental depressive and the serial murderer.

But, McManus argues, it was not only this formal manipulation of the clown that enthused the Modernists. Clowns are not just icons of the comic but can also themselves question and 'transcend genres and artistic convention'. He precedes this hypothesis with a definition of the clown, which we should look at now in order fully to understand his point about the key role clowns played in the rise of Modernism. His starting observation is that clowns are not bound by the rules of genre or of fictional worlds: 'Clown watchers generally agree that the clown seems to exist both inside and outside of the dramatic fiction' (2003: 12), citing Enid Welsford's view that clowns are 'the voice speaking from without and not from within the dramatic plot' (1935: 320). This non-obedience

> can usually be accounted for by one of two reasons. Either the clown is more aware of the fact that he or she is part of a theatrical illusion than the other characters, or he or she is too stupid to understand the rules governing the illusion being created. In other words, the clown is either too smart or too dumb.

> The clown's genius, or stupidity – is more than just a character trait. It constitutes a distinct performance mode from that of the non-clown characters ... While the behavior of normative characters is based on their emotional responses to the plot and other characters, the clown's behavior stems from an attempt to logically negotiate the arbitrary rules that govern the plot and characters.
>
> (McManus 2003: 12)

The clown stands not only outside the rules of a fictional genre but also apart from the network of social rules and cultural norms, inside the fiction as it were:

> The key feature uniting all clowns, therefore, is their ability, skill or stupidity, to break the rules governing the fictional world. But in practice, this definition of clown becomes extremely complex. The rules governing the fictional world come in two distinct categories. There are the rules of performance, governing the mimetic contentions being used, and social rules, governing the cultural norms of the world being imitated on stage.
>
> (McManus 2003: 12)

For McManus, this distancing from the norm is not a mere by-product of the clown but is a separate mode of behaviour which

> constitutes an alternate 'way of doing' or a distinct 'clown logic.' The clown will always try to think through a given situation and either fail because of an hopeless inability to understand the rules, or succeed because of a limitless ability to invent new rules.
>
> (2003: 15)

Finally, the result of not playing by everyone else's rules is that the clown is also distanced from the way in which meaning itself is produced, whether that be by the formal means of a particular performance genre or by means of socially accepted patterns of behaviour.

> Clown logic does not have an essential meaning other than to contradict the environment in which the clown appears. The meaning is defined by the individual performer, context of the specific performance and reception of the audience. There are no essentially good clowns and essentially bad clowns, at least not in moral terms.
>
> (2003: 17)

In other words, the clown has a distinct relationship to meaning itself. Or, to put it another way, as many a clown teacher is apt to say, 'A clown can do anything they want' (Cenoz 2011).

This, McManus argues, meant that clowns were already set up to do just the job that the Modernists were out to achieve:

> The general theory of clown explored in the previous chapter describes the nature of clown in any era, but is particularly relevant to clown in modernism because the

modernists were self-consciously interested in demonstrating the mechanics of art-making in an anti-illusionist fashion and breaking with traditional artistic genres. Clown was seized upon as a recognizable human figure who also transcends genres and artistic convention.

(McManus 2003: 18)

The list of artists of differing art-forms drawn to using clowns is long – Renoir, Degas, Cézanne, Picasso, Klee, Calder, Schoenberg, Busoni, Diaghilev, Fokine, Cocteau and Stravinsky – and crosses the borders of aesthetic movements: Impressionist, Symbolist, Expressionist, Cubist.

The craze for depicting clowns reached a fever pitch as the new century grew two decades old. Modernist developments in fine arts had an immediate effect on the theatre during this period. Painters [...] made countless drawings, sketches, constructions and paintings evoking the image of clown. Indeed during a period of art history when figurative art was out of vogue, Pierrots and Harlequins were among the few consistent renderings of the human form.

(McManus 2003: 24)

What had started out as a move from the theatre towards literature – Champfleury, Margueritte, Mallarmé – passed on through the hands of painting and back to the theatre, eventually returning to the clowns themselves in the form of Alexander Calder's 'surrealist dog' (Fratellini 1955: 186) used by the Fratellini in the 1920s (see illustration below). Indeed, McManus considers that the Fratellini not only bought into the Modernist story about clowns but also were a product of it:

The Fratellini Brothers were brought to Paris from Russia specifically to appeal to a high-brow clientele. The management of the Medrano circus realized that the working class audience was abandoning the circus in favor of other newer entertainments, especially films and music hall. The Fratellini specifically geared themselves, therefore to an audience with intellectual and modernist tastes.
[...]
The literati of Paris would visit the Medrano Circus, imagining that were discovering a naive kind of theater that captured the spirit of their modernist ideals. The Fratellini themselves, however, targeted their performances to this elite audience.

(2003: 27)

Although there is some truth in that, the Fratellini's own recollection of such an audience is more nuanced:

We were committed, in fact, to presenting different numbers every evening – and we didn't make our choices on a whim, but according to which kind of audience we had: the intellectuals would not have appreciated the buffoonery, the broad farces, like the one of the baker – where I managed to eat a plate full of sixty cakes. This achievement was nothing of the kind – it involved, in fact, meringues made of tissue paper, which I would spit out when out of the ring.

(Fratellini 1955: 185–186)

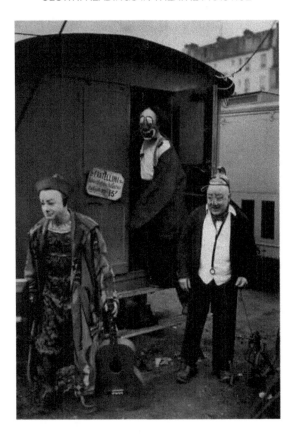

Figure 4 The Fratellini with Alexander Calder's dog
Source: Collection P. R. Lévy, Fonds Fratellini, Académie Fratellini, Paris

Once the Modernists had done with Pierrot, he was left to wander the rest of the century with no intellectual support:

> Unfortunately the 'Art' gradually stuck to Pierrot and he became dangerously 'Arty', as he was absorbed into every art form, culminating in the graphic and plastic arts of the 1920s, and the rash of Pierrot dolls, complete with painted tears, of the 1970s.
>
> (Grantham 2006: 203)

CROSS-CHANNEL CLOWNS AND THE RISE OF PARISIAN CIRCUS

But, as we have seen, the road leading from the complex Pierrot of Deburau in the direction of Modernism had not been followed by the clowns themselves. Their migration to the circus had brought about a new simplification of the role. Throughout the Modernist period, the issues for clowns were not about how to create art which disrupts, for, as McManus has shown, clowns already performed this function. A history of the clown during the decades from 1860 to 1945 tells another story – that of the rise and fall of what many regard to be the essential form of classical clowning, the clown entrée. That development was to take place principally within the world of Parisian circus.

To follow this road, we must pick up the story of the speaking clowns again. According to Rémy, it was partly they who

> after the disappearance of Joe Grimaldi [1837] and the decline of the harlequinades, maintained the English at the forefront of European clowning for another half-century.
>
> (1945: 31)

This English dominance was aided by another export to France at the time:

> the essential characteristics of the English Pantomime: the quest for trick props, the transformation of the theatre stage into a cabinet of fantasies.
>
> (1945: 31)

It wasn't that English clowns were always particularly understood or accepted in France, as the often quoted comments by Baudelaire on Tom Matthews (according to Rémy) and other English 'Pierrots' shows:

> First of all, Pierrot was not the figure to which the late-lamented Deburau had accustomed us – that figure pale as the moon, mysterious as silence, supple and mute as the serpent, long and straight as the gibbet – that artificial man activated by eccentric springs. The English Pierrot swept upon us like a hurricane, fell down like a sack of coals, and when he laughed his laughter made the auditorium quake; his laugh was like a joyful clap of thunder. He was a short, fat man, and to increase his imposingness he wore a be-ribboned costume which encompassed his jubilant person as birds are encompassed with their down and feathers, or angoras with their fur. Upon his floured face he had stuck, crudely and without transition or gradation, two enormous patches of pure red. A feigned prolongation of the lips, by means of two bands of carmine, brought it about that when he laughed his mouth seemed to run from ear to ear.

> As for his moral nature, it was basically the same as that of the Pierrot whom we all know. Needlessness and indifference, and consequently the gratification of every kind of greedy and rapacious whim, now at the expense of Harlequin, now of Cassandre or Leandre. The only difference was that where Deburau would just have moistened the tip of his finger with his tongue, he stuck both fists and both feet into his mouth.
>
> (Baudelaire 1855: 148)

According to Perrodil, in *Monsieur Clown*, clowns of the English school did eventually win over Parisian audiences, so that by the end of the 19th century they would account (according to Rémy) for 15 of the top 20 clowns, as against 2 Spanish, 1 Italian, 1 French and 1 'other'. But then by the time of the publication of *Les Clowns*, Rémy counted 6 Spanish, 6 Italians, 8 French and no English (1945: 39). From these data we could conclude that the development towards the clown entrée was also a development away from the clown of the English school.

For the moment, though, it is the English in Paris who count. Neither the Spanish 'gracioso' nor the Italian 'grotesco' are credited with having had any noticeable influence on the evolution of the French clown of the mid- to late 19th century (Rémy 1945: 39). The credit for first conquering the Parisian audiences' 'repugnance' towards English clowns goes to James Clement Boswell (1826–1859; Rémy 1945: 43). When the horsewoman had finished her act,

> Boswell, coolly, would come up and stand in front of the cloth he was to lay beneath the pink shoes of the horsewoman, and there, face to face, gloomily, scarily, whilst the audience fell about laughing, he would recite in English, to the pretty creature, some passage from Hamlet's monologue. The audience didn't understand, the horsewoman smiled. He, speaking in a kind of nervous frenzy, at once grotesque and ferocious, of *'That is a discover'd country from whose born/No traveller return...'*
> [...]
> Boswell sometimes took pleasure in scoffing at her, roughly snatching the paper hoop through which she was to leap, and staring at her with a bizarre look, uttering some guttural shout accompanied by a nervous hop.
>
> The horsewoman shrugged her shoulders and thought that this man was crazy.
> (Claretie 1881: 354–355)

The language barrier would become a key factor in the English clown's cross-channel exploits:

> The solution actually had been discovered in the previous century by Astley's clown, Billy Saunders, whose deliberate abuse of French was exemplified by his mispronunciation of 'Voulez-vous jouer avec moi?' ('Would you like to play with me?'). His atrocious 'Volé-vô joer avé moâ?' survived to become the trademark of the British *clowns parleurs* of the 1880s, who were pleased to learn that French audiences actually enjoyed hearing the British murder the Gallic tongue.
> (Towsen 1976: 197)

Those clowns more naturally suited to speech took advantage:

> One of the first British clowns to capitalize on language difficulties during this later period was Tony Grice (or Greace), who was billed as 'le premier clown grotesque du Nouveau Cirque.' He was to have a strong influence on other clowns, and his brand of comedy was perpetuated by several apprentices and imitated by many rivals. Because he was terribly overweight, it was not surprising that Grice abandoned acrobatics to concentrate on developing less physical clown sketches.
> (Towsen 1976: 197)

Today we might regard as 'physical comedy' Grice's imitation, ridiculous given his size, of a ballet dancer; or even his magician whose tricks fail. But in their day they represented a different trend:

In his various sketches, he moved clowning away from slapstick comedy and toward parody and satire.

(Towsen 1976: 197)

Disher, writing in the 1930s, had a more critical take on this trend towards clever clowns:

All who grew too fat to tumble or too stupid to play the fool in the ordinary way [...] bored the public with set speeches.

(Disher 1937: 200)

The peak of speaking clowning might be said to have been reached by Billy Hayden, to whom Towsen dedicates several pages. Hayden combined verbal jokes, acrobatics, absurd parody, animals and atrocious French:

Upon entering the ring, Hayden would shout, 'Voâla, Voâla Bonnsoar! Commoncava?' (Leading one writer to comment, 'What a treat to hear a language mistreated.') If the ringmaster was slow with his lines, Hayden would icily interject, 'Eh! Bien? tu dors?'

('What, are you sleeping?'; Towsen 1976: 201)

Entering on a donkey he would bemoan his fate, having been born a pretty little girl but later replaced by an ugly little boy, by a wicked witch, ending his story in tears (from Hughes Le Roux's *Acrobats and Mountebanks* [1890: 288], cited in Towsen 1976: 201).

The theme of confused cross-gender identities was a common one for Hayden:

Hayden: The other day, mossieu, I was with my brother Josephine.
Ringmaster: Excuse me, but you must mean your brother Joseph.
Hayden: (*Dumbfounded; then after some thought*) Obviously, my brother Joseph ... we went to see my sister Victor.
Ringmaster: You mean your sister Victoria!
Hayden: Well then, mossieu, you know the whole family!

(Frichet 1889: 93)

Rémy recounts that Hayden's eventual fall from favour could not be arrested even by his animal companions, the pig and the donkey, no longer a novelty and imitated by his competitors. He returned to England, destitute, half blind, an old and forgotten man until discovered by a journalist who had, as a child, been held in Billy's arms at an autograph session after a particularly star performance at Sanger's circus in London. The journalist, so the anecdote goes, proceeded to raise enough money from the generous British public to support Hayden until his death (1945: 97–98).

In any case, according to Towsen,

The talking clown as a distinct genre was for the most part a nineteenth-century phenomenon, but the parodies and skits he originated represented an important step toward the creation of the twentieth-century clown entree.

(1976: 205)

A major factor in that step was the end of the prohibitions on speech in French circus, in 1864, allowing for extended dialogues, which in turn permitted the development of mini-dramas (which we shall later examine in Chapter 5).

But, as we have seen, clown modes have a habit of re-appearing. The mid-20th century would see a new craze for talking, joke-telling clowns whose main proponents were of Spanish origin. This fashion followed a period of mutism, popularised by the ever-expanding size of American circus which rendered speech inaudible, a trend that also marks the beginning of the end of the smaller-scale entrée.

The height of popularity of the speaking clowns in Paris brings us to the end of the 1880s, but before moving on to the rise of the entrée we must go back a decade in order to pick up the thread of that other clown export to France, the English pantomime.

THE HANLONS: THE TRIUMPH OF ACROBATIC PANTOMIME

As we have seen, the 'English style' was not instantly comprehensible to foreign, especially French, audiences. But times change. Whereas during the Second Empire in France (1852–1870) tastes in entertainment might have been classified as frivolous, the decade following the Franco-Prussian War of 1870–1871 was distinctly gloomy, particularly in Paris, the melting pot of clowns. Economic growth in Europe was brought to a halt, particularly in France; a unified Germany under the Prussian crown had annexed Alsace and northern Lorraine, containing most French iron ore and machine shops; and northern France was occupied for three years, until war reparations had been paid. Clowns were out.

> The clown withdraws and awaits a new wave to be able to re-take a place that has been momentarily ceded to acrobatic pantomime, the last incarnation of the English pantomime before it deigns to deliver to the world its final progeny: the eccentric, fruit of its morbid vivacity and of its mind-blowing energy.
>
> (Rémy 1945: 52)

What Rémy means by acrobatic pantomime found its greatest proponents in the most successful of the 'homogeneous and disciplined' (1945: 53) troupes that now took Paris by storm, the Hanlon-Lees. The old-fashioned Shakespearean clown had had its day and was to be replaced by a new style which drew on the acrobatic high energy of English pantomime, together with elements of the old-style *pantomime sautée* ('leaping pantomime') once popular at the Funambules. This new comedy rediscovered

> The sense of the unpredictable, the unexpected, the surprise. It is based upon the body in play; it is marked by the triple hallmark of strength, skill and precision. But in its English influence, it is more diabolical than spiritual. It distorts reality; it is

thus fantasy, trickery and sham. It recreates an illusory world, made up of props, of miracles, a world upside-down, violent, tyrannical and infernal.

(Rémy 1945: 534)

The picture painted is one of a comedy driven by the high-paced age of mechanisation, which would re-appear in the cinema of Mack Sennett and others in the coming century, with its dangerous stunts and high-speed destruction. For Parisians, according to D L Murray, they were

the cynical philosophers of the fin-du-siècle, they were the incarnation of mechanized invention and the unconscious prophets of the crash of civilization.

[Quoted in Rémy (1945: 54) but incorrectly referenced, also in Towsen (1976) but with no reference. The quote probably comes from Murray (1930).]

The Hanlon-Lees took knockabout comedy to new levels of precision and inventiveness. After their London debut in 1846–1847 at the Adelphi, the six brothers, born in Liverpool and Manchester, took their first trip to Paris. It was brief to say the least, – over before the February revolution of 1848. Wandering the world, at that time their act consisted of acrobatic and gymnastic feats. But they were about to be transformed, in 1865, as John McKinven recounts in *The Hanlon Brothers*:

Figure 5 The Hanlon-Lees' trick piano
Source: Moynet, Georges (1893) *Trucs et Décors* (Paris: Librairie Illustrée)

At a Chicago engagement, they met Henri Agoust, a French juggler and all-round showman. He had experience in ballet, fencing, magic and, most importantly, in pantomime. He saw that the Hanlons were not above mixing a little comedy with their daredevil acrobatics and introduced them to the pantomime traditions of Deburau and the fantasy plays of the Théâtre des Funambules. Agoust persuaded the Hanlons to begin rehearsing two of Deburau's pantomimes, *Harlequin Statue* and *Harlequin Skeleton*. It was a seed that took a while to blossom fully, but when it did, it made pantomime history.

(1998: 20)

Their next visit to Paris, performing at the Cirque d'Hiver from 1867, was not crowned in success either, and from 1870, the troupe being without Agoust, who had enlisted during the Franco-Prussian War, they returned to England. Agoust rejoined them in 1876 in Berlin, replacing Thomas Hanlon, who had died in an accident. Their new pantomime, *Do, mi, sol, do*, started off as an imitation of blackface minstrels and ended up being a parody of the excesses of Wagner. The new work had a 13-month run in Paris. Finally, English pantomime, or at least this version of it, had had success across the Channel (Rémy 1945: 54–57).

The exotic art upset all our ideas of logic, it was in direct opposition to all our innate taste for clearness and delicate performances. However, it succeeded, for it evoked the only laughter of which we were at that time capable, a laughter without merriment, convulsive, full of terror.

(Le Roux 1890: 293)

Whilst the Romantics had fallen for the Pierrot of Deburau, and the Symbolists for the Pierrot of Margueritte, it was the Naturalist Émile Zola who found what he was looking for in the Hanlons, as Mark Cosdon's recent book describes:

Zola was captivated by the Hanlons' pantomime Pierrots, praising them for their libidinous, cruel and self-centred natures. In his seminal work *Le Naturalisme au Théâtre*, Zola marvelled that the Hanlons were 'reveling in broken limbs and battered bodies, triumphing in the apotheosis of vice and crime in the teeth of outraged morality.' For Zola, the Hanlons represented the quintessence of naturalism. Zola found the Hanlons' utter truthfulness startling, remarking, 'I wonder what outburst of indignation would greet a work by one of us naturalist novelists if we carried our satire of man in conflict with his passions to such an extreme. We certainly do not go so far in our cold-blooded analyses, yet even now we are often violently attacked. Obviously truth may be shown but not spoken. Let us therefore all make pantomimes.'

(Cosdon 2010: 49)

Zola's praise in his essay, 'La Pantomime' was not unreserved, however:

We are not in England, where can happily bear a pantomime in five acts over a whole evening. Our national flair is not at all for this kind of terrible imagination with its storm of slaps and kicks raining down for four hours, amidst a dead silence. The cruel observation, the fierce analysis of these fierce grimacers who with a gesture or a wink lay bare the whole human beast, escapes us, when it doesn't simply anger us. For us, therefore, the pantomime must only be an accessory, with moments of rest to allow the audience to breathe.

(Zola 1881: 327–328)

The content for this fierce style was ready and waiting to be re-used from the earlier Pierrot pantomimes, and maybe only needed a slight nudge further towards the macabre:

In *Pierrot Menuisier (Pierrot the Carpenter)*, Pierrot sells upholstered coffins to people. When he kills a man for declining to purchase, he is hunted by the man's ghost wearing the coffin he had tried to sell him. As gendarmes approach, Pierrot fires a gun and hits a pregnant cat producing a hailstorm of kittens falling on the stage.

(McKinven 1998: 34–35)

The Hanlon style was more than an update of English pantomime, in its fusion of the English Clown and the French Pierrot. Without doubt, the waves of its influence were to be felt for decades to come. But in Paris, which remained the melting pot from which new clown forms were still to spring, no sooner had the Hanlon-Lees arrived than they were gone again: 'Of those strange and vertiginous representatives of the art of English pantomime, what remains?' (Sangor 1892: 399).

Rémy's analysis (1945: 62) is that once the performances of the Hanlons had been seen a few times, everyone knew how they did their tricks and the glamour wore off. Repeating the formula didn't work anymore. It would now be the hour of glory for a new type of clown, the auguste, an hour that would, arguably, last more than a century. Despite undergoing various transformations, the auguste clown will bring us up to our own present moment.

Meanwhile, the fate of Pierrot was not to be so glorious, at least under his own name. Disher provides this summary from a 1920s British perspective:

The French Pierrot was shorter lived than the Clown. Legrand, who was Deburau's successor, carried the character still farther from mirth. At the time of his master's death he was acting Pierrot before the London public at the Adelphi. He had little success. In 1849 he returned to the Funambules where he acted with Charles Deburau in *Los Deux Pierrots*. At length he had a Pierrot theatre of his own. But the vogue passed until *Le Cercle Funambulesque* was formed [1888]. Their Pierrot was purely sentimental. As the hero of the play in dumb-show, *L'Enfant Prodigue*, he acted the world over. But that has nothing to do with clownship beyond its possible influence in popularising the costume until from the masquerades it passed

to the entertainments on the beach. And the seaside Pierrots – if the 'concert parties' of a derivative type be included – have supplied the town with several good
clowns.

(1925: 140)

Nearly a century later, we have little to add to this assessment, as the development of Pierrot has barely moved on, at least in name. But the lineage
which once manifested itself as 'English pantomime', drawing on mechanical tricks, fast-paced action and slapstick violence, is relatively simple to spot
throughout the 20th century, most prominent in cinema and to a lesser extent
television. This is despite the fact that the contemporary clown has generally
shied away from its brutality and vulgarity, despite noteworthy exceptions
such as Archaos's 1980s punk-fuelled chainsaw-wielding mayhem. As we
shall see, it has looked more to other traditions, which offer a vision of the
clown not so much of extreme physical action as of a heightened sensitivity
to the drama of human failure. This brings us to our next chapter.

4 Birth of the Auguste

INTRODUCTION

Any understanding of clown in our own times cannot escape the figure of the auguste clown. In its latest red-nosed aspect it has come to signify 'clown' itself. Yet despite such iconic power, the auguste clown is a relatively recent phenomenon, and its visual appearance has developed greatly during its short life. I begin this chapter by surveying its origins in the late 19th century and attempting to assess the myths, legends and anecdotal history which have surrounded the role. In doing so we will begin to understand what defines the auguste, and how the meteoric rise to popularity of the new style of clown was rooted in the new social conditions which brought mass popular audiences to the circus. I then move on to how the auguste began to forge what would become an extremely durable partnership with the older style of clown, exemplified by the first great clown duo, Footit (1864–1921) and Chocolat (1868–1917). We see how once the potential of this relationship is realised, the permutations in duos, trios and even solos take off. I look at how Little Walter's (born 1879) constant and prolific search in the field of costume and characterisation both drew on the English music-hall and also inspired a new generation of circus clowns. Walter's partnership with the great whiteface clown, Antonet (1872–1935), tells us much about the latter's subsequent pairing with Grock (1880–1959), and even more about the origins of Grock's later solo act. I look at how Grock's move from circus to variety theatre was fundamental in his development as a clown soloist, and in so doing I examine the relationship between clowning and the two distinct performing spaces of the circle and the end-on stage, finishing the chapter with a note on contemporary visions of the circle–square tension.

THE AUGUSTE CLOWNS OF THE 1880S: MYTHS, ANECDOTES AND SOME FACTS

Although we can put dates to the huge spread in popularity of the new, auguste clown (the 1880s), the search for an individual creator of the type is mired in legends with dubious credentials. Rémy is virtually the only author to have attempted to dismantle the myths rather than merely repeat them.

Despite, or because of, his dedication to clowns, he is gravely sceptical about the stories which they tell about themselves, dedicating a whole chapter, 'Birth of the Auguste', to the matter in his book *Les Clowns* (Rémy 1945). He sees that the difficulty for the historian lies in the fact that no-one seems to have bothered about the issue when the auguste clown was becoming popular, nor by the point when practically all circuses had already copied the idea, at the end of the 1880s. At the time, the critics did not think the matter to be worthy of serious study.

Not even the clowns themselves showed any interest, in part due to the fact that they regarded the auguste as an intruder and an inferior being, which didn't stop them trying to claim the credit later when they saw audiences warmed to the newcomer. Edouard de Perrodil writes of the auguste in 1889 in *Monsieur Clown*:

> With this character we descend one step on the social ladder.
>
> Never be so forgetful that you give to a clown, in his presence, the name of Auguste; he will take you for the most despicable ignoramus, for a vulgar and unintelligent lout.
>
> I give you permission, on the other hand, to give an Auguste the name of clown; he will be flattered and will offer you his hand as a mark of gratitude.
>
> (1889: 70–71)

Even though Perrodil was writing at a time when the auguste's rise to popularity was still recent, Rémy is sceptical of the veracity of his accounts, suspecting that Perrodil was falling prey to the unreliability of oral tradition, even though he would have been aware that

> some [clowns], because they are prone to the joys of mystification, others because they think to acquire more importance by exercising their imagination, alter the facts without scruple.
>
> (Rémy 1945: 66)

From Perrodil we get one of the most popular auguste creation myths (1889: 72–73). This story says that at the Circus Renz in Berlin the ringmaster hired a stage-hand named Auguste, who was incapable of doing even the simplest task, such as moving a mat or piece of apparatus for the artists. The ringmaster constantly harangued the boy, such that the audience came to join in with a chorus of 'Auguste!' Seeing an advantage to be had, the director placed the boy in a costume designed to capitalise on his stupidity.

The relationship between this Auguste, the ringmaster and the public is recognisably that of later professional augustes. The costume that Perrodil details is also accurate:

> oversized black tailcoat, huge tails, a costume of doubtful gaiety, but which, for the ordinary folk, it seems, does not detract from the utter comedy of this individual.
>
> (1889: 73)

More than a decade later, in 1900, George Strehly is still asking:

> Who is the creator of this genre that has become so popular and which tends to dethrone all other representatives of the clown genre?
>
> (cited in Rémy 1945: 68)

Another story is one which the Fratellini tell, via their biographer, Pierre Mariel:

> One evening, in 1864; an English horseman, engaged in a Berlin circus, trips as he leaves the ring, where he has just placed a prop. Tom Belling, called Auguste (it is the horseman's name), was known, *urbi et orbi*, for his drunkenness. Thus, not doubting that his fall, quite comic, be due to a state of endemic inebriation, a few funny fellows shout out at him, 'Auguste, Auguste'.

He gets up and, laughing, looks at the audience . . . Faced with his air of stupidity and his red nose, the auditorium explodes into mad gaiety:

> 'Auguste, stupid.' [the word 'august' supposedly meaning 'stupid' in Berlin slang]

> The next day, Tom Belling re-did his character and this time obtained a success that was provoked consciously, which he knew how to cultivate by dressing and making himself up in a ridiculous manner, and placidly accepting all the slaps that the clowns gave him in order to increase his confusion.

> Belling came to Franconi's in 1874, but his British reserve gained him no success.

> It is only in 1878 that James Guyon imported this role to France where for many years he was the joy of the spectators at the Hippodrome.
>
> (Mariel 1923)

Disher (1925: 196) repeats the Fratellini's story without questioning it. Towsen (1976: 208) also gives credit to another similar story about Belling which goes that he dressed up in a ridiculous way one evening as a dare to get his own back on the ringmaster who had reprimanded him previously, and then literally ran into him in front of the audience. Rémy considers that the latter 'adventure is too moral not to have been invented' (1945: 71). His source is Joseph Halperson in *Das Buch vom Zirkus* (1926), who gives another, supposedly more reliable, version, though without naming his source, which also situates the event in Renz's circus, but now in St Petersburg in 1870. This time it is a badly dressed groom who gets pushed through the paper hoops used for jumping through, and whose anger excites the audience's laughter. The groom, named Machline (or maybe MacLean), died soon after, but Renz, the circus proprietor, told the story to Belling and suggested he try something similar, which he is said to have done some time in 1873. A virtually identical account was given to Rémy in person by the clown Bébé (brother of Antonet; Rémy 1945: 72–73).

Rémy's scepticism centres on the supposedly spontaneous nature of the birth of the auguste. More likely, he considers that Belling was performing as a clown under a pseudonym, and that the events were not due to chance. Other commentators point out that the use of the term 'august' in German post-dates the story:

> Most serious historians doubt that the legend is true. For a thing, the word Auguste did not exist in the German language until after the character became popular.
> (Clowns of America International 2006: 16)

What we can see here quite clearly, though, is a common enough type of clown number involving a plant: someone whom the audience believes is a mere spectator, possibly drunk, stumbling into the ring. Indeed, the only information that Rémy accepts as factual is that Belling appeared for the first time in France at Franconi's circus in Paris on 7 January 1877, in an 'interlude' entitled *L'Écuyère 1820 (The Horsewoman 1820)*. On the 17th January, he appears as 'Belling as Auguste' (Rémy 1945: 70). By all accounts, even if Belling was the original, he certainly wasn't the first of the great augustes. Rémy cites Halperson as saying that Belling wasn't noted as being a great comic and soon left the circus to become a stage magician (1945: 76).

THE FRENCH THIRD REPUBLIC: NEW CLOWNS FOR A NEW AGE

Aside from whether the anecdotes hold any truth, or whether the auguste has precedents or not before Belling, the rise of the auguste is a notable cultural phenomenon which poses more complex questions. What was it that turned audiences on to the new clown at this moment? We have got some idea of the cultural context that nursed the Hanlon-Lees to success in the 1870s. If they and their imitators were clowning the concerns of that decade – fatalistic fears and hopes, post-war economic depression, machine- and technology-driven danger, destruction and death (two of the Hanlons died from falls) – then what does the auguste have to say about Paris, and by extension, Europe, in the 1880s and 1890s? For if we can understand clowns through understanding their time, we might also write a cultural history of the world by understanding clowns.

The late 1870s was marked by an end to the post-war stagnation of public and political affairs in France, with the decision to create the Third Republic rather than restore the monarchy:

> [N]ew circuses were opening up in the suburbs. The state of mental restriction which had prevailed under the *Ordre Moral* regime after the war of 1870–1871 was coming to an end. The world was looking for simple amusements.
> (Rémy 1945: 84)

By the end of the century, Paris would have five permanent circuses. A new mood, new audiences, a new clown:

Through his freedom of action and the spontaneity without which he could not fulfil his role, the auguste raised a protest against the select and formal milieu of the circuses of the Second Empire [1852–70].

(Rémy 1945: 83)

What kind of clown was the early auguste? Perrodil's description of the costume is not only accurate for the year of 1889 but would hold true for a few more decades yet. Strehly has more details:

The usual costume of the auguste consists of a tailcoat which is too big, a white waistcoat which is too long and black trousers which are too short. A squashed opera hat and white laced gaiters complete the outfit with a lock of hair carefully waxed up like a lightning rod on a closely shaven skull.

(1900: 102)

This is no longer the groom or stage-hand. Rémy asks, 'is this not the caricature of the ringmaster himself?' (1945: 78). He argues that for a parody to work, it must be of a figure of importance, not of a mere assistant who normally passes completely unnoticed by the spectators.

Figure 6   Piculo Fiorri in early Auguste costume
Source: Unknown photographer, fonds Soury, collections photographiques du Musée des Civilisations de l'Europe et de la Méditerranée, Paris

Perrodil's analysis of the psychology also stands the test of time:

This character's role is known: to appear incredibly busy whilst doing nothing, even getting in the way, if such is his fantasy, of those whose job it is to get the equipment ready in the ring.

He excited enough wild mirth among the masses, the hilarious Guion, of the

Hippodrome, known as Gugusse by the Parisian public always playful and endlessly cheeky.

The science of laughter has unfathomable secrets.

I give this fact to those researchers who have engaged in the study of this physiological phenomenon:

When Gugusse appears the entire auditorium jumps up and down.

(Perrodil 1889: 69–70)

The new taste for fun eventually led to Geronimo Medrano, the Madrid-born clown who took over the running of the Cirque Fernando in 1897, to establish the new concept of circus as light and colourful (despite most auguste clown's black-and-white costumes of seemingly 'doubtful gaiety'). At the Cirque Medrano, soon to become the mecca of clowns, black costumes would be prohibited.

If French pantomime managed to impose itself and to retrieve the last splendours of improvised comedy, and to rid the ring of the clown of British spirit, the splenetic buffoon and the character of a humour without sparkle, it has Medrano to thank.

(Rémy 1945: 88)

FOOTIT AND CHOCOLAT: THE CLOWN-AUGUSTE RELATIONSHIP

For a time, augustes worked semi-independently within the context of the circus, much as the clowns had done before them. Their associations with other artists, whether they were clowns, ringmasters or horse-riders, were strictly dependent on the needs of whichever numbers were to be performed. Guyon spent a decade at the Hippodrome. Buislay, at the Cirque d'Hiver, claimed to be 'the only, the unique, the incomparable auguste' (Rémy 1945: 90). William Bridge is credited with having invented a kind of 'genteel auguste', without the vulgarity of Tom Belling's drunk, which Little Walter and others would develop further, and which would make possible the best-dressed auguste of them all, Chocolat.

The auguste operated in similar territory to the traditional clown and soon looked like over-taking the latter in popularity. The distinction between the two was probably clear for all to see from the very start. As well as being a parody of the ringmaster, the auguste is also one of us, one of the new circus audience, the masses. 'Next to him, the whitefaced clown seems like an aristocrat' (Rémy 1945: 92). He has another advantage: being an imposter, he is not called upon to master any of the skills of the circus. This new clown can be as bad at anything as he wants, as long as he is funny.

But the soloists, both clowns and augustes, were to be eclipsed by the arrival of the stable duos – above all those superstars of the turn of the century, Footit and Chocolat. Rémy considers that it was Pierantoni and Saltamontes who formed the first stable partnership of clown and auguste, which lasted for six years, building a team spirit that allowed for continuous development, rather than occasionally coming together to perform sketches. This allowed them to establish a large repertoire that was played in their own style and adapted to their own tastes and creativity. The dramatic possibilities suddenly expanded: two clowns together can play longer scenes, take up more time and evolve more intricate gags.

Geo Footit, born in Nottingham, son of a circus owner, began his performing career at the age of three. He was still a teenager when he decided to give up the demanding vocation of acrobat and turn to clowning, debuting at the Cirque Continental in Bordeaux and appearing at the opening of the Nouveau Cirque in Paris. Henry Frichet describes his physiognomy as 'full of contrasts, passionate and stubborn', and often depicted by artists as 'angry, threatening, troubled and hot-tempered' (Rémy 1945: 107). By 1890, Footit was the principal clown at the Nouveau Cirque, ahead of Billy Hayden and Tony Grice.

Whereas Footit's biography is text-book circus family tradition, Chocolat's past and identity are shrouded in mystery. Apparently born in Havana, Cuba, of unknown age, unknown parentage and surname, although later he claimed it to be Padilla (first name Raphael), he turned up in Bilbao firstly as servant to a family of rice merchants, then as a porter, then a miner. Discovered by Tony Grice in a bar in Bilbao, he became the clown's family servant at age 16. His performing debut was as one half of a horse, shared with Grice's son, at the Nouveau Cirque, which he followed with various servant roles which required him to be on the receiving end of multiple slaps, blows and kicks. 'Passive roles were already his delight' (Rémy 1945: 110). Apparently sacked by Grice for spilling sauce on Mme. Grice's dress at their son's baptism, Footit brought him into his employ.

One evening at the Nouveau Cirque, Chocolat appeared in the fashionable dress of the socialite of the time: shiny shoes, silk stockings, satin culottes, red jacket and top hat. It was a costume he would only vary slightly in future, perhaps with a bowler hat or a boater. Chocolat was the perfect opposite to Footit: slow, stoic, clumsy and stupid, versus Footit's intelligence, nervousness and lightness. Together they heralded a new era for the clown repertoire: dramatic scenes with dialogue and slapstick, and an end to acrobatic trick pantomime and any remnants of the old nonsensical mock-shakespeareanism. Gabriel Astruc recalls:

I can still hear Footit saying to the unflinching Chocolat, 'You stupid idiot!' repeating the same insult ten times over, right under his nose, through a megaphone, climbing up onto his shoulders, pounding upon his head, drilling his ear-drum, and I can see him stopping, deeply discouraged because Chocolat, smiling like an angel, replied calmly to him, 'I understood you the first time.'

(Astruc 1929)

Footit's tyranny was total:

'I'm thirsty,' says Chocolat.
'Do you have any money?' enquires Footit.
'I don't have any.'
Footit, incontrovertibly:
'You have no money? Then you are not thirsty!'
And if that wasn't enough, he adds one of his typical witticisms.
'Chocolat, I'm going to have to slap you.'

(Franc-Nohain 1907)

Thanks to Footit and Chocolat, by the 1890s comedy relied as much on the personalities and relationship of the clowns as on anything else. The clown repertoire thus escapes the dynamic of the circus, being no longer dependent on the activities of trick-riders or acrobats (Rémy 1945: 113). But it also meant that their success depended on maintaining that relationship. Footit and Chocolat's ended when they left the Nouveau Cirque and found that not all audiences found their pairing hilarious (Rémy 1945: 119). In 1905, Footit left the partnership in order to work with his sons (old family tradition again). Critics now considered Chocolat to be 'not funny'. Lost without his partner, he was not of that internationalist tradition of circus families, accustomed to finding work across the globe. Despair and poverty beckoned. Footit, for his part, didn't find the same chemistry with his son as he had had with Chocolat, evidently, although he managed to retire from the circus in relative comfort. Although divergent in their origins and final destinies, Chocolat and Footit together had acquired legendary status.

CLOWN TYPES: DUOS, TRIOS AND SOLOISTS

The vogue for clowns at the circus had been set in motion. Freed from the rigours and discipline that kept acrobats and trapeze artists in strictly timed numbers, the new mini-dramas that were the clown entrées had a different notion of time, extending beyond the usual tightly timed and technically perfect circus routine. Developing entrées that had more in common with the legitimate theatre than with the primitive and freakish displays of strength or bizarre skills of the fairs, clowns 'had substituted for the suppleness of the body [...] the subtlety of the spirit' (Rémy 1945: 134). Clowns could now aspire to a nobility equal to that of the circus's founding art, dressage. The architecture of the circus programme had changed. Clown entrées sprung up in every shape and form, with the clown-auguste duo at its centre (Rémy 1945: 132–134). This 'golden age' of clowns extended all the way from the appearance of the auguste up to the 1930s.

The first three decades of the 20th century were marked by clowns' relationship to the dominant form, the duo composed of the whiteface clown and the auguste, two roles which, as well as being interpreted in many different ways by many individual clowns, also underwent significant evolution. A myriad of clown types was one result of this period. The classification of types of clown remains to this day almost an obsession with many. Dominique Denis's analysis is one of the more detailed and subtle. Speaking of the (whiteface) clown, he suggests various subdivisions:

The Elfin Clown:

The most famous was François Fratellini.

A character which is above all likeable. Elegant, supple, agile, dancing, light, ethereal. Intelligent, graceful, charming. The leader of the clown team. Jesting, joke-playing, setting traps for augustes and always ending up triumphing. He has the last laugh.

[…]

The Distinguished Clown:

The most famous were Footit, Antonet, Pipo, […]

This character commands respect. Elegant, dexterous, refined, ironic. Giving an impression of intelligence. Always shows himself superior to the auguste, making fun of him, using him as his scapegoat or punchbag.

[…]

The Jovial Clown:

The most famous were Gougou, Iles, Rico, J.M. Cairoli, […]

This is truly childlike character. Does not get angry and is the first to laugh at the auguste's jokes. The 'big brother' of the auguste…. But he knows when to be firm. A kind of intermediate figure between the elfin clown and the authoritarian clown.

(Denis 1985: 4)

Denis's classification of augustes is more complex, there being almost as many types as there were individuals. The distinctions might be based on personality: compare the 'ridiculous auguste' (Paul Fratellini; pretty much the original type who is clumsy but retains his dignity, stupid but believing himself to be clever) with the 'naive auguste' (Charlie Rivel; infantile, laughing and crying at the slightest thing) or with the 'mischievous auguste' (Charlie Cairoli) or with the 'grandiose idiot' (Albert Fratellini; outrageously exaggerated in everything). Or the traits may be based on some affinity with a particular social position: compare the 'tramp' (Otto Griebling) with the 'dandy' (Little Walter) or with the 'urchin'.

LITTLE WALTER, ANTONET AND GROCK: THE CLOWN DUO IN FLUX

Whilst some clowns, such as Footit and Chocolat, relied more on careful rehearsals than on spontaneous improvisations, others, such as Little Walter, were in a constant state of experimentation, moving from character to character, always on the lookout for some new role: the water-carrier, the goat-herd, the gas-lighter, the valet, the soldier, the toreador, the boxer, the Tyrolean singer and, above all, the woman. Walter credited the influence of his early visit to England, and his experience in pantomime there, with having ignited his creative curiosity, and Rémy considers that the influence of Dan Leno on Little Walter's style is striking (1945: 144). Like Leno, Walter was noted for his female impersonations. In any case, the imprint of English music-hall comedians is clear. Walter's costumes stretch in all directions: the waistcoat elongates to his knees and the shirt sleeves cover his hands. He was 'the first auguste whose originality surpassed that of the clown' (Rémy 1945: 143).

Figure 7 Little Walter
Source: Unknown photographer, fonds Soury, collections photographiques du Musée des Civilisations de l'Europe et de la Méditerranée, Paris

Experimental creativity or a clown in search of himself, or in search of his audience? Walter's early auguste, not caring for slapstick, was more of a pretentious figure than Chocolat's. But he later abandoned this invention, as audience tastes changed, according to Rémy, forcing a return to the auguste-as-idiot. He persevered. Rémy considers that the evening-dressed auguste finally began to lose its dominant position in large part due to Walter's constant experiments with new clothes and new styles: checked suits, saggy-bottomed culottes, trousers with intertwined legs, anything seemed possible. He was so well known for his inventiveness that anything new would automatically be ascribed to him in the decade and a half preceding the First World War (Rémy 1945: 149). After Walter, augustes were free to invent the costume that best suited their personality. Fittingly for a pioneer in clown fashion, Walter left behind a large collection of photographs of his life and work but not one word on the content of his performances (Rémy 1945: 150).

We can only speculate about his ten-year partnership with Antonet (Umberto Guillaume). Antonet was the most conservative of clowns, methodically preparing everything in advance, which would then remain set in stone. His later partner, the auguste Beby (Aristodemo Frediani), told in his memoires (1930) of Antonet's resistance to trying any new ideas. His simple, purist make-up, once found, was never modified. In the age of the prolific Fratellini, Antonet and Beby sustained a 15-year partnership (1919–1934) with only 10 or so numbers. Amongst his contemporaries, Antonet stood for purity of style: in costume, make-up, and preserving the tradition of Footit and Chocolat, developing still further the dramatic logic of the entrée. Authoritarian like Footit, both in and out of the ring, but, unlike Footit, handsome and distant, he projected a refined and aristocratic persona. 'For those in the trade, Antonet was the personification of the clown' (Rémy 1945: 174).

When Antonet met Grock in 1906 he found a potential partner with the same care for precision and detail. Grock had begun his clowning career by replacing Brock (hence the name) in a duo with Brick in the years 1903–1906. Neither one of the new pair was yet famous but Antonet took the dominant role, as ever. Grock, less experienced, served his apprenticeship, content to replace Little Walter at first. In photographs it is easy to mistake Grock for Little Walter. The copy is almost perfect. Indeed, Grock may have been the Little Walter that Antonet always wanted: methodical, conservative and obedient.

GROCK: THE AUGUSTE AS SOLOIST IN THE THEATRE

But the scales were tipping in favour of the auguste, whose popularity was still rising. The auguste attracted more of the laughs and more of the spectators' attention, leaving the whiteface clown to recede into the background, a mere foil for the comic. When Grock broke away from the model of the clown-auguste duo, he was simply following the overwhelming force of history. But it wasn't just a matter of popularity that would enable the auguste to strike out on his own. It would also need a change of space and a change of performing style. The opportunity would come in the guise of a huge flop that nearly ended Grock's career. Grock's retelling of this event is all the more striking in contrast to the remainder of his memoires – *Life's a Lark,* (1931) and *King of Clowns* (1957) – which otherwise reveal little of interest to the clown scholar. On his beginnings as a clown, his relationships with his clown partners, the content of his gags and their development, the origin of his catchphrases ('Why?' and 'No Kidding') there is virtually nothing. On the other hand, there are plenty of self-aggrandizing stories. Rémy is particularly critical: 'Clowns, notably, have a propensity to mystify' (Rémy 1945: 381). Clowns' own anecdotes of their beginnings tend towards heroism, whether they involve overcoming difficulties or shooting immediately to stardom. In order to sound interesting, presumably, Grock tells us of the many roles he is supposed to have mastered (in real life, not, like Little Walter, as clown characters): farmer, watchmaker, language teacher, orchestral conductor, accountant, gardener, fencing teacher, boxer, child-minder. He also recounted heroic actions of assisting in the Queen of Spain's giving birth, escaping from a train crash and being chased by a pack of wolves.

Laurent Diercksen's *Grock: un destin hors norme* (1999) recycles this data in the form of chronological lists and tables (father's occupations; houses lived in; hobbies; personality traits) as well as the more conventional bibliography and filmography, and the more interesting artistic output (description of his number, sheet music of musical compositions), as if by collating every known fact about the man we might get nearer to understanding him.

So when Grock speaks of failure, we pay attention. Pondering those times when it is difficult to connect to the audience, he continues:

> But a real downright frost... a complete and absolute flop – have I ever had one? Wait while I tell you [...] about the greatest fiasco in all my career.
>
> (Grock 1931: 41)

The fame of Antonet and Grock had grown such that in 1911 they secured a 14-week engagement at the Winter Garden music hall in Berlin, leading to 22 managers signing contracts with the pair. The performance was a disaster, however. Their agent, Marinelli, scolds them:

> Boys... boys... what on earth have you been thinking of? A music-hall isn't a *circus!* You're too broad... altogether too broad. Tone it down and suit your stuff to variety.
>
> (Grock 1931: 45)

The clowns attempted to adjust to the new medium, but by the fourth evening they were yet to hit on the recipe for success and all contracts had been torn up. They decided to re-work the act completely and spent a whole night doing so. Success ensued, and a re-signing of the contracts, at 1000 marks extra.

Grock's telling of the event was not simply an anecdote of the rich and famous; it opened a window on two far more interesting questions. Firstly, what is the difference between a clown in a circus and a clown in the music-hall in 1911? Secondly, what is the nature of Antonet and Grock's performance at the time, and how does it change?

GROCK: CLOWN EVOLUTION

Grock here did give considerable detail of their piano entrée, *Kubelik and Rubinstein*, and exactly where a circus audience would normally have laughed, but the music-hall audience didn't:

> we made our entrance in the approved circus fashion, a couple of conquering heroes in brand new frock coats: Kubelik and Rubinstein. Antonet was bedizened with orders and be-gewgawed as any perambulating merry-go-round, but nothing could have surpassed the air of superiority with which he turned to me and said: –
>
> Introduce me, please, Rubinstein, to these ladies and gentlemen.
>
> Ladies and Gentlemen, I have the honour to present to you Professor Kubelik, the greatest violinist that ever has been or ever will be. Professor Kubelik, as you see, has already had medals bestowed upon him from all quarters of the world – three French gold medals, eight silver and ten Certificates of Merit; seven gold English medals, twelve silver and thirteen Certificates of Merit; from Russia seventeen gold medals, twenty- eight silver and forty-three Diplomas of Merit, while from the land of Spaghetti and Tomatoes he has already acquired no less than twenty-five gold medals, thirty- nine silver and seventy-two Diplomas of Merit . . .
>
> We were accustomed to just this bare enumeration throwing our circus audience into convulsions of merriment. But our Berlin public never moved an eyelash. Whereupon Kubelik takes up his position with an air of supreme disdain and I, as his accompanist, sit down to the piano.
>
> What are you looking for, Rubinstein?
>
> The tuning crank, Herr Geheimrat. The keys want tuning up.
>
> Nonsense. Crank yourself! It's your two hands you want to use – not a crank! Come now, begin . . .
>
> Again I sit down and frantically attack the keyboard, as though I would pound the notes before me to a jelly. But not a sound results except for the dull knocking of the felted hammers and the wheezing of the notes. I get down from my stool.
>
> The brute's sick, Your Excellency!
>
> (Grock 1931: 42–44)

We might reasonably suppose that this broad and overblown style is the same as that which Little Walter would have used in the same number with

Antonet, the same number that Lavatta saw: 'It is there that I saw being created, baring a few details, all that later made Grock a success' (in Rémy 1945: 405). Antonet, being so conservative, would never have dreamed of discarding his old numbers with Walter. They are recycled. However, Grock made not one single mention of Walter in his memoires, which may be just a memory lapse, but looks more like 'an unsustainable pretension to original-ity of his beginnings' (Rémy 1945: 390), given that, with reference to his work with Antonet, Grock claims authorship:

> Our turns were really more than circus turns, being sketches, or small pieces suitable for the theatre – a fact that an English court of law later confirmed on my behalf, when I was forced to sue a fellow for plagiarism who, if left to his own sweet will, would doubtless be masquerading under my feathers to this day on the variety stage.
>
> (Grock 1931: 229)

Walter's pianist was given to obvious gags: extracting rats, a cat and shoes from inside the piano (Rémy 1945: 405). Grock's description goes on:

> I fumble about with the keyboard, grope among the pedals, open the sounding-board. A pistol shot resounds from the wings.
>
> 'There! That's a string broke... bass has gone futt. Why... what... this is a *piano*, not a *wardrobe!*' On which I extract from the piano's entrails an enormous length of wire, and a pair of crimson corsets of monstrous dimensions. On which the audience should simply be holding its sides, every member of it! But no. Not a hand. They just sat there, staring, in stony silence and disapproval. A living iceberg.
>
> (Grock 1931: 44)

Grock tells of some of the alterations he and Antonet made to the act that night in Berlin:

> It was touch and go now with a vengeance. Both our careers were at stake. From eleven o'clock that night till seven the next morning we were closeted together in our hotel room, evolving a new turn, something that should be essentially 'of the halls,' none of your 'ad lib' business, everything cut and dried. Antonet was to play an aria on his violin from *Traviata*, myself accompanying him on the con-certina, after which I should bring my comic 'cricket fiddle' out of its case and let it chirrup. We would end up with a regular Bernese *jodel* and a dance. We had got it all ready by nine.
>
> (Grock 1931: 46)

In the film of the same year as the publication of Grock's first memoires, which I partly drew on in Chapter 1, we can see the consequences: the little fiddle, the yodel and dance, and, most of all, everything 'cut and dried'. But what has been replaced?

The comedy of props which Walter borrowed from the English pantomime is, in Grock's version, completely abandoned.

(Rémy 1945: 406)

The bombastic presentation of the musicians has been replaced by a sequence of bows, intertwined with comic business with hats, gloves and back-scratching, rather than rats, cats and corsets.

Grock's costume for the piano sequence, an ill-fitting black suit and top hat, has evolved from the previous copy of Walter's more dapper auguste, but an auguste in the old style it still was. As for his other, more famous look, the long checked jacket, the bald head, it also had its history. His former

Figure 8   Grock with Max van Embden

Source: Fréjaville, Gustave (1923) *Au Music-Hall* (Paris: Éditions du Monde Nouveau), photo by C. Dobson, Liverpool

partner, Brick, is depicted similarly in a drawing by the Vesque sisters of the pair in 1904 at the Cirque Médrano. 'Brick, his head shaven, appears then with the make-up that Grock would use in his own solo performance. Grock, on the other hand, wore a large red beard' (Rémy: 389).

Grock's story is a map of the development of clown in the early 20th century. It is a convergence of two lineages, via the English pantomime and the Parisian auguste, but both curiously stripped of key elements: the former without its comedy of props and the latter without its whiteface partner. The glaring absence, compared with that fateful night in Berlin, is Antonet the clown. He has been replaced not by another clown but by a different kind of partner. In 1931 that partner was Max Embden, who left him three times no less (1916–1924, 1927–1932 and 1947–1949). After Antonet, the list is long: the first was Georges Laulhé, known as Géo Lolé, (1913–1914, 1924–1925 and 1932–1935); Alfred Schatz did several stints in the job (1936–1939, 1941–1942 and 1949–1954); and, to fill in the gaps, there were eight other short-lived partners during the period 1914–1949. Their roles were indistinguishable, non-individualised: a concert musician in evening dress. The partner's function was as a mere foil, to supply the lines and actions necessary for Grock to be able to respond. Not only that, but there were long periods when the partner would be absent from the stage. How did this change come about?

THE MUSIC-HALL ECCENTRIC

The music-hall was already the home of many solo comedians. But the solo auguste (or virtually solo, in Grock's case) was a new development. This was not the same lone figure who, in the first years of the new auguste clown, would relate to ringmaster, horse-riders or whichever whiteface clown might need a stooge. The new solo auguste was an autonomous artist. Clown terminology gives this figure the name of 'eccentric'. The eccentric has no partner on which to rely for the drama. The eccentric's drama is with their own world, with themselves. Their failures are set up not by a clown partner but by themselves. They are the victim of their own body, or of their props. They are two-in-one, having to both drive the action and fall victim to it. The whiteface drives. The auguste need only react. But the eccentric must be both intelligent enough and have enough of an idea to make things happen and set things going, and yet foolish enough to fail. The task is not easy. From the auguste as idiot, passing via the naive, the indifferent, we reach the intelligent auguste (Rémy 1945: 409).

> However, the eccentric is completely different to the auguste. Psychologically, he is the opposite. [...] contrary to the auguste, the eccentric is never an imbecile. He is a crafty auguste, resourceful, artful even, who always ends up on top. His whole science is to accumulate obstacles in sufficient quantity to have the merit of triumphing over them for once.
>
> (Rémy 1945: 369)

If the auguste wishes to be intelligent, then the clown must end up being the butt. The conservative Antonet would never have accepted such a fate. But if the auguste becomes intelligent, does he not become unsympathetic, too? In order to avoid being converted into a whiteface clown, he must remain the victim, be pitied, be out of control of his own destiny, not acquiring the power of the whiteface, a power that would turn us off. He may be no fool, but his luck is not in. It is this trait which we see clearly in Grock, and which commentators usually interpret vaguely as his 'humanity'. We warm to him. He seems harmless, without malice or power.

On the occasion of a one-off performance with his old partner, Antonet, during his month at the Cirque Medrano in 1937, Grock

> proved that has distanced himself from the primitive 'idiot'-type auguste and that, despite preserving some psychological quirk, the character was for him no more than a memory of his apprenticeship.
>
> (Rémy 1945: 394)

We are back to the servile relationship of the pre-Footit and Chocolat days, but in reverse. Now it is the auguste who holds the strings, purse strings included. When Footit and Chocolat inaugurated the age of the clown-auguste partnership, it was the clown who sub-contracted the auguste: 'He pays him, but badly' (Rémy 1945: 138–139). The auguste, Dario, earned 'a litre of milk, a few potatoes, and one sou per day' (1945: 140). And in 1910 the auguste Manrico Meschi (Bario) was forbidden under contract to work with anyone other than Léandre for two years. Clowns could always claim their overheads were too great, and their costumes too costly to spare too much on the auguste's salary. Eventually the battle for supremacy would be won by the auguste. But hand in hand with the tension of the economic power between the two went the dramatic tension of the classical clown entrée. When the economic power tipped in the auguste's favour, the dramatic entrée would be on its way out, too (Rémy 1945: 141–142).

The wheel had come full circle. Whilst Chocolat could be fired by Tony Grice for a domestic accident, Max van Embden reportedly sued Grock for 240,000 francs on account of loss of revenue having been sacked (though Grock said that it was Max who left), at a time when Grock was one of the richest entertainers in the world, and could indulge his fantasies by building himself a palace.

Grock the eccentric had his props for partners: musical instruments and chairs. It is his struggle with these that are most memorable, rather than any relationship with van Embden (there isn't one, beyond the functionality of providing the cues). The drama was musical, rather than human. Grock's battle was with himself, and it is this which keeps us expectant, awaiting the moments when the clowning will cease and the music will take over. This was managed with a 'psychological dexterity in the way he teasingly doles out or withholds the sweetmeats of melody' (Disher 1925: 218).

> At the moment of the greatest expectancy of joy, he lifts his fingers from the keys and clicks his tongue against the roof of his mouth with a resounding 'Tick'. Here, most notably, he is making his audience laugh not at him but at themselves, at their plaintive desire to have their souls tickled with mellifluous, sugary harmony. At last he satisfies them. After blowing out the footlights and throwing himself backwards on to a chair, he gazes wistfully into the spot-light and plays Verdi on a concertina with a volume of sound seemingly equal to an organ. The greatest musician might well envy the audience's veneration for this performance. The secret, however, has little to do with virtuosity or even the public's particular taste in music. Grock has satisfied their desire for the ridiculous, and they accept his idea of the sublime.
>
> (Disher 1925: 218)

FROM CIRCUS TO THEATRE, AND BACK

There is another lesson to be learned from Grock and Antonet's Berlin flop. Grock's interpretation of their agent's criticism for not realising the difference between the circus ring and the music-hall stage centres on circularity versus end-on, and how it affects one's performance:

> He had hit the nail on the head. It's one thing to have your audience all round you, and another in front of you. Your turn in the circus ring must be bold and exaggerated, even over-exaggerated, but a music-hall turn must be altogether on a smaller scale, much more sharply defined.
>
> (Grock 1931: 45–46)

Disher, observing the Fratellini in a similar setting, spotted something more subtle than the mere question of how bold one must be:

> If the Fratellini have aroused only a limited amount of enthusiasm in English Music-halls, it is because they are characteristically circus clowns. They are less funny in themselves than in what they do, which is the result of acting in the ring, where performances have to be such that they can be appreciated in the round. Take their finale, for instance. François bursts into song while wearing a top hat. Albert sets fire to it. Paul rushes to the rescue with a toy fire-engine, rests a ladder against François and mounts it, hatchet in hand. He drives the hatchet into Albert's head and leaves it there. Albert turns on a hose. François, who has never left off singing, opens his umbrella and marches off with the fire brigade in attendance and the hose pouring its ineffectual drip on the umbrella. There has been no attempt on their part to make themselves known to the audience, no confidences, no signals, no expression of emotions, no facial play, not even as much as a wink. Away from the footlights – in the arena, or the wards children's hospitals where they often perform – these negative qualities pass unnoticed in a delight in their fertile ingenuity.
>
> (1925: 198)

What is it, then, about the circle that alters the dynamic of performance? The choice of circle or stage was not a new dilemma in Grock's time. Early circus toyed with the tension between the two. Nor was it the last time the question would present itself. New Circus's push towards valuing itself on the same artistic level as 'legitimate' theatre would also lead to a move away from the circle to the stage.

David Wiles, in *A Short History of Western Performance Space* (2003), sees the distinction as one between speech and action:

> Speeches generate frontality whilst interaction and displays of physical action generate circularity.
>
> (Wiles 2003: 164)

> The political space, geared in the first instance to the speaker, is more frontal than the ritual space geared to the dancing chorus.
>
> (Wiles 2003: 169)

Speaking and hearing require that both parties face each other, such that the sound travels in a straight line from the mouth of one to the ears of the other (the ears being on the side of the head requires the eyes to be facing forward, the frontal position). Physical action which does not overly rely on facial expression does not require this configuration, however. Wiles sees the roots of the distinctions between circular and frontal performing spaces in the contrast between ancient Greek and Roman theatres, respectively:

> Whilst the Greek theatre referred the audience outwards to the *polis* beyond and a landscape inhabited by gods, the Roman theatre, completed by an awning that shut out the sun, was a contained spatial system. Autonomous Greek communities were bonded to place, but Roman citizenship conferred membership of a global community, and place slowly gave way to a more abstract sense of space.
>
> (Wiles 2003: 184)

Frontal configurations, then, by being in themselves a kind of neutral *space,* rather than a particular *place,* come to allow for the representation of a fictional place, or world, on that stage.

Although circus buildings in the modern age, or even tented circuses, do not especially give the sense of place any more than frontal theatre auditoriums, it is true that there are difficulties in creating fictional places in the circle. There are two main determining factors: visibility/invisibility and directionality.

Referring to the launch of the Theatre-in-the-Round in Scarborough in 1955, Stephen Joseph

> castigates the circle on two practical grounds. First is focus. He argues that the circle is not vectored and has but a single strong point, namely the centre, which

makes it a less interesting space to play in. [. . .] Secondly, he remarks that the circle is unsympathetic to the spaces which plays most commonly represent: rooms, roads, fields and so forth.

(Wiles 2003: 165)

In other words, fictional places need to be anchored to the cardinal points, which in the circle are lacking. Whereas the square or rectangle, particularly if the audience is not on all sides, allows for significant positioning (downstage left, upstage right, centre stage, and so on), the circle, even if it is broken by an entrance point for the performers, essentially only offers the centre and the perimeter as points of significance. A journey from A to B in the square/rectangle can be achieved via these points, thus representing satisfactorily a 'real adventure': for example, starting at upstage left, one can 'get to' downstage centre. But in the circle, any journey on the ground is virtually meaningless, as to go from one point to another on the perimeter gets you nowhere, as all points are equal. The only way to go is up. The circle cannot easily sustain fictional place and is limited to verticality for fictional journeying or narrative.

Early circus in fact combined both forms, consisting of a circular arena with a rectangular stage placed on one side:

From one point of view early circus can be seen as an awkward hybrid, pending the emergence of its natural form, the unitary ring, in the later nineteenth century. From another point of view, we can see early circus as the perfect expression of its age, reproducing the Hellenic balance of stage and orchestra. The first thesis sets up a binary opposition between circus as a space where things are done for real and the theatre as space of illusion [. . .] The second thesis helps us to see early circus as a means of resolving the aesthetic tensions evident in Wyatt's Drury Lane [. . .] Wilhelm Schlegel at the start of the nineteenth century identified the classical ideal of performance with sculpture, the romantic ideal with painting, the former emphasizing the body, the latter the face. Early circus was an oscillation between the three-dimensional acting in the ring and the pictorial display on stage, balancing the two traditions. From a classical point of view, circus set up a balance between the pleasures of the gladiator in the arena and the pantomime in the theatre. In the ring, the hero exposed himself to physical danger, whilst on stage a mythic other world was created. [. . .] In social terms, early circus was a space of relative equilibrium, not contested so bitterly as theatre.

(Wiles 2003: 199)

Circus critics of the 20th century have been divided on this issue. Pierron holds that the circus is a place of being, of fact, rather than fiction, the French word 'fait' being translatable as both 'fact' and 'act' ('that which is done'):

fact – With just this word, the fact, circus could find a definition. With no need for endless justifications, 'there', in its violence, its urge to live and to die, between joy and despair, the circus is the order of the fact. The verdict is given, immediately:

one either performs the number or one does not, the acrobat either jumps or does not jump. Things are there or they are not there, like the presence of the actor or as in life.

There are no actors and actresses there pretending to have skill: either they fall or they do not fall. Their skill is a fact. (Edmond et Jules de Goncourt (1859) *Journal*, volume I)

(Pierron 2003: 290–291)

Catalan circus critic Sebastià Gasch considered the circus to be superior in this sense to the music-hall:

The circus is the kingdom of the real. Its great strength, the secret of its success, stems from this truth. [...] Performing in the midst of the crowd, working in the circle, this man cannot cheat or lie. Everything he does must be truthful, so much more so when, finding himself illuminated by a light which falls from the roof, bare, white, more implacable than the light of the sun, he can use no artifice to fool us.
[...]
The total opposite occurs in the music-hall. [...] The music-hall is an art made of lies, or, if you prefer, of poetry, of mystery and of miracles, and pleases us because man enjoys being fooled skilfully.

('De algunas atracciones', *Destino*, 2 September 1950,
in Jané and Minguet 1998: 244–245)

Today, the predominant tendency since the 1970s New Circus movement has been to privilege the theatre stage over the circus ring, under the presumption that theatre is somehow the superior form (more of which later). Not all agree, however. A discussion about circular space in the circus journal *Zirkolika* regrets the contemporary tendency for circus performers to eschew the circle:

These days [...] circus artists find it hard to accept the circle as their stage, the ring.
[...]
One of the reasons for this fear is that in a circle you can be seen from in front from behind and from the sides.
[...]
The frontal position [...] gives us a sense of security and protection from behind. We show one side, but the other we show to the wall, to silence, to the wings, to the backcloth. The rear side remains a secret for outsiders.
[...]
The difference between circus and the theatre is between sincerity and farce.

(Aspa 2009: 33)

This obstacle to fiction in the circle, the fact that it is virtually impossible to hide anything or make it invisible, has become a key aesthetic choice, whichever side of the fence one sits.

And so we are today perhaps again at a moment of tension, between the desire to create fiction and the urge to reveal all. Indeed, perhaps this tension never really resolved itself but instead acts as a driving force for change: in the creation of early circus, in the evolution of Grock's number or in the shift towards outdoor and non-theatre spaces in the late 20th century.

Chapter

5   Clown Drama

INTRODUCTION

This chapter begins with a look at the rise to fame of the Fratellini Brothers. The Fratellini have generally attracted close to unanimous acclaim as the first great clown trio of modern times, but very little analysis has been made of just why that was the case. I here draw on Tristan Rémy's assessment of the state of circus clowning and the social forces at work in the post-First World War period. A consideration of how the evolution of the clown duo into a trio affected the repertoire leads us into a close look at Rémy's own published collection of clown numbers, *Entrées clownesques*, which today remains the definitive textual record of performances during the so-called golden age of clowns, from around 1890 until the early post-Second World War years. The entrée arguably presents the most highly developed form of clowning as drama. Understanding this mainly European repertoire gives vital clues to an exploration of the contrasting conditions of North American clowns of the early 20th century, working in far larger performance spaces. The landscape of North American clowning is complemented next by looking at the figure of the tramp clown, originating in the American Civil War and blackface vaudeville, before culminating in the huge popularity during the Great Depression years of Otto Griebling (1896–1972) and Emmett Kelly (1898–1979). I here note the development of clown performances uniquely adapted to the North American context – walkarounds and come-ins – whose dramaturgy contrasts with that of the entrée. An understanding of the evolution of clown costume and make-up is also key here, and I take this opportunity to consider Charlie Chaplin's (1889–1977) and others' claims to inspired originality in the matter. The Little Tramp also provides an example for a look at the export to early Hollywood cinema of the legacy of the English pantomime and the Hanlon-Lees, via Fred Karno and Mack Sennett, and Chaplin's first steps to distance his work from gag/action-based plot structures, laying the foundations for a new clown dramaturgy. I end the chapter with a look at how the onset of talkies gave Laurel and Hardy the opportunity to slow down the pace of comic cinema, creating a form of comedy as ritual.

THE FRATELLINI: SUPERSTAR TRIO OF THE POST-GREAT WAR ERA

The developments in the auguste clown and its relationships with other performers were partly responsible for the continuing popularity of clowns which extends from the birth of the auguste in the 1880s right up to the Second World War. But they were also aided by another force, which came from outside the dynamics of clowning as such. Just as the psychological and cultural recovery of Paris after the Franco-Prussian War created the context for the arrival of the auguste clown, so too the aftermath of another war would be crucial in renewing that impulse. Rémy suggests that only by reference to the situation post-1918 can we explain how,

> [i]n a matter of months, in fact, the Fratellini eclipsed all other clowns, apart from Grock, in the music hall, and Charlie Chaplin, in the cinema.
>
> (Rémy 1945: 213)

The Great War of 1914–1918 hit circuses hard, depriving them of many of their artists: many who were once trick riders were now dead cavalry, along with many horses; acrobats had been mobilised, dispersed, injured, amputated and were unable to work again. The circus suffered a mini-crisis. Many of its performers were no longer fit to do their job. This art form, founded upon the dream of surpassing the limits of the human and animal body, had suffered the coming down to earth of a war which had brutally crushed so many bodies.

Faced with audiences deserting to the music-hall and cinema, the Cirque Médrano dreamed up a new publicity stunt: clowns. Investing their hopes in the Fratellini (somewhat blindly since, although they had a track record, they were not yet a sure thing), the management embarked on a massive publicity campaign. Suddenly, the Fratellini were stars. Their faces, especially Albert's, were everywhere: on Paris billboards, on merchandise, on wallpaper, and advertising beauty products, shoe polish and sweets (Rémy 1945: 213).

The Fratellini were by no means averse to playing the publicity game. Their team spirit was unmatched by that of others. Their brotherly loyalty to each other caught the public's enthusiasm, who became fiercely loyal to them in return. With the mass audience in their pocket, the intellectuals were the next to succumb:

> With the general public won over, the intellectuals only had to add their voices to the chorus. Nothing could be easier. The theatre critics had prepared the way. Every day, some newspaper would lament: the theatre is dying. The worst thing is that everyone took it seriously. It was repeated that to revive the theatre it would be necessary to wade into the sources of tradition.
>
> (Rémy 1945: 216)

The Fratellini were the perfect candidates. Their name and reputation conjured up a glorious family past. Whenever asked about the facts of their family history, they would often reply: 'Read Pierre Mariel's book [their biography]. Pierre Mariel knows more than us' (1945: 218). But it was not all about history: recently returned to France after the war, the new arrivals brought audiences not just another duo but a trio. They must have seemed like the re-invention of the past.

The trio was the result of two duos minus one. The original four brothers worked the European circuit in two pairs, Louis and Paul, François and Albert. On Louis' death in 1909, the three pooled their resources in support of each others' families, adapting the repertoire for three performers: François the whiteface clown, Paul the traditional auguste, with Albert taking on a new role, a grotesque 'counter-auguste'. The success of their enterprise was such that others sought to copy this new format, and trios were all the rage from the 1920s onwards. The trio allowed for a wider range of styles. If the ideal duo looked for an explosively strong contrast between its partners, the trio allowed for greater permutations.

Rémy, rather fancifully, sees this trio as comprising three traditions: the clown of Latin origin (François), the German auguste (Paul) and the English eccentric (Albert). What is true is that the Fratellini were able to combine dialogued entrées with prop-based pantomime in the same sketch, and were capable of generating a seemingly constant flow of new ideas:

> our repertoire exceeded 180 entrées and at the Cirque Médrano we had ushered in a work rhythm that few clowns have imposed on themselves.
>
> (Fratellini 1955: 185)

TRISTAN RÉMY AND THE CLOWN ENTRÉE

Rémy's unique collection, *Entrées Clownesques* (1962), records 60 of the entrées that formed the backbone of clowns' performances for a good half-century, mostly from the period from 1890 until the Second World War, but also including some post-war numbers. Rémy's selection, made from some 150 collected, focuses on those which rely for their impact not on props or mechanical effects but on the drama of clown and auguste, a form which he notes was, by the time of writing, on its way out:

> We have therefore thought it necessary to publish them, as witnesses of a theatrical form under threat of disappearing along with its last proponents, survivors of the heroic and creative age of the art of clown, at the beginning of the century.
>
> (1962: 32)

But these are oral records, many dictated by their original performers, not works of literature:

> We have not wished to change anything of their form. They are not to be judged by literary criteria; a critique of their rudimentary style would be easy. They are only

as good as those who perform them. We must not forget that dialogue changes from one context to another, depending on the reactions of the spectators, the memory of the clown, the general atmosphere, current events and the fortunes of improvisation. Repetition is always useful. The dialogue, sparse, blunt, must be repeated by each actor to the audience he has in front of him, to whom his partner has his back. The clown entrée took the form imposed upon it by the acoustics of the circus.

(1962: 32)

One of the more complex examples is *The Bottles* (1930). The premise is an attempt by the clown to show off his newly acquired magic trick, which consists in transporting a bottle from inside a tube on one table to another tube placed on a second table. The auguste, not understanding this mysterious process, can only desire to drink from the bottle. The question is: who will upstage whom? There are many variants on this simple drama – (see, for example, Abbott and Costello's version in *Lost in a Harem* in 1944). Rémy's offering is an elaborate one for five performers. The protagonists are Dario the clown (Dario Meschi) and Bario the auguste (Manrico Meschi). Bario was an auguste of the mildly drunk type – not out of control, just a little merry. In addition, we have two further auguste-types, in descending order of foolishness: Nello and Willy Meschi. As is common, the hierarchy follows family seniority: Dario, the eldest; Manrico, his younger brother; Nello, son of Dario; Willy, son of Manrico. Finally, there is Monsieur Loyal. Loyal is the name habitually given to the ringmaster in his appearances in the cast of clown entrées, and it originates in the actual Loyal family, who produced several ringmasters, the most important being Georges Loyal.

In this version of *The Bottles*, the role of Loyal can be seen clearly. It is to him that the clown addresses himself and it is Loyal that he wishes to impress.

Monsieur Loyal is the link between the circus artists and the spectators. He presents, directs, coordinates the show. He represents the circus's direction. In general, he is the circus director himself or at least the official presenter
[...]
He represents the serious in contrast to the clown and the auguste.

(Denis 1985: 3)

The clown's initial attempts to show Loyal his trick are constantly interrupted by the auguste removing the bottle from its place:

Clown: Hey! You there! Oy! (*Auguste freezes.*) What are you doing?
Auguste (bemused): With ... the bottle?
Clown: Yes, with the bottle.
Auguste: Well, I'm looking at it.
Clown: I can see that. Please, would you put the bottle back?

Auguste: The bottle?

Clown: Yes, the bottle. (*Auguste holds it tenderly.*) Come on, hurry up. (*Auguste replaces the bottle reluctantly. Clown bats him on the head.*) Get out! (*Auguste, taken aback, removes his hat which has suffered a bit from the blow. He fixes the dents, turns around and, unhappy, retreats to the barrier, casting vengeful dirty looks towards Clown. Just as he is exiting, he recalls the insult he has just suffered and busts into tears. Then he exits.*)

Clown (to Loyal): Did you see that? What kind of interruption is that?

(Rémy 1962: 65)

By the third interruption, the clown finally gets the bottle under the tube in order to make it disappear:

Auguste (interested): What's that you say?

Clown: I said I'm going to make the bottle disappear . . .

Auguste (interrupting him and in a regretful tone): Oh! What a pity!

Clown: Why?

Auguste (unaffectedly): Because I adore bottles.

Clown (smiling): Well, my friend, that's not what this is about. This is a magic trick I'm going to show you. (*To Loyal*) I was saying, then, that I was going to make the bottle disappear from under the right-hand tube and make it re-appear under the left-hand tube.

Auguste (approaching): But it's still a shame!

Clown (brusquely): It's none of your business!

Auguste (conciliatory): Of course! But I would like to . . .

Clown: No!

Auguste (surprised, taken aback): But all the same . . .

Clown: No!

Auguste (sticking out his tongue disdainfully, his voice deep and vengeful, like a growl): Grrr . . .

Clown (to Loyal): This is unbelievable! I can't work under these conditions.

Loyal (impatient): Don't take any notice. And get to the point.

(Rémy 1962: 66–67)

As the clown begins the 'magic' of moving the bottle from one tube to the other, the second and third augustes enter. They approach the tube, which the second auguste wants to investigate and gets a slap from the clown, which makes the third auguste laugh. The second responds with a kick to the third. By this time, the principal auguste has come back. As the clown reveals his success in passing the bottle from the first to the second tube, the auguste discovers there is still a bottle under the first tube, which he steals, trying to conceal it from the clown. The clown 'magically returns' the bottle back to its original tube and everyone is waiting for the bottle not to re-appear. But at the final moment, another bottle appears under the tube where everyone thought there was none. The clown is victorious.

The drama comes from the conflict of two irreconcilable desires. The clown's desire to conclude the trick successfully is constantly imperilled by the auguste. But whereas the clown has a clear goal, the auguste does not.

It is the clown's objective which creates and drives the narrative. The clown inhabits the fictional world that he is creating, or trying to create, for his audience, Loyal, whose approval and validation is sought. The auguste, on the other hand, does not set out with any objective. He is purely reactive, and his reactions are not compatible with the fiction the clown is trying to create. In *The Bottles*, the auguste's reactions are 'non-fictional': a bottle is a bottle, a container of drink, rather than being from the imaginative world of the magician. The auguste, therefore, remains outside this narrative. The drama is thus founded not on the conflict of two characters, each with their own desires, but on this mis-match between fiction and reality.

Despite the complexity of the interactions between the five clowns, the drama is still essentially a two-clown affair. Although the Darios formed a number of different trios, or larger ensembles, throughout their careers, they could equally be effective as a duo. If there were many imitators of the trio format that brought so much success to the Fratellini, there were few, if any, who achieved the variety that the latter were capable of.

THE EVOLUTION OF THE NORTH AMERICAN CLOWN: BIG TOPS AND BASEBALL

The popularity of Albert Fratellini's new outrageous grotesque was immense. His mute, highly visual style found an echo far beyond Parisian circus, nowhere more so than in the context of North American clowning, where the extremism of the image was maintained or even surpassed. North American circus would reach such huge dimensions that large-scale visual impact was essential. In 1872 a second ring was added to the Great Eastern show, and Barnum and Bailey had three rings by 1888 with stages between. Crowd capacity was 16,000. Towsen reports that all clowns with Barnum were silent by 1885 (1976: 259). These conditions clearly worked against dialogue and dramatic entrées in the European style, and in favour of acrobatic and slapstick clowning, as well as silent pantomime. Even so, augustes of the early European type did appear (such as Marceline Orbes or Gijon Polidor), wandering around getting in the way of the setting-up of equipment. And further acts were developed which parodied the serious acts on show, including the old standards of equestrian clowning, with clowns such as Edwin 'Poodles' Hanneford (Towsen 1976: 261–263).

The later North American auguste clowns, most famously Lou Jacobs, adopted Albert Fratellini's grotesque image, which became the dominant one for clowns in the USA, together with the fashion for large-scale props or extreme visual contrasts: a tiny clown car arrives in the ring and out steps Jacobs, over six feet tall.

Non-speaking pantomime in a large space requires not facial expression, nor even gesture, but movement in space, preferably at speed. Slivers

Figure 9 Lou Jacobs
Source: Ringling Brothers and Barnum and Bailey

Oakley's best-known routine in the first decade of the 20th century was a one-man baseball game played over five minutes. In fact, the same principle of action in space applies to the real baseball field, where a tradition of baseball clowns (such as Al Schacht, Nick Altrock, King Tut and Spec Bebop, and even entire clown teams in the Negro Leagues, such as the Indianapolis Clowns) survived until the last of the greats, Max Patkin, retired in 1995 after more than 50 years and over 4000 performances. Patkin didn't just clown when nothing was happening on the field; he intervened in the actual game, if only in the early, less crucial innings:

> Patkin coaches first base, then third base, continually interrupting the game, spitting water on the players, and presumably sometimes waving a runner in from second or telling him to hold at third – how many sports would allow a clown to do this? Only baseball. The game, affected and interpreted by the clown, continues on its way.
>
> (Patkin and Hochman 1994: xiv)

Many of his gags were pre-arranged with the players, who generally played along:

> The pitcher, Robert Toth, still had his perfect game, 15 up, 15 down. Now, he had to throw three pitches to Patkin, who was lugging nine bats towards homeplate, staggering under the weight.
> [...]

> Toth [...] had to pitch to this weary old clown. First pitch was in the dirt. Second pitch was low and inside. Patkin thumped the catcher on his shoulder, who followed the script, and toppled on his backside.
>
> (Patkin and Hochman 1994: xix)

And the role of the umpires was vital:

> I depend on the umpires – to let me do my thing [...] The good guys call me out, argue back when I argue, throw me out with a flair.
>
> (Patkin and Hochman 1994: 103)

THE TRAMP CLOWN: FROM CIVIL WAR TO GREAT DEPRESSION

Another development specific to North American clowning was the tramp clown. We are accustomed to regarding this type as belonging to the Depression years of the 1930s in North America, a sad, tattered hobo representative of the times. It is true that this is the period of the early careers of the great tramp clowns Otto Griebling and Emmett Kelly. But the type has its origins much earlier. Clown historian Bruce 'Charlie' Johnson's *The Tramp Tradition* (1993) gives a detailed account, tracing the stage tramp in vaudeville to the huge growth of the tramp population following the end of the American Civil War in 1865, swollen by ex-soldiers and freed slaves newly arrived on the jobs market. Early stage tramps were Hennery and Alexander, played by Tom Heath and Jim McIntyre, who began performing in 1874 in minstrel shows:

> *Hennery:* Well, didn't that train stop?
> *Alexander:* No, it didn't stop. It didn't even hesitate.
> *Hennery:* Alexander, you got egg on your chin.
> *Alexander:* Thas jes clay from the ditch where I slep' last night.
> *Hennery:* Well, didn't that woman at the house where I sent you up give you something to eat?
> *Alexander:* No, she didn't. I saw she looked kinda hard and I thought of the old minstrel joke so I got down and started to eat the grass thinkin' that might touch her. An' she said to me – 'you poor man, you must be starvin', come around to the back yard an' I'll show you where the grass is longer.'
>
> (Johnson 1993: 9–10)

Johnson traces the tramp clown's make-up not just to an imitation of an unshaven face but also to the blackface tradition:

> Their characters were black tramps and they followed the minstrel practice of painting their mouth white to contrast with their black make up enhancing the visibility of their expressions. Tramp clowns still use a minstrel style mouth. McIntyre and Heath could be considered a transitional act between minstrels and tramp clowns, or they could be considered the first of the tramps. Old circus performers and some historians use the term 'blackface' interchangeably for minstrels and tramp clowns.
>
> (Johnson 1993: 8)

Johnson identifies four types of tramp clown in the period between 1890 and the First World War: jugglers, magicians, burglars and monologuists. We can still see what perhaps the first tramp juggler, James Harrigan, would have performed, via the films of W C Fields. Fields ('The Great Tramp Juggler') copied Harrigan's act around 1900, and, although he dropped the tramp look by 1912, he preserved the routines right up into his film appearances.

COSTUME LEGENDS: HARRIGAN, CHAPLIN AND THE FRATELLINI

In an anecdote reminiscent of the legends about the birth of the auguste, the story of Harrigan's own 'discovery' of the role claims that once when he was hired to perform at the Baltimore Press Club Camp, he pawned the dress suit he used to do his act, in order to buy a gift, which guests were expected to bring.

> That evening he borrowed odd garments from other performers, mussed his hair, and applied a beard using burnt paper. He did his act as a tramp, and according to Harrigan he was such a success the manager said, 'If you ever get that dress suit out of pawn, I'll shoot you!'
>
> (Johnson 1993: 8)

The story is reminiscent of Chaplin's tale of how he discovered his version of the auguste, the Little Tramp:

> 'We need some gags here,' [Sennett] said, then turned to me. 'Put on a comedy make-up. Anything will do.'
>
> I had no idea what make-up to put on. I did not like my get-up as the press reporter. However, on the way to the wardrobe I thought I would dress in baggy pants, big shoes, a cane and a derby hat. I wanted everything a contradiction: the pants baggy, the coat tight, the hat small and the shoes large. I was undecided whether to look old or young, but remembering Sennett had expected me to be a much older man, I added a small moustache, which, I reasoned, would add age without hiding my expression.
>
> I had no idea of the character. But at the moment I was dressed, the clothes and the make-up made me feel the person he was. I began to know him, and by the time I walked on to the stage he was fully born. When I confronted Sennett I assumed the character and strutted about, swinging my cane and parading before him. Gags and comedy ideas went racing through my mind.
>
> (Chaplin 1964: 154)

The truth is, of course, that Chaplin's costume is one more version among many of the typical auguste of the period.

An even more improbable costume story is that by Albert Fratellini, who tells of his pleasure in encountering the low life in the cities he was on tour to, in the Hamburg cafés, in Chinatown in Barcelona, or in the bars of Pigalle in Paris. On this occasion he was in London, wandering the streets and pubs of Spitalfields, Bethnal Green and Whitechapel, and he entered into conversation with the locals, who all had an opinion on clowns.

> The man who spoke to me had bare feet in enormous shoes, full of holes where his toes stuck out. His trousers, too big for him, slumped down over his shoes. These trousers swung around his waist. My interlocutor also wore a tarnished and threadbare tailcoat whose sleeves practically covered his hands and whose tails dragged on the floor. He looked like a stuffed heron, with his long nose stuck like some kind of lantern in the middle of his face.

> 'I would like to do something else in the ring,' I said to him putting a few shillings on the bar, and added, 'Sell me your clothes.' The deal was done, and we exchanged clothes. I looked like a scarecrow. To complete the character, I had made by a specialist a pair of over-sized shoes, that I paid the equivalent of a hundred francs for. These shoes completed my profile. They appeared in all the rings of Europe.
>
> (Fratellini 1955: 96)

But having dazzled us with the anecdote, Albert goes on to admit that, of course, he was well aware of other performers who used such garments, such as Billy Hayden's big shoes, 'copied in that by Little Tich, Charlie Chaplin and the Fratellini!' (Fratellini 1955: 97).

TRAMPS, WALKAROUNDS AND COME-INS

By the 1930s the tramp as performed by Griebling and Kelly had evolved from its vaudeville origins into a specifically circus clown, strongly influenced by the 'walkaround' or 'come-in' style of Marceline and Polidor. Griebling was prolific in creating permutations based on a progressive running gag format:

> For some of his routines, based on being a deliveryman, Otto used a progressive format which might begin during the come in. In one, he began with a block of ice, and with each appearance, the ice would be smaller, until finally he was carrying a tiny ice cube in his huge ice tongs.

> In another, he would go through the audience looking for Mrs. Schultz who had ordered a potted plant. Each time he returned, he was a little older, and the plant a little taller. Finally he was an old man with a beard carrying a ten foot tall plant in a wheelbarrow.

> One of his messenger boy routines caused trouble. He began by dashingly riding a bike to deliver a telegram, and ended up, his shoes in shreds, walking with the aid of a crooked stick. He had to stop performing the gag due to a threatened law suit by Western Union.
>
> (Johnson 1993: 32)

THE LINEAGE OF THE ENGLISH PANTOMIME: FROM THE HANLONS VIA KARNO AND SENNETT TO CHAPLIN

Following the trail of the auguste clown from its early experiments to the grandiosity of Grock's mature performance has told us much of the 'what', the 'when', the 'who' and the 'where' of clowning. But the old ways, the Hanlon-Lees way, didn't just disappear completely; it simply resurfaced in another context. Simon Louvish, the prolific historian of silent cinema comedy, sees a 'missing link' between the old English pantomime and the new silent movies in the company of Fred Karno, credited with being the force behind the careers of Stan Laurel and Charlie Chaplin.

Frederick John Westcott, an acrobat and trapeze artist, formed The Three Karnoes with two other gymnasts, Ted Tysall and Bob Sewall, to replace an act (The Three Carnoes) which never showed up at a music-hall in Edgware Road. They went from busking the West End, to the provincial music-halls, to touring the continent (Louvish 2001: 52). Karno (as he would thenceforth be known) graduated to larger-scale works with his 1894 box-office hit, the pantomime *Hilarity*, followed by *Jail Birds*. Although there are no surviving scripts, Louvish cites reports in the stage journal, *Era*, that in *Hilarity*, Karno is 'suspended in an inverted position high up on a house piece' (*Era*, April 1897):

> Quite what *Hilarity* was is unclear. It featured 'a humorous donkey possessed with a receptive and reflective mind, an actively funny footman, impervious apparently to hard knocks, a couple of lovers, a grumpy guardian and a domestic', living in 'rural retirement'. The *Era's* reviewer (9 January 1897) notes that 'the farce will not bear analysis. It is built simply for laughter making purposes, and fulfils its object admirably.'
>
> (Louvish 2001: 53)

Era's review of *Jail Birds* includes blasting operations in a quarry, bridges blown up, convicts playing practical jokes instead of working, lifting an official up into the air on a crane, prison bread so hard it needs a saw to cut it, and chases between wardens and prisoners (*Era*, 1 February 1896, in Louvish 2001: 53–54).

Jail Birds and *Hilarity* toured music-halls for six years. If the style had gone out of fashion at the circus, neither was it to be expected in the halls, whose entertainment was based on characters, songs and dialogue. In these silent pantomimes, Louvish suggests, can be found both the style and the themes that would later be transposed to the new context of Hollywood cinema by Chaplin. In *Early Birds* (1903),

> Karno added complicated mechanical scenery and effects to 'an original pantomime burlesque' of life in London's Whitechapel, a spoof of Dickensian degradation, representing 'the life mostly of the loafer, the thief and the dosser'. Fred himself played a Fagin-like Jew, a travelling glazier, who has a knife fight with

a brutal-looking blackguard hiding from justice' (*Era*, 10 January 1903). 'The contriver of this clever sketch', raves a later *Era* scribe, has

'caught the very essence of the hopeless gaiety, the gruesome jollity of English poverty, wretchedness and crime.... How vivid is the picture; how it reeks with life and reality! And in this twilight when virtues are vices ... looms large the typical ruffian, the "sponger" on women, the brutal, remorseless "rough". Anon night falls, and we are transported to the horrible lair where the human animals fling themselves down in their rags and tatters at the close of the day.'

It is not difficult to discern in this the origin of Chaplin's 1917 *Easy Street*, down to the ending in which the young hero beans the 'rough' with a table.

(Louvish 2001: 55–56)

We do not know who was primarily responsible for the composition of Karno's pantomimes. Louvish considers Karno himself an unlikely sole author, with performers' contributions most probably being a vital part of their creation. The point, though, is not whether Chaplin had a hand in these pieces or whether he stole or borrowed them wholesale for his own films; Chaplin's real claim to fame is that he

understood how the old characters could relate to the new medium, to the camera, in a completely new way. It was this that made Chaplin such a key figure in the history of both mime and the movies. Many of his followers, including Stan Jefferson, took a long time to discover their own relationship with the magic lens, how to make it reflect their emotions, their inner self, and their ideas.

(Louvish 2001: 77)

Karno, through Chaplin, then, was the carrier of the old tradition to the new North American screen context:

For while Chaplin brought the form of Karno pantomime to his new world, the content was Sennett's own America, contagious, nervous, always at high speed.

(Louvish 2003: 100)

This was a new post-war world, as was the Hanlon's:

This penchant for featuring the most apparently dangerous gags for no organic reason except the fun of it is typical of many of these routine two-reelers. The humble pratfall was no longer enough, at the tail end of World War I, to amuse an audience who knew that in real life, young men were being blown sky high by real gunpowder. Stuntmen performed the most amazing feats for a few dollars a day, leaping off buildings, even if the subsequent twentystorey fall was completed by a dummy.

(Louvish 2001: 129–130)

Chaplin's subsequent development, according to Louvish, entails a gradual slowing down:

All the little bits and pieces that made up the Tramp's many mannerisms, his cane-twisting, ear-picking attention to small details, were a realization in depth of Keystone's external chaos. [. . .] But though he slowed down his character, the New World surged on around him at its urban whirlwind pace.

(Louvish 2003: 101)

LAUREL AND HARDY: COMEDY AS A RITUAL

A different kind of deceleration occurred in the films of Laurel and Hardy. The director/producer/supervisor Leo McCarey, in an interview with Peter Bogdanovich, recalls that

comics had a tendency to do too much. With Laurel and Hardy we introduced nearly the opposite. We tried to direct them so that they showed nothing, expressed nothing and the audience, waiting for the opposite, laughed because we remained serious'.

(Bogdanovich 1972: 23)

With Laurel and Hardy, it is not just the characters who slow down, it is the whole action:

I came in one morning and I said, 'We're all working too fast. We've got to get away from these jerky movements and work at a normal speed.' I said, 'I'll give you an example of what I mean. There's a royal dinner. All the royalty is seated around the table and somebody lets out a fart. Now everybody exchanges a *glance*, that's all.' Everybody died laughing, but I got my point over.

(Bogdanovich 1972: 24)

This pace allowed them to meet the slowed-down demands of the new talkies. Walter Kerr, theatre and film critic, and historian, suggests that they were able to

alter silent film comedy in a way that made it possible for them, alone among their contemporaries, to pass over into sound films with scarcely a hitch of their philosophical shoulders.

(Kerr 1975: 318)

Laurel and Hardy were not the only silent film comedians to work slowly (Harry Langdon, discussed later, being perhaps the slowest of them all), but it is one thing for a solo comedian to contrast with the pace of the world that surrounds him and quite another when it occurs within the dynamics of a duo:

if the front man was slowed down by the delicacy of his nature, the second man, Laurel, had to be slowed further still, rendered all but inanimate as he waited for his master's cue. How, then, were the gags to be performed?

(Kerr 1975: 330)

The drama played out between the two is transformed, they 'showed everyone the joke, explained it most carefully, anatomized it' (Kerr 1975: 330).

> Here, you see, is Mr Hardy climbing out of bed to get a hotwater bottle for Mr Laurel who has a toothache. Here, on the floor between the bed and the bathroom, is a tack. Here comes Mr Hardy, stately in his kindliness and blind to his peril. Here is Mr Hardy stepping on the tack, howling in pain and plucking it from his bare foot. Here is Mr Hardy throwing the tack away with infinite disgust. Here is Mr Hardy in the bathroom, filling the hot-water bottle, and returning to the bedroom. Here, once again, is the tack on the floor, exactly where Mr Hardy has thrown it.
>
> (Kerr 1975: 330)

For Louvish, this is the quality which makes them appealing to so many:

> This ritual is perhaps the most important element that enabled the popularity of Stan and Ollie in almost every country of the globe.
>
> (Louvish 2001: 223)

Ritual jokes invite us to reflect consciously upon and savour their stupidity:

> Speed is not of the essence – there is little point in rushing if one can proceed more sedately, and with the proper dignity, towards inevitable disaster.
>
> (Louvish 2001: 223–224)

The formula applied not only to action, but to dialogue, too. Louvish cites an example from Laurel and Hardy's first talkie, *Unaccustomed As We Are* (1929):

> *MRS KENNEDY:* Oh, good evening, Mr Hardy.
> *OLLIE:* Good evening, Mrs Kennedy. This is my friend, Mrs Kennedy.
> *MRS KENNEDY:* Good evening.
> *OLLIE:* I brought him home for dinner, Mrs Kennedy.
> *MRS KENNEDY:* Oh, how lovely of you, Mr Hardy.
> *OLLIE:* How is Mr Kennedy?
> *MRS KENNEDY:* Oh, he's very well, Mr Hardy.
> *OLLIE:* Is Mr Kennedy home, Mrs Kennedy?
> *MRS KENNEDY:* No, he isn't, Mr Hardy. I must be going. Good night, Mr Hardy.
> *OLLIE:* Good night, Mrs Kennedy.
>   Mrs Kennedy exits.
> *OLLIE:* That was Mrs Kennedy ... Why, what's the matter?
> *STAN:* I was wondering who it was.
>
> (Laurel and Hardy 1929)

This wasn't just a ritual with 'universal' appeal but also contained a reference particular to its time:

> This exchange, with its ponderous, idiot-proof diction, [...] suggests their realization, and that of their screenwriter, 'Beanie' Walker, promoted from titling, that the very slow, self-conscious speech of early talkie actors was itself ripe for spoofing.
>
> (Louvish 2001: 251–252)

With Laurel and Hardy we have come another full-circle. Their origins are in the fast-paced physical and visual action of early slapstick-based cinema comedy, heir to the Hanlons and the English pantomime, yet their mature work rests equally upon the foundations of the drama of human relationships as manifested in the duo of the whiteface and auguste clowns. Chaplin, too, would later evolve towards another kind of fusion, between gag-driven and emotionally driven storylines, which I shall look at in more detail in the context of a closer discussion of clown plots (Chapter 13).

We can see how the evolution of clown drama is not a single story but a complex of influences. The ups and downs of clown fashions throw up action-based plots, dramas of conflict between clown types and fusions of the two, subject to the concerns of the decades, themselves subject to world events, from war to the comings and goings of political systems; the evolution of performing spaces, media and technology; and the meetings and separations of individual clowns, together with those who directed, employed and recorded them.

Death and Rebirth
of the Clown

INTRODUCTION

In this chapter I turn my attention to the origins of the contemporary clown and the way it has been perceived as being a renewal of the art-form. I begin with the situation of clowning in the aftermath of the Second World War, with reference in particular to Charlie Rivel's (1896–1983) questioning of whether clowning could be possible after the suffering of the Holocaust. I examine how his eventual return to performing and his evolution of a kind of minimalist clowning led to world acclaim, followed by his reinvention as a cultural hero in his native Catalonia. I then take a broader look at the period and at the growth in importance of the concept of tradition, posited as the polar opposite of the new approaches to clowning, such as Jacques Lecoq's, which were gaining pace in the 1960s. Claims that clowning was dead (and therefore in need of revolution or resuscitation) surface most famously in Federico Fellini's mock-documentary *The Clowns* (1970), a film which provoked resentful accusations from many clowns themselves. I then discuss some of the modern-day consequences of this split, where clowns can be variously viewed as infantile, scary or unfunny. This leads to the debate over whether clowning is about fun or philosophy, or both, as I focus on the origins of Slava Polunin (born 1950) and the company Licedei in the time of perestroika in the Soviet Union in the 1980s, where 'just fun' could signify radical statements about freedom. I follow the story to the present day and analyse whether this still holds true for such clowning in the context of huge commercial success. This also entails an exploration of the position of clowning in the globalised environment of Cirque du Soleil. I finish the chapter by looking at a selection of clowns who do not conform to these dominant forms – Andrei Jigalov (born 1966), Fumagalli (born 1956) and Jean-Baptiste Thiérrée (born 1937), all of whom have escaped the 'death of the clown' and have retained strong elements of 'tradition'.

CHARLIE RIVEL: POST-HOLOCAUST CLOWN

Clowns in the immediate period post-Second World War seem, from today's perspective, like the tail end of the inter-war period. The post-1918 years had seen Grock, Antonet, Little Walter, the Fratellini, Chocolat and others attempt to revive, to re-start or to continue their careers (with results ranging from superstardom to abject misery). Now Grock was nearing his end, finally retiring from performing in 1954. François and Albert Fratellini continued for some years, but with replacement augustes since the death of Paul in 1940. It didn't look like there were any candidates to set in motion a new golden age of clowning this time. When Grock asked Charlie Rivel why he had stopped performing, his reply was, 'Who can laugh any more after the tragedy the world has lived through?' (Rivel 1973: 220). Rivel had continued to honour his contracts in Nazi Germany throughout the war, reportedly even appearing for Hitler, but after a few shows in Sweden and London following the end of hostilities, he retired to his home in France in 1947, leaving the performing to his sons:

> My courage had deserted me, exhausted. I was supposed to make other people laugh and now I couldn't any more. I couldn't forget the war.
> [...]
> Only now, when the guns are silent at last, can people really understand what has happened; only now can they see the catastrophe of war in its full horror. In this world full of hate, everywhere you see wounded and invalided soldiers, orphaned children, widows, lonely, forlorn shadows of people wandering about without knowing where to go, on highways and byways: ruins, dead people, concentration camps, fires, and sirens which continue to wail, although the war is long since over. One still hears them, and the spectacle of the war's misery is still burned into my memory. Who wants to laugh now? What can a silly clown like me do? I have done what I set out to do for mankind. [...] All these suffering people – whether Germans or Frenchmen or Russians – they all had hearts like the rest of us and used to laugh and cry as we do. And I, the clown, am I to make them laugh, I who would like to weep over it all myself?
>
> (Rivel 1973: 220–221)

Though nervous and unsure about performing again, Rivel finally yielded to family pressure and, at the age of 56, returned to training for his trapeze number. His comeback in 1952 at the Deutsches Teater in Munich was a success, and Rivel tells us that it was a letter he received after that show that was 'positive proof that it was right to begin working again' (Rivel 1973: 227). It came from a spectator who saw him perform many times in Berlin before the war, and who associated those happy times with seeing the clown. After the war, the whole family had become depressed, not least herself, as she had been paralysed in both legs by being crushed in a bombing raid. They moved to Munich and now had come to see the clown once again. The letter continues:

> Dear Mr Charlie Rivel, when I saw you the day before yesterday I laughed so much. I laughed as much as in 1926. That night my husband, my children and I got no sleep at all. We sat and talked about you all night long. Only at daybreak,

when my husband and my son were to go off to work did I fall asleep. When I woke up, my daughter came as usual to help me into my wheel-chair. She was just going to take hold of my legs to lift me out of bed when the miracle happened – for it was a miracle! I could move my legs! Today I can walk a few steps. Thanks to you, Mr Charlie Rivel, happiness has returned again to our little family. Thank you, thank you! Your F. H.

(Rivel 1973: 225–226)

If true, it certainly would be justification for returning to work. But Rivel was not the only clown to have performed a miracle. Supposedly, one evening a group of sailors on leave attended a performance of Grimaldi's. One of them had been struck deaf and dumb since suffering sunstroke a few years earlier, but none of his fellows was surprised that he enjoyed the show so much, relying as it did so little on the spoken word,

and so deep was his enjoyment that, after one violent burst of applause, he turned to the man beside him and said: 'What a damned funny fellow!'

'What, Jack, can you speak?' cried his neighbour, who could hardly believe his ears, with all the hubbub going on around them.

'Ay, and hear too!' said the sailor, to his own enormous surprise, and he proceeded to tell his shipmates and everyone else in the gallery.

(Findlater 1978: 133)

Slightly less spectacular is Jules Claretie's 1898 short story, *Boum-Boum*. This is a tale of a sick child whom medicine had failed to cure and whose parents were desperate, having brought him all the toys he wanted, all to no avail:

'But what is it that you want, then, my François? asked the mother. Look, there must be something you would like . . . Tell me! . . . tell your mother!' And she rested her cheek upon the pillow of the little sick child, and whispered into his ear, gently, like a secret. The child, in a strange tone, sat up in his bed and, stretching his hand out as if towards something invisible, replied suddenly with a tone which was at once ardent, begging and commanding:

I want Boum-Boum!

(Claretie 1888: 7–8)

The first visit of the famous clown Geronimo Medrano (known as 'Boum-Boum') was a failure, as he came dressed in his normal clothes. Only when he returned suitably made up and costumed did the cure take effect. When asked by the father what he is owed, Boum-Boum replies: 'permission to put on my business cards: Boum-Boum, doctor-acrobat, physician to little François!' (Claretie 1888: 17)

Albert Fratellini tells a similar tale. Since 1909, the Fratellini had been in the habit of performing for free in hospitals and charitable institutions, where we fulfilled a sacred duty by becoming, for the little ones, those fantastic doctors who, through the therapy of laughter, sometimes performed miracles.

(Fratellini 1955: 216)

They are called to the bedside of a little girl who in her fever called out 'My clowns!' [...] 'I want to see my clowns!' and of whom the doctor had said 'There is no hope left, alas! .... Only a miracle can save her ... Give her whatever she asks for.'

Faced with our capers and joking, we saw her literally resuscitate, come out of the chrysalis where death had imprisoned her.

(Fratellini 1955: 217–218)

Whether these anecdotes are true, half-true or pure fiction, they have a common purpose: they articulate our belief in the clown's power to overcome suffering. When the news of Grimaldi's cure spread, he not only had cured the sailor but also

had given back sight to a blinded soldier, had raised a man from the dead. (Why not? A Clown could do anything: he broke the laws of life and death on the stage.)

(Findlater 1978: 133)

So it is the clown who can save the people from their post-war suffering – Rivel post-Second World War, the Fratellini post-Great War, the auguste post-Franco-Prussian War, and so on.

Rivel's return to performing wasn't just a comeback, however. It quickly transformed itself into a reinvention of his career. Like Grock, he had already undergone the transition from team-player to soloist. Although the trio of brothers, the Andreu Rivels, formed in 1923 in imitation of the Fratellini's success (Charlie even drawing on Albert's grotesque look for his own make-up), had indeed acquired fame, it was Rivel who was the star comedian, and he finally left in 1935 in order to perform with less equal partners.

Like Grock, too, Rivel had begun his rise to fame by stepping into the shoes of a better-known clown, his famous imitation of Chaplin on the trapeze earning him universal plaudits and giving him his new name, Charlie.

Rivel's international appeal would even outstrip that of Grock, according to some critics:

Rivel is a gift from heaven, because he makes us laugh. And we all know that laughing is healthy. Whoever is unable to laugh at Charlie Rivel is hopelessly sick.

There is none like him. He is the master, a global phenomenon. We are in the presence of a clown who combines art and culture with the most profound humanity. And who, moreover, expresses himself in a universal language, comprehensible to everyone.

There are countries which do not appreciate the humour of great clowns such as the august Miehe or Grock himself. Grock has been whistled noisily in Italy. On the other hand, Charlie Rivel has obtained a complete success. Audiences around the world have surrendered before the art of Rivel. We will keep applauding him until our hands are sore.

(Eitz, *Berlingske Tiende*, Copenhagen, 1953, in Jané 1996: 31)

In Spain, his birthplace but where he was virtually unknown, the fabrication of the living legend began in 1954 when Rivel performed in Barcelona and Madrid with the Circo Price. The reinsertion of a clown of such 'universality' into his homeland wasn't all easy-going, though, receiving mixed reviews:

In his season with the Circo Price in Barcelona in the autumn of 1954, Charlie Rivel produced no impact. As had happened with Grock, he didn't move the majority not one bit. His art was too subtle, too wise. At that time there existed the fashion for speaking clowns and for telling jokes. People wanted cheap laughs and broad humour.

Charlie wasn't a tortured soul like Grock, he didn't play with paradox. But, like Grock, he did make you think too much. The thing is that people want it all ready-cooked for them, they don't want to have to chew. And they want it hot out of the oven, even if it does burn their mouths. Charlie was too good a cook. It wasn't worth people making the effort.

(Jordi Elias, in Jané 1996: 27)

But despite the doubts about whether he was too northern European (having performed so much in Germany and Scandinavia), the new Rivel was gradually constructed over the coming years, a Spanish TV programme being made about his life (1962), followed in 1963 by a street named after him in the town of Cubelles, his birthplace, and then a film on his career, *El Aprendiz de Clown* ('The Clown Apprentice'; 1968). The centenary of his birth saw the circus critic Jordi Jané's *Charlie Rivel* (1996), which situates him amongst the great figures of Catalan cultural history, blending rigorous journalistic research with whimsical fantasies of Catalan reunification as he imagines a moment when Rivel and family perform on a tight-wire spanning the 'two Catalonias', on the Franco-Spanish border.

By 2005, Rivel's position was so confirmed that it even allowed for the moral questioning of Gerard Vàzquez's play, *Uuuuh!*, at the Teatre Nacional de Catalunya and the film spin-off, *El Pallasso i el Fuhrer* ('The Clown and the Fuhrer'; 2007), the plot of which includes a Gestapo officer who wishes to take the place of Charlie's clown partner and a supposed private show for Hitler's birthday.

Rivel's clowning had its origins in his acrobatic apprenticeship, his Chaplin on the trapeze, but as time passed he would drop first the Chaplin character and finally the rigours of physical discipline. What was left was a clown who seems the epitome of non-physicality:

When he entered the ring he was slow, almost majestic. He took his time. Thus he gave an impression of some great event to the most insignificant of his tricks.

(Jacques Fabbri/André Sallée, in Jané 1996: 26)

But this is not the slowness of Laurel and Hardy, laying bare the workings of the gag. Indeed, there are virtually no 'tricks'. The gag in the conventional sense is minimal. For example, as Charlie begins to climb on his chair, is he going to sit on it, stand on it, or do a handstand on it? Finally standing on the chair and realising his guitar is out of reach on the floor, he must get down again. But it is not the comedy of the situation, of the problem to be solved, which engages us but his descent, using only his arms, his feet hanging as they slide gently to the floor. The situation has become almost abstract, the bare bones of human action; we are watching only a man on a chair, yet the performance still seems full, but of what?

Charlie Rivel is an exception. He reacts to the audience just as they react to him. He has the secret of improvisation. When he is near you, there is no need for you to say anything because he knows what you are thinking and feeling. His eyes and his face tell you.

(*Darmstegel Tagblat*, Darmstad, 1971, in Jané 1996: 35)

This quality of self-reflection, of heightened awareness, was spotted in Rivel in earlier years by Rémy, who described the Andreu-Rivels' entrée of *The Eggs*. Polo, the first auguste, holds an egg that René, the whiteface clown, is to pierce with a bullet from 15 paces. But Polo is unable to overcome his fear, letting the egg fall and break. But then in comes Charlie, 'the imbecile who has no awareness of fear' (Rémy 1945: 360). For him, holding the egg is a great honour, since it is a task no-one else is capable of.

Oh! yes. Hold an egg. What's that?
It's an egg .... Don't you know what an egg is?
Ah! It's an egg? How nice it is!
Yes! It's an egg!
What kind of egg, René?
A hen's egg.
Ah! A hen's egg! How nice it is!

(Rémy 1945: 360–361)

When Charlie's curiosity about the egg leads him to break it, the contents running all over his hands lead him to the same innocent and wondrous conclusion: 'Ah! How nice is an egg!' (1945: 361). There is no sense of suffering in Rivel's failure, as he says to René: 'Give me another egg so I can start again' (1945: 361).

Whereas Grock's chairs were problematic and falling apart, Rivel's is just a chair. Whereas Grock's violin bow wouldn't obey him, Rivel's egg behaves just like an egg. For Grock's frustration substitute Rivel's satisfaction.

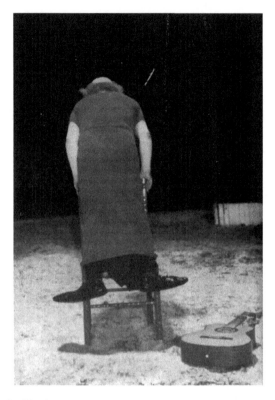

Figure 10   Charlie Rivel
Source: Rivel, Charlie with J.C. Lauritzen, trans. Ursula Hoare (1973) *Poor Clown* (London: Michael Joseph), photo by Jan Selzer

CLOWNS AND TRADITION IN THE LATE 20TH CENTURY

Most clowns in the second half of the 20th century, however, were treading different paths to Rivel's minimalism. Anthropologist Kenneth Little has written extensively about the way those clowns who strived to maintain the entrée were eventually faced with a dilemma. Either they could cede their place to the 'new' clowns, many of whom had no contact with or knowledge of the 'old' ways, but whose vocation had been developed through their experience, direct or indirect, of the teachings of contemporary clown, most prominently Jacques Lecoq, since the 1960s. These new clowns' practical experience was more likely to be in street rather than circus, and in independent theatre companies rather than in commercial circuses. Or they could recoup their strength and reinforce their 'tradition' in an attempt to out-perform the newcomers. Few of the traditional clowns saw the danger of this strategy, which is one of the focuses for Little's study of the whiteface clown, Pitu:

> Most entrée clowns are unwilling to change their work as they rely on an increasingly restricted set of traditional entrée styles, methods, and materials.

They hope that this stock-in-trade will save their art from the threat of the 'new' clowns. As a result, Pitu argues, the entrée has become unimaginative. It may be that in their attempt to protect the entrée tradition, circus clowns have exhausted its form. Relying on an increasingly restricted set of stock routines and styles of comedy in the search for purity and identity, the established entrée groups are cutting themselves off from the source of power in their tradition – the imaginative adaptation of comic elements, whatever their source of inspiration, to the entrée form. As a successful circus director complained to me, it is in the name of circus tradition that contemporary entrée clowns stick to the same entrée material year after year, constantly refining it, hoping to improve what is already mastered rather than creatively acting upon it.

(Little 2003: 142)

Little argues that entrée clowns in the late 20th century, rather than following a tradition which reaches back generations, were inventing a rigidly defined idea of tradition that never really existed:

The earliest entrée clowns engaged in free play within the tradition, relying on the imagination of family members as *bricoleurs* and constructing the tradition as open-ended; by contrast, contemporary entrée clowns resort to a more strictly defined circus authority: its rules, its laws, its morality, and its order. Proudly drawing back into its traditions as new clown forms emerge, entrée clowns have undermined their popularity.

(Little 2003: 142)

It wasn't just the new wave of self-made clowns which posed a threat, however, and stimulated a further entrenchment in tradition. Since the mid-1950s,

Entertainment forms were engulfed by a routinized industry of art and culture, which turned things, like the family circus and the circus artist's performance ideology, into commodities – i.e., images and decorations of the culture of spectacle consumption.
[. . .]
The narrative of family solidarity and of 'circus' self-reliance has been subverted by different versions of circus acts that are now determined by a contractual relationship negotiated solely through entertainment impresarios, agents, lawyers, circus associations, and the 'new' entertainments.

(Little 1991: 241–242)

FELLINI AND THE DEATH OF THE CLOWN

What Little's studies suggest is that the 'traditional' clown is only invented when it is under threat. That threat appears to be mortal, if we are to take at face value Federico Fellini's TV mock-documentary *I Clowns* ('The Clowns'; 1970). Much has been said about whether the 'death of the clown' scene is Fellini's metaphor for a long-lost innocence or a comment on the actual state of clowning, but whatever the director's intentions, the film has often been taken to be a literal document of its subject matter, by both its supporters and its detractors.

Circus historians L R Dauven and Jacques Garnier took offence in an article the following year in *Le Cirque dans l'Univers*, journal of the Club du Cirque.

> We have seen *The Clowns*. We were totally disappointed, and quite disgusted.
>
> (1971: 41)

Their fundamental criticism is that Fellini misrepresented the circus:

> What is sad is that Fellini has retained only what is sordid and ugly about the circus.
> [...]
> Fellini has offered us an image of the circus that is outrageously deformed, and totally out of touch with reality.
>
> (Dauven and Garnier 1971: 42)

We have here a now familiar battle between the circus as decadent and the circus as dignified. A more serious accusation is that Fellini deliberately manipulated the interviews he conducted with the clowns so as to get what he wanted: tears, melancholy and nostalgia. Dauven and Garnier cite a letter to the press by the family of the clown, Bario, who is interviewed in *I Clowns*.

> When Fellini came to see our father – Papa Bario is eighty-seven years old – he found him all smiles. He asked him to recount his past, but he systematically stopped him when he spoke about anything humorous. 'Tell me about your last time in the ring, when you became ill in the Circus Knie in 1956! Tell me sad stories.' To think he made our father cry. Realizing the same tactics would not work with the dwarf Ludo, he got him drunk and then had him talk. He cried then. When Maïss doubled as Papa Bario, Fellini decided on the circus at Amiens, because it is empty.
>
> (Dauven and Garnier 1971: 43)

The issue today is perhaps not whether 'clowning was dead' but whether Fellini ever intended to document the state of clowning at all, and if so whether *I Clowns* wasn't a 'missed opportunity'. In the words of the prolific clown collector, historian and performer, Pat Cashin,

> With so many great clowns still performing at that time it might have been more valuable to have interviewed more of them and interviewed them a bit more thoroughly.
> [...]
> But, since television and film producers only view clowns as monsters anymore, the chances of something like this being produced are exceedingly slim.
>
> (Cashin 2011: 'Fellini's Clowns', *Clownalley* 10 April 2009)

THE SPLITS IN CLOWNING: TRADITION VERSUS CONTEMPORARY, INFANTILISATION VERSUS PHOBIA

Whether there was a real crisis or not, clowning at this point in history seemed to split. On the one hand, partly in reaction to the perceived degeneration of circus or 'traditional' clowning, the 1960s saw the birth of a clown which finds its roots not in the past or in tradition but in a personal, essentially interior, experience in the here-and-now. The search for, or discovery of, 'one's own clown' is propelled by the teachings of Jacques Lecoq and others, and becomes a powerful ally of those seeking personal and political liberation. I will discuss this later when I come to look at the 'how' of clowning, and how the teaching and learning of clown became privileged over the performing of clown.

According to this story, if the old clown was dead, it was because it had been reduced to a superficial and empty shell, confined to going through the motions of the old routines but devoid of convincing human content. In a sense, this position was just a re-run of the Modernist use of the clown as an icon, seeming to mean laughter but empty and sad on the inside. What the contemporary clown offered, though, was a way to fill that emptiness with one's own authentic self. This would then equip the clown for communicating on a deeper level with audiences, something that it was supposed was no longer possible for the old clown to do. In Eli Simon's words,

> these Bozo-type clowns . . . are not the soulful clowns you will likely develop using this book.
>
> (2009: 4)

One clear sign for the new clowns that the old clowns were now defunct was their infantilisation. The history of who clowns are perceived to be performing for is not a simple one. In a way, all popular arts which are not clearly marked as 'for adults only' have suffered at one time or another the denigration that their lack of serious pretensions to art means that they must be for children (puppetry, pantomime, circus and so on). But the latter part of the 20th century arguably saw a marked intensity in the projection of clowns as children's entertainment.

This development is paralleled by the rise in popularity of television as a medium, and of clowns for children working in that medium. At first sight the clown whose aesthetic had been built in the medium- or large-scale spaces of circuses would not sit comfortably on the small screen. The strong visual elements – necessitated by distance – circular spaces and the acoustics of the circus were alien to the tiny flat space of the television screen with its volume control in your own living room. Despite this, television clowns for children were abundantly present, especially in the 1960s and 1970s: the Barios in France, the Aragóns in Spain and South America, and a long line of Bozos, originally created back in 1946 and franchised out across North America and beyond. This contrasts with comedy intended for adults on television, which drew not from circus clowns but from the traditions of music-hall, variety and vaudeville – forms whose frontal, verbal style adapted easily to the new medium.

The infantilisation of clowns is evidenced by the longevity of Ronald McDonald, created in 1963 and still going strong. Of course, clowns had been used in advertising before but the new strategy was aimed exclusively at children.

But this for-kids-only clown had another dual opposite, apart from the art-clown-for-adults. If the infantilised clown seemed to represent a kind of complete innocence, then the scary clown would incarnate complete evil. The myth of the evil clown took root in the late 1970s. In 1978, Paul Kelly, son of Emmett Kelly Jr, was arrested for the murder of two of his partners. Diagnosed with multiple personality disorder, those personalities included 'Weary Willie' (the clown his father and grandfather had incarnated). It was also the decade of the highly publicised case of serial killer and rapist John Wayne Gacy, who occasionally appeared as an amateur clown at parties and events and became known as the Killer Clown. Stephen's King 1986 novel *It* seemed to underpin the clown scare, depicting a malevolent character who preyed on children by luring them while dressed as a clown. Coulrophobia, the fear of clowns, became the fashionable fear to have and to boast about, despite the fact that all of these figures only resemble clowns in their masked appearance and not in their behaviour. Here is the clue: we have another manifestation of the old Modernist cliché that behind the smiling mask there simply cannot be what we expect but its opposite. That opposite varies throughout history: for the Romantics it was Pierrot's sadness; for Beckett and the Absurdists it was the nothingness of meaningless human existence; for Lecoq it was the dead tradition, mechanically repeated unoriginal gags which are no longer funny; and for the coulrophobe it was the darkness of evil.

Joseph Durwin in *Coulrophobia & The Trickster* (2002) offered a more enlightening analysis of the modern clownphobe. His argument is that although there is no inherent connection between evil and clowns, there is a connection between fear and laughter, and it is one which the clown may play with. Citing the more extreme forms of clowning that are traditional in indigenous peoples in North America (and which I will discuss later), Durwin points out that a clown is in fact a kind of fearless being which can break taboos, travel to other worlds, behave erroneously and yet survive. Such fearlessness often excites fear: for one who is enslaved by fear, witnessing someone who is not only free of such restraints but 'authorized to do things ordinary people can't do' (Durwin 2002) might be disturbing for them. On the other hand, it might be liberating through laughter.

Whichever strand of late 20th-century clowning you look at, the absence of laughter has taken on a prominent role. Kids' clowns are deemed not to be funny (to adults), scary clowns are by definition not funny, and many contemporary clowns claim that 'It's okay not to be funny. Clowns do not have to make people laugh' (Simon 2009: 31).

SLAVA POLUNIN: PERESTROIKA CLOWN

Back in the 1980s in Leningrad, 'fun' wasn't just for kids; it was a political statement with revolutionary potential upon which Slava Polunin and the company he founded, Licedei, built a new clown aesthetic:

> But when I came [to North America] with my troupe for the first time and we began running on their heads, an excessively free American spectator quickly understood that he is besieged by the true anarchists, and he cocked them a snook and said: 'Now you will see what the real freedom is'. But this game wasn't interesting to me. It made sense in Russia under Brezhnev; it was my hobby-horse there. [It] was an island of spiritual freedom in the country where there was no freedom at all. That was the reason why the audience supported us. People thought: 'At last, there is freedom somewhere, at least in the clownery some do what they want, they crush the aesthetic canons, at least it's them who get the joy'.
>
> (Polunin 2001)

For Polunin, it is this freedom itself which is the clown's meaning:

> Clown is the most spontaneous creature on Earth. When you start restraining his freedom, he loses himself and whimpers like a child. Basically, it means that you offended him deeply. Clowns are very special, and they need a special treat. Like the lunatics or, I don't know, like the drunk or the dogs.
> [...]
> At a glance you notice how unusual he is. Like, when you offer him a seat, he answers: '*I will lie down here*'. His answer is inadequate, but that is not because he wants to show off, rather it is his normal condition, the only one in which he feels happy. I always use my son as an example. I tell him: '*Vanya, bring me a teapot*'. Vanya lies on the floor, rolls to the kitchen and comes back with the pot on his head. This is his normal enjoyment of the game. To live as usual would be dull and uninteresting, he feels emptiness of this life. All his being fights against everyday occurrence, routine, and he seeks the festival and the game.
>
> Freedom is everything to the clown. The only thing I cannot stand is when my freedom is restrained. I cannot imagine the situation when I have no freedom of choice.
>
> (Polunin 2001)

The early work of Polunin exemplified this philosophy put into simple practice. The 1984 sketch *Nizzzya!* ('Can't!') 'didn't demonstrate any professional skills [...] at all', whilst *Blue Canary* turned to be a red cloth for a bull: four clowns are marking time – and that's it. One TV-maker told us: 'Take this nonsense with you and keep it for a good memory'. And he wasn't wrong: none of us was doing a double somersault, nobody could actually sing, the harmonies were paper-made. What is the trick then?.

(Polunin 2001)

In a sense, this clowning began where the abstract clowning of Charlie Rivel left off. Measured, reflective, almost gag-less: 'Sometimes I regret I cannot hold the audience without any plot whatsoever' (Polunin 2001).

As Polunin notes, the meaning of this clowning alters when it travels the world. It is one thing to clown in the last decade of the Soviet Union, and quite another to tour the world in the post-communist era, as Polunin has done since 1993 with *Snowshow*:

It's a great problem for the Americans – to keep a mind on something that doesn't move. [. . .]

This year I was 'fighting' with the French when we had performances at the Casino de Paris. [. . .] Whatever I tried, didn't work. It was so till I guessed that poetical emotion would be a place of our meeting. [. . .] Now I know exactly which countries do need me, and which do not. For example, Spain doesn't need me. All our attempts to demonstrate tenderness in Barcelona last year failed miserably. They couldn't understand a thing. The Spanish audience doesn't forgive if you do not address it personally. Columbia needs me. While in Belgium or in Portugal I am absolutely useless: their society is in such condition that my idea has no meaning there.

And our Russian audience is just like me. We are so similar. I prefer when comedy and tragedy are together.

(Polunin 2001)

But whereas 'fun' was once a serious business, now it is not enough. Alexander Kan, arts editor of the BBC's Russian Service, interviewed Polunin on his return to London in December 2011:

Slava Polunin is proud to be a clown. But when you look at what he does you see much more than conventional fooling around of a circus jester. His work is deeply rooted in contemporary avant-garde theatre and dance.

(Polunin 2011)

And we are back with the kids' clown vs. art clown duality, as Polunin explains:

I had a dream to turn it into a contemporary art form, to make it more than just fun for children. I thought there was something more profound, a mystery, a modernity in it.

(Polunin 2011)

GROCK AND POLUNIN: PHILOSOPHER CLOWNS

Polunin is by no means the first clown to have been hailed a 'philosopher'. Grock 'was called intellectual, the philosopher clown, the shakespearean clown, cartesian, bergsonian' (Rémy 1945: 392). But Grock, in a moment of rare humility, rejected the label:

> I should like to take this opportunity of painting myself in my true colours. What is Art to me, or Philosophy, either? I am no Intellectual!
>
> All these things that get said about me are charming in their way, but they don't really wash. They are merely skilfully framed advertisements, concocted in their innocent fashion by my excellent backers. From a business point of view I can in no way complain, for an 'intellectual clown' has a far greater vogue these days than does your simple-minded bucolic clown.
> [. . .]
> I am merely [. . .] a simple son of the mountains [. . .] I've no World Philosophy!
>
> [. . .] As for reading Shandy and Plutarch, I made it all up. I boasted about it, thinking it would give a nice twist to my reputation. Fancy a clown reading Plutarch!
>
> (Grock 1931: 194)

If in Grock's time the idea of a philosopher-clown seemed like an interesting, but peripheral, marketing angle, then at the beginning of the 21st century it appears to have far greater resonance in offering itself as a way of rescuing clowning from its post-war supposedly decadent state. *Snowshow* is undoubtedly a remarkable achievement in selling new clowning to a mass audience, perhaps even comparable in some respects to that of the Fratellini in the 1920s, with both the general public and intellectuals on board. Bringing the philosophical art-clown to a mass audience has been partly achieved by the use of multiple understudies, the chances being that it won't be Polunin himself whom the spectator sees, which has enabled the show to tour globally for nearly two decades. Some critics may delight in spotting the winks to serious modernity:

> The foolery on display owes something [. . .] to Beckett (the proceedings begin with a Godot-style visual gag about hanging yourself).
>
> (Paul Taylor in *The Independent*, 23 December 2011)

But others have pointed out that times have changed:

> Nearly 20 years old now, *Snowshow* was created by one of Russia's (now) most celebrated clowns, Slava Polunin, the founder and inspiration of a considerable tradition of highly evocative mime theatre, and who possibly has become somewhat trapped by its fabulous international success. When he made

Snowshow in 1993, it was soon after the fall of communism, and the grimness of that world lent its weird population of tramps an edge and pathos that now has dissipated.

[...]

And now, how does it fare nearly 20 years on?

[...]

The pace is excruciatingly slow, and I have to admit that this time round, many years after my first amazed encounter, I felt the slowness, and the cosiness, rather more keenly.

[...]

At any rate, I felt that I remembered, seeing Polunin in this long ago, something more hesitant, isolated and withdrawn in the performance.

Yes, this mattered – or at least, the robustness mattered. The street-cleaners, daily out in sub-freezing temperatures clearing the pavements for ordinary folk, are the lowest of the low in Russian society, and there isn't any hint of that brinkmanship left in the clowns in *Snowshow* now – perhaps I imagined it before.

(Ismene Brown in *theartsdesk*, 29 December 2011)

Audiences apparently also remain somewhat divided. A quick perusal of current online reviews by spectators (not a scientific survey, admittedly) reveals an almost equal divide between mostly 5-star and 1-star reviews. And although the comments are diametrically opposed – typically ranging from 'clowning at its most sophisticated' to 'pretentious tosh' (Ticketmaster 2011) – they are agreed on one thing, that the issue is meaning and not how funny the clown is.

Some critics have dropped the references to significance altogether: 'This is a show purely about entertainment with no forced narrative or worthy message' (Liz Arratoon in *The Stage*, 19 December 2011), which leaves us with 'a fuzzy warm feeling' (David Brinn in *The Jerusalem Post*, 13 August 2011). If this is Beckettian, then it is Beckett without ideas. We have come a long way from fun as political freedom to fuzziness as commercial success.

What is beyond debate is the influence on early 21st-century clowning. Since the break-up of the Soviet Union and the emigration of many clowns to the west, a shared aesthetic with common roots in the Leningrad of the 1980s, a recognisably new 'Russian style' of clowning has spawned new companies, aside from Polunin's own, such as Dimitri Bogatirev and Iryna Ivanytska's Aga-Boom in the USA, or Nikolai Terentiev's Booff Show in Canada.

CIRQUE DU SOLEIL: GLOBALISED CLOWNS

Clowning which signals its meaningfulness found its natural home in Cirque du Soleil, which specialises in circus which, though loaded with signs telling the spectator they are watching something full of meaning, leaves them guessing as to what that meaning might be, as Michael Billington did in a review of *Varekai*:

I have come late to Cirque du Soleil, who now turn up annually at the Albert Hall. What I had not quite expected was a show that, for all the skills involved, combined corporate soullessness with spiritual pretension. It pays tribute, we are told, 'to those who quest with infinite passion along the path that leads to Varekai' which means 'wherever' in Romany. To which one is tempted to say: 'Phooey.'

(*The Guardian* 10 January 2008)

Cirque du Soleil's relationship with clown brings clearly into focus two prominent forces at the turn of century: the commodification of the circus and clown artist/performer; and the duality between decadent old clowning and artful new clowning. Cirque du Soleil has become a kind of haven for some chosen performers to work solidly for a number of years, albeit at the expense of signing away all rights to their own material, and ex-company members acquire a prestigious addition to their CV. Joey Robinson-Holden spent four years performing in *Varekai* (2004–2008), a job she says she got 'despite feeling I was under-trained, because they were looking for a short fat-legged woman' (Robinson 2011). Since she was to replace another performer, Mooky Cornish, the creator of the number, she was called upon to learn and reproduce the routine in the same way as her predecessor:

We had eight days rehearsal. It was 'old school' work, no time for discovering things. We spent lots of time on make-up ... and shoe shopping. There's no time to find your own self in the number. I could see where the laughs were in Mooky's version, but mine wasn't funny in the same places. Mooky's wobbly legs and sliding around were her signature. I couldn't do that. But I'm good at falling over, so I used that. It took a whole year to nail the number.

(Robinson 2011)

Just how far clown performers can reproduce each others' work is debatable. Robinson stayed for four 'brilliant and frustrating' years, but her clown partner at the start only lasted six months, his anarchic spirit restricted by the working methods:

Every show is videoed, then the choreographer will ask you why you moved your hand at that point ... When you start with them, every show gets feedback.

(Robinson 2011)

Indeed, Cirque du Soleil's relationship with clowns seems fraught with ambivalence towards clowning itself. Audition calls to performers refer to 'comic characters' rather than 'clowns', although the continuing popularity with the general public of the idea of clowns means that they are advertised as 'clowns'. The company doesn't have clown specialists, relying instead on 'artistic directors and choreographers to guide performers' (Robinson 2001). Robinson sees them as 'comic characters in odd situations'. She became obsessed with what clowning might really offer only on leaving Cirque du

Soleil, subsequently studying with clown master Philippe Gaulier. Asked what he might have said of her work efforts, she replied, 'Not honest enough' (Robinson 2011).

Whilst there is a perception that the shows rely on the clowns for the human element, and the connection with the audience – 'you can't imagine circus without clowns, you need a representative of the audience onstage' (Robinson 2011) – there exists an alternative view that they are the weakest link. The ambivalent relationship with clowns was evidenced by the first Cirque du Soleil show ever to flop. *Banana Shpeel* (2010) brought the comic routines together into one show, but the critics were almost unanimously damning:

> To be fair, Cirque du Soleil – that prolific, Canadian troupe that seems intent on world entertainment domination – is trying for something different. 'Banana Shpeel' is a true departure from the lavish, exotic spectacles that have been popping up here for years.
>
> Cirque followers know that the laborious clown segments tend to be the show's weakest elements. And this show, written and directed by veteran clown David Shiner [. . .] is stuffed with them.
>
> (Frank Scheck in the *New York Post* 22 May 2010)

Perhaps it was the change of context:

> But the acts, though fine, are on a smaller scale than usual – and without the lavish theatricality that usually surrounds them, they seem overly familiar.
>
> (Frank Scheck in the *New York Post* 22 May 2010)

Others agreed that without the usual production standards the comedy fell flat:

> What's emerged, under the writing and direction of the great comic mime David Shiner, is a shapeless and sour enterprise, totally lacking the crispness and focus that are Cirque trademarks.
>
> (Robert Feldberg in *The Record* 27 May 2010)

The conclusion that the funniness in clowning relies on tight choreography and high production standards is indeed an odd one.

Clowning at the beginning of the 21st century is in some ways highly visible to a mass global audience through Cirque du Soleil and *Snowshow*. As we have seen, both have tapped into the key concerns about clowning at the end of the century, combined with a similar powerful commercial business strategy – one which Polunin learned from his collaboration with Cirque du Soleil:

> Polunin spent time working with Cirque du Soleil – not because he felt he could learn from them artistically, he says, but because he wanted to learn how to be as

good at business as they were. When he was offered a Broadway run, he spent months paying lawyers to teach him contract law. 'I'm now a highly-educated clown,' he laughs.

(Interview with Slava Polunin by Nuala Calvi in *The Stage*, 16 December 2011)

SURVIVING TRADITION: ANDREI JIGALOV, FUMAGALLI AND JEAN-BAPTISTE THIÉRRÉE

But that dominance doesn't mean there are not in existence other forms that are less culturally dominant. One of the many of a more 'classical' style, Andrei Jigalov works against the grain, with entrée-style numbers with a partner playing whiteface clown to his auguste. The visual aesthetic is entirely contemporary but is also a reproduction of the dynamics of a style now out of fashion: Jigalov dressed in a jacket whose armholes are ripped and trousers with the most ridiculously saggy crotch, while his partner Albert Csaba is immaculately besuited. In *The Sweets* (2009), the roles play out in familiar fashion, Csaba fooling Jigalov with a sleight of hand into believing the sweet he holds is in his other hand, Jigalov guessing wrong every time, until Csaba produces an enormous one, which Jigalov snatches. At last! He can eat! But Csaba suggests he play the magic trick back on him. Of course! Jigalov moves his hands around, hoping to confuse his partner, but we can see the huge sweet sticking out of his fist. He loses. The format may be familiar but the execution is exceptional, both partners playing their roles with the utmost dedication only to exposing the stupidity of each of them and, above all, their relationship. It is failure stripped naked. If there is emotion to be provoked in clowning, then perhaps this is it, something akin to tragedy but ridiculously hilarious at the same time.

Despite often being introduced as 'the best clown in the world', Jigalov's talent is relatively unknown outside clown circles. It remains to be seen whether the cultural context will be right for the old entrée style to resonate once again with a larger public in the future. In the meantime, being out of fashion doesn't stop high-quality clowning being performed within the old context of old circus by the likes of Barry Lubin (Grandma) or Fumagalli. The latter is descended from the old circus family tradition and his *Le Miel et la reine des abeilles* ('The Honey and the Queen Bee'; 2011) is from the classical entrée repertoire (see, for example, Dario and Bario's 1920 version in Rémy 1962: 183–186), but in his performance there is no sense of a form in decadence. In contrast, Josep Montanyès sought to revive the importance of clowns through a conscious reconstruction and recuperation of historic numbers in *Clàssics* (1996), but his success owed much to Montanyès's capacity as an auguste clown to elaborate seemingly endlessly within the structure of the entrée form, leading to numbers which were of considerable length and complexity.

Jean-Baptiste Thiérrée and Victoria Chaplin's Le Cirque Invisible is more familiar to a wider audience, partly due to its longevity. Their work spans several decades, appearing as young newcomers auditioning for the Cirque Bouglione in Paris in Fellini's *I Clowns* in 1970, and continuing to tour internationally today. Despite a vast array of props and costumes, Thiérrée's clowning style is simplicity personified:

> it is like watching an embarrassing elderly uncle at a family party. He saws his wife in half, and makes rabbits and doves appear from boxes with a charm that recalls the days of music hall; but he does it all with the air of one who is exceptionally pleased with himself.
>
> (Lyn Gardner in *The Guardian*, 5 August 2009)

This is an excellent description of what clowning does. The only thing is, Gardner's words were meant to be uncomplimentary. It seems that critics are still too much in thrall to the display of 'meaning' to be able to spot clowning, judging by her comparison with Thiérrée's son, James, in the same review:

> The triumph of James Thiérrée's work is to conjure image with context, emotion and meaning. Here, however, we just get the conjuring.
>
> (Lyn Gardner in *The Guardian*, 5 August 2009)

But for others it is that very lack of pretension to meaning which saves the show: 'Cirque Invisible swims along on a wave of whimsy but it is never twee or saccharine' (Franco Milazzo in *Londonist*, 10 August 2010).

This tension in clowning between meaningfulness and meaninglessness thus comes into focus as a major theme of post-Second World War clowning, stretching from Rivel's existential doubts over whether laughter would be possible again up to today's attempts to bring clowning with significance to a globalised audience.

Chapter

7 Clown Women

INTRODUCTION

In the final chapter of Part I we complete our journey in search of answers to the what, who, where and when of clowning by focusing on the growing importance of women clowns in our own times. I start by looking at conflicting claims about whether there are any significant historical precedents before the 1970s, and uncover the roles of women clowns at the turn of the 19th and 20th centuries, and how articulate they are in revealing gender concerns of the era of the New Woman and women's rights. I also examine how the figure of the woman clown served to express more reactionary gender roles at the same time. I then take a look at the clown career of Annie Fratellini (1932–1997) from the 1970s on, which reflected both the new opportunities of women's liberation and also the still narrow options open to women in clowning. I end with a survey of some women clowns who today demonstrate a variety of approaches to the issues of gender, femininity and clown.

WOMEN'S CLOWN HISTORY: THE NEW WOMAN

A major feature of clowning at the end of the 20th century was the large number of women clowns active in the field. In one way this is simply a reflection of advances in gender equality generally since the 1960s. Bypassing traditional power structures, such as the circus family, contemporary clown has presented itself as a personal choice open to all, such that gender inequality has in some ways played less of a role than before. Real equality might still be a way off, but something must have shifted when Bruce Johnson told of an instance in 1990 of a variety arts magazine editorial complaining that women were taking the men's clown jobs because they were more popular. The author of the article

> implied that women were hurting the art of clowning. He supported his position by claiming the only woman to star in a circus until recent times was Annie Oakley and that female clowns had not existed until late in the twentieth century.
>
> (Johnson 2010)

Johnson's written reply disputed this view of history, citing Evetta Matthews, who appeared on an 1895 Barnum & Bailey Circus poster. And elsewhere, in *Early Female Clowns* (2000), Johnson lists ancient Greek female Dorian Mimes in the 7th century BC; medieval glee-maidens; Mathurine, a 17th-century jester at the French court; and the role of Columbine in commedia dell'arte. But the truth is that uncovering the history of women clowns is not an easy task. The poster Johnson mentions announces 'Evetta, the only lady clown'. On the surface, this looks more like a publicity gimmick playing on the novelty value of a woman appearing as a clown, rather than an acceptance of women clowns in circus.

Janet M. Davis's 2005 lecture 'Bearded Ladies, Dainty Amazons, Hindoo Fakirs, and Lady Savages: Circus Representations of Gender and Race in Victorian America' situates the poster image of Evetta, dressed in full-length bloomers and whiteface make-up, in the context of the rise of the 'New Woman' at the turn of the century, part of the new forces which were pushing for the rights of women in politics, education and society:

> starting in the late 1890s, 'New Woman numbers' were a frequent part of the largest circuses: women, clad in 'becoming' bloomers, 'of the most trim fitting, advanced new woman dress reform pattern,' played all roles in the arena: ringmaster, grooms, and object holders.
>
> (Davis 2005: 2)

In the circus, this new public role for women was part of a general evolution which would enable Mabel Stark, who joined the circus in 1913, to become

> the most celebrated tiger trainer in the United States. [...] the athletic performances of Mabel Stark and other circus women celebrated female power, thereby representing a startling alternative to contemporary representations of frail, neurasthenic womanhood.
>
> (Davis 2005: 2)

From this perspective, Matthews' clown is not just a freak one-off:

> Mathews [sic] boldly sat down next to male audience members, made faces at children, and danced, tumbled and twisted 'like a rubber doll' while in the arena. Press releases noted that she had 'all of the new woman's fads' because she rode a bicycle, swung Indian clubs, 'and does everything a man does to keep herself in proper trim.' [From 'A Very New Woman,' unidentified newspaper clipping, 1896, Circus World Museum]
>
> (Davis 2005: 5)

Matthews' own words confirm that she consciously saw herself as being in tune with the progressive times:

I believe that a woman can do anything for a living that a man can do, and I do it just as well as a man. All of my people laughed at me when I told them that I was going into the ring as a clown; but they do not laugh now when they see that I can keep an engagement all the time, and earn as much money and more than they can in their branches of the business. [From 'A Very New Woman,' unidentified newspaper clipping, 1896, Circus World Museum]

(Davis 2005: 5)

Figure 11   Evetta Matthews, Barnum and Bailey Circus poster
Source: Ringling Brothers and Barnum and Bailey

LULU THE CLOWNESSE AND THE BELLE ÉPOQUE

History records only a few other women circus clowns either at this time or before, notably Amelia Butler, who toured with the Nixon's Great American Circus in 1858. Nor was Matthews' pioneering example followed up by many. Rémy mentions Lonny Olchansky in Germany, and in France Miss Loulou and Yvette Spessardi of the trio Léonard (1945: 438–446). Pierron dates the coining of the term 'clownesse' to the Belle Époque (Matthews' era), and *femme-clown* and *pitre en jupons* ('petticoat clown') to the 1920s, suggesting that part of the rejection, or appeal, of female clowns of those periods was the confusion between seduction and humour:

> For even if there are no reasons why a woman cannot clown, the pulling of faces, by she who is supposed to be seductive, is discomfiting.
>
> (Pierron 2003: 179)

This confusion is evident in Félicien Champsaur's one-act pantomime *Lulu* (1888) and his later novel *Lulu, Roman clownesque* (1901), which includes the pantomime as one of its chapters. Although Champsaur cultivated links with just about every major literary and artistic figure of his day, being a special favourite of Stéphane Mallarmé, his work is virtually unknown outside France, probably due to his reputation for obscenity and pornography, as one of many citations collected by Sophie Basch in her introduction to *Lulu* demonstrates:

> A repugnant author. He is to literature what music-hall proprietors are to dramatic art and his inspiration is scarcely ever above mezzanine level. [Jacques Vier]
>
> (Basch 2002: 587–588)

Champsaur's *Lulu* pre-dates and, according to Basch, inspired Wedekind's character of the same name, and is an eroticised clown of male fantasy:

> Lulu, creator of a type, the clownesse, united the verve of the professional clown with the exquisite grace of a woman, of a pretty girl, heady and spiritual, as well as the vertiginous suppleness and imagination of the Hanlons.
>
> [...] Lulu, in her extraordinary pre-dinner evening dress, but still in her clownesse's wig, mounts a fixed bar installed in the centre of the ring by two riders, and she bends backwards to place her sweet, cheeky face with its strange smile between the rustling frills revealed there beneath, which suddenly frame the inverted oval of her little face, delicate and wicked – her mouth calling – between her black-stockinged legs and white umbellate petticoats.
>
> (Champsaur 1901 in Basch 2002: 653)

Fantasy though it may be, the pantomime version starred real-life clowns Footit and the Hanlon's collaborator Henri Agoust, who also directed the performance at the Nouveau Cirque. In the novel version, Footit's partner, Chocolat, also makes an appearance. And Henry Gerbault's drawings of Lulu also resemble, at least in her wig, the style of the real-life Evetta Matthews and others. As Basch observes, 'fiction and reality do not cease to inter-mix' (2002: 594), and she wonders just how much Champsaur is inventing:

> The history of circus has recorded the memory of a certain number of transvestites, amongst them a certain Miss Lulu, who appeared from July to September 1870 at the Cirque de l'Impératrice. Is this Lulu the child of the acrobat,

Parini, who previously performed with his son on the flying trapeze? In any case, it is for a Miss Parini, named Lulu, his daughter, that this acrobat signed an engagement as gymnast [...] The coincidence is too troubling not to see in this intriguing Lulu the inspiration for Champsaur's Lulu.

(Basch 2002: 597)

But the importance of the various Lulus, fictional or real, resides in the 'climate of an epoch' (2002: 597). Basch cites an article in *Le Bambou* in 1893 which took fright at the 'conquest of public space by women' (2002: 597):

I glimpse the future, I foresee Western Woman playing her great principle role in the destiny of her race. [...] Today her power has become frightening – frighteningly delicious! [...] One day she will be absolute mistress. [...] in that enormous domain of the free woman which is the Salon, the Theatre, the Concert, the Circus, the Dance, in Europe.

(Basch 2002: 597–598)

Fictional or real, the female clown was the site of 'the apprehensions and hopes of the Belle Époque' (Basch 2002: 598).

We have some, though limited, information on a later Lulu. According to Vanessa Toulmin of the National Fairground Archive at the University of Sheffield, Lulu Adams, née Craston, probably performed as a clown from the Edwardian period onwards, first with her father Joe Craston, then in the 1920s with brother and sister as the Crastonians, and later with her husband, Albertino. She was with Ringling Bros. and Barnum & Bailey Circus from 1939 to 1941 and she continued performing in Britain until the 1950s. Tellingly, like Matthews, she was billed as 'The only woman clown in the world'. Not much progress, then. And, in contrast to Matthews' New Woman appeal, Lulu's 'father told her not to go for the grotesque but try to be feminine' (Toulmin 2007), hence the white curling wig.

The relative lack of women in pre-1970 circus clowning doesn't demonstrate a complete exclusion from being funny, though, as clear examples from other comic genres demonstrate: Marie Lloyd and Vesta Tilley in music-hall, Lucille Ball and Phyllis Diller in early television, and especially silent cinema, with Marie Dressler, Mabel Normand and Marion Davies. Perhaps it is here that the heirs to Evetta Matthews should be sought, such as the highly physical comedian Louise Fazenda, who appeared in nearly 300 films between 1913 and 1939 yet is nearly forgotten in comparison with her male contemporaries, Chaplin, Keaton, Arbuckle and so on.

Keystone provided young women like Louise with a perfect antidote to the conventional female roles. Neither child-women nor femmes fatales, they could muck in, indulge in the rough stuff with the male of the species, hammer people over the head and be hammered, giving as good as they got.

(Louvish 2001: 107)

ANNIE FRATELLINI, WOMEN'S LIBERATION AND CLOWN GENDER ROLES

One figure spans the two eras of pre- and post-women's liberation: Annie Fratellini. She was initially excluded from a male-dominated world, despite her privileged position as grand-daughter of Paul Fratellini:

> My father took me nearly every Thursday to Medrano's. He would always say, 'What a pity you aren't a boy, you could have been a clown'.
>
> (Fratellini 1997)

It was the clown Pierre Étaix, whom she married in 1969 and with whom she founded the École Nationale du Cirque Annie Fratellini in 1974, who encouraged her to rediscover her roots and work as a clown. When the two quarrelled, Annie remained without a partner. Her daughter Valérie recalls that Annie, in response to the question 'why don't you work with your daughter?' replied:

> Oh my God! with my daughter! Two women clowns, I had never thought of that. That's never been done.
>
> (Fratellini 2002: 110)

Although Valérie agrees with her mother that 'there is no female or male clown. There is just the clown' (2002: 111), the reality for her was not so simple:

> When I started working, I never ceased to hide my femininity just as my mother did. I was ashamed of being a woman.
>
> (2002: 111)

So what have other women made of the new opportunities in contemporary clowning since the 1960s, when clowning offered the dream of liberation from our conventional social roles, a freedom to behave as we want. What better ally for women's liberation could there be?

Sue Broadway recalls that it wasn't as easy as that:

> I am looking at a picture of myself aged about twenty. I am wearing a clown ballerina dress, giant point shoes and a funny red wig. I am looking out past the camera with an expression of open-hearted pleasure, my eyes sparkling with the sheer delight of being in front of an audience.
>
> The girl clown I see in these pictures went into hiding shortly afterwards and it took nearly thirty years to coax her out again. There were other clowns; a fat lady with a stammer, an elegant white face in a sequined frock, a manic 'beautiful assistant' causing havoc in a juggling act, a pompous trapeze artist . . . but the simple, open naïve clown seemed to be gone for good. I had stumbled on her thoughtlessly, just the first thing that came to mind, without realising just how fragile she was.
>
> (Clay 2005: 75–76)

The fragile, simple clown is not so easy to maintain in a hostile world:

> How did she get lost? Well, she was a bit lonely. [...] everywhere I came across conventional wisdoms that told me women and clowning were a problem zone. For a start, they said, the clown is androgynous and it is impossible for a woman to be androgynous. She carries her sex around with her as a constant.
>
> (Clay 2005: 76)

But, as with male clowns, the lure of 'having something to say' proved irresistible, and especially so for a woman:

> Also I began to think – perhaps too much. I wanted my clowning to say something, to communicate ideas about the female condition, to provide a role model and a character that other women could laugh with. The naïve girl who was so happy in her skin and just delighted to be out there having a go at it seemed too simple and childish to tackle the big questions.
>
> (Clay 2005: 76)

The trap is this: that whilst clown offers a radical opportunity to question our received ideas about ourselves, once we fixate on a particular idea the clown disappears. Clowns question anything that seems fixed or true, or presents itself as transcendent, which includes both the establishment and our own ideas about how to change it. The anarchic freedom of clowns risks sabotaging their own project, including the providing of role models. Maintaining this tension between clowning and social criticism runs the risk of returning to the old stereotypes:

> all-female clown troupe, Clowns Ex Machina, aims to carve out a bigger place in the profession for women, and to create humor with deeper meaning and a democratic spirit.
>
> The troupe's new show, 'Clowns Full-Tilt: A Musing on Aesthetics,' aims to explore such subjects as the pursuit of beauty, free expression and the pursuit of love, and to find humor in those topics along the way.
>
> (Barbara Chai in the *Wall Street Journal*, 1 November 2011)

Although the mere fact of women owning the freedom of clowning is in itself challenging to gender roles, even those women clowns who don't seem to 'have something to say' have not all escaped the 'role' trap. Kirsten Anderberg, writing about her experiences of owning public space as a street singer, considers that it is perhaps the very radical nature of performing as a woman which provokes a consequent conservatism in the choice of material:

> If you are a woman breaking gender roles by commanding street corners for entertainment, your safest bet is to sing sad love songs, depicting yourself as lovelorn and lost, still looking for a man to save you. Or as Joni Mitchell sings, 'There's a wide, wide world of noble causes...but all I really want to do right now is find another lover.' Although people are uncomfortable with your use of the street venue, as a woman, they are consoled by the material, which fits the female stereotypes and keeps a male focus. When I began street performing at

age 18 in 1978, I followed these gender rules. I had a confident stage presence and strong voice, yet I sang about needing a man, and of men who left me heart-broken. One day a male street performer came up to me and said, 'Is love all you can sing about?' It made me take notice of what men sang about. They sang about sex, and getting drunk and high. They were singing about traveling, and wars, and whaling, and politics. And about trying to stay away from women who would marry them. They were not singing forlorn love songs.

(Anderberg 2005)

WOMEN CLOWNS TODAY: FEMININITY, DRAG AND BEYOND GENDER

In a similar way, non-radical roles proliferate in much of the work of female clowns, such as Pepa Plana – the lover in *Giulietta* (2000) or the wife awaiting her husband in *Penèlope* (2010) – or Caroline Dream's would-be bride in *Dime que sí!* ('Tell Me You Do!'; 2006).

Others have chosen explicitly heroic, though no less stereotypical, role models, such as Gardi Hutter's *Joan of ArPpo* (1981) or even Nola Rae's *Elizabeth's Last Stand* (1990), although Rae's later famous figures are male, in *Mozart Preposteroso* (1999) and *Exit Napoleon Pursued by Rabbits* (2005). However, both Rae's and Hutter's works are concerned more with the form and aesthetics of hybrid forms of clown/mime/narrative/theatre than with gender issues. Hutter creates complete fictional worlds based around a solo clown figure inhabiting a fantasy mix of heroism and eccentricity. In this world the clown gags only occasionally stand alone and almost always serve to narrate a story. Much of the story-telling/clowning centres on the transformation of objects: in *Joan of ArPpo*, a metal tub used for washing clothes becomes a boat for crossing from the mountain of clothes to the sink, and later a piece of defensive armour. Slightly less story-centred is a routine where Hutter falls backwards into the tub, gets stuck and uses her huge wooden spoon to try free herself, hammering her legs into the tub and levering herself up with the spoon. Hutter's clown is one who creates worlds rather than breaks them, as is Nola Rae's clown, though the latter's fantasies are slightly more dual, more regularly broken by complicity with the audience.

A very different use of clown is made by Kate Pelling, who began by performing Elvis Presley imitations, which then became an impersonation of impersonators of Elvis, including a version where 'Elvis didn't die, he came to the UK to become a drag queen' (Pelling 2011), where the performer is a woman performing a man performing a woman. Pelling doesn't consider herself a clown as such but situates her work within the sub-genre of 'clown drag', which Julian Fleisher defines in *The Drag Queens of York* as one end of the 'The "Glamour" to "Clown" Scale':

Realness is a problematic notion when applied to drag. Even the queens who strive to attain it aren't really trying to attain 'real' realness. They are after a drag-informed *idea* of what realness might be if queens ruled the planet. It is often interchanged with 'glamour,' which is probably closer to an accurate description of what those queens are chasing. On the other end of the same scale is 'clown drag,' which – although no less cartoonish really than glamour drag – involves a more commedia dell arte feel. In 'clown drag,' every aspect of the costume is ballooned and exaggerated to its maximum. Few queens fully embody only one extreme or other, creating an even more problematic situation for the morphologist in all of us. As Chicklet is fond of saying, 'I fall right in the middle of glamour and clown drag. I call it "Clamour." '

(1996: 88)

Pelling uses our expectations of clowning to play with the mechanics of performance itself, such as the video *Boo* (2009), where we only see the performer's hands covering her face, certain in our expectation that she will at some point surprise us by showing herself and shouting 'boo!' But at the critical moment, the image disappears, accompanied by a limp 'boo'. It is at once clowning and a joke about clowning.

Angela de Castro's work focuses more clearly on 'pure' clown, ranging from the simple *The Gift* (1991) to the textually and technically complex *Only Fools, No Horses* (2006), which explores the world of Shakespeare's fools. Clara Cenoz's output is even more centred on the clown whose 'message' is the freedom of clown itself, as in early full-length works of Companyia d'Idiotes (*Mamiydaddy* 1994, *Clown Impromptu* 1998 and *Home Sweet Home* 2003), despite occasional forays into territory more influenced by other genres, be they theatre (*Macbeff* 1999), cabaret (*Look Into My Eyes!!!* 2001) or music (*Don't Play It Again, Sam* 2002; *Clown Klezmer* 2004). If anything, her later development has been even further in the direction of clown which relies purely on its own dynamics as a form, without the need to borrow from other genres, including moving away from the full-length theatre show and towards shorter pieces, such as *Banana!* (2009) and *Tuba* (2011). The formal structure of *Banana!* is 'classical', using the 'rule of three' (discussed in Part II). Circling the ring carrying a suitcase, the clown comes to the centre but the case won't open. Again, a tour of the ring and back to the centre. The case still won't open. Another tour and the frustration mounts. Once more the same problem. Then suddenly the case opens, but the wrong way, on the hinged side. The frustration turns instantly to pleasure. The performing style is 'contemporary', relying on a direct clown–audience relationship founded on the clown's assumption of her own 'flop'. Even the subsequent sequence of problems, slips and falls caused by a banana skin are not what the number is really 'about'; rather, it is the clown's pleasure in recognising her own stupidity, a stupidity which includes the very idea that a problem might be a problem. There are echoes of Rivel's egg here, suggesting that the contemporary/classical divide is no longer useful. Here there are no worlds being created, apart from the performance context which we, the audience and performer, are both in. The clown serves simply to guide our attention to an awareness

Figure 12   Clara Cenoz in 'Mamiydaddy', 1996
Source: The author's private collection

of the ridiculousness of the moment, a moment shared by clown and spectators.

This brief survey of women clowns reveals that what seemed like conflicting historical claims are in fact compatible with each other. It is true that women have entered clowning in greater numbers since the 1960s, and have forged new paths. But it is equally true that the history of earlier women clowns reveals how they articulated issues of gender politics.

*   *   *

So far we have come across a range of answers to the question of 'what do clowns do, who clowns, and when, where and for whom do clowns clown?'

As noted previously, the 'what' of clowning gives us strange, odd and generally 'wrong' behaviour: mishaps, failures, surprises, misunderstandings and mistakes. Some clowns speak, others are silent, some precipitate themselves into physical danger, others reflect leisurely upon the situation.

We have also seen that the answer to the unfashionable question 'what do clowns wear?' gives us some fascinating insights. The story of clown fashion reveals far more than mere personal choices, as noted in the cases of Chaplin, the Fratellini, the tramp clowns, the evolution of the auguste clown and the whole range of women clowns across time.

The 'who' of clowning gives us peasants, intellectuals, women, men, animals, star soloists, duos, trios and a wide range of nationalities, although our focus has so far fallen on those most influential in the modern European tradition: English, French, Russian, Spanish and Italian, as well as North American.

The question of 'where' clowns clown is equally fruitful: theatres, circuses, streets, vaudeville, cinema and television have all been colonised. Performing spaces have been intimate, gigantic, indoor, outdoor, purpose-built and improvised. We have seen clowns drawn at various times to Paris, London, Hollywood, Berlin and St Petersburg.

Asking 'when' also gives multiple answers: we have examined clowns by century and by decade; in times of abundance, under political repression, and in the aftermath of, or during, wars. Clowns have appeared at all times before, during and after performances of plays, circuses and sports events.

And the 'for whom' of clowning is likewise broad: for the aristocracy, for the masses, for the middle classes, for intellectuals, for sports fans and for a globalised audience.

Now, with this in mind, we are ready to move on and to ask 'how do clowns clown?'

Part

II How Do Clowns Clown?

Thinking about clowning has arguably received a new impulse over the last half-century, coinciding with the development of contemporary clown teaching, although, as we shall see, clowns have always found ways of thinking and talking about their art.

The new approach to clown of the last decades of the 20th century has been seen by some as revolutionary. One of its foundations was the notion that clown could be taught and learned, and consequently the last 50 years have seen an explosion of interest in clown training worldwide. Jacques Lecoq included clown in his school's studies from the early 1960s. Ringling Bros. and Barnum & Bailey Circus founded their Clown College in 1968 in order to supply their own circuses with new clowns. In 1975 Richard Pochinko and Anne Skinner founded the Theatre Resource Centre in Ottawa, teaching clown influenced both by Lecoq and indigenous Canadian traditions, a method which since Pochinko's death in 1989 has been continued by his former apprentice, Sue Morrison. The French centre near Toulouse, Bataclown, began in 1980 to offer training and research in all areas of clown. In the same year, Philippe Gaulier, former student and teacher at Lecoq's school, opened his own establishment in Paris, which later included a spell in London (1991–2002), before returning to Paris. In 1983 Alan Clay established Playspace Studio, New Zealand's first clown school, in Auckland, later re-established in Sydney (1998–2006), and thereafter concentrating on summer Clown Retreats in New Zealand. In 1986 Fool Time Circus School in Bristol began a programme of studies with a radical approach to clowning and fooling, led by Franki Anderson, which later metamorphosed into Circomedia in 1996. Michel Dallaire began the residential centre for clown arts, Le Hangar des Mines, in the Cévennes north of Nimes in 1998. The San Francisco Clown Conservatory, founded by Jeff Raz, began in 2000 to offer a comprehensive one-year clown training programme. Since 2002, Eric de Bont's International Clown School on Ibiza has been holding year-round workshops in clown. And in 2006 Clara Cenoz founded the Escola de Clown de Barcelona, beginning its full-time programmes first in the city of Barcelona and then moving in 2009 to its present rural residential centre further north, near Figueres. There have been countless other individual teachers, and new centres continue to spring up.

My own experience of the boom in clown training has been partly through my time as a student of Franki Anderson, Philippe Gaulier, Moshe Cohen, Jonathan Kay, Jon Lee, Theatre de Complicité and others; partly, since 2006, as a co-founder of the Escola de Clown de Barcelona, by spending considerable time with other teachers, contracting them, translating for them, advising them and observing them: Sue Morrison, Jango Edwards, Jesús Jara, Hilary Ramsden, Danny Schlesinger, Pablo Muñoz, Chris Lynam, Sara Pons, John Beale, Carlo Mô, Loco Brusca, Gary Boardman, Nuria Pereto and others; and partly, from 2007, as a research fellow in clown at Central School of Speech and Drama in London, where I taught, observed and discussed with clown and acting teachers, and academics and their students: Lenard Petit, Gerry Flanagan, Peta Lily, John Wright, Keith Johnstone, Franc Chamberlain, Chris Johnston, Jaya Hartlein and more.

It's been a privileged position to be in, as many clown teachers work in relative isolation. Acquiring a perspective on contemporary clown teaching is a new task, even though that teaching is now half a century old. I hope that Part II of this book can go some way towards that objective.

If the idea of writing about, or even thinking about, clown might be novel to some, as mentioned in the Introduction, then even more so is the idea of teaching it. The last 50 years have seen that done in a formal way, but clowns have always passed knowledge on, and not just through informal transmission of trade secrets backstage, within the family or on the road. They wrote books, made films and performed comedy lectures about how to do it. And there are plenty of biographies and autobiographies which, although generally loath to give up professional knowledge, do conceal valuable insights amongst the pages of anecdotes.

We can look at how clowns do what they do from the outside in, and from the inside out. As I have done since the beginning of this book, I will begin by looking at it from the outside in, which is the audience's perspective, and then move on to what it feels like from the inside. Of course, the performer has to look at it both ways. So, although I begin this exploration with the audience's perspective, it will mostly be the performer's words which will address the issue of 'how to clown'. When I come onto what it feels like to be, rather than to do, clown, I will be focusing more on the specialist teachers of clown.

If you are looking to find anything resembling a manual on clowning, you are more likely to come across one on the more general subject of comedy or, these days, the more specific subjects of stand-up comedy or sitcoms. Many in the clown world would say, 'Don't let's talk about stand-up: it's not clown.' Many in the stand-up world might say, 'Let's not bother with clowns: they're out of fashion.' However, as we have seen, the historical truth is more complex. What in one given historical moment we divide into clown and stand-up, or physical and verbal comedy, or perhaps even comedy and tragedy, in another moment demands a different set of categories or sub-genres. Some of the fashions in clowning of the 19th century that Rémy records decade by decade we might today place off the clown map. In any case, much of the workings of clowning belong to the common pool of comedy or even beyond. Many methods and techniques are shared. That's reason enough for clowns to look at other forms of comedy. Once we have done that, we can go back and look at just what it might be that distinguishes clown from these related genres.

Another good reason to look at some other forms of comedy, such as stand-up or sitcoms, is that their contemporary dominance of comedy has been accompanied by a considerable amount of reflection and analysis, much more than clowning has. Whole truckloads of books now attempt to work out why and how it all works, and how to do it. Even teaching comedy is no longer so frowned upon. Clown has also had its own rise in teaching, but so far it has lacked the analysis and self-reflection in print that stand-ups have indulged in.

The issue of 'how to clown' does not fit neatly into one category. Clown theory appears in many guises, to which I will attempt to do justice. Amongst the many kinds of 'hows' are how to make and perform with clown props; how to do comedy acrobatics or dance; secrets passed on within the trade; psychological and philosophical explanations of how clowning works; the spiritual and ritual meanings of clowning; anthropological and sociological hypotheses on the function of clowns; theories on how gags work; catalogues of tricks and routines; discourses on clown dramaturgy; theories of clown as mask; the mechanics of failure and the flop; physiological, psychological and political theories of laughter; theories and methods of actor training and technique; play and game theory; questions of ethics and theology; political theory, from militarism to anarchism; script-writing manuals; theories of intelligence; and profound philosophical dilemmas, such as whether truth or reality exist.

In surveying such a vast and complex field, I shall begin, after some general thoughts about theory, with the 'material' (objects and bodies) and wend my way towards the 'metaphysical' (truth and meaning).

Clown Theory, Technique and Technology

INTRODUCTION

In this first chapter of Part II, I begin by looking at the very notion of thinking about comedy and clowning, attempting to find common ground between a variety of contributors: comedians (Ken Dodd, Bob Monkhouse and Max Miller), theorists (Freud, Bergson and Huizinga), and comedy academics (Oliver Double). This includes an exploration of the mechanics of professional advice, which leads us to consider how the knowledge of experience is shared, in the context of street performers as described in fictional form by Alan Clay. Next comes a more formalised version of the passing on of tricks of the trade, in Lupino Lane's 1945 manual *How to be a Comedian*. I then look at ways of understanding the workings of clown prop technology, followed by an assessment of some of the prime practitioners in this field: the Fratellini, the Rastelli, and Pompoff and Thedy. The history of prop-based clowning assumes a political subtext in the writings of the Catalan circus critic Sebastià Gasch, spanning the work of clowns in Spain both pre- and post-Spanish Civil War. I then look at issues of technology and technique in some common prop themes in clowning: the chair, food and slosh. The latter brings us to consider the role of handling messy, dangerous or taboo substances in the wider field of clown anthropology and the ritual practices of clowns, particularly among the indigenous clowns of New Mexico. This is followed by an anthropological perspective on the European tradition, most importantly Paul Bouissac's concept of clowning as the profanation of the sacred, which he applies to an analysis of the role of animals and babies in the clown entrée. His contribution also opens up the study of gag structure, based on the notion of inappropriateness. With this in mind I look at ways of categorising clown numbers, such as Dominique Denis's *1000 Gags*, which offers us a fresh perspective on questions of gag ownership, with reference, no less, to Grock. I continue with an examination of impossible props in the work of Harpo Marx, Lucille Ball and Grock, and end the chapter by reconsidering the notion of the lazzi in commedia dell'arte, with special attention to the role of violence and 'stage crudities'.

THEORIES OF COMEDY: OLIVER DOUBLE

In his first book, *Stand-Up: On Being a Comedian*, Oliver Double's final chapter is entitled 'What's the Secret of Great Comedy?' His answer is:

> Jokes.
>
> It's as simple as that. No big secret. Just jokes, you know. That's what makes people laugh. Funnily enough, it was only when I started looking into comedy that I found that out. My idea was that you could just kind of *be* funny, and people would laugh. I'd go on stage with what I thought was a pretty funny idea, like 'Wouldn't it be great to launch a terrorist campaign against dogs?', and I'd just launch into it without bothering to think about gags or punchlines. Sometimes they'd laugh. Sometimes their eyes would glaze over and turn into little LED noticeboards like you get in the post office, and the message would flash across them: 'What is this bloke on about?'
>
> (1997: 243)

Double uses an analogy with learning to drive and realising that it's not just about getting in the car and driving but that you need to know how to do it:

> I didn't realise that it was more about going through a series of smaller manoeuvres: turning corners, overtaking, stopping at traffic lights, going round roundabouts, going into service stations and having a go on one of those novelty photo machines that makes it look like you've had your photo taken with Arnold Schwarzenegger. The journey is like a comedy routine, and just as it's made up of individual manoeuvres, so the routine's made up of individual gags. If you don't realise that, you're not going to pass your driving test. It'd be like: funny idea funny idea funny idea funny idea oh dear here comes a T-junction I don't know what to do I don't know how to take a corner whoops I've hit the opposite kerb. Let's go back to the test centre Mr Double, and I suggest you don't take your test again until you've learnt some punchlines.
>
> (1997: 244)

Although he puts the emphasis on having punchlines here, the point is not limited to formal jokes. Even non-punchline comedy will have its form and structure, which will bear thinking about, reflecting upon and working out how to do well. Steve Martin in his autobiography *Born Standing Up* tries to analyse his own evolution as a comedian and explain how he arrived at doing a 'parody of comedy':

> Afraid of falling short, I ad-libbed, wandered around the audience, talked to patrons, joked with waitresses, and took note of anything unusual that was happening in the crowd and addressed it for laughs, in the hope of keeping my written material in reserve so I could fill my time quota. The format stuck. Years later, it was this pastiche element that made my performance seem unstructured and modern.
>
> (Martin 2007: 12)

Even such a formless comedy would have a theory behind it:

> What if there were no punch lines? What if there were no indicators? What if I created tension and never released it? What if I headed for a climax, but all I delivered was an anti-climax? What would the audience do with all that tension? Theoretically, it would have to come out sometime. But if I kept denying them the formality of a punch line, the audience would eventually pick their own place to laugh, essentially out of desperation.
>
> (Martin 2007: 111)

The argument against theory in comedy is that it spoils the fun. If you analyse why it's funny, then it stops being funny, runs the mantra. Well, the theory is there to help the comedian, and a bit of theory won't harm them if they are professional about it and don't introduce it into their performance too much. Double takes his driving analogy further in order to explain the problem of how to rehearse comedy. Given that half of what makes comedy work is based on the immediacy of the actual relationship with the audience, as opposed to what your material is, rehearsing too much makes your performance rigid and stilted, he argues:

> the comedian has a glazed expression and goes through every word and gesture in exactly the same way as he or she has done a hundred times before in his or her bedroom. The audience winces and fidgets. Again, that's because stand-up's a bit like driving. You can practise handling the car all you want on a private road but what you can't prepare for is dealing with other vehicles. The heckles, the background chatter and the microphone that breaks in half when you take it out of the stand are the stand-up equivalent of other traffic on the road. It's like: oh yeah I'm all right I've practised all this turning a corner no problem 'Get off you're not funny!' what was that? Whoops, I've just smacked into the side of a milk float. Well, that wasn't there when I rehearsed, what's going on?
>
> (1997: 245)

So, if theory is useful, the question is, which theory? Again, if you are looking around for theories, you are more likely not to come across theories of clown, nor even of stand-up comedy, but theories of laughter. As with potted histories of clowning, so too potted psychological theories seem to have popular appeal. Many is the book, article or website which will cover this area with a quick reference to Bergson (on laughter), Freud (on jokes) or Huizinga (on play). Double takes them all on in his section 'Test the theories':

> Here are some simple experiments you can try yourself:
>
> 1. *Aggression theory* states that making a joke is about directing aggression at a third party so that you and the second party can laugh at them together. Try this theory out next time you're on a crowded train. Bide your time. Then, suddenly and without warning, start shouting at the person sitting next to you at the top of your voice: 'I HATE YOU!!! YOU'RE SCUM!!! I'M GOING TO KILL YOU!! YOU'RE A ROTTEN LITTLE PUDDLE OF SICK!!!!' See if any of the other passengers laugh.

Predicted result: Horrified silence, faces disappearing behind newspapers, guard comes along and warns you that if you do that again, he'll put you off the train at the next station.

2. *Incongruity theory* states that making a joke is about deviating from expected patterns. Try this out by getting on the train in a giant lobster costume with a bunch of daffodils tied round your head, a photograph of the Queen sellotaped to your tummy, and carry a big sign saying, 'Hey everybody, I'm a loony.' Sit there and read a newspaper, occasionally making sudden, high-pitched squeaking noises.

Predicted result: Puzzled silence, occasional hidden sniggers, guard has a bit of a joke with you and acts all matey.

3. *Release theory* states that jokes work by giving voice to anti-social urges, thus releasing the tension of repressing those urges. Try this out by announcing to the other passengers in your carriage in a loud voice: 'Hey I know picking your nose isn't very nice, but check this out for a stonking big bogie,' then pick your nose and wave your finger in front of people's faces, saying, 'Look how big and green that one is, eh?' See if the other passengers laugh.

Predicted result: Irritated silence, occasional tuts of annoyance, guard says, 'Yes that is a big bogie, but you should've seen the one I had last week.'

(1997: 245–246)

Double's point is that it's a lot more complicated than that, and it's much easier *not* to get a laugh by following the theories than to actually *get* a laugh. He reserves his final onslaught of sarcasm, though, for theories tested in laboratory conditions:

The experiments I've suggested might sound stupid, but next to some of the real experiments that psychologists have done, they're really quite rational. People have been trying to work out what comedy's all about for thousands of years, but it's only in this century that they've tried to test their theories in the science lab. Ha! What a waste of time! Experimental psychologists have assumed that it's as easy to create laughter in a laboratory as it is to generate electricity. Wrong!
[...]
That's one of the problems with a psychology lab. It doesn't provide the ideal surroundings for a bloody good laugh. And as if that wasn't bad enough, once you're in the lab, the experimenters do weird things to you. Stanley Schachter and Ladd Wheeler had a little test in which they injected subjects with epinephrine (adrenaline), chlorpromazine or a saline solution before showing them clips from comedy films. Schachter and Wheeler had edited the clips together themselves, obviously believing that psychologists have an innate grasp of the delicate art of comedy cinematography. The thing about experiments like this is, injecting somebody with an unnamed substance isn't an ideal way of getting them in the mood for a good chuckle. I've certainly been desperate for a laugh on occasion, but I've never thought of improving my chances by injecting members of the audience with chlorpromazine.

[…]
Given all this injecting with stimulants and wiring up to electrodes, it's no surprise that experimental psychologists Pollio, Mers and Lucchesi have admitted that, 'No one has ever reported the occurrence of an explosive, full-bodied belly-laugh under laboratory conditions.'

(1997: 246–248)

Double then goes on to give one example of real laughter in a laboratory, provoked by the very ridiculousness of the experimental set-up: jokes written on long strips of paper that were passed before the subjects' eyes in such a way that only one word at a time could be seen through a hole in a wall, the hope being that the investigators would be able to spot exactly which word of the joke was the one that made people laugh. (1997: 248)

PRACTITIONERS AND THEORISTS: KEN DODD, SIGMUND FREUD ET AL.

Maurice Willson Disher in his Foreword to *Clowns and Pantomimes* found 'the professors' equally ridiculous:

> The professors are wrong not merely because common sense finds them at fault but because they have broken their own rules. They study in laboratories while they should be delighting in circus tents and music-halls. In other words, they deduce facts from theories instead of inducing theories from facts. Their explanations are far too intricate. What can be said for an authority who could not enjoy the spectacle of two clowns beating each other until inspired with the idea that they were becoming 'solid wooden dummies,' nor of two others bounding against one another until he thought they resembled 'large rubber balls'?
>
> (1925: xiv)

The showman, on the other hand, is entirely empirical:

> There is no such nonsense about the showman. While the unscientific professors have been deriving a maximum of elaborate guesswork from a minimum of experience, he has been methodically providing facts. Laughter, he knows, can be created in more ways than the professors have noted. Yet he is sure that the explanation must be simpler than any they have put forward. Unlike them, he is willing to learn from babes and sucklings. He knows the tricks that amuse his offspring are essentially similar to those enjoyed by audiences of grown-ups. More important still, there is a hint of explanation in young laughter. A baby startled by the bobbing-up of a head behind a chair will catch its breath in fright before realising joyfully whose the face is. The child, a little older, slithering plates off the ledge of its high-chair, will wait a second in apprehension before chuckling with delight; or, watching an uncle who growls and walks on all fours, will spend some seconds in open-mouthed wonder before deciding that human quadrupeds are a joke. That momentary spasm of emotion is to be noted in adults as well.
>
> (Disher 1925: xiv)

Double is equally dismissive of Freud, whose belief that tendentious jokes are

> about giving voice to repressed aggressive and sexual urges [...] doesn't stand the test of time [since it] is so obviously rooted in the values and social habits of his day.
>
> (Double 1997: 248–249)

Double's summary of Freud comes down to this:

> So there it is: men crack dirty jokes to their friends to try and persuade women to go to bed with them.
>
> (1997: 249)

He then imagines a whole routine with a hopeless Freud trying to raise a laugh, taking his cue from Ken Dodd,

> who said that Freud's all very well, but he never had to play second house on a Friday night at the Glasgow Empire.
>
> (1997: 249)

Bergson's theory that we laugh at people's behaviour when it is like machines, or vice versa, is given a similar treatment, ending on a 'top-quality joke' if the theory is correct:

> There's a vacuum cleaner on the market with a cute little cartoon face printed on his little round red body. Put him behind the mic.-stand at a comedy club, and switch him on. Pretty soon he'll have his own series, Friday nights on Channel 4.
>
> (1997: 251)

Finally, Double knocks down the popular cliché of 'What's The Secret of Great Comedy?...Timing...' on the grounds of it being so generalised as to be useless:

> If you ask somebody what they like about their favourite comic, they'll probably say. 'Ooh, well you see it's his timing, he's got wonderful timing.' They say that because timing is the only aspect of the art of stand-up comedy that they've heard of. Saying, 'Ooh, well you see it's his jokes, he's got wonderful jokes,' would make them sound a bit stupid, because it's too obvious. Instead they refer to the mysterious skill of timing, to make it sound as if they know what they're talking about. As far as I'm concerned, saying that good stand-up is about timing is like saying that driving a car is about making the wheels turn round. They do have to turn, but when you're driving you're not thinking about that, you're thinking about the pedals, the gear-stick, the steering wheel and all that.
>
> (1997: 251–252)

PROFESSIONAL ADVICE: BOB MONKHOUSE AND MAX MILLER

So, rather than unthinkingly referencing theories that are either outdated or so outside the field of the actual practice of comedy or clown to be virtually useless, let us look at what the practitioners have to say. First, a quick look at the business of informal giving of advice. One of the better-known examples comes from Bob Monkhouse and is often to be found quoted or summarised in books on comedy, including Double (2005) and Allen (2002). Monkhouse was appearing on the bill as Max Miller at the London Coliseum when Miller, on hearing Monkhouse say he would appreciate some advice, took a chair and watched his act from the wings. Monkhouse narrates:

> After I came off, I was told to take a cup of tea to his car. [Miller was using his car as a dressing room due to the overcrowding in the theatre.] When I tapped on the car window, he told me to climb in and close the door.
>
> 'You drink the tea and I'll drink this.' He sipped from a silver flask. 'Now, let's talk about what you did on that stage.'
>
> On that chilly evening in 1949 I was given a master class in patter comedy by its greatest living exponent.
>
> (1993: 57)

After some initial comments on being audible, Miller moved on:

> 'give 'em the chance to laugh. Just now, they weren't easy but you never gave them enough rope. Wait. If the buggers don't laugh, stare 'em out. You're in charge, not them. Make them have it [...] Twinkle, like you're trying not to laugh yourself. That's infectious, you see. Take them into your confidence, my son. Create an atmosphere. Strike an attitude. Be likeable, be the people's mate, and if they don't take to you right away, act happy as if you didn't care. Don't tick 'em off'
> [...]
> There were more rules that night – about avoiding repetition except when it lends build-up and emphasis, about using movement to create a mental picture, [...] about sincerity and funny accents and the illusion of danger [...] precious tips that I've used so often and practical secrets that I've passed on with care to those able to use them.
>
> (1993: 57)

ALAN CLAY: STREET KNOWLEDGE

The passing on of tips takes place not just in comedy or even just in performance, but virtually under any circumstances that bring together a number of professionals who are in the same business. Although learning 'how to do it' is not always a conscious process, as Monkhouse observes:

Every time I perform, *every* time, I know I'm reflecting the ways and means of comedy practitioners I've admired: this little backwards check-step, that's Arthur Askey; that little trick of emphasis and reception, that's Max Miller; these gestures, they're like Max Wall's. Not conscious imitations, no, I'm no impersonator. If you're an apt pupil, you can't help but absorb technique by osmosis.

(1998: 184)

Stand-up/variety/music-hall/vaudeville, with its nights of different acts, has always offered performers the opportunity to share knowledge. Contemporary street performance can provide a similar context – one which the clown teacher Alan Clay dwells on in the fictional novel section of his *Angels Can Fly, a Modern Clown User Guide.* The book is a curious one, being part fiction, part clown exercises and part testimonials by professional clowns. Through a set of fictional characters – young street performers of varying types and experience – Clay is able to probe a little deeper than normal into what makes street clowning work:

'How was it?' he [TC] asked her [Madona] when the crowd had subsided.

She paused, looked down into the hat and considered.

'Be gentle,' she advised.

Gentle wasn't his normal style, he was more used to alternately slapping them around a little, and then being cute and sexy, and so her advice was ominous, and she knew this, and reinforced it with her eye contact.

He soon found out what she meant, for the flow of people was so sporadic that he struggled to build his crowd and had to adjust his timing and his material.

He started getting frustrated, which only made his performance worse. He hated it when it wasn't working, it made him look like a beginner, and this only made the show feel more forced.
[...]
He flipped off one hat, and set another on his head, his body took on a new posture and he glared at the audience. He was looking directly at a woman, who giggled at the intensity of the contact, but otherwise there was little other reaction.

'Oh, come on?' he cajoled them. 'We're here to have a bit of fun! He swept his eyes around the circle, 'aren't we?'

There was a little laughter, and murmurs of affirmation.
[...]
It felt like it was going to take more energy than it was worth to continue, and he decided to bail the show. It was better to conserve his energy and do a good one later, he decided, than to struggle on with this one.

'Okay, thanks for your attention,' he told them. 'I'll do one later when there's more energy.'

He dropped a hat to his feet.

'If you'd like to contribute something, feel free.'

[...]

'It's not about you,' Sugar told him as he came off, 'it's about them.'

'Them?' he asked.

'The audience,' she told him.

She was about to go on.

'You've got to give them more space,' Madona agreed.

He looked at the women, They were both older than him, and had both been working longer, but his hats were consistently bigger than theirs, so who were they to give him advice?

'How do you do that then?' he asked.

'Everyone is already doing their own performance,' Sugar explained, 'You just have to give them a chance to all do it together in a show.'

'I want them to play my game,' he told them.

'That's what we're saying,' Madona told him, and Sugar nodded.

'You're just procrastinating about going on,' he told them. 'I'll go again, if no-one else is going.'

'Fat chance,' Sugar told him. 'I'm up.'

She proceeded to build her crowd by engaging with each person in turn as they passed, and playing with something that they were doing. Each person thrilled to the contact and the reinforcement of their unique self, and as a result some stopped.

Backstage, TC paid more attention than usual.

'See how she's doing it?' Madona asked him.

'Everyone does it differently,' he told her.

Each person had a unique way of being in the world, and was inviting contact in their own way. Even an aggressive guy, who shouted obscenities at Sugar, was played with.

'Nice to see you too,' she told him. 'Don't stop, just keep walking.'

He looked like he felt honoured by her contact, but because there was no return of the anger he was putting out, there was nothing for him to engage with, and he sort of slid by.

However a couple with their arms around one another was welcomed and offered a hug. The woman accepted and was warmly embraced, and soon they were sitting on the ground at the front of Sugar's stage, delighted to be out of their normal patterns, and still totally comfortable.

'Some ways work better than others,' Madona observed.

(Clay 2005: 40–42)

Although the novel is entirely centred on street performers, Clay admits that the street is not necessarily the best place for a clown, nor are street performers necessarily clowns (his fictional characters included). His own first experiences at the Avignon Festival in 1982 brought home the difficulties:

I was broke at the Avignon Festival, staying with other performers who were regulars at the festival, and were making a killing. Meanwhile I was struggling to even get a show up,

because I was English-speaking and sweet, two things I realised the French hate.

(2005: 90)

He subsequently developed a more aggressive style that apparently appealed more to French tastes. But ultimately

the street environment is very hard for a clown, because in the chaos of the street, it is very hard to attract attention by creating more chaos, as the clown does, and at the same time bring it together into a professional-looking show.

(2005: 91)

Or, as Philippe Gaulier puts it,

Dreams of grandeur save the idiot. His ambition isn't to play in the street (not a very comfortable place) but at the Paris Opera.

(2007a: 291)

Although not strictly clown performers, these characters wrestle with how to reach the audience through honesty. These are struggles that can rarely be communicated unless you've actually been out there and done street performing yourself, and the fictional mode seems to be one of the best ways to give at least some impression of what it is that drives us to seek out strangers in the street and do silly things for them and then get them to give away their money.

LUPINO LANE: TECHNICAL KNOWLEDGE

A far more conscious example of passing knowledge on is Lupino Lane's 1945 book *How to become a Comedian*. He was experienced in a whole range of comedy, coming from a family who traced their ancestry back to Grimaldi. His advice has the tone and confidence of someone who is telling you

'This is how you do it, I know because we've always done it like this and it works.' The book emerged to address the immediate and practical purpose of training entertainers working for servicemen in the Second World War.

> The idea of attempting to write this book came to me during one of my many visits to the Factory and Camp Concerts. I noticed there was a grand lot of budding talent in these amateur performances. My hope is that the contents will help, inspire, and be of practical use to these young performers.
>
> (Lane 1945: 6)

Lane's first task is to reassure the reader that comedy can be learned, and his opening phrase is 'Do not let the remark that "comedians are born, not made" discourage you' (1945: 9). More than that, it *must* be learned:

> Many a time I have, when touring, had the local wit pointed out to me with great pride and the remark (in the local vernacular):
>
> 'He's awfu' canny!'
>
> 'He's a reet rum'un!'
>
> 'He's a broth of a b'hoy!'
>
> 'He's a proper cough-drop!'
>
> but, mostly, these natural comedians, one finds on closer inspection, have moulded themselves unconsciously on some well known and established star who is a native of that particular part of the country. Most of these 'naturally-born' funny people or comedians, you will find, are rarely very successful in getting laughter when they are before an audience expecting to be *made* to laugh, they lack proper training and experience. On the other hand, the professional is horrified when he is asked to be funny by the hostess at a party.
>
> (1945: 10–11)

For Lane, what looks like genius is just hard work:

> To my mind, becoming a comedian is just another job of long and patient training in the necessary trade of making people laugh.
> [...]
> Why does my old boyhood friend, Charles Chaplin, take months to make a picture? Believe me, it is a most depressing experience to watch Charlie at work; I have often done it in Hollywood. Surely, if these were naturally born comedians, they wouldn't have to worry: it would just happen to them.
>
> (1945: 12)

Like Monkhouse, Lane has a few anecdotes about how the older generation of greats slipped him a few hints: 'I studied "Little Tich" [...] Many tricks he taught me I still use to-day' (1945: 14). His technical knowledge is wide-ranging, covering slapstick, juggling, ventriloquism, female impersonation, dialect comedy, double acts, light comedy, low comedy and how to use an old gag. The advice is offered at a variety of levels, too. There are tips about attitude, such as:

> this kind of joke is always successful if the laugh is against yourself.
> [...]
> In fact, the more you insult yourself the better. [...] you never fail to cause merriment when you appear to injure yourself.
>
> (1945: 19)

There are lists of things you can do:

> The following are but a few of what I call 'injury laughs':
> Bumping your head accidently,
> Falling over a mat,
> Missing top or bottom step,
> Tripping over your own foot,
> Falling downstairs,
> Sitting on knitting needles,
> Receiving a pie on your face,
> Burning your fingers with a match,
> Striking a match on the seat of your trousers and finding it's a nail,
> Hitting your elbow,
> Accidentally swallowing a tack or a whistle,
> Treading on one,
> Getting your hand caught in a jug or vase, and having to
> break it to release yourself, thereby hurting your fist.
> Barking your shins ... and so on.
>
> (1945: 19)

And there are descriptions of how to execute them, starting with the simplest:

> First, let us rake the 'trip or stumble'. This is done by catching the toe of one foot behind the heel of the other, and tripping forward, you can use this to lose your hat and to step on it accidentally or whilst carrying a tray with plates, etc.
>
> (1945: 33–35)

To the highest level:

> There's the '108' fall. This is the daddy of the lot and one of the most dangerous, very few can do this, for it is really an acrobatic trick-cum-fall.
>
> (1945: 41)

In between there are details and diagrams on how to do the slide or slip, chair fall, dead back fall, throw back fall, surprise fall, pirouette fall, spin on the head and twist round the neck. Detailed information, clearly intended for real learning, is blended with family wisdom:

> Be careful to keep your head sideways, and knees straight. Any knockabout per-
> former will tell you that the knees and elbows seem to be parts of the body which

most often get hurt in funny falls. I have had some very painful elbow and knee injuries. Members of my family usually describe any injury of this kind as 'a *laugh*'. One never goes in the dressing room and says, 'Look at this bad bruise': one shows the injury and says, 'Look at this big laugh I got tonight' – or looking at someone else's hurt, 'You've got a lovely laugh on your elbow!'

(1945: 35)

Such high skill levels have been lacking for some time in the contemporary clown and comedy worlds, victims of the generalized rejection of non-improvisational skills. And health and safety obsessions have thrown their weight behind the myth that slaps must always be faked. Lane, however, discusses both ways of doing it:

'TAKING THE NAP' (a pretended blow on the face). This is done by one performer stopping the blow as the hand reaches the face, in other words, he 'pulls his punch', and the receiver of the slap smacks his hands smartly together in front of himself, or at the back, at the same time giving the impression of having received an awful smack on the face. I don't know why it is called 'THE NAP'
[…]
Of course, some knock-abouts prefer to take the actual blow. If this is done with a firm open hand using about half the palm and sliding the hand off the face at the moment of impact, it will make a good report and only sting a bit. Of course, if it is continually used it can become very painful.

When I was in a revue at the Empire, Leicester Square, the late Will Evans kidded me into doing a face-slapping routine with him. Unfortunately I found out too late that he wanted the 'straight nap' to be used. This meant at each performance I had to receive half a dozen blows on the side of my face.

(1945: 36–37)

THE TECHNOLOGY AND MECHANICS OF CLOWNING

Although Lane's methods seem very much a product of their time, similar works continue to be published, such as Clettus Musson's *World's Best Clown Gags* (2003) and Patrick Page's *150 Comedy Props* (1997) and *Book of Visual Comedy* (2005). Most likely to be found on the shelves of a magic shop (Page was a well-respected magician), they resemble the much larger number of booklet-sized manuals on magic. They belong to the school of thought: 'here are the gags, how they work and how to do them, now go out and do them'.

Both of these authors use simple illustrations and minimal descriptions to convey the mechanics of mainly props-based gags.

The Levitation

This is a real old fashioned music-hall classic. An assistant is lying down covered with a sheet. The performer folds down one end of the sheet so that the assistant's head is showing. He folds back the other end of the sheet so that his feet are also on display. Waving his hands over the assistant the performer commands him to rise. The assistant starts to float upwards horizontally. Suddenly the sheet slips off the assistant's body and drops to the floor, exposing the fact that he is standing on the floor and holding the two broomsticks out from his body with two shoes fitted on the other ends.

The assistant should be lying on a settee with his feet on the floor over one end of the settee. When he floats up off the settee it will be with a forwards and upwards motion. As he apparently floats forwards away from the settee the performer can accidentally step on the bottom of the sheet, which should be large, and as the assistant moves away the sheet will be drawn off his 'body'.

(Page 1997: 17)

Curiously, perhaps due to a sense of their own 'other-time-ness', one often finds a certain apologetic tone in these books, excusing themselves to the modern reader in case their tricks be thought old-fashioned, non-PC or just too barbarous for our own squeamish age, as in this example which Musson first describes in loving detail:

Some years back a couple of clowns performed a bit of buffoonery that was centered around a couple of illusions. The two clowns made their appearance quarreling with each other. As the quarrel became more violent, one of the clowns suddenly seized a sword and plunged it through the other's body. He then dragged the 'dead' clown to a block which resembled a tree stump, placed his head on the block, covered it with a red cloth, and chopped off the head.

The head was shown, placed in a basket, and then taken to a table where it was set on a plate. The face of this head, assuming horrible expressions, turned from side to side looking about. Suddenly, it spied its body near the block and began pleading with the live clown to give him his body back. Finally, the head was removed from the plate under cover of the red cloth, and placed back with its body. The two clowns exited, arm in arm.

(Musson 2003: 11)

That's what the audience sees. Behind the scenes it goes like this:

The sword was made of thin, flexible steel. A sheath was placed halfway around one clown's body beneath his clothing, a slit having been previously made in his clothing in the back and front. The sword, when pushed into this sheath, went around one side of the body and protruded on the other side. The block was made up to look like a tree stump. [. . .] It contained a trap door in the top. Behind it was a red cloth and an imitation papier-mâché head made up to look like the clowns face.

When the red cloth was placed over the clown's head prior to chopping it off, the real head hung down into the block. The imitation head was placed in the basket and was carried to a table on which rested a platter or plate. The plate had a hole in it large enough for a head to stick through. This was set over a large round hole in the table that was covered with dark cloth, the cloth being split in the center where two pieces of elastic had been sewn.

Consequently, when a head was thrust through this slit, the cloth would separate, and when the head was removed, the elastic would pull the cloth back to its original position, closing up the hole. A third clown made up to look like the dead one was hidden beneath the table by the use of two mirrors ... The dummy head was apparently removed from the basket under cover of the red cloth and was placed on the plate. When the cloth was removed, naturally ii was the third clown's head that was seen on the plate, he having popped his head up through the table under cover of the cloth.

(Musson 2003: 12)

But having presented us with such a gift, Musson seems to want to take it all away again:

It isn't likely that one would go to all this bother today to present such an act, but the following might be usable. A penetrating needle or sword can he bought from magic dealers today. Two clowns come out quarreling, after which one runs the needle or sword through the other. (A substitute which may also be obtained from magic dealers is a rod that can be pushed through the body or a spike that goes through the neck.) The needle is removed, and the live clown, realizing what he has done, suddenly becomes panicky and begs his friend to return to life. Then, struck by a sudden thought, the live clown takes a large can marked 'Life Powder' and sprinkles ii over the body of his 'dead' friend. The friend comes to life and they exit arm in arm, or continue on around the sawdust ring, whatever the case might be.

The head chopper could also he used advantageously by two clowns.

If you possess one of the mirror tables shown, the curtain could open with a clown's head resting on the table singing, 'I Ain't Got No Body'. The second clown could then enter with a large sheet, hold it in front of the head by standing on a ladder on the table, say, 'Abracadabra', and remove the sheet showing that the head now has a body. Then the two could go on with their usual buffoonery.

(Musson 2003: 12)

The attempt here to de-brutalise the clowning is surely part of that process of infantilisation which we touched on earlier. This particular number itself, in many various versions, is a classic and has been around since who knows when. Kimberley Webber's book on Sydney Powerhouse Museum's collection of the Australian Jandaschewsky clowns' props and costumes suggests a link to the French Revolution:

The Jandaschewsky's Louis XVI act was an elaborate performance that drew strongly from French theatrical tradition. Having two similar velvet burgundy costumes allowed a dummy with a detachable papier-maché head to be substituted after Guillaume lay down at the guillotine.

(1996: 54)

TRICK PROPS: THE FRATELLINI, THE RASTELLI, AND POMPOFF AND THEDY

The name most associated in clowning with the use of trick props has to be the Fratellini. Their famous dressing-room, open to spectators to visit during the interval, was crammed full of them, as Albert relates in his autobiography, *Nous, les Fratellini* ('We the Fratellini'), although in reality it only contained a fraction of the total properties and costumes they possessed:

> Moreover, our stock was always growing, as our repertoire had passed 180 numbers and we had a work rhythm at the Medrano Circus that few clowns have imposed upon themselves.
>
> I have already spoken about the elephant head but our dressing-room was also decorated with five horse's heads for 'The Bull Fight' – and a complete bull – not a real one, don't worry! The animal, in the ring, ended up gutted and its insides rolled out in a long red stream. Not far from there, suspended from the beams, hung a horse skin beneath which slipped the children who brought it to life and moved the beast's ears and the dressage parody.
>
> Amongst the flying personnel, I could mention a batch of flies and wasps.
>
> This Noah's Ark was completed by a swan, a donkey, a giraffe, a monkey, a lion, a bear, a surrealist dog, made of articulated pipes.
> [...]
> Our ingenuity in dreaming up and creating new entrées made such an immense deployment of accessories absolutely necessary.
> We possessed several umbrellas: one soft, which folded up completely and fitted inside a hat; another, more sizeable, when opened let fall a shower of hats.
> [...]
> Many axes in amongst our stuff; used in the Firemen number – not to mention the one that stuck in my skull in the Massacre scene.
> [...]
> Our arsenal included a great number of rifles: one was a curved cannon, for 'The Fratellini in Africa'; another, equipped with a syringe, which sent a shot of water into my face, whilst I ate William Tell's apple.
> [...]
> Our visitors would only sit with great care upon our chairs, as the treacherous things might break with one blow and shatter in a thousand pieces on the floor. Some would bring themselves back up onto their feet when sat on. The smartest ones had the ability to do the splits or to throw you up into the air thanks to a powerful spring.
>
> (1955: 185–188)

Although the Fratellini are sometimes cited as being the originators of a certain kind of reliance on trick props, Rémy, in his introduction to *Entrées Clownesques,* considers that they never forgot that the clown needs no intermediary between himself and the audience:

The Fratellini understood that, and of all the clowns of the ring, they are the ones who used with most tact the comedy of props. In more than twenty years of success, never did we see them dominated by trick technology, or use a prop in order to shrink from the gaze of the audience, or in a way which could hinder the expression of their personality, their talent, their kindness. And that was despite the abundance of their material – three trucks would not have held it – bric-à-brac of incredible richness, a renewal of the so-called English pantomime.

(1962: 20)

Even the Rastelli, often regarded as the heirs to the Fratellini style, could not follow in their footsteps, according to Rémy:

The Rastelli aside, who are in reality manipulators of trick props, none of the imitators of the Fratellini were able to achieve a success of which we cannot determine the exact cause.

(1962: 20)

The mistake of the imitators of the Fratellini was that

This success was attributed to the material, which is complicated *ad infinitum*, without regard to the qualities of the individuals. The 'surprise' thus obtained, the clowns were left standing in front of their machines like puppets with broken springs. And the audience, eyes fixed on the equipment, kept expecting 'something' that never came. It is the same today.

(1962: 20–21)

Sebastià Gasch, the Catalan art critic turned circus critic, who in many ways held a comparable position in Spain to Rémy's in France, at times seemed even more radical, as here in his dressing-down of Pompoff and Thedy:

Pompoff and Thedy close the proceedings at the Circ de les Arenes. 'Above all, no props,' exclaims the great Beby, companion of Antonet, well known to the Barcelona public. 'Above all, no props. The clown has his face, his voice, his stick. Nothing else. I admire the silent one. Who is silent? Charlie Chaplin. Charlie has only his face with which to say everything.'

No props. Here we have the pure orthodoxy of the art of clown, which is not shared in the slightest by these Pompoff and Thedy, who do not know what to do with their faces, and who have to resort to props, to multiple props, musical and others, or even to their own children, in order to provoke the coarse laughter of an easy audience, and to build long drawn out and heavily laden sketches, deprived of the least grace.

(From the article, 'Circ a les Arenes', *Mirador,* 30 July 1931,
reprinted in Jané and Minguet 1998: 131)

By the way, Beby's example of Chaplin rings a little false in the light of Chaplin's own words:

In a state of quiet desperation, I wandered through the property room in the hope of finding an old prop that might give me an idea: remains of old sets, a jail door, a piano or a mangle. My eye caught a set of golf clubs.

(Chaplin 1964: 281)

SEBASTIÀ GASCH AND JORDI JANÉ: A POLITICAL HISTORY OF PROPS AND JOKES

Gasch's writings on circus and clowns, collected by Jordi Jané, himself a prominent contemporary circus critic, reveal more than just an aesthetic, however. The above article dates from the period when Gasch had just turned his attention away from fine art and towards the circus and other popular entertainments. Most of his reviews from the 1930s are sharp, critical and demanding of the highest standards and, in these pre-Spanish Civil War days, always written in Catalan. But when we arrive at his post-war writings, in the 1950s and 1960s, not only is he now writing in Spanish, of course, since Catalan was prohibited in public under Franco, but the tone has softened considerably. Jané considers that Gasch's changes of heart are due to the artists themselves actually improving their acts over time and because Gasch is noble enough to admit this and give praise where it is due. But surely it is more than this and there is a note of subservience in these later articles, one which cannot admit to the failing of native artists. Here, Gasch is writing at the end of the 1960s, but he is referring to the same Pompoff and Thedy working way back in the 1920s:

In the 1926–27 winter season, there made their appearance at the Circo Olimpia the popular clowns Pompoff and Thedy, members of the glorious Aragón family. Pompoff (José María Aragón) wore a suit of rich glowing apricot, white silk stockings, low shoes with silver buckles and finished off with the classic skull-cap as hat. Thedy (Teodoro Aragón), buried in a loose coffee-colored jacket and a waistcoat down to his knees, sporting his huge wristwatch, dragging his gigantic shoes and looking around bewildered, as if he had slipped into the ring without permission. [..] They meet, their dialogue full of humor, without obscenities: then Thedy's hilarious mime, and Pompoff's burlesque innuendo. And the first number, which is called in the circus a 'comic entrance', is already a success. Then came other 'numbers' each one funnier than the previous one, and, to finish, the musical number and with it the crowd's enthusiasm cannot contain itself.

The two brothers gained an uproarious success at the Olimpia. We should add, by the way, that, back in 1914, Chicharrito, from Malaga, who was at that time one of the best 'Augustes de soirée', suggested to Thedy the idea of telling jokes to the audience, in the style of those told in Andalusia. Pompoff and Thedy did so, using for the first time in the history of Spanish circus a plain, pure, one hundred per cent Castilian.

('Evocación del Circo Olimpia -V-', *Destino*, 11 October 1969,
in Jané and Minguet 1998: 131)

The reference to the 'pure' Castilian language is full of political resonance, using the word 'castizo', which is loaded with Spanish imperial overtones. And although here it ostensibly refers to the way Pompoff and Thedy had taken a style of joke very typically Andalusian and converted it from dialect into standard Spanish (Castilian), the phrase grates in the context of the Catalan Gasch re-writing the history of Spanish clowning, a history that he himself had been so instrumental in penning.

Not only that, but it was for joke-telling clowns that Gasch often reserved his harshest criticism (along with his anti-props crusade), even in this decade:

> The Brothers Cape, seized by an overwhelming verbiage, lost sight of the fact that jokes, as the sole means of humour, are unacceptable in the circus, that patter is rigorously prohibited in the circus, which is a visual rather than aural spectacle, in which the word is to play a secondary role only. Currently there are few clowns that give preference to action over the word.
>
> ('Evocación del Circo Olimpia XII', *Destino*, 29 November 1969, in Jané and Minguet 1998: 134–135)

But Pompoff and Thedy's time had passed, their height of popularity had been in the 1920s, 1930s and 1940s, and they only returned to Spain in 1967, having left in 1952. Gasch's re-write seems to be pointing somewhere else, towards their nephews, *Los Payasos de la Tele*, the ever-present *Clowns on TV*, first in Argentina, then Cuba, before becoming a cultural staple of late Francoism in the 1970s. Their repertoire had developed, or degenerated, beyond even joke-telling and towards songs for children.

GROCK AND TORTELL POLTRONA: THE THEORY, TECHNIQUE AND TECHNOLOGY OF THE CHAIR

For Rémy, complex mechanical props only served to slow down the action and go too far beyond the framework of clowning. The good clown, on the other hand, uses a simple object to hand, such as a chair. But even this prop is doomed in the hands of those clowns in search of greater effects via mechanical means:

> This commonplace chair, which in the circus is often rickety, which is to say already prepared for comic effect, in the hands of a skilled clown, is not enough for the clown who lacks comic vision. The latter, always on the lookout for prop-comedy, transforms the chair into an exploding machine, the explosion, like the kick up the backside, putting an end to the progress of the clown's problems. Think instead of Grock. The chair which gives way under his feet allows him to show his skill. Having fallen through the broken seat, he jumps back with a thrust of the hips and takes his place on the back of the chair, his two feet resting on the seat frame. The feat is executed at an explosive speed, provoking laughter.
>
> (1962: 23)

The chair is indeed one of the most commonly found props in clown history. One of its great strengths is perhaps its 'unquestionability'. An audience will rarely ask itself 'Why is that chair there?', 'Why is she sitting on the chair?' or even 'Why does she want to sit on the chair?' By using commonplace objects that no-one questions the presence of, the clown can move swiftly on to the business in hand and avoid wasting energy on convincing the audience. It is one of the ways in which clowns avoid those problems that beset so many actors, of the type 'What is my motivation?' In the end, this is just another way of understanding how the clown 'can do anything she wants to' as justification never comes into it.

But even the chair has its limits. The Catalan clown, Tortell Poltrona, has a well-known number where he balances a vast number of chairs on his forehead, all stacked up in a fan-like way. It's a number he has done for many years (his career started back in the 1960s). Apparently, he was once performing the number somewhere in Guatemala in an area where people don't use chairs. They use hammocks. It's not that they didn't know what a chair was, it was simply not a very meaningful object in that densely forested part of the world. By all accounts the number, though received sympathetically, didn't provoke a lot of laughs that day.

FOOD COMEDY: CARROTS, BANANAS AND FISH

Other objects, as well as being deemed to have a close relationship with clowns, like the chair, also supposedly possess inherently comic qualities. Disher didn't just think the banana was funny – he traced a history of comic fruit and veg:

> When food is stolen, laughter depends on whether some peculiar association of ideas is stronger than our disapproval. Vegetables have a variety of humorous possibilities: carrots are the symbol of auburn hair, turnips and cabbages denote stupidity, potatoes and tomatoes can be made to rhyme, asparagus is a test of social decorum, onions are eloquent of the results of cutting or eating them. Offal of any kind, sheep's heart, bullock's kidney and horse's lights, are related to a medical consultation. Fish is difficult to handle if not wrapped up. Live creatures, especially lobsters, are troublesome. Bread suggests hunger too strongly for humour, and clowns have to counteract the impression by returning purloined loaves immediately, as missiles, or, copying Grimaldi, use them as boxing gloves. Associations, however, change from generation to generation, and what was humorous in the knavery of the Harlequinades of fifty years ago is less than serious now. Carrots, for instance, have been ousted by bananas.
>
> (1925: 18)

It is an intriguing list and one which makes you want to go and find examples to demonstrate. Two will suffice, whose form is distinct from each other. In Fatty Arbuckle and Buster Keaton's short film *The Hayseed* (1919), Buster feeds Fatty a bowl of onions in order to strengthen his voice before he sings. It is not, therefore, Fatty's lyrics which have the whole audience in tears: 'Roses have lost there scent and lilacs, too/I yearn for a sweet fragrant kiss from you/With each breath I recall your delicate perfume/My eyes keep watering in deepest gloom'.

In Monty Python's *Fish-Slapping Dance* (Series 3, Episode 2, 1972), Michael Palin delivers several small slaps to John Cleese's face using two small fish, performed in a mock-folkloric style. But it is Cleese's big fish, when revealed, which wins and knocks Palin into the canal.

In the first example, the onions behave as expected: they cause tears. The sentimental song also provokes tears, also to be expected. The audience are crying at the right moment but for the wrong, although logical, reason.

In the second example the fish are not used in a way we expect, as weapons, but the action of slapping each other's faces is an expected one in the context of a fight, albeit a ritualised dance. But fish do indeed 'slap', so their use to slap each other is logical. The other gag is one of size: two normal fish, the third unexpectedly big.

So although the role of the food is formally different in the two examples, in both there is only one 'wrong' or unexpected element. I will discuss 'wrongness' in more detail later when considering the question of gag types, but for now let me say that personally, having dissected those two gags, I am in no way less inclined to laugh at them.

SLOSH: TECHNOLOGY AND TECHNIQUE IN PANTOMIME

Closely related to food is slosh, recipes for which abound on websites and in books on contemporary British pantomime, of which there are quite a few. One of the better books is Millie Taylor's *British Pantomime Performance* (2007), which has a chapter entitled 'Chaos and Disruption in Slapstick and Slosh Scenes', which embraces buckets of wallpaper paste, custard pies and anything you can throw at each other which is, well, sloshy. Taylor, following Paul Harris, gives us the stage manager's perspective:

> Slapstick scenes have always been very popular in pantomimes and are loved by both children and adults. They are also fun for the actors to perform, but stage managers generally hate them.
>
> (Harris 1996: 94)

> It can take the Assistant Stage Managers several hours each day to prepare the slosh for custard pies etc. to the required consistency. Men's shaving sticks are grated, with water and colouring being added very slowly, and the mixture whisked for hours. The stage management team would allow three hours per day to prepare the 10–15 buckets of slosh per show (they might need up to 45 buckets on a three-show day). [...] Joanna Reid and Ian Liston both identify the cost

of cleaning up as the principal reason for no longer including slosh scenes in their pantomimes.

(Taylor 2007: 28)

Some clowns, such as Alesis and Tweedy, always make their own slosh because the consistency is so vital to the timing of the scene.

(Taylor 2007: 31)

Taylor goes into detail about how the handing down of slapstick and slosh scenes has changed in recent years:

Until the last twenty years or so, the training ground for pantomime included the last vestiges of variety and music hall, but largely consisted of an apprenticeship in pantomime itself. Now the training grounds are street theatre and circus. [...]
This process of apprenticeship has all but disappeared.

(2007: 39)

This has disastrous consequences for the survival of such a difficult art, as described by Ian Liston, working with Charlie Cairoli:

It was very funny, but my goodness me, it was worked out with years and years of knowledge and experience and precision. It was quite an astonishing scene to watch and it never varied, it was exactly the same every night.

(Taylor 2007: 39)

And Norman Robbins, quoted in Taylor (2007), describes Ken Wilson's slosh scenes with Lauri Lupino Lane:

The special mix, devised by the Lupino family, was prepared for each performance and unlike modern 'slosh' only went where it was intended to go. In addition, each 'mishap' appeared to happen by accident; there was none of the 'your turn, my turn' about this act; the timing was perfect. By the time the scene was finished, the pair were almost invisible beneath the quaking and glistening multi-coloured foam while the audience were helpless with laughter.

(Robbins 2002: 212)

Today's multi-skilled performers just don't have the skills, nor is a three-week rehearsal period anywhere near enough time to come up with original slapstick business, 'whereas the old pantomime routines had been honed in variety over many years' (Taylor 2007: 40).

Sometimes actors don't know how to play it and you actually have to go 'Do this – beat – in you come – beat' and you have to do it exactly the same or else it won't work. Some of them get it brilliantly and some of them don't. Then you just have to teach it. You have to say 'You need to see it – beat – look – beat – back again' and they'll pick it up eventually in performance.

(Joanna Reid quoted in Taylor 2007: 40)

Taylor goes on to discuss the different ways in which slosh scenes can occur in pantomime, whether they are interchangeable or specific to particular shows (such as make-up and hairdressing scenes for the Ugly Sisters in *Cinderella* or clothes-washing scenes in *Aladdin*); or specific to characters, most likely performed by the Dame and principal comic (the Dame usually coming out on top); or the type involving accidents, as in the decorating scene (2007: 41–42); finishing with the dynamics of audience participation in the slosh scene, as here described by Roy Hudd in *Mother Goose*:

> We then have the Kitchen slosh scene.
>
> At the end, enter the Squire. He leans on the table and falls about laughing at the mess. Billy picks up big trifle.
>
> Billy (to audience): Shall I?
>
> (Taylor 2007: 42)

Taylor's chapter on slosh concludes with:

> The play for the audience comes from the fear of being doused in egg, water or slosh, even as it becomes complicitous in the anarchy and competitiveness of slosh and the mayhem of slapstick and chases.
>
> (2007: 49)

CULTURAL ANTHROPOLOGY AND THE MEANING OF THROWING

Such an analysis seems to us almost banal, stating the obvious about something so commonplace in our culture as clowns throwing, or threatening to throw, buckets of water and custard pies at each other and the audience. Is there not some more hidden significance to be found? Well, cultural anthropologists have been interested in clowns just about ever since they have existed – cultural anthropologists, I mean. If it is generally presumed that cultural anthropology as a recognisable discipline takes off following the publication of Charles Darwin's *On the Origin of Species* (1859), then Adolf Bandolier's *The Delight Makers* (1890) must be counted as a relatively early output. For, in his preface, Bandolier informs us that his book is

> the result of eight years spent in ethnological and archaeological study among the Pueblo Indians of New Mexico. The first chapters were written more than six years ago at the Pueblo of Cochiti. The greater part was composed in 1885, at Santa Fé, after I had bestowed upon the Tehuas the same interest and attention I had previously paid to their neighbours the Queres.
>
> (1890: v)

Bandolier was the leading expert on the archaeology and ethnology of the southwestern United States and Mexico, and he had been publishing in the field since 1877. *The Delight Makers* puts the Koshari, the indigenous clowns, at the centre of the narrative. And a narrative it is, for the work is in fact a novel.

> I was prompted to perform the work by a conviction that however scientific works may tell the truth about the Indian, they exercise always a limited influence upon the general public.
>
> [...] The descriptions of manners and customs, of creed and rites, are from actual observations by myself and other ethnologists, from the statements of trustworthy Indians, and from a great number of Spanish sources of old date
> [...]
> The plot is my own. But most of the scenes described I have witnessed.
>
> (1890: v–vi)

Barton Wright, in his survey of the clowns of the region in *Clowns of the Hopi –Tradition Keepers and Delight Makers* (1994), prefaces his own book with a testimony to those early anthropologists upon whose work he partly draws, many of whom were not setting out to study clowns at all:

> Few of these individuals were trained in the new field of anthropology, instead they happened to be on the scene at the right time and interested enough to record those observations. Alexander M. Stephen was in Keams Canyon because of an interest in mining, but he left behind the most comprehensive document written on the Hopi. [...] The prolific writer J. Walter Fewkes incorporated much of Stephen's findings, as did Cosmo Mindeleff, in his published material. However, he and the romantic Frank Hamilton Cushing were the only nineteenth-century observers with even a modicum of training. The other eminent writer of that era was Matilda Coxe Stevenson, whose opportunity consisted of being the wife of an Army man assigned to make an expedition into the region.
> [...]
> many of the writers of the early twentieth century were women trained in the field of anthropology and who had specific goals. Elise Clews Parsons, with her interest in the role of women in other cultures, probably wrote more on a greater number of Pueblo cultures than any other author.
>
> (1994: vii–viii)

RITUAL CLOWNS: MUD, URINE, FAECES AND MENSTRUAL BLOOD

So what objects, which props and which messy substances do these scientists find in use? Laura Levi Makarius, who in *Le sacré et la violation des interdits* ('The Sacred and the Violation of Taboos'; 1974) brought together a vast amount of research dating back to the late 19th century, devotes a chapter to 'Ritual Clowns':

> Amongst the Zuni, the clowns connected to medicine are the Newekwe, of whom it is said they would drink whole bowls of urine and that they ate excrement and

all kinds of revolting things. As for the Koyemshi, another kind of Zuni clown, they showered the audience with urine. They themselves, during the ceremony of Shalako, are sprayed with water by the women.

(Cazeneuve 1957: 197–198, 186, cited in Makarius 1974: 62–63)

Makarius argues that 'water is probably a substitute for urine' (1974: 63), referring to the parallel that Parsons made between the two liquids:

Water or urine being thrown over the Koiemshi by the women during the ceremony of Kokoawia, and before that, at the time of the ritual called dukuyada, which I presume derives from the term 'kukuya' which means 'throw', and to have been applied to the rite in question.

(Parsons 1923: 183)

Makarius also cites Alexander Stephen's more pantomimic example:

Stephen saw, during the initiation of a child into a clown society, how a clown woman who had had fixed under her skirts a bladder full of diluted coffee, opened this bladder and pretended to urinate during the course of her pantomime.

(Stephen 1936: 366, quoted in Makarius 1974: 63)

Stephen continues to describe how those present then placed grains of sand moistened by the 'urine' on their tongues and on the child's, thereby passing on 'wisdom'. Such powers being ascribed to the 'urine' leads Makarius to the conclusion that

This 'wisdom' magically acquired shows well that this is a question of the breaking of a taboo. If the urine, which in principle must be female, does not actually represent menstrual blood, then it is its nearest substitute.

(1974: 63)

This is one of Makarius' principle themes, which we might summarise as follows. First, there are practices or substances which are taboo, such as urine (which should not be drunk), excrement (which should not be eaten) and menstrual blood (which should not be touched). Second, there are those people who are able to break taboos, including shamans and also clowns. It is in the nature of clowns to break taboos – they are beings whose function is to break rules. It could even be said it is their defining trait. Third, those who break taboos, and survive, acquire more power than those who live by the norms of society. Fourth, not only are they stronger than others but they can use the taboo substances as medicine.

Makarius gives many more examples of men dressed as women showering the young men with water, clowns drinking bucketloads of stale urine (two or three gallons at a time, according to Stephen), chasing the audience with it and so on. Blood, too, is a common prop, sometimes belonging to a taboo animal, such as a dog (1974: 64).

However, when blood appears in the clowns' pantomimes, it is generally animal blood. As in the Assiniboine's 'Dance of the Fools', who splash the spectators with deer's blood. These clowns, who are characterised by the wearing of a mask and costume that is as bizarre as possible, perform a pantomime around the carcass of a deer, which represents that of a buffalo. They feign fear, approach the body gradually, and finally share the flesh. They fill bladders with its blood, which they hang round their necks and waists. If the spectators get too close, they scare them off by splashing them with blood.

(from Lowie 1909: 62–65, quoted in Makarius 1974: 64)

PAUL BOUISSAC AND CIRCUS ANTHROPOLOGY: THE PROFANATION OF THE SACRED

Compared with the large amount of anthropological literature on the clowns of New Mexico and neighbouring regions, that which addresses clowning from the European tradition is exceedingly limited. One important exception is the work of Paul Bouissac, who has dedicated a number of articles to the subject of clowns and circus.

In 'The Profanation of the Sacred in Circus Clown Performances' (1997), he analyses some examples of classic European clowning and draws some radical conclusions about what clowning does, conclusions which will lead us straight back to the practical business of actually producing clown material.

Bouissac considers from the outset that clowns engage in ritual activity, or 'traditional patterned actions' (1997: 195). These actions can be either 'demonstrative' or 'transformative'. Demonstrative actions are those which represent or enact something. Transformative actions are those which produce a change of state for some or all of the participants. Bouissac considers clown actions to be basically demonstrative, although in the light of what Makarius had to say about clowns and magic, one could argue that they can also be transformative.

> The nature of these operations, which amount to an acted meta-discourse on the tacit rules shaping the culture concerned, is usually characterized as being transgressive or subversive and, as such, are contained within strict boundaries, both in time and space. It is suggested in this paper that circus clown performances demonstrate the basic but unwritten rules on which our construction of a culturally bound meaningful universe rests.
>
> (Bouissac 1997: 195)

In other words, the norms of our culture are revealed by clowns, whose job it is to transgress them. This 'profanation of the sacred', as Bouissac refers to it, is also responsible for the 'stigmatized social status of the clown' (1997: 196). These rules of behaviour are distinct to the written laws of a country, which are consciously articulated for all to refer to. These need no revealing by the clown. It is instead the rules which are unwritten, unspoken and therefore hidden from view, which require the clown's attention. By stepping on or over the line of these norms, clowns reveal them to the rest of society:

> Profanation is not so much the breaking of a rule made explicit in a legal code as the exposure of the rule of the rules, the principle or principles that are so fundamental for the holding together of the regulative system that they cannot be formulated.
>
> (1997: 197)

To illustrate this, Bouissac uses the instance when a man was discovered one morning sitting on the bed of Queen Elizabeth II. The problem was that no important law had been broken, so the legal punishment for the man seemed to many to be too small for such a supposedly outrageous action. But it would be impossibly embarrassing, or indeed impossible, for parliament to pass a law specifically prohibiting such an action:

> For instance to make explicit and to publicize the following rule, 'it is forbidden to British subjects to sneak into the Queen's bedroom unannounced at dawn,' is unthinkable, in terms of the system, because it would imply that this action is indeed a possibility.
>
> (1997: 197)

In the end there was no prosecution and the only way out in such a case is to

> disqualify the profanator by presenting him as an insane person, i.e., by excluding him from the system that his action jeopardized.
>
> (1997: 197)

The only other route would have been an accusation of treason. Bouissac's conclusion to all this is that:

> In a way we could say, metaphorically, that every morning a clown sits on the Queen's bed, at the risk of losing his passport.
>
> (1997: 197)

The practice of clowns is therefore to express the tacit rules upon which a culture is based. This doing and saying the unthinkable and the unspeakable (a notion closely related to Makarius' taboo-breaking), precisely because it is unthinkable and unspeakable, can only be done in the 'ritualistic mode', and by ritualistic figures: clowns. Bouissac here touches on

> the issue of whether such rituals are devised by society as cathartic outlets, as collective dreams of the cultural unconscious, or whether there is in all social systems a built-in irrepressible cognitive drive toward a representation of the system itself, or whether any other better explanations can be found.
>
> (1997: 199)

Refreshingly, he decides to steer clear of the issue, and instead look in detail at some actual examples of clown numbers and how they do the job of profaning the sacred. Although, as Bouissac himself admits, not all clown actions are up there in the category of major profaning of a vital linchpin of society.

> However there are quite a few scenarios that address head-on some of the great themes upon which most if not all societies focus their rituals, namely: birth, matrimonial alliances, and death. [...] Questions concerning the borderline which distinguishes humans from animals, or the precise moments when human life starts and is terminated, or the structure of identities.
>
> (1997: 199)

TABOO-BREAKING IN EUROPEAN CLOWNING: BABIES, PIGS AND CANNIBALISM

Such big issues need special treatment in order for a society to be able to both acknowledge the arbitrariness of the norms and at the same time work out a way of coming to some agreement. The special treatment is the clown number.

In the classical repertoire of European clowns there exists, in many variations, a number which goes something like this. The auguste clown enters dressed as a woman, grotesquely, with a push-chair, behaving like a mother with baby. Cries are heard from the push-chair and the auguste asks for milk. A large bottle is brought and a tube fitted between it and the inside of the push-chair and we see the milk level rapidly go down in the bottle until it is empty. The crying returns and the auguste picks the baby up, at which point we see that it is not a baby but a piglet. A variation involves the auguste giving someone the 'baby' to hold, who then gets wet from the 'baby's' urine.

Bouissac makes a number of points in his analysis. First, on the substituting of the piglet for a baby:

> Two powerful cultural themes are thus brought together: on the one hand the care that humans have to take of their offspring as a prerequisite for the survival of the species and the ensuing sacralization of infants; on the other hand, an animal species, the pig, which is the focus of intense cultural attention in many parts of the world, including ours.
>
> (1997: 200)

In the variation there is a third theme, that of the urine and its polluting effect.

The pig is an animal which receives a lot of attention from anthropologists ('obsessive attention', admits Bouissac), due in part to its being the object of strict taboos, rules or rituals in many parts of the world, including our own culture where still 'the pig is loaded with taboo values' (1997: 201). In the clown number, the pig can convincingly stand in for the baby:

> Many characteristics both anatomical and ecological concur to situate the pig in the immediate proximity of humans: the pigmentation of its skin; the unusually light body hair which makes it appear almost naked; the relative expressivity of its face which lends itself so well to anthropomorphization.
>
> (1997: 201)

Then there is the 'rumor that nothing tastes more like pork than human flesh', or that in the Middle Ages, when animals were under the scrutiny of the church, 'pigs were accused of crimes more often than any other animal' (1997: 201) – to say nothing of the status of the pig as an insult, as a symbol of the animal or the inhuman. The baby is the human form which is supposedly closest to the pig: dirty, smelly, squealy and without speech. Bouissac sees here a blurring of the borderline between human and animal, which accounts for our insistence on socialising infants into proper human beings so as to distance them as fast as possible from animals – animals that we might be tempted to eat.

Finally, in the peeing variation, this

> pollution crisis occurs only when the categorical confusion spreads, so to speak, in the social group since it follows someone else's agreement to enter the Auguste's game by accepting to look after the 'baby.'
>
> (1997: 202)

BOUISSAC AND GAG THEORY

Before I leave Bouissac, here is his breakdown into categories of what profanation actually means in practice:

> 1. a particular object assigned to a certain place or position is moved to and placed in an inappropriate place or position,
>
> 2. an object that should be manipulated in a certain manner (or simply be seen) by a particular person or class of persons, is manipulated in this manner (or is seen) by an unqualified person, or is manipulated in an inappropriate manner,
>
> 3. a patterned behaviour that should be performed in the presence of an object or person is performed in the presence of an inappropriate object or person,
>
> 4. a patterned behaviour that is prescribed in a specific context is performed in another context or is not performed in the prescribed context,
>
> 5. a word or text to which a prescribed interpretation is attached, is interpreted in another manner or, still worse, the consequences of this new interpretation are actually implemented.
>
> (1997: 196)

We could simplify this to:

1. things are in the wrong place;
2. things are used by the wrong people or are used wrongly;
3. doing something for the wrong person;
4. doing something when you shouldn't, or not doing it when you should;
5. misunderstanding words, and maybe acting on the misunderstanding.

This simple scheme reveals itself to be a powerful tool – not just for the analysis of clown material but also for its production. Without wanting to get too obsessive about categorizing things, looked at through this filter we can revisit much of the material we were considering earlier – Lane, Page, Musson and so on – and see more clearly how and why these gags work.

What otherwise can seem like a long list of ideas – a hat that releases smoke when you raise it; going to lean against the wall and missing it and falling; pouring yourself a drink then drinking from the bottle instead of the glass; putting your hat on only to find it is on someone else's head who was standing right behind you; bending down to pick something up such that your trousers fall down; tripping up; bending down to pick something up but instead kicking it away with your foot; taking your jacket half off in order to look at your wristwatch; bending a teaspoon in half so that it doesn't stick up too high in your cup and poke your eye; cleaning your glasses which have no lenses in them so that the cloth passes straight through (all these examples being from Page) – can now start to order itself according to how the gag works, or which category of 'wrongness' is present. And if you know how the gag works, it is very simple to come up with a hundred new examples based on the same structure.

The principle is that one (and only one) element must be in some way 'wrong'. The basic possible variables are person, place, time, action, word, behaviour and object. So we can have the right person doing an action correctly in the right place and with the right object but at the wrong time, such as raising your hand to catch a ball when it's already hit you on the head. And so on.

With such a map in hand, a glance again at Grock throws up plenty of examples of this 'wrongness': the use of a violin bow for back scratching (wrong use of object); the violin balanced on a foot (wrong place); the single violin played by Grock and Partner simultaneously (wrong number of people); the constant misunderstandings in dialogues; carrying a tiny violin in a suitcase (either wrong size or wrong place).

GAG STRUCTURE, CATEGORISATION AND OWNERSHIP: DOMINIQUE DENIS'S 1000 GAGS

Many books of clown gags do indeed already present them in categories, but those categories rather than being functional or formal are usually generic. Dominique Denis in *1,000 gags de clowns* (1997), which actually contains more than 1000 gags, has the following sections: 'Introduction', 'Music', 'Costume', 'Food', 'Body parts', 'Water comedy', 'Attitudes', 'Juggling', 'Kitchenware', 'Flowers and balloons', 'Furniture', 'Bicycles', 'Sports', 'Crazy cars', 'Magic', 'Animals', 'Acrobatic gags', 'Parodies', 'Characters', 'Parades' and 'A few more'. These are useful for referencing and finding the information, but less useful for understanding or producing ideas. However, Denis does provide some analysis of gag structure in his introduction to the book, covering albeit very briefly the composition of gags which are binary, ternary, episodic, running, delayed, substituted or defused (1997: 8–9).

Denis's descriptive style is simple and to the point, omitting any unnecessary words about how you should play a gag, or even about what you should find funny in it. In a way it is a perfect clown authorial style, each gag consisting of two or three lines of text, stating purely the action and not the interpretation, with just the addition at times of the name of the artist who performed it, as here in one of Denis's largest sections, on costume, divided into sections such as:

Shirt, shirtfront, tie and others

4 – At the time when Grock and Antonet were a team, Grock had the following gag: one tail of his shirt would be sticking out from under his waistcoat. His partner warned him that his dress was a little messy. Then Grock lifted up the offending end of the shirt and tore it into tiny pieces. The shirt tail was made of paper.

7 – Farruchio Zacchini had an excellent entrance to the ring: to make himself comfortable, he took off his jacket and then his shirt cuffs which he threw noisily to the ground, as they were made of iron.

(1997: 64–66)

The classification of gags by category rather than by individual clowns gives an impression of common sources, from which each performer may draw according to preference:

Due to its impressive shape, the grand piano has always fascinated the great comedians, from Grock to Liberace, via Victor Borge. They have all had a distinct approach to this majestic instrument. Whilst some gags are purely mechanical, many depend for their effect on the personality of the performer, and consequently are unscriptable.

17 – Gin sits on the stool, ready to play. However, he is not happy with the height of his seat. He then takes a telephone directory and puts it on his stool. He takes his place . . . but he seems concerned. He stands up again, tears one page from the directory, then sits down again, finally satisfied.

19 – in the midst of his concert, Liberace feeling a little peckish, cooks himself an omelette.

26 – Jean-Pierre Farré has a whole game of miming whilst playing the piano. Tackling a difficult piece, he doesn't hesitate to pick his nose.

28 – Chico Marx indulged in a little fantasy playing with an apple that he made roll along the keyboard.

(1997: 34–37)

Whilst it may be true, as Denis says, that each performer has a distinct approach to the piano, in that each has a different personality, what is not necessarily so different between performers is the choice of gags. Since Denis names only one performer per gag, we get the impression that the gag originates and belongs to that one person. In some cases this is so, but many times the truth is otherwise and the same gag migrates between performers. Here is gag number 20:

> Grock sits down at his piano. The stool is placed too far away on relation to the keyboard. He stands up, rolls up his sleeves and pushes the piano towards the stool.
>
> (1997: 36)

The gag has become almost a Grock icon, but John Towsen draws our attention to Max Linder's version of the same gag in his 1921 film *Be My Wife*:

> Max is disguised as a piano teacher so he can get closer to his beloved. When he discovers the piano is too far from the bench, he tries to move the piano rather than the bench. His girlfriend's aunt Agatha shows him the easier way.
>
> (Towsen 2011: post 108)

IMPOSSIBLE PROPS: GROCK, HARPO MARX AND LUCILLE BALL

It is impossible to know who got there first, and it doesn't really matter. In all likelihood it was probably done by some predecessor of both Linder and Grock. Clowns re-visit the same concept constantly, finding slight variations on a theme. For example, Grock claimed to be able to play an impossibly bizarre instrument, called the 'wztdhp' (a strange noise pronounced somewhere between a hiccup, sneeze and whistle), a conglomeration of keys, valves, levers, mouthpieces and strings. His partner impatiently wants to know how it works:

> *Max:* What is at the end of these strings, this keyboard, this mouthpiece?
> *Grock:* Cheese.
> *Max:* Cheese? Why?
> *Grock:* To eat.
>
> (Rémy 1945: 400)

This is an instrument we never see and, of course, never hear. On the same theme, Harpo Marx's impossible instrument is also unplayable, although it does exist. Appearing on the *Kraft Music Hall TV Programme* with Milton Berle in 1959, Harpo takes from under his coat a double trumpet, two trumpets joined end to end, with two mouthpieces but nowhere for the sound to come out:

> *Berle:* You invented this?
> [*Harpo replies in gesture that he did and that he is very clever.*]

Berle: Oh good, it's very peculiar. It's got two mouthpieces. You play in both sides, at the same time?

[*Harpo nods.*]

Berle: How do you do that?

[*Harpo shrugs. He doesn't know.*]

(Marx 1959)

Lucille Ball, on the other hand, does succeed with her impossible instrument. In the pilot programme of *I Love Lucy* (1951) and re-used in episode 52 (1952), she is challenged to play an unheard-of instrument. Lucy, taking the place of the clown Pepito (José Escobar Pérez), who is ill, has been trying to get herself into Ricky's band by auditioning with the cello, which she can't play. (The number was Pepito's.)

Ricky: Look, Professor, I'm sorry but I haven't got any use for a cellist.

Lucy: No?

Ricky: I tell you what, though, we have a brand new instrument.

Lucy: Eh!

Ricky: And I've been looking for someone who can play it.

Lucy: Oh!

Ricky: And if you can play it . . .

Lucy: Eh!

Ricky: You got yourself a job.

Lucy: Oh . . . eh . . . oh . . . eh . . . oh

Ricky: You wanna try it?

Lucy: Well, what is it?

Ricky: A saxo-vibro-trombo-phonovich.

Lucy: Oh! A saxo-vibro-trombo-phonovich!

Ricky: That's right. You think you can play it?

Lucy: Oh sure.

Ricky: Well, wonderful, bring it out here, the Professor can play it.

(Ball 1951)

Lucy seems to have met her match. But the instrument turns out to be a hooter-phone for circus seals, which she impersonates in order to play successfully. It is a classic auguste-imposter number. Clearly knowing nothing but saying yes to everything, all of Lucy's attempts to impress Ricky with the cello fail. Then just when all seems lost and the impossible approaches, success suddenly arrives. An inverted success, of a human non-musician playing an instrument that no-one else can play, but as an animal.

LAZZI: STAGE CRUDITIES AND VIOLENCE

In a similar fashion to clown gag books, those books on commedia dell'arte that give information about lazzi generally tend to present them in categories. Mel Gordon's *Lazzi, the Comic Routines of the Commedia dell'Arte* (1983) makes a brave bid to be definitive, in part aiming to fill in some perceived gaps in previous works. In the Introduction he notes the quality of the first books on the early 20th-century revival of commedia, such as Winifred Smith's *The Commedia dell'Arte* (New York, 1912), Constant Mic's *The Commedia dell'Arte* (Petrograd, 1914), P. L. Duchartre's *La Comedie italienne* (Paris, 1925), Cyril Beaumont's *History of Harlequin* (London, 1926) and Allardyce Nicoll's *Masks, Mimes, and Miracles* (London, 1931).

But from the perspective of the late 20th century, something is lacking, according to Gordon:

> So, when the Commedia again inspired new kinds of theatre in the early 1960s, much of the avant-garde theatre practitioners' knowledge of it came from these books.
>
> If the reader looks carefully at the rich iconography in those books, he will find drawings, mezzotints, and paintings of perverse sexual play, nudity, vomiting, defecation, and all sorts of activities involving enemas and chamberpots – images of actions that are almost never described in the texts. For instance, in the authoritative Duchartre book where captions accompany most of the pictures, a drawing of the Doctor administering an enema to Arlecchino's exposed buttocks is described as showing an 'injection' with a 'syringe.' In other books, the authors completely ignore this visual documentation. In fact, the Commedia's celebrated *lazzi*, or comic bits, are rarely discussed in more than a couple of paragraphs. Certainly these seldom even refer to the obscene *lazzi* which make up a good portion of the whole. It is as if these scholars, publishing in the early twentieth century, were psychologically or morally inhibited from accurately documenting the Commedia's best-known performance innovation, *lazzi*.
>
> (1983: 3–4)

He also has a go at bringing to order the arguments about the definition and meaning of the word 'lazzi' (as most commedia scholars do), but his main concern is practical, the focus being more on their function than on matters of etymology. The question for Gordon is whether the lazzi tie narrative action together or unravel it:

> From the beginning of Commedia scholarship, there has been a heavy concern with the derivation of the word *lazzi*. Luigi Riccoboni in his *Histoire du Theatre Italien* ... (Paris, 1728) wrote that it was a Lombard corruption of the Tuscan word *lacci*, which meant cord or ribbon. The term *lazzi*, Riccoboni reasoned, alluded to the comic business that tied together the performance. Of course, the practical reality was quite different; *lazzi* functioned as independent routines that more often than not interrupted or unraveled the Commedia plots or performance unity.
>
> (1983: 4)

In any case, it is their usage which matters to us now:

> Whatever the origins of the word, the definition of *lazzi* is relatively standard; 'We give the name *lazzi* to the actions of Arlecchino or other masked characters

when they interrupt a scene by their expressions of terror or by their fooleries,' declared Riccoboni. In 1699, Andrea Perrucci simply defined the *lazzo*, a single *lazzi*, as 'something foolish, witty, or metaphorical in word or action.' Later scholars have described *lazzi* as 'stage tricks' or 'comic stage business.'

(1983: 4)

And we should not get too fixated on the one word, given that it was only one among many:

trionfi, triumphs; *azzi*, actions; *burla*, joke; and the French *jeu*, or play.

(1983: 4)

In addition, Gordon accepts Constant Mic's three categories of lazzi. The first is when they 'arose out of the scenic occasion', being used to re-engage audience interest or inject new energy into the rhythm. The second is when they were expected high points or speciality acts within the larger show. And the third is when they form part of the plot itself, which, if extended, would became a *burla* or *jest* (1983: 5).

Gordon's book is both scholarly and practical, but where there is conflict the practical takes precedence. He lists over half of the 300–400 lazzi that survive in some form or other in descriptions of scenari from the period between 1550 and 1750, but he omits any that exist only in name without descriptions. Instead of including copious reference notes, he limits himself to describing the lazzi's use, the characters who play them and the first known performance or publication date – not dissimilar to Denis's clown gags, in fact.

Gordon's 12 categories are: 'Acrobatic and Mimic Lazzi', 'Comic Violence/ Sadistic Behavior', 'Food Lazzi', 'Illogical Lazzi', 'Stage Properties as Laz'zi', 'Sexual/Scatological Lazzi', 'Social-Class Rebellion Lazzi', 'Stage/Life Duality Lazzi', Stupidity/Inappropriate Behavior', 'Transformation Lazzi', 'Trickery Lazzi' and 'Word Play Lazzi'. These correspond to different types of humour though, as Gordon admits, overlap is sometimes inevitable and

it is not clear whether the spectator laughs at the *lazzo* for one reason or another, for instance whether because Arlecchino is making a fool of Pantalone, an authority figure, or because Arlecchino is savaging the Latin language.

(1983: 7)

In the lists of lazzi, Gordon is true to his declared intention of restoring to their rightful place the sexual and scatological lazzi, the 'stage crudities' which he claims were among the most popular yet 'remain the least analysed by scholars', and which include the

infantile and adolescent aggressions of shit and urine throwing, humiliation through exposure, of mixing food and feces, of placing one's ass in another's face, and the telling of dirty jokes.

(1983: 32)

Examples range from the simple *Lazzo of Vomit* [Venice 1611],

> At the beginning of a performance, or just after drinking some of the Doctor's medicine, Arlecchino vomits,
>
> (1983: 32)

to the more elaborate *Lazzo of Water* [Rome 1622]:

> The mistress (or Turchetta) has fainted and the servant-girl cries for water. Pulcinella (or Coviello) brings her all kinds of water: rosewater, jasmine water, orange water, mint water, lily water. Finally, he pisses in a cup and splashes it on his mistress. This revives her, and he sings the praises of 'the water distilled by our rod.'
>
> (1983: 33)

Such examples are more than a match for the clowns from New Mexico and their magical powers.

'Comic Violence/Sadistic Behavior' is another large-ish section. At times this obeys the logic of status relationships between servants and masters and the consequent acts of punishment and retaliation between such characters:

> *Lazzo of the Knock* [Rome 1580]
>
> Pedrolino, just arising from a sleep, bumps his head into his master, Cassandro, and then crushes Cassandro's bunioned toes with his enormous shoes. When Cassandro kicks him, Pedrolino unconsciously responds by striking him in the face.
>
> (1983: 15)

Sometimes, the victims are chosen for other reasons:

> The victims of the violent *lazzi* are usually Pantalone and the Captain. This is especially true in the early 1600s, when the Captain was still associated with the Spanish conquerors.
>
> (1983: 14)

In the *Lazzo of the Innocent By-Stander* [Venice 1611], Arlecchino and Pedrolino meet to fight but it is the Captain who receives the blows whilst trying to restrain them.

And sometimes the violence takes on a life of its own, seemingly outside all limitations of status relationships or plot:

> In the 1700s, a new character, neither master nor servant, became involved with sadistic or violent *lazzi*; this is the humpbacked Pulcinella, whose sole purpose seemed to be to torment other characters. His puppet outgrowth, Punch, violated all normative standards through his 'dropping the baby' routine.
>
> (1983: 15)

Clown theory is indeed a complex area. It occurs whenever we think about clown practice, when the question of 'how to do it' throws up a vast range of responses. And I have so far only looked at the 'how' of clowning from the outside in, as I have not yet begun to examine how contemporary clown performer training has delved deeply into the way failure in front of an audience can form the basis of a whole way of clowning or being in a clown state. I shall come to this soon, but before that I shall explore some of the ways clowns create: the 'how' of clown authorship.

9 Clown Authors

INTRODUCTION

Clowns appear as authors in a number of ways. I first look at some of the ways they write about themselves, and what clown autobiographies reveal, and do not reveal, about their subject's art and how they clown. I ask why clowns such as Coco (Nikolai Poliakoff 1900–1974) and Buffo (Howard Buten born 1950) are so unconcerned with communicating clown knowledge? Despite being packed full of anecdotes of the rich and famous, Harpo Marx's (1888–1964) offering does contain a fascinating account of the conflict between performing styles – clown versus Stanislavski – on the occasion of his visit to the Soviet Union. Bearing this in mind, I analyse part of the screenplay of the Marx Brothers' *Duck Soup* in search of the relationship between narrative and clowning, and to determine whether clowns belong outside, or inside, the script. I look at Philippe Goudard's theories about clowns and other circus performers as authors of their own performances, which contrasts with the signing away of authorial rights by performers with today's Cirque du Soleil. I then examine the growth of the status of clowns as authors as a result of the demands for written records put upon them both by censorship, in the Soviet Union, and by public funding of circus, originating in France in the 1970s, which was instrumental in impelling the growth of New Circus. The subsequent desire to fuse circus/clown with other performance forms brought problems of its own, especially with regard to theatrical narrative and whether circus/clown is fact or fiction. I look at the urge to create fictional worlds, or 'theatre', and how clown as 'self-expression' or as 'art' has recently tended to split itself off from clowns as 'bozos'.

Clowns have often functioned as authors on screen. I look at a range of such cases: stories told about clowns by clowns in the cinema, another form of autobiography (Leonid Yengibarov [1935–1972] and Charlie Chaplin); and clowns depicted by film-makers in the form of fiction (Raj Kapoor) and documentary fact (Jean-Pierre Melville). Occasionally, clowns have chosen cinema as the medium through which to articulate their theories, as is the case with Jacques Tati (1907–1982) in *Cours du Soir*. Here I supplement Tati's philosophy with his biographer's account of the creation of Monsieur Hulot, and a discussion of Tati's theory of the structure of gags, and how he used it to distance himself from Chaplin. I end the chapter by looking at Rowan

Atkinson's television guide to visual comedy, where analysis of how comedy works serves both to understand and to create material.

AUTOBIOGRAPHIES AND TRADE SECRETS: COCO AND BUFFO

Descriptions of gags and how to perform them are not only to be found in books whose stated purpose is collection and classification, or to offer training and advice. Occasional gags do crop up now and then in performers' autobiographies, but they are usually few and far between, hidden amongst the many pages dedicated to childhood family experiences or anecdotes involving the rich and famous.

Nikolai Poliakoff, the Latvian clown known as Coco who spent most of his career in Britain, on the occasion of accompanying his mentor, Vitaly Lazarenko, on a trip to a hospital, can only tell us:

> During the five minutes it took us to get to the hospital, I tried to think of all the things I could do to make the children laugh. And we did make them laugh. So much so, that we could hardly get away to get back to the circus.
>
> (1941: 56)

It does not seem to be a poor memory which prevents us from learning more:

> That night, lying in bed in a cheap lodging-house, I went over all my gags and turns in my mind, and wondered whether I had forgotten any. But gradually they all came back to me, and it seemed to me that I had forgotten nothing.
>
> (1941: 113)

And on Lazarenko himself, one of the most influential clowns of the pre- and post-revolutionary period, Coco is only scarcely more forthcoming:

> with a shout he dived headlong down into the ring. He was followed by a seemingly endless stream of old pots and pans.... I cannot remember all the things he did, but I know he gave a wonderful exhibition of clowning.
>
> (1941: 42)

Coco does give us tiny glimpses of what clowns are, or aren't:

> Suddenly I found that there were tears rolling down my cheeks. A clown in tears, what a grotesque idea!
>
> (1941: 179)

> an august must be funny at first sight, and funny all the time [...] they are always wrong. Everything they do is wrong.
>
> (1941: 198)

In contrast, we are treated to several pages of detailed descriptions of circus workers putting up the big top.

The North American clown, Buffo (Howard Buten), whose career has been spent mostly in France, is just as tight-lipped, though when he shares knowledge it is practical and re-usable:

I thought up a way to hide a big red balloon in my mouth: by inserting the mouth of the balloon into a rigid mouthpiece – a slice of hosepipe one centimetre thick did the job –, you just have to hold it under your tongue with the rest of the balloon rolled up inside your mouth. When the moment comes, you open your mouth, keeping the ring under your tongue, you blow and the balloon unrolls, comes out and inflates.

That way it looks like it's inflating all on its own.

(2005: 68)

HARPO MARX IN THE SOVIET UNION: THE CLOWN-ACTOR-AUTHOR AND STANISLAVSKI

Harpo Marx's autobiography, as well as focusing on the Marx Brothers' rags to riches story, is crammed full of anecdotes of the rich and famous in New York and Hollywood, and may well have fascinated his readers at the time of publication (1962). But today there is one chapter that stands out from the rest where Harpo, telling of his eight-week visit in 1933 to the Soviet Union, reflects on how his comedy works.

Arriving at the Moscow Art Theatre, he is asked by the director to show him what he does:

I asked if somebody would volunteer to be my straight man for the bit. 'No,' said the director. 'We must see you perform alone. To perform alone is the only true test of the pantomime artist.'

So I had to play both parts, straight man and comic. I made some faces, winding up with a Gookie, then shook hands with myself to start the knives dropping. The silverware fell to the carpet of the office, not with raucous clatter but with polite, soft thuds. Nobody cracked a smile. The room was deathly silent. Cold as it was there, I was drenched with flop sweat. It was the most miserable performance I'd ever given.
[...]
The director said my juggling of the cutlery was not exceptionally clever. I said I could do any of a dozen different bits, but they wouldn't mean anything without an audience.

'I shall be the judge of what your acting will mean to an audience,' he said. 'You will please return tomorrow morning at eleven o'clock.'

(1962: 310–311)

In the event, Harpo finds the Russian audiences extremely gratifying:

One thing I wasn't prepared for, however. I never knew any people who laughed as easily as the Russians. [...] Walking the streets, working, or waiting in line, these were the most self-controlled people I had ever seen. In the theatre, the same people couldn't hold themselves in. Every move I made threw the joint into a new riot. The director of the Moscow Art Theatre, the guy who'd almost auditioned me out of town, still had tears in his eyes from laughing when he came back to congratulate me.

(1962: 315)

Harpo was assigned four spots in a kind of revue-show and decided to do a harp solo, his bubbles-coming-out-of-a-clarinet bit, a comedy pantomime, and another harp solo to finish. He had predicted the pantomime sketch would be the easiest part but was proved wrong:

The scene I worked out was the opening of *Cocoanuts,* with a few variations thrown in out of *I'll Say She Is.* I come to check in at a hotel. I tear up the telegrams and the mail. I decide I'm thirsty. I take a swig from the inkwell on the desk. The ink – after I've swallowed it – tastes like poison. I make a Gookie. I need an antidote. I take out a rubber glove, inflate it, and milk it. The milk does the trick. I feel great now. I jump on the straight man's shoulders and throw pens like darts until I hit a plaque on the wall and a bell rings and I win a cigar. Blackout. The second part of the scene was the old knife-dropping routine. For a local-gag finish, I dropped, not a silver coffeepot, but a miniature samovar.

The first time I ran through my bits, at the first rehearsal, the staff applauded the harp solo. They howled and clapped when the bubbles came out of the clarinet. But throughout the comedy scene, which I had worked on all night with my Russian straight man, they sat on their hands. When it was over they smiled politely, nothing more. *Oh, no,* I thought. *Here we go again!*

(1962: 316)

The sticking point is the question of meaning:

The English-speaking writer who looked like Kaufman lumbered onto the stage. 'Your movements are extraordinary,' he said. 'But please forgive us. We don't know the story. If I may say so, the point eludes us.'

'Point?' I said. 'There isn't any point. It's nothing but slapstick. You know – pure hokum.'

'Yes, yes, of course,' he said, like he understood, which he didn't at all. 'But may I ask why you were compelled to destroy the letters? Why did you drink the ink, knowing it was ink? What was your motive for stealing the knives that belonged to the hotel?'

I was flabbergasted. I'd done these pieces of business hundreds of times, and this was the first time anybody had ever asked me *why* I did them. 'All I know,' I said, 'is that if something gets a laugh you do it again. That's all the reason you need. Right?'

Now the Russian was puzzled. He said, 'No.'

I said, 'No?'

He said, 'Forgive me. Perhaps it is different in your American theatre. Here you must tell a story that answers the audience's questions, or your performance will fail.'

(1962: 316–317)

In order to 'correct' this, Harpo agreed to having his bits of business incorporated into a script, which his hosts would write. The end result was a ten-minute play with three extra characters ('a doctor, a dame and the dame's jealous husband'), although Harpo's part was still the original two minutes of comedy. He relied on the director to cue him in each time, not understanding any of the rest of the action in Russian. When he asked what was going on, the answer was 'It is not important to you' (1962: 317).

This unlikely mise-en-scène was a huge success:

I'll be a son of a bitch if it didn't knock them out of their seats.[...] I only had to wiggle an eyebrow to bring the house down, that's how ready they were to laugh. I didn't give a damn what the plot was about. It was a comedian's dream.

(1962: 317–318)

THE MARX BROTHERS: NARRATIVE AND HOKUM

But just how far from a Marx Brothers script in Hollywood was this experience? What is the relationship between the hokum, or lazzi, and the rest of the characters who inhabit a rational narrative? If Harpo could function without even understanding, what does that say about the relationship between the clown and the fiction? Here is the beginning of a scene in *Duck Soup* (released in 1933, the same year as Harpo's trip to the Soviet Union), where Chico (Chicolini) and Harpo (Pinky) arrive at Trentino's office to report on their spying activities:

[*We see Chicolini and Pinky standing in the doorway, both wearing bearded masks and hats. The eyes on Pinky's mask whirl round. Chicolini removes his mask and grins, then spins Pinky round to reveal his face on the other side.*]
Chicolini: We fool you good, heh?
[*Shot of Trentino.*]
Trentino [*genially*]: Gentlemen! [*He starts forward.*]
[...]
[*Trentino advances towards Chicolini and Pinky with open arms, but they suddenly dive past him to the desk as a bell rings. At the desk, Pinky answers first one phone, then the other, but the bell goes on ringing.*]
Trentino: Gentlemen, what is this?
[*A closer shot excludes him as Chicolini replies.*]
Chicolini: Sssh! This is spy stuff!
[*Pinky listens to both phones at once but the bell still goes on ringing. Finally he gives a grin and pulls a large alarm clock out of his pocket. Chicolini laughs.*]
Secretary [*off*]: A telegram for you sir.
[*As she finishes, we see her and Trentino.*]

Trentino: Oh!

[*Chicolini and Pinky rush round beside him. Pinky grabs the telegram, looks at it, then screws it up and throws it on the floor in a rage.*]

Chicolini: He gets mad because he can't read.

[*The Secretary exits and Pinky leers after her.*]

Trentino: Oh, I see. Well, gentlemen, we have serious matters to discuss.

[*Camera pans with them to the desk, then cuts to show them from a high angle.*]

Trentino: So please be seated.

[*Chicolini and Pinky slide under Trentino as he sits down. Pinky whistles while Chicolini sings.*]

Chicolini: Rock-a-bye ...

[*In a medium shot of the group, Pinky continues to whistle and puts his feet up on the desk while the other two get up again.*]

Trentino: Gentlemen! Gentlemen! Now, about that information I asked you to get.

(1933: 113)

Comic business with cigars follows, with Chicolini and Pinky continuing to run rings round Trentino, and Trentino continually trying to get Chicolini and Pinky to concentrate on the matter that concerns him – their spying on Firefly (Groucho Marx): 'Now, let's concentrate. Have you been trailing Firefly?' (Marx Brothers 1933: 115). But each time Trentino thinks they have got back on track and are finally advancing with the plot, Chicolini and Pinky throw in some more business with cigars. Or some other diversion:

Chicolini: Look. We find out all about this Firefly. [*He pulls out a letter.*] Here, look at this.

[*Trentino grabs it and sits down.*]

Trentino: Ah very good, very good. Wait a minute. We must not be disturbed.

[*Close-up of his hand pressing a buzzer on the desk. The trio are seen from the side as the Secretary enters in the background and comes up to the desk.*]

Secretary: Yes, sir?

Trentino: Oh. This is a very important conference, and I do not wish to be interrupted.

[*Shot of Trentino, Pinky and the Secretary.*]

Secretary: Yes sir.

[*She sees Pinky leering at her and backs away nervously. Pinky starts to follow, but Chicolini restrains him.*]

Chicolini [off]: Ah-ah! Ah-ha! [*He snaps his fingers.*]

[*Resume on the three of them beyond the desk. Trentino gets up in exasperation.*]

Trentino: Gentlemen, we are not getting anywhere.

(1933: 114–116)

When finally Chicolini addresses himself to the conversation with Trentino, the outcome is equally useless in terms of the spy plot:

Trentino [wagging a finger]: ...I want a full detailed report of your investigation.

[*Pinky is partly visible to the right.*]

Chicolini: All right, I tell you. Monday we watch Firefly's house. But he no come out. He wasn't home. Tuesday we go to the bail game, but he fool us. He no show up. Wednesday he go to the ball game, and we fool him. We no show up. Thursday was a double header. Nobody show up. Friday it rained all day. There was no ball game so we stayed home and we listened to it over the radio.

Trentino [exasperated]: Then you didn't shadow Firefly?

Chicolini: Oh, sure we shadow Firefly. We shadow him all day.

Trentino: But what day was that?

Chicolini: Shadderday.

  [*Cut to include Pinky. Trentino clutches his head in his hands.*]

Chicolini [laughing]: At'sa some joke, eh, Boss?

  [*Pinky snips at Trentino's hair, which is standing up between his fingers. Resume on Trentino and Chicolini.*]

Trentino: Now, will you tell me what happened on Saturday?

Chicolini: I'm glad you asked me. We follow this man down to a roadhouse and at this roadhouse he meet a married lady.

Trentino: A married lady?

Chicolini: Yeah. I think it was his wife.

Thicolini: Firefly has no wife.

Chicolini: No?

Trentino: No.

Chicolini: Den you know what I think, Boss?

Trentino: What?

Chicolini: I think we follow da wrong man.

  [*We see the three of them again, facing camera. Trentino gets up.*]

Trentino: Oh, gentlemen, I am disappointed.

(1933: 117–118)

The final shot of the scene is Trentino alone with his fingers in a mousetrap, a newspaper stuck to his backside and an agonized expression on his face. As in much of The Marx Brothers' film output, there is an almost total split between plot and gags.

At least in the case of the Marx Brothers we have the films to study (though not the live vaudeville performances), which makes up for the usual frustration of combing through clowns' autobiographies in search of trade secrets. Cinema clowning has always enjoyed a privileged position in this respect. It is far easier to speak of Chaplin, Keaton or Tati than of Grock, Deburau or Grimaldi, for the simple reason that there is so much of the screen stars to look at. This has tended to bias the study of clowning in favour of cinema, as if clowns had found their natural home on the two-dimensional screen.

CLOWN AUTHORSHIP: PHILIPPE GOUDARD AND CIRQUE DU SOLEIL

Several commentators note the reticence of clowns to give away their secrets, whether through fear of plagiarism (Rémy 1962), fear of censorship (Gordon 1983), or simply because 'it never occurred to many [. . .] popular performers to write out and preserve their *lazzi*' (Gordon 1983: 6).

Philippe Goudard is an active campaigner for clowns and circus artists being recognized as authors of their own work. In *Lire et Écrire le cirque*

['Reading and Writing Circus' 2005] he identifies the act of creation with the act of writing. So when circus artists (clowns included) create their own performances they should be considered as authors. As Goudard points out, though, the reality is that most artists have little contract security, the most extreme case being *Cirque du Soleil*:

> He must even, as with the Canadian 'Cirque du Soleil', when signing the contract, cede all rights to the producer, who may then exploit his number without the artist.
> (2005: 84)

This signing over of authorial rights leads to franchising. In Cirque du Soleil's shows it doesn't really matter which performers are doing the acts. They are interchangeable. They are not the only company engaged in this practice. Slava Polunin's *Snowshow* also uses interchangeable performers, as already noted.

It is debatable whether authorship, with its subsequent powers and rights of ownership, can be reduced to creation in general, or to the 'production of meaning', unless there is a physical, sellable product. Traditionally, writing refers to 'the representation of words and of thoughts by means of conventional graphic symbols' (Goudard 2005: 84). Much of what happens in clowning can be written down without difficulty, in the manner of a play-text: direct speech for dialogue, present tense prose for describing physical actions, even if sometimes it takes a whole page of description to cover the simple act of falling through a chair seat and getting out of it again.

And if the physical actions belong to some other genre, one can always have recourse to the surprisingly large number of systems of notation that exist. Goudard refers to a number of these (2005: 90–94). For the art of equestrianism we have 'diagrams and illustrations to indicate the directions and paces of horses and their riders' from early examples of modern dressage, such as riding master Antoine de Pluvinel's *L'instruction du Roy en l'art de monter à cheval* (c.1630), to circus empresario Victor Franconi's *Le cavalier, cour d'équitation pratique* (1855). Juggling has many systems, principally siteswap and its derivatives (Bruce Tiermann, Paul Klimek, Mike Day, Martin Probert, Charlie Dancey and others), which date from the 1980s to 1990s and notate both movement and timing, not only of throws but also of when hands are empty, using one axis (vertical or horizontal) to transcribe time in a fashion parallel to musical notation. The needs of acrobatics are served by illustrated figures in series of positions, modern systems following older ones, such as Mercuriale Girolamo's *Arte Gymnastica* (1569). Finally, all these systems may be combined and used together for a more complex show score, as in *Le chant des balles* by Éric Bellocq and Vincent de Lavenère (2004):

> The scores, reading horizontally and vertically, use several types of notation: musical, juggling, acrobatics and words for stage directions.
> (Goudard 2005: 91)

AUTHORS, CENSORSHIP AND CULTURE: ART AND ACT IN THE SOVIET UNION AND POST-WAR FRANCE

Goudard interestingly draws our attention to the widespread use of notation systems, including for larger-scale circus works, in the Soviet Union, where artists were required,

> before the work entered into production, to submit written projects to the organs of ideological control. Thus there exist in the ex-USSR circus number scores in a whole variety of disciplines; bear-training, trapeze, acrobatics.
>
> (2005: 92)

Contemporary circus in the West might end up with a similar 'library':

> The system of public funding of circus in France for the last 20 years could have the same effect.
>
> (2005: 92)

Pierron pinpoints the precise date of this shift in France, the first western country to subsidise circus:

> *Ministry of Culture* – supervisory body which funds certain circuses under contract.

> Before 1981, circus artists, due to the presence of animals in menageries and shows, were under the responsibility of the Ministry of Agriculture. They were considered to be without fixed abode.
>
> (2003: 398)

Moving from agriculture to culture had a series of related consequences, one of which was the need

> to present a 'project'; a word which is whispered in our era with as much indulgence as there is a feeling of powerlessness in possible success. So much so that energy is displaced from action to paper and computers. The perverse effect is that a well put together project has more chances of being accepted than a superb number which the 'decision-makers' will never see. Creators risk much in wasting their energy on this little game imposed on them by the administrative workers who do not breathe the same air as them.
>
> (Pierron 2003: 227)

The 'promotion' to culture leads to the invention of 'circus arts', similar to that of 'street arts', both of which then slot neatly into 'performing arts' and can now take their place in the academy, alongside theatre, opera, dance, mime, puppetry, music and so on. For Pierron, 'this may help those who teach it, but not the artists'. More than that, it 'takes away artists' creative independence' (Pierron 2003: 58).

Here she is touching on one of her principal themes throughout her *Dictionnaire de la langue du cirque*:

> Rather than an art, [circus] is an act. This is why, moreover, it does not belong to the bourgeoisie: it is aristocratic or popular.
>
> (2003: 58)

In other words, if circus (clown included at this point) must first write (project proposals), before doing (its act), then that creation becomes something imagined, in the mind of its creator, then committed to paper. It is now the fantasy of an artist, something that may, or may not (if you don't get the funding), be realised in action. So, rather than consist of an act (actions performed in front of an audience), it now becomes a piece of writing (a piece of fiction). Act becomes art.

I have lumped circus and clown together here for this discussion as the point of change we are talking about happens at a moment in history when the two are still inextricably, though not exclusively, bound together. Later, clown and circus will follow their own, often separate, roads but the first steps of what will become known as 'New Circus' are still closely related to those of contemporary clowning.

CLOWN DRAMATURGY AND NEW CIRCUS

Pierron analyses a further consequence of this, which is the re-appearance of dramaturgy in circus since the 1980s.

> *dramaturgies* – A word recently appeared in the circus; it dates from the 1980s. It is a word taken from theatre and pasted onto the circus. Whilst the theatre needs a plot, an ensemble vision, the circus is made up of individuals; it is a juxtaposition of heterogeneous numbers each of which is the fruit of a personal universe, of the dreams and the poetry of an artist.
>
> (2003: 229)

The word 'dramaturgy' might be of recent appearance but the concept is not. Despite New Circus's claims to novelty in this respect, dramaturgy in different forms has been part of circus at various times and places. Early circus is marked by Andrew Ducrow's equestrian dramas – *Mazeppa* (1831) and *The Courier of St. Petersburg* (1827) – as well as various retellings of Napoleonic events and other wars. A century later, Vladimir Mass's *Makhno's Men* (1930) revisited the genre but with a Stalinist rather than British Imperialist ethic. Indeed, Soviet circus throughout the 20th century privileged the artistic director, who was responsible for a unified aesthetic experience, though not necessarily a narrative one, distinct from the more individualistic variety format of western circuses at the time.

For Pierron the circus is made up of individuals, since

> A circus artist, unlike an actor, does not play a character. He is himself or, if you wish, the character which is himself.
>
> (2003: 344)

The circus artist just 'is', rather than pretending to be someone else. Consequently, for Pierron, as we saw earlier, the circus performance is 'fact', not 'fiction' (Pierron 2003: 290–291).

This 'fact-ness' of circus poses serious problems for fiction and hence narrative. The circus seeking justification or to increase its cultural value by borrowing concepts from theatre is, in this light, doomed to failure. Dramaturgy does not only 'drown individualism' but 'reduces circus to the stereotypes of a school essay' (2003: 300).

ART-CLOWNS AND BOZOS

What is clearly true for the acrobat can also be applied to the clown, as we will see. The clown makes us laugh, or does not make us laugh. Laughter is the fact that anchors the clown in reality and prevents flights into fiction. The only way to circumvent this would be to deny the necessity of laughter (which, as we saw earlier, Eli Simon's claim that 'It's okay not to be funny' does in his *The Art of Clowning*).

In parallel with the introduction of dramaturgy, narrative and fiction into New Circus, this opens the door not just to clowning which is not defined by an audience's laughter but also to clowning which seeks to express the performer's own fantasy, or fictional creation. Not needing to be funny, clowns can do whatever they want. But this is not the same 'clowns can do anything' we discovered in another context. In the latter case, the freedom is one which causes laughter, since it entails a shocking or surprising break with expectations or normal behaviour. In this new case, however, the freedom, having no root in the reality of laughter, can only be guided by the performer's own fantasies and is thus limited to 'self-expression'. Clowning which is the expression of the performer's own fantasies is very different from clowning which is determined by the duty to 'contradict the context'.

However, for those in favour of removing the obligation to be funny, the result is supposed somehow to be clowns with greater profundity than the 'maniacal clown who freaks out the neighbourhood', given that

> these Bozo-type clowns [. . .] are not the soulful clowns you will likely develop using this book.
>
> (Simon 2009: 4)

Simon's claim that 'you will be deeply connected to truths rather than just gags' (2009: 6) sets high expectations, but the exercises in the book do not go beyond standard impro games of the 'take an object and transform it' type.

Meanwhile, circus has moved on since the 1980s and begun to distance itself from representational and narrative forms that it had once borrowed from theatre. Circus today reaches towards abstraction and 'circus for circus's sake', no longer feeling a need to ape theatre. But along the way, by appropriating for itself the functions of narrative and drama, it ousted clowns, who had until then been those who provided drama in the circus. If acrobats, jugglers and trapeze artists could now act, then what use for clowns? In fact, couldn't the acrobats, jugglers and trapeze artists now do the clowning?

In Reg Bolton's seminal book *New Circus* (1987), a work that influenced a whole generation of performers, clowning is held to be central to the new approach: 'New Circus [...] concentrates on [...] clowning and physical skills' (1987: 6), but actual references to clowning are few and far between, and are almost always in a negative context:

> when I look at the American 'weekend' clown from a European perspective, I shudder.
>
> (1987: 38)

> 'Clowning Around', an activity I normally steer clear of.
>
> (1987: 50)

In a way, this seems to pre-figure Cirque du Soleil's ambivalent relationship with clowns, which I have already explored.

If clowning is act/fact and not art/fiction, and thus cannot be sold to other performers in the commercial market-place of art-products, except under the franchise format, and excepting the requirements of funding or censorship, what is the reason for 'writing clown'?

CLOWN AUTOBIOGRAPHY IN THE CINEMA: LEONID YENGIBAROV AND CHARLIE CHAPLIN

We have seen how clowns can be writers both in the sense of creators of their own work (live performance) and also in reflecting on that work (in written autobiographies). The medium of the cinema makes possible a combination of both these functions, giving us the sub-genre of the 'clown biopic'.

The plots of these films have much in common, despite telling the stories of distinct performers in very different times and places. The basic narrative is often a simple clown-as-hero one: young would-be clown discovers their vocation, tries to realise their dream, is given a chance, fails and is forced to wander in search of their own personal style, finds it and returns triumphant.

The life of Soviet-Armenian clown Leonid Yengibarov follows this route in Путь на арену ('The Path to the Arena'; 1963). His first efforts in the circus are grossly derivative – desperately trying to make the spectators laugh, Yengibarov throws himself around the ring in the hope that his falls will gain approval and save him, but his act is greeted first by silence and then by jeers and whistles. It is the classic failed clown scene. Sacked from the circus, he has a vision where clowns masters, amongst them Marcel Marceau and Charlie Chaplin, spur him to go in search of his own style. Yengibarov wanders the country, turning his hand to manual jobs and finding meanwhile that he can entertain his fellow brick-layers with his comedy mime and acrobatic skills. Then one night, asleep by a canal (is he pondering ending it all in the dark waters?) he has a dream of a new act, a remarkable balancing trick with a broom and his clothes. Awakening, Yengibarov returns to the circus with hope, keen to practice and sure that now he will succeed. And so he does, the film ending with an extended sequence featuring his most famous numbers, appearing in between the best of Soviet circus artists, with those who had doubted him now convinced, those who had always believed now vindicated. The film seems to be telling us: you all know these famous numbers by your favourite clown; well, this is how he got there. And at the same time the message is 'find your own clown'.

Though not a biopic, the 'failing clowns' also crop up in Chaplin's *The Circus* (1928). But here the situation is reversed: our hero is now the only clown in the circus who is funny, all the others being flops. The lesson here is that the clown makes us laugh in spite of himself, whilst those who believe they possess the right to make us laugh are shown up to be frauds. Of course, in reality Charlie Chaplin was anything but 'a clown who makes us laugh in spite of himself', being a highly skilled manipulator of technique.

CINEMATIC CLOWN FICTION AND DOCUMENTARY

Raj Kapoor's *Meera Naam Joker* ('My Name is Joker'; 1970), though its creator is not a clown, does claim to be partly autobiographical. If we re-constructed the storyline chronologically, it would begin with the teenage boy who finds that he has a gift for making others laugh. But having discovered his vocation it is revealed to him that his dead father was a clown who died from a fall in the circus. For his mother, a tragic destiny must await him if he were to follow in father's footsteps. But now it is too late to turn back. The failures of this clown-as-hero will not be aesthetic, however, but amorous. The film actually begins with the hero, Raju, about to give the final performance of his life, with all three of the failed loves of his life present in the audience.

In the number, Raju is to have an operation to have his heart removed by a team of clown doctors, since his heart is too big for this world. Raju protests: 'Then operate on the world' (Kapoor 1970). The anaesthetists, wearing huge boxing gloves, sedate Raju. The surgeon, using a huge pair of pliers, and with the help of his colleagues pulling as if in a tug-of-war contest, wrenches a big red heart from under the sheet covering the patient. The doctors pass it around, examining it as it gets bigger and bigger, warning Raju: 'It's very dangerous to have a large heart. Look after it well. If it continues to grow, it will engulf the world!' (Kapoor 1970)

The message is clear: the world is no fit place for a clown. The story to come will inevitably be tragic. Indeed, *Meera Naam Joker* is threaded through with messages, more or less explicit, about what clowns are. When other circus workers express concern about Raju's health they are scolded by the circus owner, whose belief is that clowns are not like ordinary humans but must continue to bring joy whatever the risks to themselves. Clowns have a greater purpose beyond personal tragedy.

As an adolescent, Raju's trials and tribulations are about the dilemma of being a clown. The way of the clown seems joyous, but the clown must always laugh at himself, according to Raju's teacher, Mary (his first love).

There is a higher purpose, though, which David, Mary's husband, explains to the young man. Ultimately, a clown is happy, no matter what, since all he does is done for others' happiness. His own sorrows are nothing compared with the joy this service brings him. In this he is like God, who does all for others, nothing for himself.

Raju takes up the challenge, and vows to make even Christ laugh, whose sadness and suffering he has seen in crucifixion statues at the school chapel.

Jean-Pierre Melville's short documentary, *24 heures de la vie d'un clown* ('24 Hours in the Life of a Clown'; 1946), which follows a supposed typical day in the life of the clown Beby, creates a different kind of fiction about clown's lives, which is that their qualities as clowns are not limited to their performances but somehow infuse their everyday lives with clown-ness. In *24 heures,* Beby's normal day, the humdrum activities of which resemble those of any non-clown, are just slightly odd enough not to be 'normal': the reading of books about clowns in bed at night, followed by prayers in which Beby's dog also participates before joining the clown under the bedcovers to sleep, even the plate of spaghetti for dinner or having a drink with friends. It says, 'Beby is like us, but different.'

THE CLOWN LECTURE: JACQUES TATI AND THE PERFORMANCE OF CLOWN THEORY

Jacques Tati made a short film in 1967 called *Cours du soir* ('Evening Class'), much maligned by Tati connoisseurs. In a style distinct from his major films, it presents Tati as a live and speaking performer rather than as a part of an integrated cinematic canvas. In the role of a teacher, he attempts to explain to his students the principles of observation which form the foundation of his notion of how comedy works. The unlikely looking students, all dark-suited men who seem to have arrived straight from the office, are indistinguishable apart from one bespectacled and enthusiastic intellectual who is ever ready to give the best answer to the teacher's questions. Tati the teacher's method, though seemingly forming part of this mild parody of education, referring as he does to page so-and-so, paragraph such-and-such in the textbook, actually consists of demonstrations of what he means by observation. These demonstrations are his own mime pieces, of the sort he made his living from before entering cinema: the angler, the smoker, the horse-rider, the tennis-player and so on. In addition, Tati puts the students through their paces in a practical lesson on slapstick, firstly on how to trip up steps, conducted in a formal way which is completely out of place with the foolishness of such simple slapstick techniques. The students' failure to achieve even a simple trip leads the class's star pupil to explain the technique by means of geometry on the blackboard, but this does nothing to improve their performance. Although the students are hopeless and the teacher is frustrated, as is to be expected in a clown classroom, *Cours du soir* successfully explains much of Tati's method and philosophy to a general audience.

MONSIEUR HULOT AND THE VILLAGE IDIOT

David Bellos in his biography of Tati discusses those methods and philosophy at length. The early mime acts and the sporting impressions marked Tati out from his contemporaries: 'it was neither impersonation nor slapstick, neither ballet nor acrobatics' (1999: 63). Tati's claim was that his models were not professional comedians:

> I realise that for sheer comic effect, no clown, no supposedly amusing film, can match the first riding lesson of a squad of raw recruits.
>
> (1999: 22)

As an expert rider, during his time in the army Tati had been given the role of training those hopeless beginners. It was during that time that he found what he was looking for:

> the character that, according to Tati, had the greatest impact on his sense of comedy and of life was a hairdresser named Lalouette. Lalouette was a happy, inoffensive fellow who seemed simply not to notice that the army was different [...] undaunted and as it were blind to the reality of his situation [...] Lalouette wandered through his military service like the 'Ivan Durak' of Russian folklore – stupid and innocent to a degree that made him untouchable, almost a holy fool.
>
> (Bellos 1999: 25)

The non-professional is not only inept but also unaware of the joke:

> Tati explicitly attributed the original inspiration of Hulot to [Lalouette] [...] In Tati's description, Lalouette was never able to see or share the joke that he constituted;

the humour of the situation lay in the exaggerated reactions of the officers, rather than in the inappropriate, but unremarkable and never malicious behaviour of Lalouette. From this Tati extracted the first principle of his own kind of comedy, which he was forever at pains to distinguish from Chaplin's: 'Comedy lies not in the actions of the comedian, but in the comedian's ability to reveal the comic dimension of others.'

(Bellos 1999: 26)

In fact, this leads us not to a new type of clown but to a well-known one:

The character created by Tati for his role in *Jour de Fete* is [...] not far short of being the village idiot [...] [He] has no wife, no family name, and as far as we can tell no home of his own. He is taunted by children.

(Bellos 1999: 138)

The belief in the non-professional would later lead Tati into trouble, when working in 1969 in a doomed partnership with the director, Fred Haanstra, on *Trafic*:

Tati had insisted as usual on using non-professionals for the walk-on roles, and, as always, he had insisted on showing them how to be themselves. His mime acts of how the extras should walk had the entire crew and cast falling about with laughter. Then it was the extras' turn to do it: and nobody laughed at all. Haanstra felt embarrassed on behalf of those people, who were first made ridiculous by Tati's flamboyant exaggeration of their deportment and gestures, and then made doubly foolish by their failure to recreate themselves as comedy acts.

(Bellos 1999: 295)

Although the clown is not called upon to play a character, but instead must simply 'be himself', this playing oneself is not immediately available to most non-professionals when they are placed in front of an audience or a camera. So the 'being oneself' must be trained, in this case by the director. I will look further at the issues around 'being oneself', and whether it can be seen as authentic or trained, when I come to discuss clown training later on.

GAG TYPES AND THEIR AUTHORS: TATI AND CHAPLIN

If the comedian is not really a comedian – in Tati's terms, being unaware of the joke – then the consequences for the structure of the gags are far-reaching. Bellos maps out three types:

Reduced to its simplest structure, *Les Vacances de M. Hulot* consists of a number of gags of the form: X (or somebody) takes Y (or something) for Z (or something else). [...] for the formula to be applied to the raising of a laugh, X's error in taking Y for Z has to be revealed, at some point, to someone, be it X (type A), another represented character (type B), or the spectator alone (type C).

[...]

Most typical of Tati's comedy style are type-C gags, where only the spectator – provided he or she pays attention – is undeceived over the length of the joke.

(1999: 173–174)

As an example of a type-C gag, Bellos gives the instance in *Les Vacances de Monsieur Hulot* (Tati 1953) when Hulot believes a woman's gesture in rubbing her foot up against the calf of her other leg to be a sign of seduction; it is only later on that we, the audience, see her perform the same gesture before entering her villa, where it is revealed to be a simple act of cleaning her feet. The deception is multiple here: Hulot thinks one thing and is never aware of the truth; the woman is unaware of any misunderstanding; and we are at first deceived and then realise the truth later. Type-C gags in Tati's work are often aural, as in when X (the spectator) takes Y (the sound of ping pong balls) to be Z (footsteps).

Type-A gags also occur in Tati's films – for example, when in *Mon Oncle* (1959), nosing around his sister's ultra-modern kitchen filled with gadgets, Tati drops a container, which unexpectedly bounces on the floor and returns to his hands. Exploring further, he deliberately drops a glass, expecting the same result. Unfortunately, the glass breaks, as we would have expected. Here, the hero is both the perpetrator and the victim of the error, and is aware of it.

But type-B gags, according to Bellos, 'are almost entirely absent from Tati's work', whereas 'Laurel and Hardy shorts use almost no other type of gag' (1999: 173).

Type-B gags are where a 'wise guy' understands (and perhaps laughs at or profits from) the mistake made by X about Y' [...] Type-B gags set one character above the other, even if only temporarily [...] they also require, or imply, some kind of interaction between characters. In Tati's world, though, characters do not interact, but pass each other by at a distance.

(1999: 173)

Bellos has uncovered an interesting set of variables with which to analyse comedy, consisting of not only 'who knows what' but also 'when do they know it'. This leads him to compare and contrast comedy with tragedy:

The typical Tati gag thus has the same ironical structure that underlies many more serious forms of theatre. Oedipus takes his father for a stranger, and tragedy ensues [...] Tragedy and comedy both deal in errors of perception and their unveiling, a device known to the Greeks as anagnorisis. But in Tati, [when X takes

Y for Z] nothing happens. There are no neat resolutions [...] no punch-lines, no conclusions. Structurally perfect though they are, Tati's comedy gags do not drive plots or make stories. They just are: quirks of a world that is *just like that*.

(Bellos 1999: 175)

It is a feasible comparison, despite failing to explain why we laugh at Tati and not at Oedipus.

The analysis of gag types also allows us a greater understanding of how and why Tati was often at pains to distance himself from but compare himself with Chaplin.

The gag which Tati used as his regular example of the difference between Chaplin's comedy style and his own is the 'cemetery scene' in *Les Vacances*.

(1999: 177)

In this scene, Hulot and Fred happen to drive into a cemetery during a funeral. Hulot, looking for tools in the boot of the car, tosses an inner-tube to the ground, where wet leaves stick to it. The leaf-covered tube is mistaken for a wreath and Hulot is mistaken for a family member. But the inner-tube, hung on a hook, punctures and deflates embarrassingly.

Tati insisted that had this gag been Chaplin's, then the clever chap would have been responsible for the transformation of a rubber tube into a funeral wreath, and the spectator would have been invited to admire his ingenuity and to laugh with him at the gullibility of the world. Whereas he, Tati, made the comedy emerge not from the comedian, but from the situation; and that, he said, was a much more respectful and realistic understanding of life.

(1999: 178)

ROWAN ATKINSON'S GUIDE TO VISUAL COMEDY

Bellos's biography paints a picture of a Tati keen to present his own comedy as an advance on Chaplin's. Clowns are not usually anxious to explain themselves, despite the existence of a veritable genre of the comedy lecture. These do not usually address an aesthetic or philosophy of comedy in the way that Tati does but instead make a general joke about the absurdity of a lecture about comedy, as with the contrast between Graham Chapman's pompous mock-articulate Oxbridge professor and the demonstration by Palin, Gilliam and Jones of trips and pie-throwing, all done in a dry, mechanical, very unslapstick style, in *Monty Python Live at the Hollywood Bowl* (1982). A different contrast drives Dick van Dyke's attempt to explain to television producers that today's comedians do not rely on pain and cruelty but on sophisticated verbal means to get their laughs, whilst accidently demonstrating a whole series of falls, bumps and general physical mishaps (*The Dick *van Dyke Show*, 1962, Series 1, Episode 30). John Towsen, discussing the form, considers:

> Good as these are, the ultimate to my mind is Bill Irwin's *The Regard of Flight*, which borrows this notion and transforms it into a brilliant 46-minute, post-modern theatre piece. Irwin's efforts to deliver a manifesto on the founding of a 'new theatre' are constantly undermined by a nettlesome critic who forces him to admit to his reliance on the tried and true props of the variety stage.
>
> (2011: post 199)

Towsen's evaluation may be true but the basic gag is still reliant on the idea that talking about low comedy in highbrow language is funny:

> *Critic:* Say, have you any hat tricks?
> *Bill:* Well, this is a contemporary performance piece. It's post-modern. All of the imagery which you are seeing is laid within a formalist construct.
> *Critic:* So, no hat tricks?
> *Bill:* Oh no, I do hat tricks ... or, hat moves.
>
> (2011: post 199)

Rowan Atkinson's *Laughing Matters* (1992), which serves as both analysis and as a series of prescriptions for creating comedy, is thus unlike most comedy lectures. The pretext appears similar to the Monty Python example: posh professor talks highbrow about lowbrow comedy. Except, in fact, Atkinson's language is not highbrow, nor is it comic in itself. The lecture derives its comedy mainly from the role of Kevin, the mime artist (played by Atkinson as well), in demonstrating the principles of comedy. The rest of the comedy is provided by the many excerpts from film and television used to illustrate his points. The advantage of this mixed method is that the specially created sequences by Atkinson counter-balance the fact that the excerpts are necessarily all drawn from film and television, a common failing in television documentaries on comedy in general, which tend to rely exclusively on their own archives and the easily available silent films, thus writing live performance out of the story.

Whilst maintaining a reasonable degree of comedy by means of these devices, Atkinson manages to get through a large amount of serious analysis of what makes comedy work, organised into categories and principles:

> Principle number one: an object can become funny by behaving in an unexpected way. [Shot of a banana wilting]
>
> Principle number two: an object can become funny by being in an unexpected place. [Shot of a banana on Kevin's head]
>
> Principle number three: an object can become funny by being the wrong size. [Shot of a tiny banana on a plate]

What applies to the banana can also apply to Kevin himself. Take principle number one. Kevin is an adult human being, so he can immediately become funny by behaving like something else. Like an object, for instance. [Shot of Kevin standing with a lampshade on his head, switching the light on and off.] Or like an animal. [Shot of Kevin on a lead, barking.] While an animal can become funny by behaving like a human. [Shot of a dog riding past on a bicycle.]

(Atkinson 1992: my transcription from video)

Although the programme contains a lot of these principles and categories, it is in fact relatively easy to simplify them down to some broader ones. Many of Atkinson's principles are founded on one element being in some way wrong, within an otherwise correct and normal context. We have already seen wrong size, wrong place and wrong behaviour. This wrongness can often be expressed as 'too...something'. Other examples from Atkinson include wrong body shape (tall and thin or short and fat); wrong clothes size (too big or too small); too aggressive or too affectionate.

So, you see, the world of visual comedy is one where doves lurk in our underpants. Where cats are fifty feet high and buses can turn somersaults. The jokes depend on sudden shocks and strange transformations that undermine the normal laws of our existence.

(Atkinson 1992)

Bouissac's 'inappropriate' and Atkinson's 'wrong', 'too' or 'unexpected', or other related terms – mistake, error, failure, abnormal, incongruous, contrary or out of place – are talking about the same thing: they refer to things which are 'not right'. With this simple definition of what acts of comedy are, we can then deduce something about the nature of those who perform them (the comedians). Firstly, their behaviour is different from the norm:

The first thing to say here is that the physical comedian is an alien. He comes from the other side of the looking glass. He is like us, but different.

(Atkinson 1992)

In addition, they are rule-breakers:

If we take Kevin into a fashionable restaurant, the one thing he won't do is sit there and behave himself. In order to amuse, he needs to be uncivilised. He either doesn't understand social conventions, or he is incapable of following them.
[...]
If he were to conform to social expectations, he wouldn't be funny anymore. One way or another, the physical comedian has got to be a threat to decent and respectable people.

(Atkinson 1992)

Finally, there are consequences if you commit errors:

In order for funny things to happen, he must constantly make mistakes, and he must constantly be susceptible to accidents.

[…]

The physical comedian is really the ultimate outlaw. As we've seen, he breaks all the rules of decorum and convention. He does all the things we can't, couldn't and shouldn't do in real life. You can't break the rules without getting into trouble and consequently the physical comedian is suffering most of the time. He is an eternal victim, subject to constant hostility from all quarters.

(Atkinson 1992)

A large part of the same material and arguments that Atkinson presents also appears in the introduction to the Spanish translation of Tristan Rémy's *Entrée clownesques*, edited by Edgar Ceballos. Ceballos's book *El Libro de Oro de los Payasos* ('The Golden Book of Clowns'; 1999) doesn't make any reference to Atkinson, even though much of the text of the introduction is virtually identical to his. It may be that there is a common ancestor, not cited in either case. *El Libro de Oro de los Payasos* refers to itself as being 'based on' Rémy's work rather than as a translation of Rémy's transcripts of clown entrées, which it basically is but with some additional contributions. Confusingly, the editor's note states that

we are sure that this book represents the first contribution in theoretical notes on this art, but mainly focuses on dramaturgy, intended for those who are clowns or are aiming to be.

(1999: 8)

It is unclear whether the claim refers to Rémy's book or to its appearance in Spanish for the first time. Conversely, the English translation, *Clown Scenes* by Bernard Sahlins, does present itself as being Rémy's book in English, but only includes 48 of the 60 original entrées and Rémy's original introduction is vastly truncated.

In general, we can see that clowns hold a position in relation to authorship which is precarious or at least ambiguous. We have already seen how Grock's performance is at once his own and pertaining to his predecessors and contemporaries. And in the same way that clowns often exist in part outside the context in which they appear, so their status within a text or performance is by nature disputed. We expect the Marx Brothers, for example, to mess around with what the official screenwriter has composed – it is in the nature of their clowning. We saw earlier how a state of being both outsider and insider might also be observed in the way Will Kemp related to the Shakespearean text. Attempts such as Goudard's might seem counter-intuitive for this reason. On the other hand, such exclusion from ownership as occurs in Cirque du Soleil might also appear to be disturbing the outsider/insider balance of clowns.

Chapter

10 Clown Training

INTRODUCTION

Having touched on how clowns create and reflect upon their creations, I now look at perhaps the dominant manifestation of clown theory, if not of clown practice, over the last half-century: clown training and teaching. I start with the red nose, symbol both of continuity and a break with the past, as the element of pre-1950s clowning chosen by Jacques Lecoq and others to carry forward the revolution in clown training and performance which would be undertaken from the 1960s onwards. I trace a story which starts with Albert Fratellini's popularisation of the oversized nose, via Jacques Copeau's vision of the Fratellini as models for the new actor, on to Lecoq's incorporation of the red nose into his scheme of mask-based actor training. I then look at how his pupil, Philippe Gaulier, developed some of the most influential elements of clown training today, centred on the acceptance of failure and the flop. I also look at failure as a technique and the faking of spontaneity already present in clowns and other comedians. This leads to a further look at laughter as a response to failure, and how this gives it a disruptive power which has at times attained political significance. I then look at the consequences of basing clown presence on failure and pretence, and how this brings Gaulier's teachings into direct confrontation with Stanislavski. Here I look in more detail at how Gaulier's class actually works. In relation to another key concept of Gaulier, his emphasis on pleasure, we see how the concept of play has entered mainstream drama training, and I look at how orthodox training deviates from Gaulier's methods. In doing so, we come across more advanced theories of play, such as Roger Caillois' vertiginous play or James Carse's infinite play. In parallel with play questions, I examine the role of rule-based games in clown and drama training, and refer to those, such as David Mamet, who believe that obedience to rules spells danger for the actor. Here I branch out to consider some other 20th-century actor trainers whose work touches upon clown training, such as Michael Chekhov. I then draw together some of these strands again to see how clowning can suggest a performance mode based on the fake (or the failure of truth) rather than on the true, and how this might offer a solution to Diderot's actor's paradox. I also examine those currents of clown training which, though accepting the centrality of failure in clowning, seek truth through the expression of emotion. The cross-currents between clown and actor training and practice have been strong over the last century, and I turn my attention here to the influence of clowning on Brecht and Beckett, two pillars of 20th-century theatre.

THE RED NOSE AND THE CLOWN-ACTOR: THE FRATELLINI, JACQUES COPEAU AND JACQUES LECOQ

As we have already seen, contemporary clowning over the last 50 years has largely rejected the notion that we can know what clowns do, claiming clown to be above all an authentic, personal and in-the-moment experience. How has this arisen?

Jacques Lecoq, four years after founding his school in 1956, when he introduced clown into the programme of studies, found that it was the most popular area of study with his students, reaching a peak at the end of the decade:

> He ascribes this interest as being deeply rooted in a quest for liberation from the 'social masks' we all wear [...] it has at its heart a subversive and radical dimension which chimed with the spirit of 1968.
>
> (Murray 2003: 79)

According to Murray, for Lecoq, circus clowns were 'limited', stating on Lecoq's behalf: 'the circus clown [...] has little to offer theatre' (2003: 79). Murray doesn't elaborate on what those limitations are supposed to be, allowing him thereby to sweep clown history neatly under the carpet while no one is looking, as in: 'Like the circus clown, the pantomime mime has little to offer theatre' (2003: 70). Despite the huge influence on contemporary clowning which is ascribed to Lecoq, he actually had very little to say on the subject in print. There are more clues in the writings of the precursor of many of Lecoq's ideas and practices, Jacques Copeau, actor trainer and theorist of some decades earlier. He was also interested in clowns, but unlike Lecoq he turned to actual working clowns, the Fratellini, to inspire his students. In Copeau's forward to the Fratellini brothers' autobiography, he wrote:

> What I call your 'purity of style' is that technical perfection and especially the muscular perfection at the service of a spontaneous and sincere feeling. And I call 'kindness' everything that you do with the smile of your true natures.
>
> (Mariel 1923: 19)

Copeau's idealised vision of clowning is still with us today, which is odd given that he was disillusioned when he saw that the Fratellini's rehearsal and performance techniques were not based on some kind of innocent playfulness but in large part on set routines.

He [Copeau] greatly admired their improvisational ability, for instance, but the form of improvisation that his school developed, and that is still used in theater train- ing around the world, serves an entirely different purpose from clowning. Rather than recognizing that clowns like the Fratellini based their improvisation on an understanding of structure and character as well as an acute sensitivity to the audience's perceptions of these aspects, improvisation in theater pedagogy, as developed by Copeau and his disciples, focuses on 'freeing' students from their intellectual selves.

(McManus 2003: 38)

Curiously, despite dismissing working clowns, Lecoq retained the red nose, which has since become a symbol of clown itself, a veritable fetish even. Red noses have a long history, but it was Albert Fratellini in the 1920s who began the vogue for the outlandishly sized prosthetic version that was copied the world over. The irony is that the symbol of the most grotesque of all clowns was to become the symbol of the new, authentic contemporary clown. In addition, by concentrating on the red nose, Lecoq seemed to demon- strate that clown is a kind of mask, thus slotting neatly into his mask-based pedagogy. John Wright describes the red-nose-as-mask:

We see 'Le Flop' in the actor's eyes and the little mask of the nose directs our attention to them. We want to look behind the nose to see who it is that looks so stupid and we find ourselves looking into the actor's eyes. The red nose becomes 'a tiny neutral mask for the clown.'

(2002: 80)

The red nose is thus made to appear responsible for our perception of the performer's flop, leaving aside the fact that one can clown without a red nose.

Indeed, some teachers, such as Moshe Cohen, prefer to steer clear of the red nose:

Some of you who know me are aware that I am not known to put on a clown nose very often, or to encourage their use in the workshop setting, mainly because I am wishing to reach the inner clown, the humor from the deep inside. Too often people tend to hide behind their nose, or lose the inner connection, relying on the nose to do the clowning for them. As I like to say the more you are connected within, the more you connect with the world beyond.

(Cohen 2012)

The assumption that the red nose is necessary to clowning often leads to a further one: that the red nose is also sufficient for clowning to occur. At its worst, this results in actors in red noses who not only fail to be clowns but also fail to be actors, a fact that would be visible to all if they took the nose off. In this case the nose does not reveal the performer's flop in a clown way but instead disguises his or her failure to convince us as an actor. Fooled into believing we are watching a clown, the audience excuses poor acting.

So, what is behind this revolution in clowning which sweeps away its history, bar the appropriation of the red nose? The clue is in those words of Copeau's quoted above: 'a spontaneous and sincere feeling'. This is a search for truth, a truth that is perceived to be absent, both in the actors of Copeau's time, and later in the circus clowns of Lecoq's decade. These same assumptions are still with us today. For example, 'Nose to Nose' advertises clown workshops thus:

> We prioritise authenticity in the learning process above the acquisition of external skills. We believe the expression of this inner authenticity is the ground for learning clowning.
>
> (Nose to Nose 2011)

Louise Peacock states that 'the concept of performing truthfully is common in clowning' (2009: 107), but without telling us why or how. As we saw when discussing Tati's use of untrained actors, just 'being oneself' is problematic and questions to what extent clown presence consists of some kind of attainable authenticity. But aside from whether we can answer that question or not, we can go some way to understanding just why and how this new clown orthodoxy has come about, and ask how much of that clown revolution was a product of its time and place, and how much of it is still of relevance to us today.

PHILIPPE GAULIER: FAILURE AND THE FLOP

The key here to understanding how clowning produces the sensation that we are witnessing something authentic is the dynamic of failure.

A clown enters then performs an action for the audience. There are two possible outcomes: either they laugh or they don't laugh. If they laugh, that is a clown success. As the clown, I can continue with my next action or repeat the first one, depending on what I want to do with my material. If on the other hand they don't laugh, then this is a clown failure. There are two possible responses to a failure. I can either accept it as a failure or not accept it. If I accept it, and the audience sees that I have accepted it, they will most probably laugh. In that case, I am in the same position as if my original action had made them laugh and I can continue or repeat my action in the full knowledge that my audience is with me. In other words, I have converted my failure into a success. However, if I choose not to accept my failure, but instead to soldier on, bravely resisting the stage death that is looming, forging on despite boring my audience to death, then my failure will remain a failure. The dynamic of the accepted failure is what Philippe Gaulier calls the 'flop' and explains why it is the clown's 'friend'.

But there is a contradiction here. This manipulation of failure is a learnable technique, though admittedly a subtle one. However, many students and teachers, and I include myself here, have the feeling that when they work with failure in this way they are coming into contact with something deep and authentic in themselves rather than a mere technique. And they are not the only ones, for audiences often share this perception. Herein lies the origin of contemporary clown's alliance with authenticity and with those practices and ideologies that claim to produce authenticity in performance or behaviour.

So, how does authenticity enter the picture? Trying to succeed, sooner or later we must fail. We can accept this failure in full view of an audience, who will see everything as long as the performer lets them. This creates an effect, for the audience and for the performer, that something that is usually hidden is being revealed. This revelation convinces us that what we are witnessing is in a sense fuller, more authentic or more real than what we normally come across (our 'social masks'). We might call this 'clown presence'. So, when clowning, when we flop, when we fail, is this some kind of revelation of truth, beneath the veneer of our mask of pretence; or is it simply a theatrical truth-effect, just like those we can find in all acting styles, from Melodrama to Naturalism? If we accept that this is a learnable technique, can we then say that there is something in the technique that remains hidden, or unrevealed, from the audience?

FAKE SPONTANEITY: CHARLIE CAIROLI AND STAND-UP COMEDIANS

Audiences will often believe that comedians are improvising, making it up on the spot, when the performer knows all too well that he is manipulating his technique in order to create this 'spontaneity effect'. Often you only need to have seen the act on two different occasions to realise the trick. Let us watch Charlie Cairoli on film at the London Hippodrome in 1966 and then again at the Cirque Bouglione in Paris in 1973, and observe the moment in the *Milk Number* when Charlie has a mouth full of milk. The set-up for the gag is that Charlie has already been the victim three times, receiving a faceful of milk. It is now Charlie's turn to get his own back. Filling his mouth with milk, Charlie prepares to ask Jimmy Buchanan to press his tummy and so receive the milk in his face. But he is so eager to do so that he can't control himself, and getting the giggles he spits the milk uncontrollably from his mouth. Blaming the audience for his laughter, as they are laughing too, Charlie tells them to shut up, provoking more laughter in the spectators and himself. Only after two or three attempts to hold the milk in his mouth does Charlie succeed and manage to play the trick on Jimmy, although the final pay-off is another squirt of milk in Charlie's face when Jimmy also asks to have his tummy pressed, revealing that he had his mouthful of milk prepared all along.

The combination of apparently uncontrollable laughter and the complicity with the audience makes it all seem as if it's happening right now. Both actions – laughing and gagging – are of the kind which are normally assumed to be spontaneous. But it is the same every time – it's in the script. In fact, uncontrollable food in the mouth pops up quite often in clowning. More than one classic number involves eating apples and trying to hide the fact (see, for example, *William Tell* and *The Hidden Apples*, Rémy 1962). The food is real but the effect is a manipulated one.

Oliver Double devotes quite a few pages to analysing stand-up comedians who use what he calls 'fake spontaneity'. He gives the example of Duggie Brown seemingly forgetting the punchline to a joke on the television show *Comedians*:

> It seems like an extraordinary moment. On national TV, a comedian is potentially messing up his big break by forgetting the gag, then winning out over adversity by getting laughs from his mistake. But all is not what it seems. The joke, complete with mistake, is a set piece which is so strong that Brown uses it to conclude his stage act. A book published in 1971 gives an account of the sequence performed at the Batley Variety Club, and it's played out almost word for word as it is on *Comedians*.
>
> (Double 2005: 177–178)

Double's examination of the role of fake spontaneity in comedy reveals it has always been a vital part of what most performers do, giving a variety of examples, dating from the music-hall era to the present day (Gladys Morgan, Tommy Cooper, Ken Goodwin, Billy Connolly, Eddie Murphy, Bill Hicks, Billy Williams and Randolph Sutton), although he reports that

> comedians can feel rather sheepish about the fact that apparently spontaneous material is actually planned. Ellen DeGeneres says that 'the whole secret' of stand-up is that the audience 'really think it's something that is brand new'.
>
> (Double 2005: 179)

On the other hand, there are those who don't hold by it:

> Tony Allen attributes his own inconsistency as a stand-up to the fact that he 'couldn't hack the fundamental deceit' of fake spontaneity.
>
> (Double 2005: 179)

And even some of those famous for it don't hold by it:

> Lenny Bruce, who championed the idea of improvising, once estimated that about eight minutes of his forty-five-minute act would be 'free-form'.
>
> (Double 2005: 179–180)

LAUGHTER TRAINING

A performer's laughter is highly convincing as a sign of authenticity, as noted. It is maybe the most convincing of signs that something has cracked and that we are seeing 'inside', beyond the controlled exterior, and into the 'real' person. Surely we can tell the difference between fake laughter and the real thing?

Some years ago I developed a clown exercise, which I still use today, based on a technique intended for use in laughter therapy. My source was a book called *Lighten Up – Survival Skills for People Under Pressure* (1992) by C W Metcalf and Roma Felible. Their source for the exercise was

> from classes I took in the seventies with one of my Tibetan Buddhist friends, a monk named Thon. Thon told me that if I was ever to understand life, I would have to first discover the 'silliness in seriousness.' Because I took myself more seriously than anything else, I was to start by finding the silliness in me.
>
> (1992: 59–60)

Metcalf describes how you should stand in front of a mirror (it's better if it's full-length and you are naked, but a small mirror and fully clothed works too) and laugh, looking at your reflection. The laughter doesn't have to be real. The exercise is to be repeated first thing every morning until you find yourself 'laughing from the heart'. Metcalf reports that it took him several weeks to reach this point,

> until, one morning – I still don't know why – my reflection in the mirror struck me as genuinely funny. I noticed how sour I looked. My forehead knotted furiously when I laughed my phony laugh. At that moment I looked myself in the eye and *knew* that I was God's punch line. I lost it.
>
> I tried to stop laughing, but could not. My knees buckled and my chest and stomach ached. The more I looked at myself, the harder I laughed. I ended up on the floor, gasping for breath, and abruptly began crying. Sorrow filled my heart as I began to remember many painful incidents in my life. I was crying as hard as I'd been laughing only a few moments before. Then I saw myself in the mirror again, and even my teary, puffy eyes and miserable expression looked silly. I was crying about things that weren't happening any more. And I started to laugh again!
>
> (1992: 60–61)

Lighten Up is, as its subtitle *Survival Skills for People Under Pressure* makes clear, about learning techniques. In the introduction, Metcalf explains that the point of the book

> is that the humor which gives us 'grace under pressure' isn't some cosmic quirk but rather a set of specific, learned skills. And just as in any other discipline, before we experience the benefit, the skills need to be developed.
>
> (1992: 5)

Not only are we dealing with learnable techniques but we are learning them in order to achieve a specific objective:

> Humor can help you thrive in change, remain creative under pressure, work more effectively, play more enthusiastically, and stay healthier in the process.
>
> (1992: 5)

This objective is presented reassuringly as attaining a kind of calm happiness:

> The Third Humor Skill: A disciplined sense of joy in being alive.
>
> (1992: 17)

But it is tinged with the drive for efficiency. The book is a manual for higher productivity in the workplace, despite its attempt to convince us that it stands in opposition to the work ethic:

> I have no argument with hard work, brains, talent, a solid sense of values – even a great education, loads of charm, and fabulous connections. I recommend these goodies to everyone I meet but there's not much I can do to help you get them.
>
> (1992: 5)

This is Metcalf's selling point, and the book is clearly an adjunct to a successful and lucrative career as a business consultant:

> *Lighten Up* is based on the absurdly successful seminars I've been giving to businesses and other groups around the world for the past ten years.
>
> (1992: 5)

So, laughter produces more capitalism.

CLOWN EXERCISES AND ACCEPTING FAILURE

In the mirror exercise, Metcalf's objective is firstly to attain real laughter. But as a clown exercise, this achievement is unnecessary. In clowning, the objective moves further away, away from the effect on the performer themselves and towards making the audience laugh. The consequence of this is that we can discover a more complex relationship between what is fake and what is real. In the clown version of the exercise, the laughter can be fake or real, as in the laughter-therapy version. But the difference is that things can happily stay that way. In the clown exercise you do not need to seek, or even wait for, the real laughter. The only laughter to avoid is one which is fake but is trying to convince us that it is real – a kind of 'actor's laugh', if you like, which we interpret not just as fake but as dishonest. Better to stick to the openly fake and let the real be real. What happens is that the fake laugh, when accepted as fake, provokes our real laughter (that of both the student doing the exercise and those watching), as it is an attempt to be real (to laugh, which is something we believe must be real) which has visibly flopped. As for the real laugh, there are no questions to be asked – it is a convincing 'success'. It is only the fake-disguised-as-real which we reject, as a failure un-admitted. All this is parallel to the failure we discussed earlier. The openly fake laugh corresponds to the failure admitted, the disguised laugh is the unadmitted failure and the real laugh is the success.

The other main difference in this clown version is the presence of the audience. Instead of devoting 100 per cent of your time to looking at your reflection in the mirror, it is shared between the mirror and looking at the audience. This gradually shifts the responsibility from the reflection towards the audience, which is the normal situation for the performing clown. Both the mirror and the audience could, ideally, be seen to perform the same function, which is to reflect back to the laughing person whether their laughter is a flop or not.

The reason this works so well as a clown exercise is the very close correlation between laughter and what we believe to be reality. It is so obvious when the laugh is fake that it easily creates the sensation of having flopped, which then sparks off the real laugh, which is in itself so believable. And it is this failure–success cycle that is at the heart of the dynamics of clowning. This is a different cycle to the laugh–cry cycle that Metcalf's Buddhist friends taught him, although crying can obviously occur when doing the clown version. The link between crying and laughing in clowning is certainly important in that, essentially, it entails laughing at suffering, but it is also the case that any state, emotion, idea or action which we take seriously or with which we closely identify is ripe to be shattered by laughter.

What we also see here is that in clowning we do not need to resolve the fake. The fake and the true play off each other. Or we could say that the fake is resolved into the genuine by admitting its fakeness. This is one of the great feats of clowning and one of the aspects that give it its liberatory feel. We no longer have to try to 'correct' our failures. Instead of being told 'you should improve' or 'you should develop such-and-such an aspect of yourself more', instead of being told to change, in clowning we are told to admit, to accept and to carry on being who we are.

> If the teacher corrects the student, hoping to change the person in his entirety, the teacher is making a big mistake. The teacher corrects the student hoping that, maybe one of these days, the student will have fun with their 'disorders'. The teacher doesn't change anything but rather teaches how to use these things.
>
> (Gaulier 2007a: 183)

Happy with our failures, the pressure to succeed disappears. We are no longer in the business of improving productivity: laughter produces less capitalism.

The laughing exercise can be extended further in clown training. The next stage is to use your own laughter as the motor to drive your action. Now, whenever real laughter occurs, you move, gesture, act – it doesn't matter how. When the laughter is fake you remain still. Actions performed in this way, riding the crest of the wave of laughter, have a very different quality from actions driven by mere willpower. They seem already ridiculous, being laughed at as they even begin. And being ridiculous, they often generate still further laughter, which demands more action, and so on. Variations include eliminating the fake laughter, so we have either real laughter plus action, or silence plus stillness. The exercise can also be done in pairs or with more people. And once the performer has learned to get the same reflective effect from the audience, the mirror can be dispensed with.

We are more used to thinking in clown training that the clown has a relationship with the audience's laughter rather than with their own. Focusing on the performer's response means that the actions are done in a heightened sense of self-ridicule. In any case, laughing at yourself more often than not leads to others laughing too, which is another way of defining what clowning is. Almost all forms of comedy have a relationship with an audience's laughter, but not all of them imply self-ridicule.

On the fake/true issue, there remains the question of whether there is any qualitative difference between the fake and the true. Sociologist Erving Goffman, in *The Presentation of Self in Everyday Life*, explicitly warns against accepting that the behaviour that discredits our social mask (which we could align with the behaviour that appears in clowning, or the failure to convince the audience) can be judged as somehow more authentic than the social mask itself:

> While we could retain the common-sense notion that fostered appearances can be discredited by a discrepant reality, there is often no reason for claiming that the facts discrepant with the fostered impression are any more the real reality than is the fostered reality they embarrass [...] For many sociological issues it may not even necessary to decide which is the more real, the fostered impression or the one the performer attempts to prevent the audience from receiving. The crucial sociological consideration [...] is merely that impressions fostered in everyday performances are subject to disruption. We will want to know what kind of impression of reality can shatter the fostered impression of reality, and what reality really is can be left to other students. We will want to ask, 'What are the ways in which a given impression can be discredited?' and this is not quite the same as asking, 'What are the ways in which the given impression is false?'.
>
> (1990: 72–73)

But our analysis of clown dynamics may resolve even this issue. Instead of the clown being identified with his or her failure, with that (supposedly authentic) part which is revealed to lie beneath the social masks, we could say that the clown resides in the laughter provoked by the play and tension between the desired success and the revealed failure. We thus have a third area, which is neither 'inner life' nor 'outer experience', perhaps akin to Winnicot's

> intermediate state between a baby's inability and his growing ability to recognize and accept reality.
>
> (1971: 3)

BIM AND BOM: LAUGHTER AS (COUNTER-)REVOLUTIONARY

Whether laughter is pro- or anti-capitalism, pro- or anti-work, productive or not, is examined in a related issue (laughter as pro- or counter-revolutionary) by Joel Schechter in *The Congress of Clowns and Other Russian Circus Acts* (1998), in his analysis of *The Laugh*, a number by Russian clowns Bim and Bom:

> The laughter of Bim and Bom almost stopped the Russian Revolution. In Alexander Serafimovich's novel, *The Iron Flood*, Red Army troops on the march find themselves paralyzed with laughter after they hear the two Russian clowns perform an act known as *The Laugh*. The novel is based on oral history: but even if Serafimovich's report of the paralysis is an invention, it portrays the laughter of Bim and Born as a counter-revolutionary act – a comedy which endangers the survival of a revolutionary army. That tribute entitles *The Laugh* to join the satires of Mayakovsky, Bulgakov and Platonov as Russian humor which was condemned in the Twenties for inciting counter-revolutionary laughter.
>
> (Schechter 1998: 33)

It is not just pure laughter, however:

> Several circus historians have discussed *The Laugh* of Bim and Bom previously, but evidently they did not hear the routine before writing about it. Tristan Rémy in *Les Clowns* and John Towsen in *Clowns* seem to have based their description of the act on Serafimovich's inaccurate account. They write that it consists wholly of laughter; in fact it contains verbal dialogue between the two clowns, as well as their laughter.
>
> (1998: 34)

Here is the dialogue:

> *Bom:* Hello, Bim.
> *Bim:* Hello, Bom. What's new?
> *Bom:* No, tell me what's new with you.
> *Bim:* Listen, listen. I go out for a walk in the woods and I see three trees. Then I come out of the woods and I see three trees again.
> *Bom:* And what next?
> *Bim:* And then I see three trees again. And then I go further and meet three trees again. And then as I come out of the woods – three more trees. And then I go

home and, what do you think, in front of the house – three more trees. And then, listen to this, I am on my way to the bazaar and I meet a young lady.
Bom: And what then?
Bim: I get to the bazaar and – the same young lady. I walk [some more] – the same young lady. I walk back again – the same young lady.
And then I come home and again – the same young lady.

(Schechter 1998: 39–40)

Serafimovich does not present the sketch as counter-revolutionary because of its overt political content as it has none. The 'danger' is that the laughter 'goes on for no apparent reason but the clowns' own amusement' (1998: 35). Schechter describes how in Serafimovich's 1924 novel a group of revolutionary soldiers, retreating from the Cossacks and hoping to rejoin the Red Army, starving and exhausted, listen to *The Laugh* on a portable gramophone. 'Their paralysis becomes complete when they hear Bim and Bom's laughter' (1998: 36). Schechter quotes the following passage from the novel:

the gramophone was sending out of its trumpet staggering peals of laughter. Two people [Bim and Bom] were laughing, first one, then the other, then both together.

Laughing in the most extraordinary way, sometimes thinly, like little boys when they are tickled, sometimes in roars so that everything around shook. They laughed choking and one could imagine them waving their arms helplessly; they laughed hysterically, like women in fits of nerves; they split their sides, sounding as if they could never stop.

The dismounted cavalrymen began to smile, glancing at the [gramophone] trumpet which could laugh so madly in all sorts of ways. A ripple of laughter spread in the ranks, people began to join in the merriment of the trumpet, and the laughter grew, swelling, rolling further and further away along the column.

It rolled down to the slowly marching infantry. There, too, the men laughed, ignorant of the cause that had released all this jubilation; they laughed because the laughter all around infected them, and, without check or restraint, the laughter was caught up by those in the rear . . .

When this wave of laughter rolled down to Kozhukh [their commander], his face became the color of tanned leather, then, for the first time in the campaign, white.

(Serafimovich 1935)

Their leader, Kozhukh, saves his men from this paralysis by breaking the record with his whip, and they move on, escaping the Cossacks. The lesson is clear. Laughter removes suffering, and without suffering there can be no action, no revolution and no war. Schechter fantasises about a modern day use for *The Laugh*:

If broadcast in zones of international dispute before hostilities begin, *The Laugh* might leave both sides rolling in their tanks, before the tanks roll. National leaders who offer their country absurd apologies for hunger, poverty or war could be met with *The Laugh* and waves of laughter whenever they speak, until they speak honestly.

(1998: 39)

As Coco says, 'A circus clown in a revolution! There is something comic in the idea' (Poliakoff 1941: 130).

CLOWN AND THE ACTOR'S PARADOX: GAULIER VS. STANISLAVSKI

We have seen how the dynamics of clown failure and success, whether through laughter or otherwise, might resolve the fake-versus-true dilemma. This dilemma is the age-old problem for actors – the famous actor's paradox, in Diderot's words – which concerns how one can be convincing (or 'real' or 'truthful' or 'natural' or 'successful' or whatever term you prefer) by means of theatre, which is 'fake' or 'fictional'. This has vexed and provoked actor training since at least Stanislavski, becoming a key issue in 20th-century training.

The same solution to this that clown dynamics offer is applicable to the more contemporary obsession with 'presence', which is perhaps the same issue. Clown presence depends on failure. It is through the clown's inability to convince us, and his or her admission of that fact, that the spectator is led to 'believe'. The failure to convince, the 'flop', could thus be seen as a kind of absence: the absence of success. Thus we could say that the clown achieves presence (believability) by admitting his or her absence (failure to convince). In other words, in clowning we do not need to fret about the difficulty of being fully present, or the ideological impossibility of fullness. Clowns escape the actor's 'problem' of having to pretend that what they are doing is 'really real'.

A side-effect of the clown solution to the actor's paradox is a lack of interest in the 'content'. As a clown, what is of interest is not what I am doing or trying to communicate, which the 'flop' reveals to be laughable. The question then is: what am I trying to convince the audience of? That it is real? That this is authentic?

Gaulier is untroubled by all this:

Theatre equals the false, lies, fibs, spiel, invention, untruths, mystification, tall stories, deceit, treachery, imposture, simulation, falseness. Consequently, the kingdom of the apocryphal, of the inauthentic, and of the supposed, rejoices. It is the triumph of artifice, subterfuge, adornment, costumes, masks, buskins. This land is more joyful than that of the authentic, the true and the sincere.

(2006: 177)

Gaulier's theatre is thus diametrically opposed to Naturalism and realist theatre, as described here by Shepherd and Womack in their chapter tracing the political and social roots of this late-19th-century shift:

> Victorian middle-class culture included a puritan strain still deeply inimical to the stage, with its artifice, eroticism and gratuitous physical display. The values of nineteenth-century Nonconformity – moral seriousness, self-restraint, sincerity – are a 'uniform integrity of the self' (Auerbach 1990: 4) which is the logical opposite of the theatre's playful shifting of identities. Here, autonomous theatricality is as far as possible suppressed, the theatrical sign is to appear not in its own right, but by virtue of its contribution to the task of imitating life as it really is; the essential attitude of the actor is one of deference to the non-theatrical humanity he seeks to reproduce. In short, realism is the sign that the theatre possesses that vital talisman of cultural validity, seriousness.
>
> (1996: 256)

Gaulier is well known for his diatribes against Stanislavski and the acting styles associated with him, as here in an 'editorial' a few years ago on his school's website:

> I had fun some time ago, in the brochure I sent out about my School, saying bad things about Stanislavsky. I had conscientiously read his two books and at one point I was so completely bored I penned my lines of revenge. Every day since, I have regretted not having been nasty enough, or polemical or venomous enough with this man who seemed to me such a pedant, so pretentious and vulgar. In short, Stanislavsky has never been my cup of tea, as the English put it.
>
> (2007b)

For Gaulier, the idea that an actor should summon up real tears, for example, is an 'abasement':

> The actor cries when it's useful to do so at a particular moment in the story. He cries the better to surprise his public, never going back to his personal sadness but rather turning to the pleasure to tell a story. Can one cry with pleasure? Some sensitive people do it every day.
>
> (2007b)

Otherwise, one must use 'artifice', which is at the root of theatre itself:

> Artifice is the deceitful and artful vehicle that disguises so well the truth that everyone believes. In theatre, artifice is truer than the real.
>
> (2007b)

This game of artifice is pleasurable for actor and audience, unlike 'personal misery', which destroys our pleasure. For Gaulier, those who would have us believe in 'truth' are 'fanatics' and 'morons'. For him it is pleasure which is the basis of an actor's training: 'The pleasure of the game. A child who plays forgets his sadness. Why not an actor?' (2007b).

In recent years, having been relatively ignored by the theatre establishment, there has been an increase in writings and reflections on Gaulier's work, by academics, ex-students and other commentators. Gaulier's pronouncements are habitually blunt, as well as being laced with a playful sense of humour. This combination sometimes leads those for whom his opinions are uncomfortable to say that he is being 'ironic' and 'doesn't really mean it like that'. I myself have been told off for citing Gaulier as 'he didn't really mean what he said'. I will therefore focus on his own words here more than on those of his interpreters.

In place of the imitation of reality – 'A huge error is the confusion between the actor and his character' (2007a: 175) – Gaulier proposes pretence:

> It is better to enjoy pretending, rather than to 'be' water. So many patients are locked up in mental hospitals because they think they are Napoleon.
>
> (2007a: 184)

This pretence is a game, and produces pleasure:

> The game of hide and seek: hiding behind a door, or under a mask or a disguise. Enjoying disappearing. When the joy of the game wavers, the character in the play appears heavy, true, too true to be honest: theatre dies.
>
> (2007a: 193)

So it is not how true to reality the actor is but his or her pleasure which convinces us.

> The Game allows things which are unbelievable and marvellous, not feelings. Enjoy pretending to feel, without feeling. The pleasure of lying will give your lies the appearance of truth. You will be believed. Theatre lives off this 'lying truth'. Why don't you feel anything? To liberate the joy of pretending, so you will not be soiled by truth. People who look for the real truth in the theatre, rather than the not-real truth, are fanatical preachers and true (not pretend) arseholes.
>
> What a shame!
>
> The truth kills the joy of imagining.
>
> (2007a: 196)

For Gaulier, pleasure is what underpins the effectiveness of the performance in all theatrical genres – tragedy, melodrama, buffoon, clown and so on. In clown, where the freedom from having to produce a successful imitation of reality is so evident, the performer's pleasure becomes bound up with the joy of laughing at yourself and how stupid you are. The connection between the performer's self-laughter and the audience's laughter in response is what defines clown: 'A clown who doesn't provoke laughter is a shameful mime'

(Gaulier 2007a: 289). This is the guide for the student of clown, rather than any attempt to imitate what we might imagine clowns to be, which is a dead-end:

> I begin a class on clown. It's not easy. What people imagine about the clown is extremely irritating. They are praised to the skies as being a devilishly poetic little character.
>
> (Gaulier 2007a: 289)

CLOWN TRAINING WITH GAULIER

Gaulier's accounts of moments in class are pretty accurate descriptions of what actually happens and how he relates to students working on an exercise. The focus is on the reality of whether we find it funny or not, thus trying to lead the student to see when it works and when it doesn't. In the following example the student is supposed to be an electrician checking for electrical current (juice):

> Frantz begins. He's big. He's constructed a little cramped character who walks slightly on his heels, fidgets all the time and even shakes a bit. He looks in his pocket for is little piece of wood, but can't find it. Heavy silence from the audience. Annoyed at not hearing any laughter, Frantz yells.
>
> 'There's juice.' No laughter. I stop the improvisation, telling Frantz that he wants to be funny, but he isn't, because the little character he is hiding behind is a mean shit. I ask him to stand in the middle of the space.
>
> 'Frantz, stand up straight. No, Frantz, straight! Now, repeat: 'I'm not funny'.'
>
> 'I'm not funny.'
>
> We howl with laughter.
>
> I tell Frantz that this big idiot who regrets not being funny is his clown. Frantz is not having it. He prefers the other character who is funny in his head but doesn't make anyone laugh.
>
> (2007a: 300–301)

The clown is our failure to be what we think we are, including when we think we are funny. It is always the audience who will tell us if we are funny or not, laughter being a clear and unequivocal signal:

> 'Your name?'
>
> 'Gregor.'
>
> 'Where do you come from?'

'England.'

'Are you ready, Gregor?'

'Yes, sir.'

'I have the feeling you might be too ready, Gregor.' (Gregor doesn't understand. Everyone laughs).

'I'm sorry, sir?'

'I meant, Gregor, that, in your head, you have already done this exercise so well that you will serve it up cold to the audience and meet Monsieur Flop.' (Gregor doesn't understand, everyone laughs).

'Gregor, did you hear people laughing when you don't understand?'

'Sorry, sir?'

'Gregor, why do you think your classmates laugh when you simply don't get it?'

'I don't know, sir.' (Everyone laughs).

'I'm going to tell you why, Gregor. They're laughing because when you don't understand, your face is full of comic foolishness.'

'I don't know, sir.' (Everyone laughs).

Gregor does the exercise. A catastrophe. He gets angry and even more angry. No one likes him. I stop him. I ask the class who liked Gregor. No one answers. I tell Gregor no one liked him. I ask him if he knows why.

'No,' he says. (Everyone laughs).

I ask the class if they like Gregor when he doesn't understand. Everyone says they love him. I tell Gregor that when he doesn't understand, people laugh at his vulnerability and his foolishness and that his clown must be found somewhere around there.

'Ah, good,' says Gregor. (Everyone laughs).

Gregor doesn't understand anything. Will he be able to sell his stupidity?

(2007a: 301–302)

For Gaulier, it is the acceptance of how bad we are which marks clowns out from other forms of comedy:

A question:

'Why do clowns choose bad jokes?'

If the jokes were good, they would be comic actors. They wouldn't meet Monsieur Flop. They wouldn't perform with the feeling of having committed a blunder. They wouldn't have been born by chance, like tarte tatin or even penicillin.

(2007a: 307–308)

PLEASURE, PLAY AND DRAMA TRAINING

If Mark Evans' assessment is anything to go by then clown seems to have been accepted as part of an assorted bag of techniques, inspired by the legacy of Copeau and Lecoq, to be incorporated into the contemporary actor's training:

> Talk to any student actor at an established drama school and they will tell you about the animal studies they have been doing, the neutral mask work which underpins their movement work, the group and ensemble exercises they do, and perhaps the classes they have had on commedia dell'arte or clowning. These exercises are the backbone of contemporary actor training, deeply informing much of the student actor's development, shaping and building their psycho-physical technique [...] Copeau's ideas have become part of the international language of occidental actor training.
>
> (2006: 117)

But can such a radical way of seeing theatre, which is Gaulier's approach to clown, really be so easily appropriated and sit comfortably within this broad syllabus that Evans speaks of? Has clowning joined the establishment? As Lynne Kendrick points out, the absorption of play into drama training has been done without much theoretical under-pinning:

> The practices of play are commonplace in actor training, as the warm-up or the group bonding exercise, play is predominantly used as a precursor to performance. Moreover, theories of play frequently appear in academic analysis of performance, for instance play was expedient in broadening the territories of Performance Studies. However, save Clive Barker's use of games to demonstrate a strategic 'scientific basis' (McCaw 2007, p. 337) for actor training, there is little to no research into how play functions in the training for, and therefore the construction of, an acted performance. Such lack of practical analysis has come to the attention of play theorists; in 2001 Sutton-Smith raised the question 'where is the appropriate ludic *performance theory?*' (Sutton-Smith 2001, p. 192).
>
> (Kendrick 2011: 73)

Kendrick suggests that the way in which play has slipped into actor training is due in part to the perception that it is easy:

> Gaulier's techniques also emerge in UK university drama programmes and have even influenced actor training. This is because his technique appears readily attainable, as it is based entirely on *play.*
>
> Everyone can play. Everyone knows how to play. It is an accessible activity which does not appear to require any specialist skill or acting technique. Play is immediate, its results can be instantaneous and performance can easily be conjured from

the playful engagement in a game in a fraction of the time that more complex actor training techniques demand.

(2011: 73)

But there is no short cut, at least in Gaulier's case, whose 'technique is more complex and confounding than his use of play suggests' (Kendrick 2011: 73). There is a gulf between the presence of play in the syllabus and the lack of understanding of how it works, at least in Gaulier's case:

Despite Gaulier's use of the familiar territory of play – and all its dangerous as well as pleasurable possibilities – there is little understanding of how the ludic functions in Gaulier's training, specifically how his adaptations of play produce his performance aesthetic. This is curious considering how ubiquitous play *is* in the conservatoire and the academy.

(Kendrick 2011: 73)

There is also a gulf between Clive Barker's:

My early use of games work was entirely confined to the practical problems of movement training.

(Barker 1977: 63)

And Gaulier's:

As a child I never liked gymnastics, nor movement, nor teachers of gymnastics, nor those who taught movement.

(Gaulier 2007a: 235)

The 1960s and 1970s saw clown become associated not just with the search for authenticity but with other related concepts. 'Being in the moment', play, and improvisation all became key concerns. Stephen Nachmanovitch in *Free Play: Improvisation in Life and Art* recalls that

Since the 1960s, the psychological issue of being in the moment has become a conscious preoccupation for many people. It came to be seen as one of the keys to self-realization, and variants of it are on the lips of a thousand teachers and gurus.

(1990: 22)

Simon Shepherd and Mick Wallis, in *Drama/Theatre/Performance*, date play from the following decade:

Barker's thoughts on play, by contrast, fit into the (counter-) cultural context of western Europe in the 1970s. So, too Csikszentmihalyi's final chapter (1975), the 'politics of enjoyment', celebrates the value of 'non-instrumental' behaviour for creativity and pleasure. Indeed so much of the work on play seems to date from this decade.

(2004: 126)

And Anthony Frost and Ralph Yarrow in *Improvisation in Drama* assume that it is a self-evident truth, without need for justification, to state that 'Clowning is one of the purest forms of improvisation' (1990: 91).

GAMES, THEATRE AND RULES

Gaulier's emphasis on the pleasure of playing the game seems at face value to place clowning firmly into the 'play' camp. But what kind of play or games are we really talking about here? When I returned to work in Britain a few years ago I was struck by how ensconced the use of theatre games had become in actor training, in contrast to Spain, where I had spent 15 years performing and teaching. In British actor training, games and play have acquired high status. Many proclaim total faith in games as theatre.

> For John [Wright], games are how we make dramatic action real. To discover the play is to discover the games at work in the play, the games that generated the play in the first place.
>
> (Toby Jones' Foreword in Wright 2006: ix)

The identification between games and theatre is already explicit in one of its post-war pioneers, Clive Barker, in *Theatre Games*:

> The elements of play [...] are also the seeds of drama because they are expressive forms of human personal and social behaviour, and because drama is itself a game or a play activity. The use of games is therefore not only a means of technical training and of exploring human behaviour and acting, but a springboard for exploring the nature of drama and theatre.
>
> (1977: 88)

Wright believes that games, or rules even, can do all the work of making theatre:

> Theatre as game and acting as play are the two most radical ideas to hit theatre-making over the last twenty years, and they're still rattling the doors and windows of our most august theatre institutions. Games aren't 'icebreakers' or 'warm-ups' that you abandon when you decide to start work. The games *are* the work, particularly when you're making physical comedy. Games contain all the raw ingredients we need for creating material and evolving comedy of amazing richness and complexity. Games work because they give us restrictions. Rules, if you like. Not rules to live by, just rules to make things happen.
>
> (2006: 80)

And clown and clown teacher Avner Eisenberg states: 'The clown searches to create a game and to define the rules, which then must be obeyed' (Eisenberg 2005).

TYPES OF PLAY: ROGER CAILLOIS AND JAMES CARSE

But what do these rule-bound games, as generally understood in actor training, have to do with clowning's 'pleasure in pretence'? Hasn't there been a slippage here from pleasure, to play, to games, to rules? Indeed, the very use of the word 'play' is notoriously confusing. Roger Caillois in *Man, Play and Games* (originally published in 1958) wondered whether

> The facts studied in the name of play are so heterogeneous that one is led spec-ulate that the word 'play' is perhaps merely a trap, encouraging by its seeming generality tenacious illusions as to the supposed kinship between disparate forms of behavior.
>
> (2001: 162)

Caillois states that those kinds of play that seem most to resemble theatre – 'make-believe' games or 'mimicry'– are actually opposite in nature to rule-based games:

> No fixed or rigid rules exist playing with dolls, for playing soldiers, cops and rob-bers, horses, locomotives, and airplanes – games, in general, which presuppose free improvisation.
>
> (2001: 8)

> games are not ruled and make-believe. Rather, they are ruled *or* make-believe.
>
> (2001: 9)

Theatrical play is even definable by the absence of rules:

> With one exception, *mimicry* exhibits all the characteristics of play [. . .] However, the continuous submission to imperative and precise rules cannot be observed.
>
> (Caillois 2001: 22)

According to Caillois, the driving forces of theatrical play are improvisation, fantasy and inspiration. Rules are required, however, in non-theatrical play, such as competitions or games of chance.

James P Carse in *Finite and Infinite Games* goes a good deal further:

> There are no rules that require us to obey rules. If there were, there would have to be a rule for these rules, and so on.
>
> (1986: 10)

His distinction is not between the rule-bound and the rule-free:

> Finite players play within boundaries; infinite players play with boundaries.
>
> (1986: 12)

Carse sees the playing of what he calls finite games (games bound by rules, space, time and so on) as a mere reinforcing of the controlling mechanisms of society, whilst his concept of infinite play would transcend such subjugation and lead the way to a liberation via a playing with, rather than at, games. Seen through Carse's perspective, rule-based games are allied with the repressing drives of a controlling society, as opposed to the liberating forces connecting to the unconscious that Barker sought. Society requires that we do not depart from the script (or rules):

> Society is a manifestation of power. It is theatrical, having an established script. Deviations from the script are evident at once. Deviation is antisocietal, and therefore forbidden by society under a variety of sanctions. It is easy to see why deviancy is to be resisted.
>
> (Carse 1986: 53)

It is not the existence of rules as such which differentiates finite from infinite play but taking them seriously or not:

> Since finite games can be played within an infinite game, infinite players do not eschew the performed roles of finite play. On the contrary, they enter finite games with all the appropriate energy and self-veiling, but they do so without the seriousness of finite players.
>
> (Carse 1986: 18)

It is not in some abolition of rules altogether, then, that society might be revolutionised:

> What confounds a society is not serious opposition, but the lack of seriousness altogether.
>
> (Carse 1986: 66)

According to Carse, not taking the rules seriously is subtly different from disobeying them or cheating. In competitive sport (a highly serious rule-bound activity), cheating is frowned upon less than not taking the rules seriously. This tells us that non-seriousness is more challenging to the established order than is cheating or breaking the rules. For example, if a 100 metre sprinter takes illegal drugs in order to run faster and win, they may be banned from the sport but their motives are not questioned. After all, they were only trying to win, which is what you are supposed to do. But if the sprinter walks along the track, or runs in the opposite direction, then the very seriousness of the system is ridiculed, which is a far greater sin than cheating.

Deviant behaviour, departing from the script, not taking the rules seriously: not a bad description of clowning.

If rules, or at least obedience to them, are not obligatory in play, then might their establishment in actor training be due to ideological and historical reasons more than because they actually work for us today? Chris Johnston (2006) in *The Improvisation Game* (a survey of the history and state of improvisation today) calls for a balanced historical perspective:

> there is arguably some comfortable leaning on the past. One consequence is a too-easy acceptance of those tenets established early but more recently losing their relevance. The Johnstone/Spolin axis was born from a desire to liberate performers via game disciplines into a spontaneity that was imaginatively liberating. Perhaps now it's time to move to a stage in which those now-liberated imaginations can dream a science that moves beyond game-dependency.
>
> (2006: 269–270)

In other words, what may have been revolutionary and liberating in the late 1950s might not be so in the early 21st century.

BREAKING THE RULES

There are several problems with rule-based games in the context of clowning. One of them is how they can easily attract more and more rules. These rules have nothing to do with how to play the game and much to do with creating a network of social and behavioural obligations between participants – a society, if you like. These are different rules from the ones that define the game. The latter are the basic rules which are needed to generate the particular action that occurs in each game. They are the rules that kids will state first when asked to describe a game, as, for example, with this girl describing how to play the game 'Ball He' in Iona and Peter Opie's major collection *Children's Games in Street and Playground*:

> If she hads a person when she is he the person she hads becomes he.
>
> (1969: 65)

These rules are necessary and sufficient to play the game. But what commonly happens when we play a game is that other rules, unnecessary for its playing, become added. For example, the game of 'Queenie' consists of throwing a ball over your shoulder and then guessing who's caught it. A typical occurrence, at least amongst acting students, is that players will attempt to create a democratic version thus: saying that the thrower has to wait before turning around, in order to give the receivers a chance; or even sometimes the thrower themselves, after having caught someone, says 'oh, sorry, I turned round too quick, I saw you'! If we were to play it like this we might as well pack up and go home because nothing interesting is going to happen. A balanced and safe system like this does not produce interesting theatre, and still less engaging clowning. Conversely, when we play without these safety nets, clowning takes off: there is surprise, unfairness, imbalance, cheating even, all of which inspire clowning.

I recently taught a clown workshop for a large group of undergraduate acting students. After the lunch break I proposed a simple game to start the session. I explained the game in brief and the students' response was: 'Oh no, not that game, we play that every day in class!' I insisted, though, as my intention was merely quickly to get everyone moving again. The game as I described it went as follows. There are the same number of chairs as people. Everyone bar one sits down. The standing person has to sit down on the empty chair but can only walk – no running. The others, who can run, have to stop them sitting down by occupying any chair as it becomes empty. As the students began to play, I became curious: 'What are they doing,' I asked myself. 'This doesn't look like that game.' Stopping them, I asked what they were doing. They explained, for example, that an empty chair must be occupied by the person sitting furthest away from it. Or that you can't sit back down on the chair you've just got up from. In other words, they were following a series of additional rules of behaviour. This was the way they had been taught to play this game. I asked them 'why?' 'Because our teacher told us to.' 'But why do you think your teacher told you to play it like this?' It wasn't easy for them to find an answer to this, but in general it was agreed that the extra rules made the game 'fairer', 'more balanced', 'more equal' and so on. I asked them which way they thought was most fun: my 'free-for-all' or their 'democratic'. The class split more or less down the middle, even after playing both versions. For me, I saw half a class of clowns and half a class of collaborative theatre-makers.

My comment is not wholly flippant. It seems that the dominance of game-playing in British theatre training has produced another confusion, which goes more or less as follows. Game-playing, beyond its use or otherwise in the making of performers and performance, has been seen as aiding in the formation and cohesion of a group. Thus the best way, it is assumed, to build a new company of performers who want to work collaboratively, rather than hierarchically, is to use games. Now it may be true that building cohesive groups who work in mutual respect and equality is aided by recourse to rule-bound games that promote fairness, inclusion and group awareness. That is good for interpersonal relationships in a company. But is it good for onstage dynamics? Isn't the production of fair and equal systems inimical to good theatre, especially good clowning, which thrives on imbalance, unfairness and the failure of relationships?

There is another way to develop games in order to produce more, not less, clowning. In the game of 'Queenie', instead of democratising it, we can expose still further the elements of failure. For example, if we reduce the group who are receiving the ball to two people, we can see better what's going on and their mistakes will be more exposed to the audience's view. We can also demand that the two receivers look at the audience, as well as keeping their eye on the ball, about half the time. Try looking at critical moments, like when the ball is in the air. Whether you catch it or not, share with us your situation. Let us see your desire, thought and emotion. This variation of the game increases the likelihood of failure as there are only two players, so it is easier for the thrower to catch them out. Not only that, but the need to maintain contact with the audience makes it even riskier. But the key here is to learn to play *with* each other (as in any game of this kind) and at the same time *for* us, the audience. This *for us* in reality simply means looking at the audience. In this way we gain access to the thoughts, feelings, intentions and impulses of the clown. It is enough to let us see; there is no need to add anything or to try to communicate anything as it's all out in the open anyway.

The aim of the game boils down to having to fool the thrower. This is always the case: when you don't have the ball, if you fool the thrower into thinking that you do have it, they will guess wrong; and if you do have it, you want to fool the thrower into thinking that you don't have it.

A further level can be attained by reducing the number of receivers to just one person. Absurd? Maybe. Impossible to play? Only if you think that the only point is to convincingly deceive the thrower as to who has the ball. In the one-against-one version, the thrower will always win by these rules, of course. So let's say that the receiver, in the event of the audience laughing (at their attempts to do the impossible and conceal the facts from the thrower), wins the game and stays in their place. In clowning, even when failure is inevitable, success is possible.

We thus have another definition of clown, based not upon game- or play-theory but on clowning's own dynamic. The clown attempts to convince us of something that is patently not true. And the greater the gap, the more ridiculous the attempt is. This definition can encompass a range of 'clown phenomena' in different contexts. It applies not only to the above example of 'visual error' where the clown is saying 'the ball isn't here, it's somewhere else', but also to social failure, as in the case of a high-status figure with pretentions to dignity taking a fall. Clowning is failing to convince the audience that we are who we maintain we are. In Erving Goffman's terms, this failure to keep up appearances means we break ranks from our team. He uses theatre as a metaphor for social behaviour, viewing the latter as a kind of 'performance':

> I would like to add a further general fact about maintaining the line during a performance. When a member of the team makes a mistake in the presence of the audience, the other team-members often must suppress their immediate desire to punish and instruct the offender until, that is, the audience is no longer present. After all, immediate corrective sanctioning would often only disturb the interaction

further and, as previously suggested, make the audience privy to a view that ought to be reserved for team-mates.

(Goffman 1990: 94)

This mechanism of polite behaviour, of 'not doing your dirty washing in public', is exactly what we don't want in clown performance. We want the opposite. Which audience prefers to see 'polite behaviour' rather than 'dirty washing'? Goffman's comments could easily be put to use for clowning by re-writing them in reverse, perhaps something like this:

> When a member of the team makes a mistake in the presence of the audience, the other team-members often must *reveal* (not 'suppress') their immediate desire to punish and instruct the offender *as long as* (not 'until'), that is, the audience *is* (not 'is no longer') present. After all, immediate corrective sanctioning would often only disturb the interaction further and, as previously suggested, make the audience privy to a view that ought *not* to be reserved for team-mates.

What audience would want to watch people not getting caught out? Perhaps here there is a clue that may help us to avoid boring audiences to death. The emergence of game-playing in theatre over recent decades has led us sometimes to consider that what is important is for the performer to be in a state of play, of pleasure as Gaulier has it, in order to create that presence that fascinates an audience. So far, so good. But the trap here is then to assume that if I, as a performer, am having a good time, then it must mean it's because I'm playing, which must mean that the audience will like what I'm doing. However, we must be clear about what we mean by play. There are many ways in which I can sense that I am enjoying myself. It may be that I enjoy myself when there is a complete absence of risk, when I will not be called on to expose anything of value. In this case the audience will certainly be snoring away. The mistake, then, in theatre-training through games can be to focus on the security of the performer at the expense of the enjoyment of the audience.

In clowning, the eradication of the masking of failure is highly dependent on vision. Looking is therefore paramount, and not just at the audience. This might seem a banal thing to say, but one of the common ways of playing, for example, the game of 'Queenie' 'politely' is to give the receivers too much time to hide the ball. That means you will be reduced to telepathically guessing who has it. 'Peripheral vision' is a concept that many theatre practitioners promote. But in clowning we have no problem or shame in looking directly at other performers or the audience, so there is no need for us to pretend that acting techniques also include mind-reading. If you turn too soon, the potential catcher will not take the ball – if they're using their intelligence, that is. You aren't obliged to catch the ball. If you catch it in full view of the catcher looking at you then that's your failure.

CLIVE BARKER AND DAVID MAMET: CONTROL AND LIBERATION

Taking things a step further, David Mamet judges that polite obedience to training in general spells disaster for the actor:

> To serve in the real theatre, one needs to be able to please the audience and the audience only. This has nothing to do with the great chain of being, or the academic model. The opinion of teachers and peers is skewed, and too much time spent earning their good opinion unfits one for a life upon the stage. By the time one is twenty-eight years old and has spent twenty- three of those years in a school of some sort, one is basically unfit to work onstage as an actor. For one has spent most of one's life learning to be obedient and polite.
>
> Let me be impolite: most teachers of acting are frauds, and their schools offer nothing other than the right to consider oneself part of the theatre.
>
> (1998: 42–43)

Strangely enough, what Barker started out believing would be a means to bypass our control mechanisms has returned to haunt us as play has been steadily infiltrated by urges towards risk-free fairness:

> If we accept that the subconscious, back brain body/think processes are automatically self-righting, we are looking for three factors. Firstly, what are the means by which we can by-pass conscious control, to allow these processes to work naturally? Secondly, what inhibits or interferes with those processes acting naturally?
>
> (Barker 1977: 31)

But our urge to control the situation with rules, to control outcomes (our own and others'), remains present, even if we manage to play the game freed from the extra layers of rules. Furthermore, I would even say that it is vital for clowning that it does remain. The gap between what we want others to do ('don't turn round yet!') or what we would like to happen ('I'm going to stand close and catch the ball quicker') and what actually does happen (the thrower turns quickly and the ball hits me in the face as I'm very near) remains in full view. It is my very urge to control which leads me into inevitable failure. And thus the clown appears. Our urges to control ourselves, others and the world are as essential to the production of clowning as are our urges towards freedom. This would all remain nearly invisible were it to be smothered by endless rules of fair engagement. This excessively rule-bound play is a widespread problem in clown training, although it is particularly common in Britain.

Incidentally, *Children's Games in Street and Playground*, being a vast survey of children's games as described by children, without any moralising filter or judgements on the usefulness of games, is therefore more valuable than most books on games as applied to theatre, which often contain additional rules that seem to be there for reasons other than to enable play.

VERTIGINOUS GAMES: PLAY BEYOND RULES

So, can we salvage anything from game-playing? Can we play without rules? Caillois identifies a category of playing which he calls vertiginous games:

> The last kind of game includes those which are based on the pursuit of vertigo and which consist of an attempt to momentarily destroy the stability of perception and inflict a kind of voluptuous panic upon an otherwise lucid mind. In all cases, it is a question of surrendering to a kind of spasm, seizure, or shock which destroys reality with sovereign brusqueness.
> [...]
> Various physical activities also provoke these sensations, such the tightrope, falling or being projected into space, rapid rotation, sliding, speeding, and acceleration of vertilinear movement, separately or in combination with gyrating movement. [...] This vertigo is readily linked to the desire for disorder and destruction, a drive which is normally repressed.
>
> (2001: 23–24)

Caillois's descriptions of vertiginous play, or 'ilinx', combined with mimicry, or theatre, often resemble a kind of possessed clowning:

> The alliance of mimicry and *ilinx* leads to an inexorable, total frenzy which in its most obvious forces appears to be the opposite of play, an indescribable metamorphosis in the conditions of existence. The fit so provoked, being uninhibited, seems to remove the player as far from the authority, values, and influence of the real world, as the real world seems to influence the formal, protected, regulated, and protected activities that characterize the wholly inhibited games subsumed under the rules of *agôn* and *alea*.
>
> (2001: 75–76)

This freedom is opposed to the intellectual qualities of civilised behaviour:

> Vertigo and simulation are in principle and by nature in rebellion against every type of code, rule, and organization. *Alea*, on the contrary, like *agôn* calls for calculation and regulation.
>
> (Caillois 2001: 157)

In Caillois's opinion, it is this association between ruled games and 'civilisation' which accounts for the unruly having been neglected by sociologists, psychologists and other theorists, who have implicitly morally judged its 'unproductive' and 'uneducational' nature. Huizinga, so beloved of modern play-theorists, is singled out as the main culprit:

> Thus, games of vertigo are no better analyzed by psychologists than are games of chance. Huizinga, who studied adult games, pays no attention to them. He no doubt holds them in disdain, because it seems impossible to attribute a cultural

or educational value to games of vertigo. Huizinga derives civilization, to whatever degree necessary, from invention, respect for rules, and fair competition.

(2001: 169)

This is not entirely fair on Huizinga, who does refer to non-ruled play, the problem rather being that he is not as clear in making distinctions between different types of play as Caillois is. Nevertheless, Huizinga does have some relevant things to say about the issue which concerns us here, which is the relationship between clown and ruled games:

When we call a farce or a comedy 'comic', it is not so much on account of the play-acting as such, as on account of the situation or the thoughts expressed. The mimic and laughter-provoking art of the clown is comic as well as ludicrous, but it can scarcely be termed genuine play.

(1970: 6)

And if clowning is not playing then the converse is also true:

The category of the comic is closely connected with folly in the highest and lowest sense of that word. Play, however, is not foolish.

(Huizinga 1970: 6)

Training activities inspired by vertiginous play – dancing, jumping, chasing, laughing – will give us a different approach to the clown-state than will rule-based games.

THE ACTOR AND THE CLOWN: MICHAEL CHEKHOV, LENARD PETIT AND SANFORD MEISNER

Stanislavski might not be Gaulier's 'cup of tea' but there are other actor trainers in the 20th century who would sit more comfortably with contemporary clown training. In the case of Stanislavski's pupil, Michael Chekhov, the link with clowning is explicit. In *To the Actor*, Chekhov points up the freedom from psychology and 'logical emotions' that distinguishes the clown:

Also bear in mind the important difference that exists between a comedian and a clown. While a comedy character always reacts naturally, so to speak, no matter how peculiar the character and the situation might be, he is still afraid of things when they are frightening, indignant when the situation requires such an emotion and always obedient to the motivation. His transitions from one psychological state to the other are always justifiable.

But it is quite different with the psychology of a good clown. His reactions to a surrounding circumstance are completely unjustified, 'unnatural' and unexpected: he might be frightened by things which do not give the slightest cause for fear; he might cry when we would expect him to laugh, or he might utterly disregard a danger that perils him. His transitions from one emotion to the other do not require any psychological justifications. Sorrow and happiness, extreme agitation and complete poise, laughter and tears – all might follow one another spontaneously and change lightening-like without any visible reasons.

(1953: 129)

Many teachers who use the Michael Chekhov technique incorporate clowning. Lenard Petit at the Michael Chekhov Acting Studio in New York teaches clowning not as an 'add-on' skill or as part of a vast mixed bag of techniques as is common in British drama schools, but as a central part of the actor's training and on its own terms, which he believes coincide with the global aims of the Chekhov approach. Petit's 'immersion into stupidity' in the clown work is not an alternative to the Chekhov technique but a way of exploring it still further:

This is an approach to character and comedy utilizing the acting techniques of Michael Chekhov. This workshop is intended to give actors an opportunity to be able to put into form elements of their creative individuality in search of a clown. We will work with the dynamic principles of movement and the psychological gesture, archetype, imagination, imaginary body, imaginary center, atmosphere, and improvisation. A time to explore performance skills, relationship to the audience, and basic stagecraft. This is a course in being and doing, play, simplicity, and truth.

(Petit 2011)

Sanford Meisner's focus in *On Acting* is more on the actual here-and-now impulses and reactions that are happening between performers than on the fictional world of the play. This approach thus emphasises the real riskiness of being an actor on stage. Meisner's only explicit reference to clowning refers to that sense that it could all flop:

My mind goes back to Ed Wynn, who was Keenan Wynn's father and a truly great clown. He had an act which consisted, among other things, of inventions. He was trying to sell the audience a very complicated machine that was designed to let you eat watermelon without getting your ears wet. Now that's ridiculous, right? But the feeling of desperation, the feeling of fear that he wouldn't succeed made it first-class clowning.

(1987: 45)

Meisner elsewhere identifies breaking out of the straitjacket of socially engineered inhibition as a vital aim for the performer:

the tendency nowadays is to follow your instincts only when they are socially acceptable. We fear being branded as uncivilized for liking or disliking something.

(1987: 30)

Although Meisner's focus is on emotion, if we were to substitute 'failure' for it, we would have a statement about clowning:

> There's another thing you have to realize about emotion. You can't hide it. You can mask it but you can't hide it.
>
> (1987: 120)

Other advice needs no such re-writing for it to sound straight out of a clown class:

> Don't make up anything; you're better off saying, 'I'm stuck, let's quit.'
>
> (1987: 31)

CLOWN AND METHOD ACTING

David Mamet runs Gaulier close in the virulence of his attacks on Stanislavski, as here in *True or False*:

> The Stanislavsky 'Method,' and the technique of the schools derived from it, is nonsense. It is not a technique out of the practice of which one develops a skill – it is a cult. The organic demands made on the actor are much more compelling, and the potential accomplishments of the actor much more important – the life and work, if I may say so, much more heroic – than anything prescribed or foreseen by this or any other 'method' of acting.
>
> (1998: 6)

Mamet has no time for what he regards as Stanislavski's 'amateur' approach, preferring the practical philosophy of those who are obliged to make their living by pleasing audiences:

> Stanislavsky was essentially an amateur. He was a member of a very wealthy merchant family, and he came to the theatre as a rich man. I do not mean to denigrate either his fervor or his accomplishments – I merely note his antecedents.
>
> The busker, the gypsy, the mountebank, come to the theatre to support themselves. As their support depends directly upon the favor of the audience, they study to obtain that favor. Those who have, in the perhaps overused phrase, 'come up from the streets,' have little interest in their own performance, save as it relates to their ability to please an audience. This is, I believe, as it should be.
>
> (1998: 8)

As we have already seen, the clown is completely at the mercy of his or her audience, whose permission must be won in order for the clown to continue the performance.

And, like Gaulier, Mamet states that the actor need feel nothing:

The actor does not need to 'become' the character. The phrase, in fact, has no meaning. There *is* no character. There are only lines upon a page. They are lines of dialogue meant to be said by the actor. When he or the she says them simply, in an attempt to achieve an object more or less like that suggested by the author, the audience sees an *illusion* of a character upon the stage.

To create this illusion the actor has to undergo nothing whatever. He or she is as free of the necessity of 'feeling' as the magician is free of the necessity of actually summoning supernormal powers. The magician creates an illusion in the mind of the audience. So does the actor.

(1998: 9)

If clowning can be defined as self-ridicule, then everything I can do, think, feel or be is up for grabs. In clowning, emotions are just as ridiculous as are actions, ideas, thoughts, costumes, bodies or anything else. Emotions in a clown are just as likely to be failures as anything else. This might be in terms of how the emotion is expressed – for example, the case of someone who when they get angry makes us laugh, because the way they show their anger is so unconvincing. Included in this category are emotions which are too big or small – over-statement and under-statement – or which break normal boundaries, as in excesses of affection or aggression. Or it may be that the chosen emotion is erroneous somehow – for example, if I get happy when I hear the news that I have lost all my money. Clown training works simultaneously on two levels, therefore. On the one hand, we need to be uninhibited, unafraid of feeling and showing emotion. On the other hand, we need distance from our emotions so that we can be aware of how foolish they are and so be able to play with them rather than identify with them and be ruled by them.

Hence, Mamet's view

that nothing in the world is less interesting than an actor on the stage involved in his or her own emotions

(1998: 10–11)

will serve us nicely.

In place of a theatre which indulges in emotion, Mamet sees engaging theatre happening in moments of risk on stage. The performing act itself is all that is necessary for the performer to 'reveal' something. Like the clown doomed to fail but who must save the show and dredge success from flop, the actor must not seek to maintain control and balance:

If the actor had simply opened his mouth on cue and spoken *even though* he felt uncertain, the audience would have been treated to the truth of the moment, to a lovely, unexpected, unforeseen beautiful exchange between the two people onstage. They would in effect have witnessed the true lost art of the actor.

(1998: 21)

Clowning as we have discussed so far may have the potential to avoid the pitfalls of emotion that Gaulier and Mamet warn against:

Any method of acting – any interchange in life, for that matter – which is based upon the presence or absence of emotion sooner or later goes bad.

(Mamet 1998: 116)

CLOWN TRAINING AND EMOTION

It is also the case that a certain confusion on the matter of emotion has encroached on parts of the world of clown training. Some clown practitioners and teachers have sought to place emotion – rather than 'pleasure', the 'flop' or self-ridicule – at the centre of the clown performer's art.

In a way that parallels how New Circus felt the need to borrow concepts from theatre (plot and character) in order to qualify as 'art', some contemporary clowning has shown a similar urge to escape a perceived superficiality, or lack of refinement, and attain emotional depth via an appropriation of what is perceived to be the actor's art par excellence: the play of emotion.

The French clown organization Bataclown has been instrumental in developing contemporary clowning since 1980. Bertil Sylvander, one of its founders, in an article entitled 'Looking For Your Clown ... And Finding Yourself' (first published in 1984 in *Art et Therapie* and reproduced in translation online by the British group Nose to Nose), begins by stating that

The clown is essentially an emotional being.

Clowns feel and express powerful and intense emotions. They respond to events which often seem to us, normal people, trivial. If all of a sudden a beam of sunlight crosses the room, one clown may become happy as if this was the greatest and most wonderful thing that had ever happened in his or her life, another however might become completely and inexplicably depressed.

(Sylvander 1984)

We are far from Gaulier's 'Enjoy pretending to feel, without feeling' (2007a: 196). For Sylvander, the proof that the clown is 'in the moment' is that they are 'in their feelings':

The clown lives 'the now' of every second.

The intensity which clowns experience is due to the fact that they live the present moment of each second. Feelings and emotions in the present are the most important things in the world for them, and they are not preoccupied by what the next second will bring.

(Sylvander 1984)

This leads to an emotional relationship with the rest of the world:

> For a clown, the emotional state generated by an event is perceived as an over-whelming experience; it is this obsessive and frantic perception of feelings which forces the clown to identify with the world around: the clown is in empathy with the world. The clown is a professional empathiser.
>
> (Sylvander 1984)

This kind of clown, rather than being liberated, seems to be weighed down:

> If someone's crying, the clown might be overcome with sadness and not know why, simply through empathy and mimicry.
>
> (Sylvander 1984)

Though liberation through laughter finally comes:

> It is important to realise that when feelings and emotions in clowning become too strong, clowns have the freedom to play with them. It is this 'breaking free' which releases relief and laughter from the audience, because it de dramatises a tense situation, it exorcises tragedy.
>
> (Sylvander 1984)

But despite this relief, Sylvander's clown is still primarily driven by emotion rather than by self-ridicule. The consequence of this is that clowning is not so much put to the service of 'contradicting the context', in McManus's words, as to a personal agenda:

> Seeking one's clown is primarily working towards self-expression.
>
> (Sylvander 1984)

The idea that the clown is a tool for self-expression and the elaboration of personal fantasy is a very different conclusion to arrive at compared with the clown as 'this big idiot who regrets not being funny' (Gaulier 2007a: 301).

In clown as self-ridicule, clowning based on failure, as we have seen, the audience experiences the effect of witnessing something convincing, something present, something they might even interpret as 'authentic'. This appearance of the clown we can call any number of things: pleasure in one's own stupidity; the revelation of one's vulnerability through failure and its acceptance; clown presence; even the truth of the moment, or an illusion of truth; and so on. In any case, the audience has a response to this moment, to this 'seeing the clown'. In effect, they are getting what they came for, experiencing that 'something' for which they go to see performance and for which it is worth paying. The point of reference, ultimately, is the audience, who come to be pleased:

> The audience, on the other hand, can be pleased. They come to the show to be pleased, and they will be pleased by the honest, the straightforward, the unusual,

the intuitive – all those things, in short, which dismay both the teacher and the casting agent.

(Mamet 1998: 50)

This audience-centredness demands that the performer is not self-centred:

I assume that practitioners of these crafts put their attention on the legitimate demands of their profession and of their clients; and I, as a client, patient, audience member, do not expect these professionals to burden me with their life story.

(Mamet 1998: 8–9)

But the slippage occurs if we view this audience pleasure, and indeed the performer's own pleasure in playing, as being just emotions like the other ones we experience as 'personal' and in need of 'self-expression', albeit perhaps more 'special' than our everyday ones. So, if the 'moment of truth' – when 'clown appears' to the audience (and performer), when the clown in the flop reveals his or her stupidity and we are 'liberated' from our stupid attachment to what we believed to be true, real or necessary – if what we experience in this moment is now to be returned to being a mere part of the personal emotional world of the clown (and audience), then have we not simply tricked ourselves back into believing that 'emotions are true'? Or (in a shorter sentence than the last one), how can we be liberated from emotions if that liberation is deemed to be an emotion itself?

Attachment to emotions is addictive, and in clown training the work of detachment without becoming disconnected and fearful of them is a tricky balance to attain. It is far easier to indulge. Jesús Jara's *El Clown, un navegante de las* emociones ('The Clown, a Navigator of the Emotions'; 2004) has achieved extensive popularity and influence in the Spanish-speaking world. This is partly due to its being virtually the only recent work in that language to reflect on clowning, and to offer guidance and exercises for those who are studying it.

Jara's words on emotions echo those of Sylvander:

The emotions of the clown are his springboard for action, that is to say, behind every action there is an emotion which motivates it.

(2004: 73)

However, not all feelings are equal:

Whichever emotion the clown feels, it is essential that they always transmit tenderness.

(2004: 73)

This close identification of clown and emotion seems to be a relatively new phenomenon. In older works on the subject, one is more likely to find views such as Disher's, in his 'Forward on Laughter and Emotion', who sees the two as alternating desires of the audience:

> The merrier they are the more they want to be thrilled. The more they are thrilled the more they want to be merry. How he can alternate the sublime and the ridiculous is the test of the showman.
>
> (1925: xiii)

Laughter happens just when emotion has subsided:

> A baby startled by the bobbing-up of a head behind a chair will catch its breath in fright before realising joyfully whose the face is. The child, a little older, slithering plates off the ledge of its high-chair, will wait a second in apprehension before chuckling with delight; or, watching an uncle who growls and walks on all fours, will spend some seconds in open-mouthed wonder before deciding that human quadrupeds are a joke. That momentary spasm of emotion is to be noted in adults as well.
>
> (1925: xiv)

The two are opposites, although linked:

> Consequently, out of the depth of his knowledge of humanity gained in barn or tent, the showman believes that laughter is directly related to emotion. All opinions agree that it tends to take away fear and anger, tenderness and wonder and so forth. That is obvious to the showman.
>
> (1925: xiv)

CLOWNING AND THE FOUNDATIONS OF 20TH-CENTURY THEATRE: BERTOLT BRECHT AND KARL VALENTIN

It is one thing to find parallels, influences and disputes across the fields of clown and actor training. Quite another thing is Donald McManus's tracing of the influence of clown techniques on the whole of 20th-century theatre, via their presence in the work of two major figures, Bertolt Brecht and Samuel Beckett.

McManus holds that Brecht's main theoretical foundations – epic theatre and the *verfremdungseffekt* (alienation effect) – pretty much owe their foundation to clowns:

> This new poetics, broadly known as 'Epic Theater' [...] grew out of an interest in, and experiments with, clown and popular theater.
>
> (2003: 53)

> Brecht's theoretical concepts stem from his notion of *vertrackte Dialektik* [perverse logic] which is at heart a related idea to 'clown logic.' (2003: 54)
>
> (2003: 54)

Verfremdungseffekt [...] is easily understood when considered as part of clown technique. The clown continually breaks with mimetic conventions, thereby disturbing the effect of illusion [...] Brecht simply adapted clown technique [...] shifting its use away from the comic mode and toward serious debate.

(2003: 54)

According to McManus, this role of clown in Brecht's theories is somewhat masked by terminology, as Brecht does not use the term 'clown' due to its close association with the purely comic:

As a result, be referred to 'the actor Chaplin' as the model epic performer.

(2003: 55)

It wasn't just for matters of theory and acting technique that Brecht borrowed from clowns. McManus cites various examples of content borrowed from them. In *Mann ist Mann*, the English soldiers, having got Galy Gay to buy an elephant, convince him that it belongs to the army and that he should be shot as punishment. McManus recalls the Fratellini's elephant routine where the front and back halves of the animal are in conflict with each other, citing from Pierre Mariel's biography of the Fratellini. The story goes that the Fratellini heard about an elephant act that went wrong and turned it into a successful number:

One day, the two pairs of legs got into an argument during the show and engaged in a monumental exchange of blows. The comic effect was incalculable, but the clown to whom this mishap happened was unable to take advantage and sacked the two wearers of the elephant costume.

The Fratellini got wind of this, and made the argument the main attraction of their entrée.

(Mariel 1923: 183)

In Brecht's scene the elephant players also quarrel:

[*Polly inside Billy Humph, laughs loudly. Uriah hits him.*]
Uriah: Shut up, Polly!
(*The front of the canvas slips, leaving Polly visible.*]
Polly: Damnation!

(Brecht 1994: 46)

To back up his contention that this is a steal from the Fratellini, McManus notes that Brecht was completing the play in the same year Mariel's biography appeared. The evidence might only be circumstantial but the clowning is clear. McManus is on surer ground in noting the influence of Karl Valentin, however, whose relationship to Brecht is well documented. Following Joel Schechter (*Durov's Pig* 1985), McManus cites Valentin and Liesl Karlstadt's

The Bird Seller (1916–1924) as the source of Brecht's dialogue for the exchange of money for the elephant:

> *Valentin:* Here is the canary with the cage, and here is the bill.
> *Karlstadt:* That is all correct, but wait, where is the little darling? The cage is empty. Where is the bird?
> *Valentin:* It must be in there.
> *Karlstadt:* What do you mean 'must be in there?' It is not in there.
> *Valentin:* That Is impossible Why would I bring an empty bird-cage? . . . Here is the bill. I want thirteen marks to pay for everything.
> *Karlstadt:* What do you mean, everything?
> *Valentin:* The cage and the bird.
> *Karlstadt:* The bird is not in there. I can't pay for something not received.
> *Valentin:* Then I'll take the whole thing back with me
> *Karlstadt:* 'Whole thing' is good. You can only take the cage, though. The bird is not inside.
> *Valentin:* Madame, the bird must be inside. The bill says 'Cage with bird.' 'Cage with bird,' if you please. Therefore the cage must be with bird.
> *Karlstadt:* I've never heard of anything so stupid . . .
>
> (Valentin 1976: 128–129) (translated by Schechter 1985: 29)

SAMUEL BECKETT, BUSTER KEATON AND ROBIN WILLIAMS

Turning to Beckett, McManus notes, as have many commentators, the clown origins of many of his characters:

> Jean Anouilh [. . .] described *En attendant Godot* as 'Pascal's *Pensées* as played by the Fratellini clowns.'
>
> (2003: 74)

A discussion of Buster Keaton's involvement in Beckett's *Film* (1964) illustrates the formula: Beckett equals clowns minus the gags. McManus maintains that despite, or even because of, Keaton's admission that he never really understood what *Film* was about,

> He looks more alive because of the very pointlessness of his action. Beckett understood this aspect of clown and simply utilized Keaton's ability without the gags [. . .] The core of this clown-man ('O'), according to Beckett's notes, is his awareness of self despite lack of awareness of anything else.
>
> (McManus 2003: 88)

In the end, this is simply a formal trick which Beckett performs, converting a clown with gags and a context into something 'more':

> Clown *sans gags*, or social context, looks profound simply because we instill the characters with our own sense of the profound.
>
> (McManus 2003: 88)

But although 20th-century theatre was more than happy to beg, borrow and steal from clowning, the transaction rarely went the other way. Most critics couldn't cope with the 1988 New York production of *Waiting for Godot*, with a cast of clowns and comedians, including Steve Martin as Vladimir, Robin Williams as Estragon and Bill Irwin as Lucky. For although, as McManus claims, there is a good case to consider Williams as 'the contemporary American Auguste' with Martin as the whiteface clown (2003: 139), the critics seemed incapable of understanding the clown logic at the heart of Beckett's work. But it also surely has to do with the re-introduction of what we saw removed in the case of *Film* – the gags. The production was criticised for being 'overly comic'. Mimi Kramer in *The New Yorker* was scathing:

> What can have been the point of casting two such idiosyncratic performers in roles created to embody universality and anonymity? Robin Williams is the guy who makes us laugh by assuming an oddness of manner – by talking too fast or in a funny voice. His signature role is that of an alien – the Russian émigré or the non-conformist d.j. so zany he appears to be from outer space. Martin, meanwhile, has made a career of sending up universality. What the outward elements of his style – the aura of colossal oafishness and ineptitude, the nasal monotone, the squint, the seemingly unmanageable frame – add up to is a portrait of the average American male as a grotesque.
>
> (Kramer 1988: 135)

As McManus notes, Kramer's angry criticism is also actually a very good analysis of the auguste and whiteface clown relationship in a contemporary context, and he claims that this suggests that the performers were in a way perfect for their roles. The lesson remains, though: in the 20th century you can intellectualise a clown but you cannot clown an intellectual.

Chapter

11 Clown Politics

INTRODUCTION

Although politics has been continually present in one sense or another in many of the chapters of this book so far, here I focus on some more explicit examples of how clowns have been allied with or appropriated to political ends, stated or otherwise. I start with the 1959 Clown Congress in the Soviet Union and how political changes of the post-Stalin era had important bearings on the development of the 'realist' clown, as epitomised by Oleg Popov (born 1930). Popov's own writings contribute to an understanding of the development of Soviet clowning, and I uncover the changing representation of clowns that paralleled the political developments from revolution to Stalinism, as illustrated by the career of Vitaly Lazarenko (1890–1939). The role of clowns and representations of patriotic military display has an earlier history, too, which I explore in the story of the Ducrow family, near the beginnings of the modern circus in the early 19th century. Having sketched out this ancestry, I return to the Soviet Union to look at how clowns took forward the new realism in the Khrushchev era, and how this has surprising parallels with the move towards the 'theatre clowning' of Lecoq in the West. I then leave the Soviet Union to consider the role of clowns as social critics among the indigenous peoples of Vancouver Island, whose clowning tradition was once strong. Further south on the same continent we see how the Koshari clowns of the Pueblo people of New Mexico act as figures of both political and religious power, and at once function as rebels and social police. Finally, we see how the recent phenomenon of the Clandestine Insurgent Rebel Clown Army attempted to unite the theory and practice of clowning with that of political activism and direct action.

REALISM VS. THE GROTESQUE: THE SOVIET CLOWN CONGRESS AND OLEG POPOV

Curiously, at the same time as Lecoq in Paris was setting off on a search for a new clown which would reject clowning's grotesque history, Russian clown Oleg Popov was becoming the spokesman for a different, yet parallel, search for a new, realist clown that might better serve the new, socialist society. Popov, like Lecoq, saw no use for the old-school circus clowns, as here in the chapter 'What is a clown?' of his autobiography entitled *Russian Clown*:

> Let us move on to the Fratellini. Wonderful artistes, they perform in the age-old manner of buffoons, a thick layer of make-up on their faces. They are perfect connoisseurs of human nature, sharp and intelligent. But they do not try to reflect anything in their performance except such faults as stupidity, clumsiness, absent-mindedness. As a result it is hardly surprising if the most common outcome of their conflicts is a slap in the face. And the spectator hears a positive deluge of slaps. Certainly I understand that the Fratellini are the guardians of an old circus tradition, a tradition respected down the centuries. But the times demand that this tradition should be broken and it is this that accounts for the appearance of the realistic clown.
>
> (Popov 1970: 93)

For Popov, the old grotesque clown is dead:

> The ancient art of clowning, with its methods and its rules for constructing the entrée and with the working method of the red-haired comic, is dead, above all because the spectator wants to see a real, natural man. The appearance in the ring of degenerates, paralytics, rheumatics, idiots, madmen and maniacs (and it is precisely this which is the basis of the burlesque red-haired comic) does not rouse the interest of spectators.
>
> (1970: 91)

And the new 'real, natural man' has finally taken his place. This new Soviet clown

> looked for new, less extravagant means of expression.... The spirit of clownery joined more and more harmoniously with that of the other acts which were trying to create a realistic appearance.
>
> (Popov 1970: 81)

This is a remarkably blunt statement of the realist aesthetic. In their discussion of the late 19th-century shift towards realism in the legitimate theatre, Shepherd and Womack use Pinero's 1898 comedy *Trelawny of the 'Wells'* to analyse what this shift represents. The play stages the move of Rose Trelawny from the status of actress – characterised as 'emotionally uninhibited, playful, changeable, diffusely expressive' – to that of a lady, which is marked by 'restraint, gravity, stillness, concentrated self-assertion'. The actress thus represents the values of the old theatricality, whereas the lady stands for the new realist mode (Shepherd and Womack 1996: 252).

This new mode is essentially a blueprint not only for the new, bourgeois-dominated theatre but also for new bourgeois-dominated ethics of behaviour:

Here 'ladylike' is the bridge by which Rose makes the tricky crossing from 'actress' to 'human being'. Her acting feels real because it is not 'actressy' – that is, it is quiet, simple, reserved, devoid of willed or unnatural emphasis. In other words, it is informed by exactly the code of physical and emotional restraint which governs behaviour in good society. Refinement –freedom from gestic and linguistic excess – has been adopted as the hallmark of the human.

(Shepherd and Womack 1996: 252)

Popov describes the 'realistic clown' in similarly 'neutral' terms as 'human':

At first sight the buffooneries of the clown do not seem to contribute anything at all to the presentation of human qualities, qualities which, if anything, they are more inclined to mock.

(Popov 1970: 81)

It is not entirely clear whether Popov's words are descriptive of the actual situation and that audiences really had lost interest in the old style, or whether they are prescriptive, and he is advocating a new aesthetic, for the good of the audience, even if they don't realise it yet. The thing is that Popov was not alone in his crusade. This was official Communist Party policy. Joel Schechter in *The Congress of Clowns and Other Russian Circus Acts* tells how in 1959 the First National Conference on Clown Craft, known popularly as the Congress of Clowns, was held:

That year an assembly of circus clowns, critics and government officials had been convened by Soviet Premier Nikita Khrushchev, after he found the circus lacking in satire.

(1998: 5)

At the congress, circus historian Yuri Dimitriev accused contemporary clowns such as Yuri Nikulin of comparing poorly to earlier clowns such as Durov:

'what you do now,' Dimitriev told Nikulin and company, 'is trivial by comparison.'

Nikulin asked: 'Why do you offer us the example of Durov? We cannot perform now as was done in Czarist times.'

The speaker asked him why not, and Nikulin replied: 'Who will be the subject of our parody? The government is marvellous.'

(Schechter 1998: 15–16)

The result of the congress, coming only three years after the revelation of Stalin's crimes by Khrushchev, would be that

clowns mocked low-level bureaucracy, as well as idlers and incompetent doctors, with state approval.

(1998: 20)

In other words, although clowns were given back some of their historical rights to parody, their targets were strictly limited by the party. The choice of content fits neatly alongside Popov's stylistic overthrowing of the grotesque.

What Shepherd and Womack have to say about that earlier aesthetic revolution might, with only minor alterations, be applied to this one:

> the emergence of the new drama is not primarily an artistic development but a sociological event: that the occasion of English naturalism is the theatre's breaking with its old plebeian and popular associations and forming a new alliance with the ruling class.
>
> (1996: 251)

In the Soviet Union of the 1960s, clowning was finally brought into line and converted into an art:

> it must be said that in those days comedy in the circus was not an art as we understand that word today.
>
> (Popov 1970: 81)

Popov maintains that this evolution towards the new clown was constant since the revolution:

> In 1945 Vyatkin went back to work in the circus. But he was no longer the traditional red-haired zany. We saw a man without a wig, wearing a green hat and a quite ordinary suit.
>
> (1970: 83)

> [on the clown Shliskevich] The spectator does not laugh, he smiles warmly, the smile of one acquiring an insight into someone.
>
> (1970: 89)

> When Sereda appears in the ring, the children generally ask: 'But where is the clown?' They can't believe that this artiste, dressed without make-up, dressed in an ordinary suit, is actually the clown who is trying to make the public laugh [...] They are, of course, not seeing a conventional clown, but a man like other men.
>
> (1970: 91)

ANARCHY AND THE STATE: VITALY LAZARENKO AND JOSEPH STALIN

Popov's rewriting of Soviet clown history in order to prove the inevitability of victory for socialist clown realism is not altogether convincing. For whilst it is true that Stalin in the 1930s had already hijacked the circus to the socialist realism cause, the clowns, such as Lazarenko, generally portrayed the baddies, as in *Makhno's Men*, a 1929 circus pantomime vilifying the Ukrainian anarchists of the Russian Civil War. Joel Schechter analyses thus:

The fact that Lazarenko ceased to leap over three elephants, and began to leap over three automobiles placed side by side [...] suggests he was quite capable of acknowledging Soviet industry and its infatuation with machines after the revolution. But his leaps over automobiles hardly embodied the brawny, Stakhanite ideal; that would have required construction of cars at record speed, not a jump over them. In any case, he was hired to portray a villain in *Makhno's Men*, not a pleasing or socially productive character.

(1998: 48)

Makhno's Men, written by Vladimir Mass and subtitled *An Aquatic Pantomime in Three Scenes with a Prologue and Apotheosis*, was a production on a grand scale. James von Geldern and Richard Stites, who reproduce the script in their edited collection *Mass Culture in Soviet Russia* (1995), note that the show had echoes for some decades to come:

notice the similarities with the film script for the *Little Red Devils*. *Makhno's Band* was also the inspiration for an operetta of the 1930s and a 1960s film, both called *Wedding at Malinovka*.

(1995: 139)

Makhno's Men played more than 250 times including touring to Leningrad and Kiev. It was also an echo itself from circus's distant past, with its re-enactment of battle scenes on a grand scale (with 50 horses), which run throughout the show from the Prologue:

Prologue: Red Headquarters

The field commanders of a Red Army brigade are discussing the timeliness of liquidating Makhno's band. A railroad worker, Obukh, informs them of a sudden raid by Makhno's men, who have blown up the tracks near their camp so they can capture an approaching supply train. The commanders cannot contact the necessary military unit to order a detachment sent out, because Makhno has cut the telephone wires. Obukh decides to use a bypass to stop the train and deliver the order to the army unit to attack Makhno immediately.
[...]
A train approaches the station. According to the calculations of Makhno's men, it's the very supply train they have been aiming for. However, Red cavalry unexpectedly spring from the train. A battle scene ensues which results in Makhno's retreat The Reds pursue them. Peasants and railroad workers aid the wounded. One of the wounded Red soldiers gets up and walks off, leaving his horse, which was shot in the crossfire. The horse gets to its feet and limps off after him.

(1995: 140)

to the final scene:

Scene III: Sabotaging a Bridge on the Outskirts

A bridge outside town. Anarchy in town. A group of local residents prepare to meet the Reds. Suddenly the rumor circulates that the Whites are approaching. The citizens appropriately change their colors. Makhno's men unexpectedly burst into town. General pillage ensues. Anyone caught is tossed into the water from the bridge. The Red cavalry bursts in. A battle scene follows. As he retreats, Makhno orders the bridge blown up. The destruction of the bridge follows. Calamity strikes. The Reds are cut off. The cavalry halts before the dynamited bridge section. After several seconds of indecision, the cavalry wades into the water and, riding up to the other side of the bridge, attacks Makhno, There is confusion in the bandit ranks. Makhno's men flee, pursued by the Reds.

(1995: 141)

The politics are specific to the early years of Stalin's rule, but the methods are old. As Schechter points out,

While *Makhno's Men* brought a new historical 'realism' into the Soviet circus, the pantomime's river flood and its military battle reconstructed with circus artists riding horses were hardly avant-garde innovations. Charles Dibdin staged 'aqua-dramas' in England as early as 1804. The 1824 London pantomime, *The Battle of Waterloo*, featured riders dressed as Cossacks in cavalry battles more than a century before the Red Army's cavalry chased Makhno's Men across the ring in Moscow. Like the Russian pantomime of 1929, the Cossack spectacle at Astley's Amphitheatre in London included the blowing up of a bridge.

(1998: 43)

Indeed, early circus is partly defined by its origins in, and obsession with, the military. And it was not only London that had its Waterloo show. The same period saw its fair share of Napoleons and naval dramas at the Cirque Olympique and elsewhere in Paris (see Disher's chapter entitled 'Napoleon's Circus Wars' 1937: 175–187). The genre, though it lent itself to enactments of imperialism, was neutral in that respect.

MILITARY AND PATRIOTIC DISPLAY AND THE ORIGINS OF CIRCUS: THE DUCROW FAMILY

Circus history usually starts with Philip Astley's first purpose-built circus in 1768 (actually, a riding school), followed by Andrew Ducrow's rise to fame with his act *Courier of St Petersburg*. Much attention has been paid to the Ducrow family – father Peter the Belgian-born 'Flemish Hercules', and sons John the clown and Andrew the equestrian – the latter being credited with founding a whole genre. But there is a pre-history and a context in which this success might be possible.

The origins of circus equestrianism are in the tricks that idle cavalry used to earn some cash from wherever they could find a willing public to show off to. In *Greatest Show on Earth* (1937), Disher first gives us a quick summary of how horse-riding ended up at Islington, where 'Haunts of health and happiness abounded' (1937: 11) and where he paints a picture of 18th-century Londoners seeking holiday pleasures:

Mid-way through the eighteenth century Islington took a sudden fancy for trick-riding. This was highly significant of the social history of the times. Fully to understand why, you must consider the decline of the tourneys of the middle-ages after royal combatants had received fatal injuries in the lists. Jousts changed into *carrousels* in the seventeenth century with tilting at the quintain amid pageantry that cost vast sums. When a curb was put on the spending powers of kings, these gave place before the eighteenth century to riding-schools, built by the nobility for the exercise of horsemanship and arms. These, in turn, suffered from the pinch of economy and riding-masters had to turn showmen. Jacob Bates, the first of note, made the Continent ring with his praises. His example was followed by many, including Johnson, the Irish Tartar, who rode three horses together at Islington.

(1937: 11–12)

A 1766 advertisement suggests the tone of these occasions:

Mr. Price will exhibit Horsemanship, this and every afternoon, if the Weather permits, in a field adjoining to The Three Hats, at Islington: Where Gentlemen and Ladies may be accommodated with Coffee and Tea, Hot Loaves, and Sullybubs, the Loaves to be ready at Half an Hour after Four O'Clock every afternoon, by your humble servant, Joseph Dingley.

(Disher 1937: 12)

Islington didn't have a monopoly, however:

'Mr. Sampson, lately discharged from Lord Ancram's Light Dragoons,' at the Weaver's Arms, Mile End – 'Admission one shilling'.

(Disher 1937: 13)

Disher reports that Sampson 'kept the tea-parties in a state of constant surprise' with his tricks:

standing in the saddle on one leg, while putting his horse to the gallop [...] He rode at full speed, hanging so low that his hand swept the ground; he dismounted at full speed, discharged a pistol, and remounted in an instant; he rode two horses at once, besides putting them to a jump; he rode at a gallop, head on the saddle and feet in the air.

(Disher 1937: 13)

And at the Jubilee Gardens, the hero was

a Mr. Coningham, who would vault over two hones as they jumped the bar, or play a march on a flute as he stood on their backs.

(Disher 1937: 15)

Whilst Price 'retired on a fortune', his rival Sampson had a bumpier ride, falling into debt, then enjoying 'great popularity at a shabby little ale-house called the Dog and Duck', then opening a riding-school in Tottenham Court Road where he announced 'the grandest feats of horsemanship that were ever attempted', the closing-down of which obliged him once more to 'offer himself for hire to any showman that would have him' (Disher 1937: 15).

But the bizarrest of all is Daniel Wildman, who in 1772 gave a display of trick-riding and bee-keeping at the same time.

> While balancing himself with one foot in the saddle and the other on the horse's neck, he let the swarm cover his head and face; he would also stand on the saddle with the bridle in his mouth and fire a pistol as the signal for one part of the bees to march over a table and the other part to swarm in the air before returning to their hive.
>
> (Disher 1937: 15)

With such oddities on show, what room for a clown? The distinction between clowns and trick-riders is not always discernible, though the division of roles at Astley's is clear in the following example, a transcription from memory by Henry Angelo in his *Reminiscences* from 1828:

> One evening I was very much entertained at Astley's Theatre, at the time he amused the public with his dialogue with Master Merryman. Having a pencil in my pocket I could not refrain from writing it down. He seemed so confident and pleased with every word he uttered, bawled so loud, smiling at his own wit, and the superiority which he *must* convince the audience his eloquence displayed over the clown's. He excited my curiosity to retain it in my memory. Those that have seen him, cannot forget what Astley's erudition was.
>
> *Astley – Alto –* Mister Merryman, Mister Merryman, where are you, Mr. Merryman?
>
> *M.* I be coming directly, master.
>
> *A.* Coming directly, Mister Merryman, so is Christmas.
>
> *M.* I am glad to hear that, master.
>
> *A.* Why, Mister Merryman?
>
> *M.* Because I likes plum-pudding and roast beef, dearly.
>
> *A.* Plum-pudding and roast beef, dearly! that's very good stuff; Mister Merryman; but come, Sir, get up upon the top of that there horse, and let the ladies see as how you used to ride before the Emperor of Tuscany, and the Grand Duke of Switzerland. Mister Merryman, ladies and gentlemen, has had the honour to attend me in my different excursions out of the kingdom, and has been much admired for his wit and his activity. Come, Sir, mind as how you sit upright on that there horse, Sir. What are you about?
>
> *M.* Why, master, I am only combing his wig.
>
> *A.* Combing his wig, Sir; did you ever hear of a horse wearing a wig?
>
> *M.* Yes, master; and an ass too.
>
> *A.* Vastly well, indeed, Mister Merryman. Ladies and gentlemen, Mister Merryman has a great deal of wit.
>
> *M.* Yes, master; I should like to be a poet laureate.

A. Poet Laureate, Mister Merryman? What! I suppose as how you would write manuscript on horseback, like the Roman Arabs in the time of Pontius *Pirate* – you would never want a bridle or saddle.

M. No, master; I would write a book about the French war.

A. About the French war, Mister Merryman? Why, you know nothing about it. You must leave it to Mr. Parnassus, and people of high breeding and learning[1]; but come, Sir, let us see you off.

M. I go, Sir.

A. I go, Sir! but you have got your face the wrong way.

M. Never mind, master; it will be right if I go to fight the French.

A. How so, Mister Merryman?

M. Why, master, if my horse was to take fright and run away, I should not like to have it said I turned my back on Mounseer.

A. Vastly well, indeed, Mister Merryman; but as our brave countrymen will prevent the French from coming to eat up all our roast beef and pudding, you had better turn about; so off you go.

(Angelo 1828: 94–97)

In a footnote on Astley's warning to the clown to leave writing books about the war to others, Disher draws our attention to Astley's own volumes – *Remarks On The Duty and Profession of a Soldier* and *A Description and Historical Account of the Places Now the Theatre* of *War in the Low Countries* – which, although claiming to be 'chiefly written in camp', Disher judges to have been 'compiled from some bulky *Universal History*' (Disher 1937: 39).

So, what was special about the Ducrows? However they managed it, most commentators agree that their influence was long-lasting. Disher states that John Ducrow's 'style stamped the stock jests of circus clowns for years to come' (1937: 103).

He was the perfect fool to the ring. Though lost under the chorus of praise for Woolford and Widdicomb, Gomersal and Andrew Ducrow, evidence enough can be found to show that he was to the circus what Grimaldi was to the pantomime. While no more the inventor of Mr. Merryman than Joey was of the clown, he perfected the part.

(Disher 1937: 114)

And Helen Stoddart in *Rings of Desire: Circus History and Representation* (2000) considers two aspects of Andrew Ducrow's power. First was his directorship of Astley's from 1825 to 1841, which although it

may have, until its final hours, been absent of great upheaval or revision, his management brought not only physical/institutional but also an artistic and cultural readjustment for circus as a whole. He launched an extensive building programme to erect permanent circuses in the provinces while the circus basked in a level of financial success, respectability, stability and royal patronage (the Royal Family attended in 1828) it had not previously known.

(2000: 19)

And second were his aesthetic feats:

Artistically he was most famous for his 'poses plastiques', a kind of dramatic equestrianism in which he mimed popular versions of famous characters from myth, history and literature on horseback. His equestrian version of Byron's *Mazeppa and the Wild Horse; or The Child of the Desert*, first performed on 4 April 1831, was very much in this vein. [...] Both this and his other famous adaptation of *The Courier of St Petersburg* (1827), which involved a messenger straddling two horses, each of which bears the national flag of a different country. This continued to be performed internationally until late into the 1890s. Ducrow then, can be seen as consolidating the (connected) pantomimic, equestrian and internationalist dimensions of circus spectacle whilst at the same time lending it a certain cultural respectability, through his demotic dramatisations of myth, opera, history and literature which, though they may not have constituted the majority in the audience, proved an irresistible combination for the Victorian middle classes.

(2000: 19–20)

LEAPING CLOWNS

As if that wasn't enough, Andrew Ducrow was also capable of playing a kind of second clown to the clown proper, as in *The Peasant's Frolic*, where he entered the ring from the audience impersonating a drunken lout, dragged the clown off his horse, refused to leave and ended up on horseback in reverse, facing the tail.

The peasant fell off, got astride again, stood up and kept his feet even though the horse got into its stride, threw off greatcoat, waistcoat, under-waistcoat, a third and fourth, and ten other waistcoats – traditional business of First Gravedigger in *Hamlet* – and then his trousers fell down. The next instant, drawing his shirt off in a twinkling, Ducrow revealed his fleshings and classic grace.

(Disher 1937: 97–98)

This kind of act, known as a 'Flying Wardrobe' act, is still around. Ducrow's version actually combined several elements which could be developed according to the performer's taste, skills and comic abilities – the fake spectator, the drunk, the 'bad' acrobat, the metamorphosis from clown to star and the champion equestrian. Variations abound. Jacques Tati's last completed film, *Parade* (1974), features Karl Kossmayer doing his regular act as a bespectacled hen-pecked spectator who mounts the mule that no other (real) volunteer can master, suffering an array of slips, falls, throws and kicks, as well as a triumphant moment fully mounted facing the mule's tail, and a later losing of his trousers, though no graceful circus artist is revealed underneath, just his underwear.

The link with 'jumping clowns' is also apparent:

> Jean-Baptiste Auriol, a favourite of London as well as of Paris, was Franconi's clown. Laughter broke out directly the bells of his motley tinkled before he entered the ring to take a standing jump and pirouette three or four times in the air. From the tremplin, he would vault over eight horses and their riders, over twenty-four soldiers with fixed bayonets, or over twelve horses flanked by soldiers who fired during the leap. He would dive through fireworks, or through a circle bristling with 'churchwarderns' without breaking a stem, and march, drill, and fire his musket while balancing on the tops of a dozen wine bottles. He could climb walls 'like a fly' and throw himself, seemingly with foolhardy recklessness, from the topmost frieze of the Cirque Olympique.
>
> (Disher 1937: 173)

And so I return to Lazarenko. Physical prowess and military propaganda aside, there is one more link between Ducrow and Lazarenko. Ducrow was as a child known as the 'Little Devil' (as well as the 'Infant Wonder'). Lazarenko also, it seems, was in demand as a devil, playing one in a 1921 production of Mayakovsky's *Mystery Bouffe*, directed by Meyerhold. According to Schechter, citing Lazarenko's biographer, Slavsky (1980), he was also asked to play Makhno as a devil – a drunken, violent one – but found it difficult to elicit any humour from the role. Although Lazarenko matched Makhno in being able to ride horses at full tilt, just how to conform to Stalin's views of the anarchist leader and remain a clown was not obvious. He opted for

Figure 13 Vitaly Lazarenko executing a jump somersault, Irkutsk, 1914
Source: Mosarchiv

portraying him as a coward posing as a military leader, complete with a routine where he was afraid of falling off his horse (Schechter 1998: 47).

CLOWNS IN THE POST-KHRUSHCHEV ERA

Returning to the 1960s, we can see that other Soviet clowns of that period are clearly marked by the drift away from the grotesque that Popov proclaimed. We have Yuri Nikulin's slightly sour-faced, ironic clown resigned to not sharing a glass of vodka with his clown partner, Shuidin, and instead using it to wash his hands, gargle with and then spit out, all under the watchful and controlling eye of the ringmaster. Or Leonid Yengibarov's handsome young mime-artist look, with his tight-fitting sweater, no permanent hat and no noticeable make-up.

But it was Oleg Popov, known as the 'sunny clown', who was the face that Soviet clowning presented to the world, acting as the great ambassador abroad. Travelling to the West with the Moscow Circus's first ever visits outside the Communist countries, Popov was always at hand to speak to the press about the merits of the new Soviet clown/citizen. In contrast, most other clowns were only for domestic consumption. Yengibarov, whose tours outside the Soviet Union were strictly limited to Eastern Europe, reportedly offered to be kept in a cage meant for circus animals and only let out in the ring when it was time to perform to prevent him from defecting. His request was refused.

Popov was feted in the West, but the praise was by no means unanimous. In the Preface to Tristan Rémy's *Les Clowns*, Bernard de Fallois judges against:

> At the occasion of one of the first shows in Paris by the Moscow Circus, the clown Popov explained in a press conference that clown comedy in the West expressed the class war. The white clown was capitalism and the auguste the proletariat. For him, the Soviet circus had put an end to this unpleasing opposition, such that laughter no longer came from malice and oppression. Now, it is true that Popov's number, in the great tradition of Russian *augustes de soirées* – talking, whistling, joke telling clowns – was without malice. He was even of a great kindness. But neither did he make us laugh. He had replaced the laugh with poetry. The clash, the emotion of the art of clown were absent. What Popov had not seen was that the duo of the white face and the auguste had never had the sense which he was ascribing to it.
>
> (Rémy 1945: XVI)

Popov had never set out to be a clown, in fact. His studies at circus school had focused on the great range of techniques that he mastered to such a high degree – juggling, slack rope and balancing. It was only when called upon to replace a clown at short notice that Popov's career as a comic began (Rémy 1956). Looking at his performances today on film, there is a clear distinction between the quality of his presence when his focus is on gags and when it is on his circus skills. When he looks directly to find that gag, telling us when to laugh, that 'sunniness' grates somewhat as we see Popov 'playing the clown'. Surprisingly, it is when he is immersed in his skill, jauntingly trotting along his slack rope or casually tossing a myriad of kitchenware high into the air, that Popov is more engaging, lighter, transmitting a warm pleasure – 'sunny', in fact.

LECOQ, POPOV AND CLOWN REALISM

We can see how Popov's socialist clown realism is at once an aesthetic and a political choice in keeping with its time and place. So too the post-Lecoquian clown, despite Gaulier, has drifted towards a concept of the everydayness of things. This is an easy step to take, as we have seen, from the clown in the flop to the idea that we can discover the 'truth' of the person through the 'mask' of the outside, if we scratch the surface a little. Realism demands that this surface mask resembles as much as possible what we see in our everyday world. The style must not draw attention to itself but look like ordinary activity which has no significance: like drinking tea. Hence the 'cup-and-saucer' style of the late 19th-century English theatre, as here described by Nicholas Dromgoole in *Performance Style and Gesture in Western Theatre*, with reference to Pinero's plays in particular:

> For the cup-and-saucer plays, and perhaps for the first time on the English stage, actors were trying to behave as much as possible in the way people behaved off stage. It was deliberate and it was new. It meant building up a character with little touches of stage business, little details of behaviour.
>
> (Dromgoole 2007: 189)

For confirmation of the contemporaneity of clown realism, see this blurb for a course by Jos Houben in 2006:

> Every day we get up, we eat, we get dressed, work, go to bed, sleep...so many banal and obvious activities that we repeat day after day and that makes our lives. This daily routine is so private, so close to us that we no longer see it...In this workshop we take some distance, we observe it as if for the first time. By replaying our daily life we will perhaps be able to discover a hidden side, a poetic depth that might nourish our clown universe...To extract, from daily gestures and situations, rituals, music, grand themes such as Solitude, Love, Death... Going from the table to the door: a Melodrama; slicing an apple: a Tragedy; taking off your shoes: Spiritual Ecstasy! To render that which is simple and banal into something surprising and sublime, what a beautiful mission for a Clown!

Cup-and-saucer clowning, anyone? If that is what our times demand, then that is what clowning shall become.

Whilst Popov wanted clowning to show us how to live by providing a positive role model, there is another, opposite method which uses the wrongness of clown behaviour in order to show us how not to live.

SOCIETY'S MORAL CONSCIENCE: TRADITIONAL CLOWNS OF VANCOUVER ISLAND

Anne Cameron in *Daughters of Copper Woman* (1981) re-tells some of the stories she was told by the indigenous women of Vancouver Island. In her Preface, Cameron makes clear that her, and the original tellers', purpose in passing these tales on is 'that the mistakes and abuse of the past need not continue' (1981: 7). There is a whole chapter on clowns, which begins with the granddaughter, Liniculla, worrying about what costume to wear for Hallowe'en. Granny's suggestion that she go as a clown doesn't go down well, as Liniculla thinks that just means she couldn't think of a real costume. Granny explains that she is thinking of 'an Indian clown, like in the days before the invaders came' (1981: 109), and proceeds to explain the importance of their traditional clowns, who were 'with us all the time, as important to the village as the chief, or the shaman, or the dancers, or the poets' (1981: 109). Their function was to comment on anything that was foolish. This could be anything from politics, where they might go to the tribal council meeting and imitate the leaders if they thought they were about to take a rash decision:

> the clown would imitate it in such a way every little wart on that person would show, every hole in their idea would suddenly look real big
>
> (1981: 109)

to fashion, where vanity might get you being followed by a clown dressed up with 'bits of bark and twigs, and feathers, and dog shit, and old broken clam shells' (1981: 109).

This wrong behaviour can be seen as the opposite of model behaviour in that it is eminently visible and it makes itself noticed as 'strange'.

According to Granny, the clown's motivation wasn't to hurt but to remind you of common values 'like bein' nice to people, and bein' lovin', and trying' to fit in with the people you live with' (1981: 110). The clowns were respected in their carrying out of their duties:

> And nobody would ever dare blow up at the clown! If you did that, well, you were just totally shamed.
>
> (1981: 110)

Although clowns might be called upon to bring clowns into line, too:

> Sometimes a clown would find another clown taggin' along behind, imitatin', and then the first one knew that maybe somethin' was gettin' out of hand, and maybe the clown was bein' mean or usin' her position as a clown to push people around and sharpen her own axe for her own reasons.
>
> (1981: 110)

Having explained how and why clowns did what they did, Granny goes on to tell a story that dates back to an earlier time when the Europeans (the 'Christians', as Granny refers to them) were carving up Vancouver Island. They were tempting the people to go to church in exchange for worthless gifts like mirrors and pictures. One particular clown, famous at that time, felt that things were going too far when the preachers were not only telling the locals what to believe and how to behave but also using religion to impose strict dress codes of trousers for the men and long dresses for the women.

> Well, one Sunday didn't the clown show up. She was wearin' a big black hat, just like a white man, and a black jacket, just like a white man, and old rundown shoes some white man had thrown away. And nothin' else.
>
> (1981: 111)

The preacher can't believe that the people are treating this naked woman with respect as she sits at the front during the service and so, having ranted about sin and disrespect for god,

> he came down from that pulpit and he grabbed ahold of that clown to throw her out on her bum.
>
> The people just about ripped him apart. You don't put violent hands on a clown!
>
> (1981: 112)

The clown intervenes, calms everyone down and gives a speech about how everyone has different customs that shouldn't be judged, before leaving with everyone behind her. 'And that church is still there today and it's still empty' (1981: 112).

In Granny's second story the clown has an even higher purpose and a more difficult mission. People were going down to the town of Victoria to trade more and more furs with the Europeans, despite knowing they were depleting the stocks of seals and otters, and often getting very little in return, especially from private traders who were buying furs in exchange for rum. The clown sets up a stall next to the Hudson Bay Company's (who had a monopoly on trading rights), offering to buy furs. Whilst the Europeans offer molasses in exchange, she has wild honey. The whites give rum, but the clown pays with swamp water. Granny says that some people got the message and went home without trading, some ignored her and some even traded with her. The Hudson Bay Company complain to the governor about the loss in trade that they have suffered that day, but the governor takes the locals' side, resulting in more dignified deals for a time. Encouraged by this, the clown decides to bring up the issue of the rum trade.

> The Americans were sendin' lots of ships up here, and they wouldn't trade nothin' but rum for furs. First they'd just put a small barrel of rum on the beach, free gratis, and then when the men were all into the rum, why the Americans would come and trade, and the result of that was pretty awful.
>
> (1981: 114)

But the clown never made the trip back to Victoria and was found dead by her canoe, shot in the head. 'Hadda be a white man done it. We would never do violence to a clown' (1981: 114).

POLITICAL AND SPIRITUAL POWER: THE KOSHARI AND SOCIAL ORDER

Not all non-European clowns are necessarily so noble. In Bandelier's novel, the plot revolves around Tyope, the Koshari (ritual clown) leader, and his personal political ambitions and the inter-clan rivalries that threaten to destroy the whole tribe. Even the legitimate functions of the clowns seem questionably repressive in their pursuit of evidence that a woman, Say Koitza, has indulged in black magic in order to cure her illness using owl's feathers. Her father, Topanashka, a political enemy of Tyope, worries over his daughter's fate:

> 'Woman, your ways are wrong. I know it, and the Koshare know it also. They may know more, much more than I could wish,' he added
> [...]
> 'My father, I do not ask you to tell me how you come to know all this; but tell me, umo [father], what are these Delight Makers, the Koshare? At every dance, they appear and always make merry. The people feel glad when they see them. They must be very wise. They know of everything going on, and drag it before the people to excite their mirth at the expense of others. How is it that they know so much? [...] since I hear that the Delight Makers wish me no good, I want to know at least what those enemies of mine are.'
>
> (Bandolier 1890: 32)

Nevertheless, he respects the judgement of the clowns over and above his love for his daughter:

> 'And yet you have used owl's feathers!'
>
> Her face grew pale. She asked, hoarsely, –
>
> 'Where should I keep them?'
>
> 'The Koshare know it,' was the equally husky reply.
>
> She started, her eyes gleamed like living coals.
>
> 'Have the Koshare sent you here, father?'
>
> 'No,' was the gloomy answer; 'but if the old men come to me and say, 'kill the witch,' I must do it. For you know I am Maseua, head-war-chief, and whatever the principals command I must do, even if it takes the life of my only child!'
>
> The woman rose to her feet; her attitude was one of defiance.
>
> 'Let the Koshare speak, and do you as you are commanded. The time must come when I shall have to die.'
>
> (Bandolier 1890: 35)

But there is another side to the clowns. Bandolier tells us of the Koshari's role in the fertility ceremonies performed to bring rain and better crops, explained by the story of their origins as entertainment for the wandering people who founded the tribe of the Tehua:

> But, lest the people might get weary on their bag journey, [they] commanded that from Shipapu [the place of the gods] there should come forth a man whose body was painted white and black, and who carried on his head dried corn-leaves instead of feathers. This man began at once to dance, to jump, and to tumble, so that the people laughed and their hearts became glad. This man led the summer-men southward, and as often as they grew tired he danced again and made jest; and the tribe followed him until they came to where we are now, and all met again. The summer-people never suffered hunger in all their wanderings, for their leader was precious, and wherever they went he caused the fruits to be ripe. That man was the Koshare. Since that time there have been Koshare in every tribe. Their task it is to keep the people happy and merry; but they also fast, mortify themselves, and pray to Those Above that every kind of fruit may ripen in its time, even the fruit in woman's womb.
>
> (1890: 34)

As with all power, clown power may be on the side of good, or in the hands of those who want to use it for domestic politics. It seems that there are good clowns and there are bad clowns. The husband of Say Koitza, Zashue,

> was a Delight Maker himself, and one of merriest of that singular crew. Among them he was perhaps the most popular; for while good-looking, his strength and agility enabled him to perform in a conspicuous manner, and his ready wit and quick conception of everything ludicrous caused him to shine as a great light among that society of official jesters.
>
> (1890: 39)

On the other hand,

> Tyope was a Koshare rather than an agriculturist, he spent his time mostly in other people's homes and in the estufa [common house] of the Delight Makers, leaving his wife to provide for herself and for him also.
>
> (1890: 42)

Barton Wright tells of how the Hopi people sometimes use their clowns not just for ridiculing their own faults but for satirizing those of their enemies, particularly the Navajo people. The Piptuka are a type of non-religious clown who, unlike the Koshari, do not take part in ceremonies and whose actions are not ritualized. They can therefore choose when, where and how to use their skills. On one occasion, two Piptuka play a Navajo medicine man and his wife, and offer to cure two of the Koshari who have stomach and leg pains, for a fee. The Piptuka parody the Navajo curing song and ceremony using feathers, sticks and soot.

Next, [the 'medicine man'] takes a large cloth ball wrapped with string, and, standing behind his patients, throws it against their backs, knocking the wind out of them, which is always vastly amusing to the audience. Finally he pushes the clowns down full length on their faces, yanks off their breechclouts, and taking a large handful of the grass pulp from the metate [mortar], slaps it on their buttocks. He then pretends to insert a large feather into their anus. However, the quill is stuck between the clowns' legs, which leaves the feather upright.

All the other clowns demand to be treated, and the medicine man soon has all of them lying in the plaza with feathers waving in the breeze. He then gathers up his fee and he and his wife leave the plaza (1994: 44–47).

RELIGIOUS CEREMONY: THE PURPOSE OF CLOWNS IN NEW MEXICO

The Koshari and other clowns regarded as sacred, the Tsukuwimkya, follow strict ceremonial scripts, although with freedom to improvise at some moments, as in the previous example. Wright offers full descriptions of their actions. Their arrival in the village plaza, where they will perform, is across the rooftops, as the clowns are supposed to arrive from the clouds. They walk right through or over any obstacles or spectators, 'behaving like ignorant, rude children' (Wright 1994: 13). Reaching the edge of the rooftops, they look down upon the plaza and make it known with shouts that they have arrived. The pretence is that they are on a mountain-top and they discuss noisily whether and how to get down to the valley below (the plaza).

Because it is supposed to be a long and difficult trip, the clowns enter the plaza from the rooftops in the most ill-conceived, inefficient, awkward, mirth-provoking method they can devise. Head first down a ladder and falling in a heap at the bottom, or lowered clinging to the end of a long pole or swung inside a tire at the end of a length of rope, invariably they end up in a heap on the plaza floor amid loud exclamations and protests (Wright 1994: 14).

In the plaza they discover the kachinas' dance. The kachinas are the spirits and those who represent them in their dance, which is serious. The clowns push and prod the kachinas and shout questions at them, none of which puts them off their serious business. The leader of the kachinas explains that their dance is to bring rain and fertility and blessings from the gods. The excited clowns want to get in on the act:

Greedily they ask for all the wrong things, such as 'mountains of corn,' 'goodlooking girls,' 'a Cadilac,' etc.

(Wright 1994: 15)

The kachina dancers complete their dance and leave the clowns alone. The clowns make a small tree their 'home' and they gobble chunks of food, wasting large amounts. Cans of soft drinks are poured down their throats, both inside and outside. In general, they behave as wasteful, thoughtless gluttons.

(Wright 1994: 16)

Then comes another kachina dance, which the clowns are hopeless at joining in with. The clowns are left alone again and next set out to build their house in which they place their 'sister', represented by a rag doll possessed by the clown's leader.

This self-appointed 'boss' tells the other clowns what they will need in the way of supplies to build their house. Suggestions fly, and one clown will ask for 'French doors,' another for 'picture windows,' or 'a stair case,' 'a Jacuzzi,' or whatever other incongruous thing the clowns can think of installing.

The leader then sends them off to get these items. They return almost immediately, not with anything constructive, but with handfuls of ashes and charcoal with which they mark the outline of their 'house' on the plaza floor. Often they make believe that they have locked themselves in or out of this ash outline.

(Wright 1994: 17)

Then comes a clowning routine making fun of whatever issue is prominent, as we have seen elsewhere. The Koshari also engage in contests, one of which, as described by Wright, is a tug-of-war with their penises tied together. At the point when the clowns' behaviour is at its most outrageous, another group appear, the 'Warrior Kachinas'. After warning the clowns three times, with no effect, their role is to punish them,

thrashing them with willow switches, stripping them of their breechclouts or shorts, piling them in a heap, and committing other indignities before drenching them with water.

The clowns plead for forgiveness and one by one, in acts of 'atonement,' they 'confess' to the most outrageous events, usually sexual in content, and occasionally involving a relative.

(Wright 1994: 19)

Finally, the clowns leave in a serious fashion.

Wright notes that the question 'what are clowns for?' has several answers:

Most preliterate cultures have clowns who behave in a manner similar to the jester, giving unsolicited advice through the medium of humor. However, the role of these clowns is far more complex than that of the court fool because, in addition to offering humor and advice, they are often believed to be quasi-inhabitants of the supernatural world or to personify beings from there. Such clowns are therefore sacred and are a combination of jester, priest, and shaman.

(1994: x)

Figure 14 Koshari playing tug-of-war
Source: Northern Arizona University, Cline Library, Jo Mora Collection

It depends on who you ask.

> When Hopi are asked about the importance of the clowns, their actions, and their purpose, the explanation depends upon the age and position of the one who answers. The elders or chiefs justify clowning by saying, 'They are worth something. They do it for rain, crops, fertility.' Others, somewhat younger and often more acculturated, will express a humanistic philosophy with the statement, 'The clowns represent ourselves. They do all the things we do. They act like children. They don't know how to behave. They come down the ladders head-first and they make jokes. The clowns always realize their bad behavior and confess it in a funny way and the crowd laughs.' [...] When the youngest are asked they declare, 'It is just to make the people laugh.'
>
> (Wright 1994: 2–3)

At the root of all these explanations, though, is the fact that deviant behaviour provokes laughter:

> Although their avowed purpose is to amuse, the direction their humor takes is, as usual, concerned with that which is beyond the accepted Hopi way of life, be it outsiders, neighboring tribes, individuals, or attitudes that seem aberrant to the group.
>
> (Wright 1994: 35)

Deviance from the norm can be understood in another way to explain the sacredness of these clowns. Wright, whilst recognizing that not all cultural anthropologists are agreed on the matter, suggests that the connection is to be found in a relationship between underworld and upper world. For the Hopi, the underworld is the opposite in every way of the upper world. Winter in one means summer in the other, beauty in one is ugliness in the other. To inhabit the underworld one only needs, as a clown, to say the opposite of what you mean, or swim in the dust, or ride a horse backwards.

> One of the characteristics of all pueblo sacred clowns is the fact that that they often speak in reverse or behave in opposites. For example, clowns will tell the men to do the women's work and the women to hunt rabbits, or declare that the most respected elders in the village are guilty of obscene actions.
>
> (Wright 1994: 61)

Not only this, but the clowns' patron amongst the spirits is Paiyatamu ('Sun Youth'),

> a handsome young man with a healthy libido, a prototype for lovers, one who plays a flute from which comes not only music that causes the flowers to bloom but also draws the butterflies of the world to him.
>
> (Wright 1994: 60)

He represents all that is beautiful, positive and life-giving and is thus the opposite of the crude and ugly clowns. In a sense, it is through this opposition that the clowns stand in for the god, which accounts for their power over the corn crop.

So we could say that the answers to the question 'what are clowns for?' whilst operating on vastly differing levels are closely inter-related.

CLOWN ACTIVISM: THE CLANDESTINE INSURGENT REBEL CLOWN ARMY

Clown as fun, clown as liberation, clown as political intriguer, clown as altruist, clown as ridicule of the other, clown as enemy of the people, clowns as gods, clown as moral guardian – the list is perhaps endless. In May 1968, so one story goes, Lecoq's was the only class still running in Paris, saved from the wrath of the revolutionary students who found in clown an ally for the breaking apart of the old order.

One initiative that sought to harness clowning as a tool against power itself was the Clandestine Insurgent Rebel Clown Army. Begun in 2006, it enjoyed great popularity among political activists, spawning groups of 'rebel clowns' in many countries. It has only recently begun a revival, following several years when the founders had all but abandoned the project. The group's philosophy was rooted in the convergence, as the founders conceived it, between the nature of clowning and the politics of anarchism:

We are clowns because what else can one be in such a stupid world. Because inside everyone is a lawless clown trying to escape. Because nothing undermines authority like holding it up to ridicule. Because since the beginning of time tricksters have embraced life's contradictions, creating coherence through confusion. Because fools are both fearsome and innocent, wise and stupid, entertainers and dissenters, healers and laughing stocks, scapegoats and subversives. Because buffoons always succeed in failing, always say yes, always hope and always feel things deeply. Because a clown can survive everything and get away with anything.

(CIRCA 2006)

Although in many cases it was taken to be simply another weapon of protest, something else to throw at the authorities, or even merely a way of having fun on a political demonstration, what was interesting about the project was its subtle politics. Reasoning that the usual demonstrations of protest often only brought a stand-off with the authorities, an unproductive result of aggression on both sides, the Clandestine Insurgent Rebel Clown Army sought to learn and pass on new techniques to be used to face these situations. Encountering police lines, instead of simply shouting and pushing, clown activists would engage the police in game-playing, or offer to help clean the building they were guarding.

One example will give us the idea. During a training weekend at the Barcelona Clown School some years ago led by one of the movement's founders, Hilary Ramsden, the army of clown activists found themselves in front of the town hall. Offering to dust the building, they were humoured by a relaxed police guard for a time. Soon, though, the guard's superior officer appeared and his angry remonstrations obliged the clowns to move away. They began to play a children's game, but this was too much for the officer, who unilaterally and spontaneously declared that the playing of games was not allowed within a metre of the building. The clowns moved the requisite distance and continued to play. Crowds witnessed the scenes, joined in for a while and commented, and the clowns moved on to find another line to cross.

There is something of the clear insight we have seen in Bouissac's analysis of profaning here, as the officer invents the one-metre rule on the spot in order to enforce what is normally an unspoken law, which in reality would be more something like: 'no being silly near serious representatives of authority'. Unfortunately, not all the groups that sprung up around the idea of rebel clowning were able to spend as much time either on the politics or on the practical clown training, or this combination of the 'how' and the 'why' of clowning that makes CIRCA so interesting. The immediate appeal of clowning was enough for many activists, as Ramsden recalls:

Activists get hardened, by being involved in violence and close to danger near nuclear facilities, for example. To create nonsense was liberating, it went to their heads, but clowning takes time to craft. People focused most of all on the make-up and costume, they didn't have enough time to find their clowns. In a couple of days they assumed things quickly. Those things worked for a time.

(Ramsden 2011)

And the balance between goal-oriented political objectives and open-ended clowning is not an easy one to achieve:

For me, clowning is about 'mixing it up', pointing out the stupidity of authority. That's as far as I go. But other activists might be more goal-oriented and that might end up end up conflicting with clowning.

(Ramsden 2011)

We can see that clowning in the realm of politics holds an ambiguous position, at once critic, police, hero, enemy, representative of the people and a threat to the social order. Having seen such slippery behaviour already in other fields of clown endeavour, this should come as no surprise. The clown is apt to be assimilated into the needs of the moment, yet never completely so, it seems.

Chapter

12 Clown Television

INTRODUCTION

Having just considered the political and, to an extent, ethical power of clowning, I begin this chapter with a contrasting subject: the existence of clowning in the commercial world of television, and specifically that of sitcoms. I am guided in part by Scott Sedita's classification of eight sitcom roles, two of which are patently clown-like: the 'In Their Own Universe' character and 'The Dumb One', described in great detail for the benefit of the aspiring comedy actor in a practical language which is rarely found in the world of contemporary clowning. I follow this with an assessment of where clown stands in relation to other forms of comedy, such as parody, satire and buffoon, returning to television for some contemporary examples to illustrate this, analysing some recent clown- and buffoon-related trends in the work of Andy Kaufman, Ricky Gervais and Larry David.

SITCOM CLOWNS 'IN THEIR OWN UNIVERSE': PHOEBE, KRAMER AND MORK

Clowns do not always proclaim their morality or seek to change the world. Clowning that reaches mass audiences, attaining commercial and popular success, perhaps sees no need to explore the possibilities of ethics. Neither do such successes have motive to question their methods – they simply 'do what works'. They are Mamet's 'busker', 'gypsy' and 'mountebank' made good, with 'little interest in their own performance, save as it relates to their ability to please an audience' (1998: 8). I have already trespassed into the territory of stand-up comedy, but it is in the world of sitcoms that we can find more highly developed examples of analyses of 'how to do it'. Scott Sedita's *The Eight Characters of Comedy* (2006) unashamedly advertises itself on its back cover: 'Buy This Book and People Will Laugh at You!' The blurb continues:

> *The Eight Characters of Comedy* is a Hollywood 'How To' guide for actors and writers who want to break into the world of situation comedy.
>
> (2006: back cover)

In the first part of the book, Sedita's topics include how to analyse a comedy script, how jokes work, techniques of comic delivery and the history of sitcoms – not much you can't find in the many other books available on the subject, to be honest. But he then moves on to analyse in rich detail each of eight 'specific character archetypes that will help you discover your niche in half-hour comedy' (2006: back cover). At least two of these characters could easily fall within the ambit of clowning.

Sedita calls his character number 8 'In Their Own Universe' (ITOU) and he begins by citing one of the most obvious examples of the type, Kramer on *Seinfeld*, played by Michael Richards. The responses of Kramer to most situations and other characters typically function to demonstrate that he is in some way 'somewhere else', as when asked whether he really intends to move to California: Kramer replies that he has 'already gone' (Sedita 2006: 195).

But it's not just a question of some kind of generalised wackiness or show of craziness. The defining trait of being ITOU is that the character thinks, acts and lives by their own rules. These rules resemble those of the normal world but are oddly different.

> The In Their Own Universe (ITOU) characters are some of the weirdest, edgiest and funniest characters of all time, mainly because they are allowed to do and say almost anything and everything. [...] They are 'free-wheeling' on what they believe, what they do and how they do it. That makes them unpredictable and a lot of fun.
>
> (Sedita 2006: 196)

We only need the slightest remnant of logic in order to accept this other way of seeing things, as when Sedita's other main example, Phoebe in *Friends*, played by Lisa Kudrow, spells aloud her own name, the final letter being 'E as in ... 'Ello there mate' (Sedita 2006: 196).

ITOU characters can be split into different types, according to how their otherliness is justified. There are those which actually do come from other universes – aliens such as Mork (Robin Williams) in *Mork & Mindy* (1978–1982) and Uncle Martin (Ray Walston) in *My Favorite Martian* (1963–1966). Others come from another time, like Jeannie (Barbara Eden) in *I Dream of Jeannie*, or another dimension, like Aunt Clara (Marion Lorne) in *Bewitched*; or from some distant and unknown country, such as Latka (Andy Kaufman) in *Taxi*. And then there are those, like Kramer and Phoebe, who were just born odd. Finally, whole casts might be 'different to us', as in *The Addams Family* or *The Munsters*.

> And then of course, there is one show that features a cast In Their Own Universe *from their own universe*, the aliens on '3rd Rock From The Sun.'
>
> (Sedita 2006: 198)

When the whole fictional world is from another universe, this strangeness becomes the norm. This allows for one or more of the characters in this strange/normal world to be strange within the strangeness, whilst the remainder will revert to conforming to other types of characters which, according to Sedita, come from his list of eight.

> Think of '3rd Rock From the Sun.' The entire Solomon family is from another universe, and most of the humor on the show revolves around them trying to adapt to life on Earth. Still, they each take on a specific character. Dick (John Lithgow) is The Dumb One. Sally (Kristen Johnston) is The Manizer [Sedita's female equivalent of the Womanizer]. Tommy (Joseph Gordon-Levitt) is The Logical Smart One and Harry (French Stewart) is...well, he's In His Own Universe. He's a rare character that is In His Own Universe *in his own universe*. As an example, here's Harry doing something 'normal,' like looking for a job in the newspaper.

> Harry: Here's a job that I can do! 'Police are seeking third gunman.' Tomorrow, I'm gonna march over to the police station and show them that I'm the man they're looking for.
>
> (Sedita 2006: 198)

In the end, though, the point is not whether these characters are 'justified' in being different from us or not. At no point do we really believe that beings from other planets, times or countries actually behave like this. The point about these characters is that reason as we know it is absent – they are outside the normal parameters we use to explain and justify behaviour. Thus they are, in Chekhov's sense, clowns and not comedy characters. Their behaviour is not 'obedient to the motivation' but instead 'unjustified, unnatural and unexpected' (Chekhov 1953: 129). For Sedita, '[t]hese are the most dangerously exciting, unpredictable and interesting of characters' (2006: 198). They also recall the dual nature of the clown as both a stage role and a socially defined type. In 16th-century England 'a clown' who arrives from out of town and thus has no idea of how to behave in the capital city is someone who is ITOU and becomes 'the clown', a type, or character, or role, which is a way of talking about ourselves outside the bounds of the norm. In our own historical moment, that 'normal' way of thinking about behaviour is still dominated by notions of 'realism' and the restrictions of 'psychology'. This is strikingly obvious in the world of acting, where despite the existence of many alternatives, the obsession with character analysis and motivation still rules. 'Unlike most of the other characters, there isn't much of a background for the ITOUs' (Sedita 2006: 200), which is why clowns don't obey the rules of psychology.

It is not just a question of behaviour. All means are used to communicate the oddness of ITOUs:

> For most of these characters, it starts with their physical appearance. Think of Jim's hair on 'Taxi' or Kramer's on 'Seinfeld.' Think of Phoebe's clothes on 'Friends.' Or think of anything the girls were wearing on 'Absolutely Fabulous.'
>
> (Sedita 2006: 201)

Sedita's method doesn't just consist in identifying the traits of the role, though. His advice for the actor is still coming from the belief that actors themselves do obey psychology, even if the role does not:

> Now before you go doing something crazy to your hair or putting together ridiculous ensembles, remember that being eccentric is more organic than that. Look into your life and think of those things that you do that your friends or family consider kind of 'out there.' Think of those times you've let go, stepped out of yourself and gotten crazy. That's how you must approach the ITOU character.
>
> (Sedita 2006: 201)

But mostly he is concerned with giving details and examples of the dynamics of the role. The ITOU uses 'illogical logic':

> Karen [in *Will and Grace*]: Grace, it's Christmas for goodness sake. Think about the baby Jesus, up in that tower, letting his hair down so that the three wise men can climb up and spin the dreidel and see if there are six more weeks of winter.
>
> (2006: 203)

They are 'unflappable'.

> Kramer was convinced that The Bro (the bra for men) was something that every guy needed and wanted and he was perplexed as to why others were ridiculing him for it. Nevertheless, that didn't stop him from going forth with a prototype.
>
> (2006: 202)

They are 'childlike', 'positive' and optimistic':

> Jim [in *Taxi*]: Hey, you know the really great thing about television? If something important happens, anywhere in the world, night or day, you can always change the channel.
>
> (2006: 204)

They have a 'skewed train of thought'. 'They are either thinking one-step ahead, one-step behind or one-step removed' (2006: 204).

They are 'direct' but without malice, as when Phoebe (in *Friends*) replies to Joey's request for help with 'Oh, I wish I could. But I really don't want to' (2006: 207).

They are 'shameless', having 'no internal censor':

> Marni [in *Committed*, when her boyfriend asks her what she wants to do in the morning]: Well, usually I poop first thing in the morning, but I can put that off.
>
> (2006: 208)

Consequently they are free of regrets or guilt. The ITOU's obliviousness to the norm is not due to stupidity. As we have seen already, the clown sets himself apart from the illusion of normality by not playing along with the rules, which can be because 'the clown is either too smart or too dumb' (McManus 2003: 12). The ITOU is smart:

> *Mork:* I know about jail. It's when you get free food, free clothes and no rent.
> *Prisoner:* It sounds better the way you say it. I got caught shoplifting.
> *Mork:* Wow, you must be strong!
>
> (Sedita 2006: 209)

DUMB CLOWNS: JOEY

The trait of stupidity belongs to another of Sedita's characters, 'The Dumb One'. Sedita's prime example here is Joey in *Friends*, who thinks 'omnipotent' means 'impotent', for example (Sedita 2006: 115).

Like the ITOU, the Dumb One is childlike, direct, positive and honest:

> There is nothing false about them. They are true to themselves and more often than not, they are proud of it. They always tell the truth, even if they say something that is obviously incorrect.
>
> (Sedita 2006: 126)

We have already seen how the clown, not playing by the rules, can be left outside the logic of the plot, whether it be due to lack of understanding or due to lack of interest. Clowns are unlikely, therefore, to be at the centre of the narrative.

> Perhaps because of the childish and simplistic nature of the character, there have not been many shows that have put The Dumb One in the lead.
>
> (2006: 117)

But clowns' self-sufficiency and freedom from plot logic allows for easy combination with other types of character:

> The Dumb One is a character that seems to work well with most of the other characters because of the humor they bring by simply being themselves. They definitely work well with The Neurotic (think of how frustrated Monica gets with Joey at times). They also work well with a Logical Smart One who is trying to explain something The Dumb One can't comprehend.
>
> (2006: 128)

If the stupidity of the Dumb One is what distinguishes them from the ITOU characters, then it is their obliviousness which marks them out from the other of Sedita's eight characters which habitually suffers failure, the Lovable Loser.

> I called The Lovable Loser 'consciously oblivious,' meaning they are aware that something is wrong or that their idea might not be the best one, but they are

blinded by their own want. The Dumb One is actually the opposite. They aren't aware in the least that this would be a bad idea. Otherwise they wouldn't do it. Their messes are a result of their simply being oblivious, not consciously oblivious to a situation. That's a big difference and an important one between these two characters.

(2006: 129–130)

Finally, the one characteristic that differentiates the Dumb One from all other characters is that they are never sarcastic:

Sarcasm requires intelligence, something The Dumb One lacks. They are such honest and sincere people, they don't really understand the concept of sarcasm, and as such, it comes off as false. The Dumb One isn't good at lying and *sarcasm* is telling a lie. Also, sarcastic remarks are a way for some characters to lash out at the world. The Dumb Ones don't want to lash out, not even for a second.

(2006: 128)

These lacks – intelligence, the ability to lie and malice – are key to defining clown.

Sedita's advice to the actor in this role is: 'Find the disappointment (not the resentment) when things don't go your way' (2006: 121). Good advice for a clown, as is:

to play The Dumb One, latch on to those things that you know *nothing* about (and use how you feel in those situations) for playing this character.

(2006: 124)

But perhaps the best clown acting advice comes, as Sedita himself admits, from the Dumb One himself (2006: 131). In one episode we find Joey actually teaching an acting class. In order to provoke facial expressions which match the emotion the actor wants to express, Joey suggests a number of tricks. In order to cry, the actor should pull their own hairs out with tweezers through a hole in their pocket. When receiving bad news, the actor can do some difficult mental arithmetic like dividing 232 by 13, in order to obtain a tortured look (*Friends* Season 3, Episode 7). Elsewhere, Joey explains how to do a meaningful pause, and buy time in order to remember your next line, by imagining he is smelling a fart (*Friends* Season 2, Episode 11).

NON-CLOWN COMEDY, PARODY AND SATIRE

If some of the qualities which clowns lack explain how sarcasm is not in their repertoire, then we can perhaps go further and try to define clown by observing what it is not in relation to its closest cousins – other forms of comedy. John Wright at the end of his book gives a series of detailed explanations and clarifications of what the most common forms of non-clown comedy are. He defines these in terms of their relationship to parody.

He starts by giving an example of clear parody, performed by a student on a course given for teachers:

> 'Well. Leroy What's this?' Her voice was dripping with sarcasm. The audience bellowed with laugher. 'Not only did you hand it in on time but you actually did the work! Why do you think you get bullied, Leroy?' she said, tauntingly. Then suddenly incandescent with rage she shouted, 'Look at this – you've actually backed it in brown paper! […] Have some pride! What's the point in coming to a school like this with an attitude like that?' She was in tears now and digging into her bag for a tissue. 'We'll never get you excluded at this rate; I'll never get to be head of department.'
> […]
> As she spoke she ripped the pages out of the exercise book, screwed them up and crammed them into her mouth until her speech became too distorted for us to understand.
>
> (2006: 251–252)

Wright comments that the teacher's focus on meaning was what made this parody rather than clown.

> She had too much to say about being a teacher to play clown. There wasn't a trace of bafflement, she knew exactly what she was doing, she had a clear target.
>
> (2006: 252)

Clowns, on the other hand,

> have nothing to say other than, 'This is me, and this is what I'm doing': that's the vacuous freedom of clown, and to many performers it is an appalling freedom.
>
> (2006: 253)

The clown's function is to make us laugh, whereas the parodist must make us think and laugh. Clowns do this by being completely honest, in the sense that they do not hide anything. In parody, honesty is not so simple. What you say is not what you mean. 'It's the world of "only joking"' (2006: 253).

Clowning and parody are not completely mutually exclusive, though – they can contain elements of each other. The example of the teacher includes much of what we find in clowning, as it was 'silly, playful and performative', but the parody is entirely intentional, 'whereas clown drifts into parody unintentionally' (2006: 253).

As an example of unintentional clown parody, we have Max Wall's piano-playing business. In a way, he dresses like a concert pianist, though ridiculously. His actions are those of a pianist, as he tries to play the piano, thwarted absurdly by the lid to the keyboard being down. But suddenly he is up and doing his eccentric dance, and the piano is forgotten. At no moment do we see a real concert pianist. Unlike the teacher, the parody that Max Wall was playing was completely incidental. He had nothing to say about classical pianists; that was his theme and not his target.

(2006: 252–253)

So our laughter is at the performer and not at any particular aspect of pianists. Whereas with the teacher we are not laughing at the performer herself but at the absurdity of trying to teach kids who don't want to learn, in a system that is failing and so on. It may be great parody,

but in comparison with Max Walt, we saw nothing of her, because everything she did was exaggerated to the point of ridicule thus obscuring her own personality.

(2006: 253)

Having a target other than yourself and your own ridiculousness means that non-clown forms of comedy can easily be driven not just by fun, silliness and awareness of one's own stupidity but by anger, frustration and hatred. The outcome is that the target won't be happy: 'parody is at its best [...] when it's on the verge of offending us' (2006: 260). Whilst clown thrives on the performer's vulnerability, '[i]n playing parody, the idea is to feel empowered'. (2006: 268)

Wright distinguishes between parody, conceptual parody, satire, pastiche, caricature, burlesque, grotesque and buffoon (bouffon), giving examples mostly, though not exclusively, from late 20th-century British television:

pastiche: *The Royle Family* and Steve Coogan's Alan Partridge;
caricature: Harry Enfield's *Loadsamoney;*
satire: *The Frost Report* sketch written by Marty Feldman and John Law about the British class system, which begins:

> *John Cleese:* I look down on him [looking down at Ronnie Barker] because I am upper class.
> *Ronnie Barker:* I look up to him [looking up at John Cleese] because he is upper class. But I look down on him [looking down at Ronnie Corbett] because he is lower class. I am middle class.
> *Ronnie Corbett:* I know my place.

(Feldman and Law 1966)

burlesque: *Jerry Springer: The Opera,* with its juxtaposition of two unrelated genres;
grotesque parody: *The Young Ones, Bottom* and *Spitting Image;*
conceptual parody: *The Bacchae* (Kneehigh Theatre Company, 2004), where a 'chorus of men who made their first entrance naked except for old-fashioned women's underwear' (2006: 261) 'attack the means to the end and not the end itself' (2006: 262).

BUFFOONS: PUNCH AND LOUIE DE PALMA

Wright finishes his book with the buffoon (although he uses the English term 'buffoon', the French 'bouffon' is the more generally accepted term to refer to a precise definition, coined by Lecoq and Gaulier). The buffoon is so extremely grotesque that its very form (hunchbacked, typically) provokes rejection or disgust, rather than laughter. It is only when it performs the most ordinary tasks, particularly ones which are supposed to be graceful, beautiful or pleasing, that we perceive the absurdity and laugh. Wright's main example used to illustrate how buffoons function is Punchinello (otherwise known as Pulcinella, Polichinelle or Punch), whose 'ludicrous shape turns anything he does into a parody of the real thing' (2006: 300). Buffoons are indeed a kind of parody of a human being. Their target is a dangerous one: his or her own audience. Gaulier asks students to imagine parodying the Nazis in front of an audience of racist skinheads, for example. The buffoon must take the audience to the brink, where they laugh, then realise they themselves are the butt, when the performer must shrink back with apologies for having offended.

Wright considers that buffoons are harder to find in our contemporary culture:

> *Little Britain's* caricatures certainly touch the grotesque but they lack sufficient malevolence and mystery to give their work the sardonic edge of buffoon.
>
> (2006: 267)

And he believes that historical examples are easier to spot: Richard III, Quasimodo, Ubu. More modern comic figures with traits of meanness or nastiness can be found, such as Wilfred Brambell in *Steptoe and Son* (1962–1974), but they are mostly simply a character that fits logically into a fictional world, more a kind of Pantalone rather than a true buffoon, whose dynamic is more transgressory.

A better example might be Louie de Palma (played by Danny DeVito) in *Taxi* (1978–1983), who possesses the requisite complete lack of moral values. In an episode from the first series, Alex is pleading with Louie not to humiliate Bobby when he returns to being a taxi driver, having failed to make it as an actor:

> *Alex:* Louie, I'm warning you. Don't screw around with Bobby, you hear me?
> *Louie:* What do you mean, you're warning me? Are you threatening me with physical violence, Alex? I'm not saying it won't work. I just want to know.
> *Alex:* No, I'm not threatening you.
> *Louie:* Well, do you got something on me? Are you blackmailing me?
> *Alex:* I'm just telling you this very simply, Louie. Don't do what you're thinking of doing to Bobby. Just don't do it.
> *Louie:* Oh, yeah? Why not?

Alex: Because . . . you shouldn't.

Louie: I shouldn't? That's the reason I shouldn't? I shouldn't? I shouldn't? I shouldn't! Oh, no, no, no, no! I shouldn't. I shouldn't! You shouldn't, you shouldn't! I shouldn't.

(1979, Season 1, Episode 18)

Louie's pleasure hits its height exactly at the point when Alex is left with no more moral arguments. But despite the extremity of the character's moral void, it remains just a character, played in the same performance mode as the rest of the cast.

TRUTH AND HOAX: ANDY KAUFMAN AND RICKY GERVAIS

However, *Taxi*'s other clown, Andy Kaufman's 'Latka', does function in a different performance mode – up to a point. The role ultimately proved too restricting for Kaufman, who left the show despite the fame it brought him. Kaufman's body of work as a whole relied to a great extent on breaking apart our expectations of a genre. His appearances on television chat shows allowed for ample opportunity to break the rules. On one occasion on the Letterman Show he appears ill, claiming it is due to his divorce and the resulting poverty. Scolding the audience for laughing, he slowly rises from his stool and, reaching a hand towards the studio audience, he approaches them, begging for money. Walking past the cameras, breaking the illusion of television, he is finally removed from the studio by force (Kaufman 1980).

The television chat show is supposedly the place where people speak the truth and 'are who they really are', yet which we know is a 'show', a context for self-publicising with its own conventions and limits on behaviour. Kaufman seems to present another, 'more real' reality beyond that, which breaks apart the fictional reality of television. Paradoxically, in order for him to convince us that 'TV is not real', he must convince us of the utter truth of his other reality. Kaufman played on the doubts that the public had over whether his behaviour was 'real' or a practical joke. This is the strategy of the hoax, which demands a huge investment of energy in order to convince us, in contrast to an approach which only breaks up our belief in an illusory fiction without seeking to put anything else in its place.

Even Ricky Gervais in *The Office* (2001–2003) becomes assimilated into the world of the fiction, although initially the programme shocked many who found his character, David Brent, too 'real', unable to distinguish 'fact from fiction'. There is a clue here: a buffoon, or indeed a clown, their dynamic lying outside the conventions of the fictional world, cannot rely on the construction of a mere 'character' in order to convince us but must instead seem 'really real'. For if they do stand outside that fiction, they must by definition be standing 'in reality'. Of course, one of the ways in which that reality-effect is performed is by contradicting the rules of the genre. On television, a simple way to do this is the look to camera, a device which is central to *The*

Office, and which is basic to its premise of being a documentary, and therefore a window on reality. But, of course, the documentary is in itself a conventional genre, which ends up assimilating any belief that what we are seeing is 'really real'. The buffoon, and clown, therefore, must be constantly finding new means to escape from this assimilation, always on the look-out for ways to slip out of the illusion, and thereby appear not to be of that 'false' world. Gervais's move from television series to stand-up comedy is in some way a move in this direction, an attempt to be able to speak truths by being less mediated, and his public haranguings of his audience – for example, at the Oscar award ceremony – are a further step towards a buffoon who inhabits the 'real world'.

With this perspective we can see why his latest work, *Life's too Short* (2011), despite having the trappings of buffoonery, has been unsuccessful. The hero is a dwarf actor (played by real dwarf actor Warwick Davis), whose pretensions to grandeur are ludicrously and evidently misplaced. They are seen as delusions not because of his size but because he is so clearly a failure – divorced, out of work. Whatever comedy there is in this series, it is clear that it comes from our laughter not at dwarves failing to reach the doorbell, for example, but at Davis's expectations that people will recognise him as a famous actor and help him, which doesn't happen (Gervais et al. 2011: Episode 1). *Life's too Short* also might qualify for buffoon-status if the amount of offence it has provoked is anything to go by. But the offence is not on behalf of Gervais's supposed target, the pretentiousness in all of us, but in aggrievance at a perceived belittling of the programme's actor and the group he represents, dwarves. Ultimately, the layer of fiction is too thick, the protagonist fitting too well into his fictional world. Davis's pretensions are all fictionalised, a mere 'story', and thus a conflict which is far weaker than the potentially much more 'real' conflict which haunts the series, that of a dwarf in the 'real world', an issue which is side-stepped, in spite of the protests.

AMORAL CLOWNING: LARRY DAVID

Gervais's mirror image in North America in some ways, Larry David, is also engaged in a struggle with dramatic conventions as a means to 'speak the truth'. *Curb Your Enthusiasm* (2000–2012) creates a hyper-real world by means of improvised performance, which ostensibly shows us David's life having acquired fame and fortune as the co-creator of the television series *Seinfeld*:

> As for the improvised scenes, while the situations sometimes felt *Seinfeld*-like, they played out very differently. There was no quick banter and smashing punch lines.
>
> (Levine 2010: 60)

But these improvisations are guided by very painstakingly scripted plot-lines:

> Larry did not write conventional thirty-five to forty-page scripts for the episodes. Instead, he wrote outlines six to nine pages long, a series of scene descriptions with the general feeling and the key plot points laid out. The story was not to be improvised, but the dialogue was, although Larry might feed a key line or two to an actor – something he did increasingly as the show went on.
>
> (Levine 2010: 73)

In terms of the conventions of the genre, David himself does not stand out from the other performers. They share the same style, as it were. But within the world of the social conventions of the world portrayed, David is in constant conflict and contradiction due to his disobedience of the rules of behaviour:

> The personality that Larry David developed for the first season of the show has a reduced super-ego and a runaway id. He speaks his mind, acts selfishly, tries to fulfil his wants, and avoids obligation.
>
> (Levine 2010: 67)

David himself describes the role in similar terms:

> 'I'm playing – yes – I am playing myself. I'm playing the part of myself that doesn't censor my thoughts.'
>
> (Levine 2010: 81)

He has emphasised that the source of his comedy are the unspoken rules, unknown and untrodden paths where no-one has yet decided how we should behave. And his job is to seek them out and tread on them.

But is this achieved by not understanding those rules, or by regarding them as ridiculous and not to be taken seriously? The issue has confused some:

> Larry David has developed a saleable attitude about the character that he can trot out whenever interviewed, a useful but simplified version of his fictional self. For the Larry of *Curb* is not as consistent as commentators like to pretend, or as free to speak his mind. He sometimes gets into trouble because of his brutal honesty, but often as not his predicaments are the result of lying.
>
> (Levine 2010: 81)

The confusion Levine notes is one based on a moral judgement: is he 'brutally honest' (morally good) or is he 'lying' (morally bad)? Is he an innocent victim of oppressive social decorum that he cannot understand or is he self-centred and uncaring, able only to express and act on the stirrings of his *id*? But if we examine the issue in purely clown terms, the question becomes: is he too stupid to understand or is he too clever to believe in the rules? The answer is that Larry David plays both types of clown at the same time. Or, as he puts it in an interview with Gervais, 'We all have good thoughts and bad thoughts. The bad ones are funny . . . when we say them' (Gervais 2006). This idea of good and bad is distinct from the moral judgement above. Here, good means that which conforms to society's rules, and bad means that which breaks those rules. This kind of 'bad' can appear to be part of an ethical stand and a desire to change society for the better; or it can be seen as a voicing of the individual's egotistical lack of concern for others. In the former case, 'being bad' is a fight against unjust power; in the latter, 'being bad' is a bid to impose one's power unjustly. The confusion occurs because of this mis-match between the amorality of the clown and the ethics of the humanist view.

The strangeness of lumping together the ethical and the selfish is recognised openly in the episode 'The Hero' (2011, Season 8, Episode 6), in which a series of seemingly disparate events all demonstrate Larry's 'hero' status: saving an air hostess from a drunken and aggressive passenger (by accident, tripping over his extra-long shoelace and thus doing what no-one else would dare, pinning the passenger to the ground); collecting his and Jeff's lunch from the counter without waiting for the slow waiter to serve them (deliberately circumventing the rules of customer–waiter relations) – 'If you do that you're a hero! . . . This man is a hero. He just revolutionized the way restaurants work, my friend. No one is ever going to go hungry again'; and finally in the closing scene, in which he altruistically saves Ricky and Donna from a mugger on the subway using his stick of hard Italian bread as a weapon. Lying about an accident, not waiting for the waiter and risking attack from a mugger may seem to be from separate moral categories but, in Larry David's world, they are all examples of 'heroism'. The result is that our systems of moral categorisation are put under unbearable strain.

In the episode 'Palestinian Chicken', this moral questioning covers a range of events from the most banal discussions about whether or not one should say 'LOL' in public to the politically charged dilemma of whether, as Jews, Larry and Jeff should be appreciating the Palestinian restaurant where 'they know what they're doing, chicken wise' (2011, Season 8, Episode 4).

The even greater pleasure of sex also evidently trumps religious bigotry, but it is not just the fact of Larry, a Jew, having sex with Shara from the Palestinian restaurant which creates the comedy, but the intensity of the sexual pleasure of a kind of sado-masochism based on religious hatred, Larry taking the role of 'occupier' and Shara begging him to show her 'the promised land'. All this is coupled with Larry's friend, Marty Funkhouser, who has recently turned ultra-orthodox Jew, overhearing the scene from downstairs.

Again, it is not just one particular moral issue which is examined but our whole system of moral-coding, or what Bouissac calls 'the exposure of the rule of the rules' (1997: 197). As before, when we looked at politics, or the fictional world of the play, we find clowning occupying ambiguous territory, this time in the region of ethics and our reasoning about how we should live our lives.

Chapter

13 Clown Plots

INTRODUCTION

I previously touched on the subject of dramaturgy in the chapters on clown drama and clown authors. Here I look in more detail at some of the mechanics of generating action which are key to understanding certain types of clown plotting. Our first example is Avner the Eccentric's description of problem-solving, which can be used to teach a style of clowning based on the overcoming of obstacles, or to analyse such performers as Keaton or Harold Lloyd. Clown solutions are often, as we would expect, odd, inappropriate, surprising or extraordinary. This leads us to explore the role of magic/surprise and circus skills/virtuosity in clowning. We can then begin to understand the functioning of an anti-virtuosic clown, such as Harry Langdon (1884–1944), and how both Langdon and Chaplin developed their work in directions opposed to the prevailing chase-dominated Hollywood style. In Chaplin's case, this would be towards a delicate balance between emotion and gags, here analysed in detail with respect to *City Lights*. In contrast, we see how Langdon dispensed with virtuosity almost completely, leading him to create an almost plot-less, character-less clown.

PLOT STRUCTURE AND PROBLEM-SOLVING: AVNER THE ECCENTRIC

Not all contemporary clown teachers use the post-Lecoquian clown-as-play model. Avner Eisenberg ('Avner the Eccentric'), although Lecoq-trained, focuses his teaching on techniques of breathing to build audience complicity and stage presence: 'Clown's job is to make the audience feel things, and to get the audience to breathe' (Eisenberg 2005). Drawing on his knowledge of martial arts and hypnotherapy as well as his experience as a performer, he focuses on the functioning of inbreaths and outbreaths, and how they habitually match up to perceiving new information (inhaling is a response to danger) and being satisfied that all is well (exhaling is a response to safety). The clown performer who is aware of these patterns and can consciously manipulate them brings an increased subtlety to their relationship with their own action, with objects and with the audience. If we breathe in on first seeing the audience, for example, then the audience will also breathe in and a relationship based on reserve and distance, or even fear, has been created. But if the clown, on seeing the audience, breathes out, then so do they, and the rapport created is one of trust.

Breathing also has an intimate relationship with thought and action. When we observe someone who is breathing in and who is still, we often interpret this to mean that the person is 'thinking'. As a clown performer, you can make an audience believe you are thinking just by inhaling. You don't actually have to 'think'. Conversely, an outbreath which follows this 'thinking moment' will accompany the subsequent action. Again, it is the audience who interprets this action as being 'a result of' the previous 'thought'. So it is the performer's job to do (and breathe) and the spectator's to interpret. As a conscious performer, I can choose when to use outbreaths and inbreaths, and how frequently. If every action and thought is marked by a whole cycle of breathing in and out, for example, as well as a look to the audience, then each bit of action seems significant, asking to be interpreted. Or I can choose to apply the whole breathing and looking cycle to a longer sequence of actions. This then becomes one 'thought chunk'.

Eisenberg also links breathing to the concept of problem-solving, a large area in his teaching. Problems provoke inbreaths, solutions go with outbreaths. Problem-solving basically entails identifying a problem and finding a clown solution to it. It is a kind of clown dramaturgy. Let's look at this in more detail and see how it easily combines with other concepts we know about 'how clown works'.

Firstly, it is assumed that the clown has an aim. Let's say it is to open the door. It's important to clarify exactly what the objective is. It is one thing to aim to open the door and another to want to simply leave the room. Once you know your objective then there must be an obstacle to achieving your desire. This is the problem. So the door won't open, for example. Again, the problem must be specific. The door being locked is different from it being painted shut, because different problems will require different solutions. Let's say it's locked. In normal life, if all goes well, I simply take the key from my pocket and unlock the door. Problem solved. But let's say I don't have the key. How do I open the door? Again, in normal life, I might try some normal solutions. Push the door. Doesn't work. Call for help. No answer. In clowning, the rule of three states that we can do something twice but that the third time it must be in some way surprising, unexpected, ingenious, strange, excessive, inappropriate . . . in other words, funny. In finding a solution, this rule translates easily into two first attempts that are 'normal', but which fail, followed by a third solution which is successful and taken from the many categories of 'what clowns do' which we have been examining.

The dynamics of problem-solving also give us two added categories of unexpected behaviour: 'a clown is someone who finds complicated solutions to simple problems, and very simple solutions to complicated problems' (Eisenberg 2011).

The 'rule of three' isn't a hard-and-fast law, but it is based on an observation of how we understand and how we learn. The first time we encounter something is, well . . . the first time. The second time we encounter the same thing – in the example above, the second encounter with a door that won't open – it is a repetition of the first time which confirms what we observed initially. For whatever reason, we tend to draw conclusions from observing the same thing twice. We assume that it is 'true' or 'real'. One person seeing a ghost may be hallucinating but two people seeing the ghost means it's really there. As we only need two occurrences to convince us of something, another repetition would be superfluous. An audience is already expecting the same thing again, so to deliver this would merely confirm their expectations, which would be, frankly, boring. Having learned our lesson (that the door is definitely not opening), we must try something special. Or something special must happen to us. This could be any number of things: the door opens alone when we are not trying or not looking; or we use dynamite to open it – an excessive solution which destroys the whole door in the process. What then generates more clown action is a new problem, preferably created by the last solution. So we now have no door, so it's cold. What's our solution for that? And so on.

One more thing: not only is the surprising solution to be drawn from the category of the unexpected, erroneous or inappropriate; the problem itself is, by definition, 'wrong'. Our expectation is what we consider to be normal. When it isn't, you have a problem. Identifying wrongness means identifying a problem. Or, the clearer and more narrowly defined are our expectations and rules of behaviour, the more likely they are to be over-turned, and the more problems we are likely to encounter. Highly rule-bound systems generate more 'mistakes'. To put it simplistically, it is easier (in the sense that it is more probable or likely) to be a clown in a regime which is authoritarian rather than libertarian. This explains why clown students have more fun going into a posh department store and asking for non-existent products (the usual answer from the attendant being, 'We don't have any in at the moment but we're expecting a delivery') than they do trying to draw attention to themselves by acting like fools amongst a teeming crowd of holiday-makers. This also vindicates both Clay and Gaulier's warnings that clowns don't do well in the street.

Chaplin comments that

> My means of contriving comedy plot was simple. It was the process of getting people in and out of trouble.
>
> (1964: 227)

As a clown script-writer, then, you are looking for problems. But the clowns themselves 'are foremost problem-solvers' (Eisenberg 2011). Whereas what the audience sees are the failures, as in this sequence from Avner's show *Exceptions to Gravity*:

Avner is sweeping up a mess which is on the stage. He shakes a cigarette packet to get a cigarette, but it jumps out and falls onto the floor. He bends down to pick it up and put it into his mouth, but the packet facing downwards means all the cigarettes now fall out. He picks them up but they keep falling as he picks more up. Finally gathering them all, the broom he is holding drops to the ground. He throws the cigarettes into the pile of rubbish and continues sweeping. Pausing to light the cigarette in his mouth, he searches for a light, takes out a large box of matches from his pocket, opens the box which, being upside down, lets all the matches fall to the ground, too. He bends to pick up a match but his cardigan snags on the top of the broom handle and doesn't let him reach the floor. Unhooking himself, he gets a match, strikes it but it doesn't light. Striking a second match on the box makes the box itself fly out of his hands to the floor. Bending to pick up the box, his foot kicks the box further away. He takes the cigarette from his mouth and puts it behind his ear, seemingly in order to be better able to solve the matchbox problem (an action which goes unnoticed by the audience, but which is an essential set-up for later). He stamps on the matchbox to stop it escaping and picks it up. Now he lights a match successfully but, putting his fingers to his lips to hold the cigarette while he lights it, he finds that it is now longer in his mouth. Searching for the cigarette in his pockets, he finally discovers it behind his ear, just too late, as the lighted match has burned down and burns his fingers. No match, no lighted cigarette. He returns to sweeping but the broom falls off the handle, leading to another picking up and dropping sequence involving three objects: broom head, broom handle and hat. (Three objects are good for this, as we only have two hands, leaving one object to fall.) The hat ends up on the broom handle, out of sight and reach. He balances the stick on his forehead, the hat on the top, knocks the stick away and the hat falls onto his head. After some more problems sticking the two pieces of broom back together, which he solves by licking the end of the handle to make it stick, he picks up the litter by hand, scrunching it into a ball, and then opening it out into a single sheet.

(My transcription from video.)

MAGIC, SURPRISE AND TOMMY COOPER

The final two solutions are the most extraordinary, which is appropriate in order to end a number, as they draw the largest applause and act as a climax. They are both from non-clown techniques which are often used in this way (if you have those skills): the stick balancing and hat-onto-head bit from circus, and the paper trick from magic. From a clown perspective, both these disciplines provide surprising solutions – ways of doing things which seem beyond the norm and beyond the reach of normal mortals.

Magic makes achievable those outcomes which in the real physical world are impossible solutions. Magic here performs a similar function to a trick prop. It allows for something to happen in reality, or so it seems, that can normally only happen in our imaginations. For example, the Rastelli clowns, inheritors of the Fratellini style in many ways, have one clown playing a tuba whilst another puts a lighted stick of dynamite into the bell end of the instrument and stands back to see the result. The explosion sends the bell flying off the tuba into the air, landing perfectly on top of the waiting clown's head. It is something we could imagine, and is as such still logical to us, despite being normally impossible. Brass instruments are commonly associated with explosions and substances being shot from them, partly because of their shape, which resembles a shotgun or a cannon, and partly because of their sound, which is explosive, depending on pressurised air for the instrument to be played. With each instrument we will imagine different logical-but-impossible outcomes, depending on their nature and how they produce their sound.

The other way of achieving these impossible results is through cartoon animation and trick photography, of course. In *Hic-cup Pup* (1954), when Spike the dog rams a trumpet down on Tom the cat's head, not only does Tom's head pop up out of the other end but it appears tiny, in proportion to the mouthpiece, which is smaller than the bell which rests on Tom's shoulders. In a way, reality is being falsified in order to look more like how we would imagine it to be.

Rowan Atkinson draws parallels between jokes, which 'undermine the normal laws of our existence' (Atkinson 1992), and magic. His main category of magic as comedy is that of 'appearances and disappearance':

> a lot of visual jokes are based on people suddenly appearing or disappearing. The sudden appearance and the sudden disappearance are important elements in slapstick. If someone falls over it is funnier if they disappear at the same time.
>
> (1992)

Of course, a clown magician, or someone failing to do magic well, is a different question. Here what is interesting is the clown's unconvincingness, their inability to lie. The clown will most of the time be a victim of reality rather than a creator of illusions. Here, the magic does not function as something 'better than ordinary reality'; instead, reality keeps bursting through and ruining the illusion. Tommy Cooper's endless series of unrelated tricks are constant flops, although there are occasional moments of success, when he is one step ahead of us. His biographer, John Fisher, cites Kenneth Tynan's analysis that it is this clown-ness – Cooper's acceptance of failure – which put him in a different comedy league:

> The most important young critic in the country, Kenneth Tynan went out of his way to eulogize him in the *Evening Standard*, describing him as our best new clown: 'Cooper is the hulking, preposterous conjuror, who is always in a jelly of hysterics at the collapse of his own tricks. Convulsed by his own incompetence, holding his sides, he staggers helplessly from trick to trick; no man was ever less surprised by failure. Cooper, you see, has a distinct attitude towards life; a stoic attitude, a gurgling awareness of the futility of human effort. And this is what raises him above the crowd.'
>
> (Fisher 2006: 97)

THE NARRATIVE OF CIRCUS SKILLS, VIRTUOSITY AND
ANTI-VIRTUOSITY: YENGIBAROV, KEATON AND HARRY LANGDON

From a clown point of view, circus skills have something in common with magic in that they are a seemingly impossible manipulation of reality. Whereas the normal person, if they were to balance a broom on their head which has on the top a waistcoat, a scarf and a walking stick, would get all the objects falling on them, a clown – in this case Leonid Yengibarov – simply knocks away the broom handle and the next second he is wearing the waistcoat, scarf and hat, and carrying the stick

Circus manipulation of objects is not only already a 'strange' or 'unexpected' way to behave as judged by the norm, and hence already potentially in a useful category for clowns, but is more specifically an excessive solution to the problem of getting those objects to do what you want them to do. The skill used is more than required to achieve the objective. In this sense it is virtuosic. The performer has more skill than is necessary. The converse is the clumsy clown, who has less skill and dexterity than is required in order to complete a task.

When Buster Keaton in *Neighbors* (1920) plans to elope with a girl who lives on the third storey of a three-storey building, his solution to the problem of getting the girl out without her father noticing is to go through the window – not an unsurprising choice, and one that we are used to seeing in such a plot. But his means of entry into that third-storey window is completely unusual, virtuosic and yet logical. Appearing at the third-storey window in the house opposite, he climbs out at the same time two others come out of the second- and first-storey windows below. They form a three-high (each standing on each other's shoulders) and cross the street, all three entering the respective windows opposite. A moment later they re-appear, Buster (at the top) carrying a huge suitcase, and the three go back across the street and into their house. They return to the girl's house in the same manner and Buster carries her out on his shoulders. They start the journey back but the father comes out of the door onto the street so they go back into the girl's house. The father, forgetting something, also goes back into his house and the three-high plus girl over shoulder come out again and run off round the corner. And off they go, passing through scaffolding, over a washing line, where the middle man gets caught and the others keep going down the street until the bottom man disappears down a man-hole, leaving Buster carrying the girl, until they too fall down into a cellar belonging to the judge who was to marry them, who does so then and there.

Joyce Rheuban in her in-depth study *Harry Langdon – The Comedian as Metteur-en-Scène* (1983) looks at Langdon's dramaturgy with reference to his contemporaries and other major stars of North American silent comedy: Charlie Chaplin, Buster Keaton and Harold Lloyd. In Keaton, we typically find a 'long-distance dash [...] an exhibition of strength, speed, and endurance' (1983: 195). This obstacle course forms the narrative of a Keaton film:

> Keaton's performance demonstrates his comic character's ingenuity, perceptual acuity, superior intellect, and Keaton's own physical agility and acrobatic expertise. These qualities are displayed in comic situations in which Buster solves the problems that confront him and adjusts to the abrupt changes of fortune and circumstances that constantly beset him.
>
> (Rheuban 1983: 194)

Lloyd also uses physical skill and feats of strength to progress past problems, but his is often a 'vertical ascent' (1983: 195). As with Keaton, the dramaturgy is problem-based:

> Lloyd describes how, in the 'building' of a gag sequence [...] 'one gag led into the other.'
> [...]
> The attraction, or feat, of overcoming a vertically or horizontally plotted obstacle course is central to the narrative structure of a Harold Lloyd film [...] It also provides the basic architectural structure of the thrill comedy.
>
> (Rheuban 1983: 194)

Simon Louvish considers this reliance on problem-solving by Keaton and Lloyd to be 'quintessentially American':

> their need for problem resolution through action – Keaton's tremendous chases; Lloyd's rush through life's perils to win true love – are defining icons of 1920s America, the urgent social climb, the necessity of speed.
>
> (2001: 223)

In contrast, Langdon in *Tramp, Tramp, Tramp* (1926a) 'wins the [walking] race in his own slow time and only in spite of himself' (Rheuban 1983: 196). Langdon does not act consciously on the problems that beset him, lacking the skill, either physical or mental, to overcome them. His films therefore lack the narrative-dominance of Keaton's and Lloyd's, instead being composed of a loose succession of situations.

Rheuban considers that Langdon is unique amongst the major comedians of the genre in his abandonment of virtuosity. Her tracing of the development of his performances from his beginnings in vaudeville in 1906, where he created the character and style previous to moving into cinema in 1923, leads her to believe that, rather than through any lack of skill, this was part of a wider process and development as an artist:

> In the evolution of Langdon's vaudeville act [...] Langdon gradually reduced the comedy talk, jokes and gags.
>
> (1983: 170)

For high skill Langdon did indeed possess, as in the rare example of his trick bicycle routine which occurs in *Long Pants* (1927).

BEYOND CHASES: MACK SENNETT, LANGDON AND CHAPLIN

Ignoring certain conventions of comedy in fashion at the time, Langdon resisted the dominant model of the Sennett comedy 'of broad farce, fast-paced action, and slapstick violence' (Rheuban 1983: 33). There are no chases in Langdon's films, for instance. Rheuban cites the director, Hal Roach:

> He would rehearse a scene exactly the way you wanted him to play it. Great! And as soon as you started the camera it was like slow motion.
>
> (1983: 38)

And Edward Bernds, one of Langdon's writers, considered that

> the moment you tried to speed him up and make an ordinary two-reel comic out of him, you were dead. He wasn't funny unless he could pace himself.
>
> (1983: 39)

Another rebel against the chase-dominated style was Chaplin. In his autobiography he quotes Sennett as saying:

> 'We have no scenarios – we get an idea then follow the natural sequence of events until it leads up to a chase, which is the essence of our comedy.' This method was edifying but personally I hated a chase. It dissipates one's personality; little as I knew about movies, I knew that nothing transcended personality.
>
> (Chaplin 1964: 151)

But Chaplin was in fact a master of the chase and in his early years in cinema did follow the Sennett way, taking a simple situation, such as a park or a café, and building as many gags as possible into the context.

> Although I hadn't a story, I ordered the crew to build an ornate cafe set. When I was lost for a gag or an idea a café would always supply one.
>
> (Chaplin 1964: 180)

But there would soon come a time when gags were not the be-all-and-end-all for Chaplin, as his attention turned to more complex structures. Speaking about *A Dog's Life* (1918),

> I was beginning to think of comedy in a structural sense, and to become conscious of its architectural form. Each sequence implied the next sequence, all of them relating to the whole. [...] If a gag interfered with the logic of events, no matter how funny it was, I would not use it.
>
> (Chaplin 1964: 224)

In any case, as Simon Louvish points out, 'Keystone movies were, by 1915, extensively scripted' (2003: 126). Even the early years were not so free:

From the beginning, there had been writers and gag-men on the payroll, despite the mythology that Keystone films were made up as they went along.

(Louvish 2003: 80)

As Chaplin's plots gain more presence, the density of gags decreases,

with each succeeding comedy the tramp was growing more complex. Sentiment was beginning to percolate through the character. This became a problem because he was bound by the limits of slapstick. This may sound pretentious, but slapstick demands a most exacting psychology.
[...]
As my skill in story construction developed, so it restricted my comedy freedom.

(Chaplin 1964: 225)

This hybrid form had its doubters, as the writer, Gouverneur Morris, commented on *The Kid* (1921):

'It won't work. The form must be pure, either slapstick or drama; you cannot mix them, otherwise one element of your story will fail'

We had quite a dialectical discussion about it. I said that the transition from slapstick to sentiment was a matter of feeling and discretion in arranging sequences.

(1964: 252)

In the final scene of *City Lights* (1931), when the flower-seller has been cured of her blindness and is now working in a flower shop, we first see Charlie pass by the spot where she used to work. Then the rich car-owner enters the girl's shop. Recognising the sound of the door closing, she thinks 'he', her love, has returned. But he leaves without even noticing her. The narrative has worked its way round and is now ready for one big climax. Chaplin, more tramp-like than ever, wanders past the shops, as the boy news vendors shoot peas at the back of his neck. So far it is pure sentiment, no gag in sight. But just then, as Chaplin turns to the boys, out of the florist's doorway behind him comes a woman sweeping with a broom. He is moving towards her without looking. Surely there must be a fall here? But no, Chaplin turns as she goes inside. Instead, he spots a flower in the gutter that she has swept out of the shop. He bends to pick it up and the boys take their chance to pull the ripped seat of his pants. Surely now there will be some rough and tumble? But no, the boys run off and their practical joking ends, although it awakens the attention and laughter of the girl and woman in the shop. Instead of generating gags, each opportunity for something to happen is generating a further step in the narrative. Only now, when we see in the same shot Chaplin and the girl behind him through the shop window, and we know they will meet again, does Chaplin allow himself a little joke, blowing his nose on the piece of ripped material he has retrieved from the boys. Our laughter is secondary, both to the girl who laughs at him kindly and to our anticipation of a further crescendo of sentiment. From this point until the end of the film, there are no more gags, nor even potential for them, as they would only obstruct the emotional consistency of the story. The girl, handing Charlie a flower, only now recognises him by touch, from before, when she was blind. And, like us, she moves from laughter to serious emotion. The final frames are Chaplin's own smile, barely breaking through the intensity of the emotion. And Chaplin's discretion in arranging sequences of slapstick and sentiment comes to a triumphant climax.

Figure 15   Charlie Chaplin with Virginia Cherrill and Florence Lee in *City Lights*
Source: Screenshot, © Roy Export S.A.S.

As we can, see, Chaplin's rejection of chase-based comedy is not an attempt to escape narrative, as in Langdon's case, but a move towards character-based rather than action-based narrative.

VIRTUOSIC PANTOMIME AND THE BOOB

Going back to virtuosity, or Langdon's lack of it, the contrast with Chaplin's virtuosity is not so much a question of narrative but of gestural language:

> Langdon's performance lacks the density of allusion, articulateness, and psychological subtlety of Charlie Chaplin's pantomimic acting.
>
> (Rheuban 1983: 110)

Rheuban qualifies Chaplin's mime as 'dense' and 'articulate'. It is 'dense' in that many meanings are crammed into a short space of time and action.

And it is 'articulate' in that one element may denote and connote multiple references. Chaplin typically uses a kind of 'metaphorical pantomime', where an action is performed or an object is used as if it were another action or object, similar in function but from another context.

Take, for example, the sequence in *The Pawnshop* (1916) when Chaplin examines a clock that a customer has brought into the shop. Chaplin first shakes the clock and puts it to his ear. So far, normal. Next he listens to the clock using a stethoscope, as if he were a doctor listening to a patient's heart. Then a few taps, also doctor-like, followed by flicking the bells. Then he hits it with a hammer and listens again. Using a drill to make a hole in the clock, he then opens it as if opening a tin of food, with gestures appropriate to a chef. He smells the contents, and his facial reaction is almost of disgust. Having examined inside with an eyepiece used by jewellers, he squirts oil inside, as if it were a piece of machinery less delicate than a clock. Using pliers, he wrenches out some of the inner mechanism of the clock, perhaps as if extracting a tooth. Listening again, he takes a hammer and chisel in order to get the rest out. He stretches the long spring of the clock mechanism along his arm, as if measuring a length of rope or cloth. Listening to the clock again to see if the extracted parts were the culprit, he is not yet satisfied. He takes the hammer again, in a sequence of flamboyant juggling moves, far too skilful for his purpose, and ends the movement by banging the hammer on the counter and nearly hitting the customer's hand. Now he looks for a piece of the mechanism which is on the counter, as if doing a jigsaw puzzle. He looks at it, with the eyepiece placed in his other eye, then uses it to wind up what is left of the clock and listens to the clock again. The pieces on the counter move around as if by magic. He tries to stop them moving around by using the hammer to hit them, as if killing mice. Finally he resorts to the oil gun, spraying them as if killing insects. They cease. He casually begins to put the pieces back in the clock, but finding there is no room puts the rest in the customer's hat which is on the counter and gives the customer his hat with a shake of the head which says, 'I'm sorry, I can't do anything for you.' The customer protests, and Chaplin gives him a blow to the head with the hammer, and he stumbles out of the shop. (My transcription from the film.)

Virtually every gag is metaphorical, denoting one thing and connoting another, with very few exceptions, such as the eyepiece put in the wrong eye. This is not an isolated routine:

> This density of reference is not reserved in Chaplin's work merely for set pieces [...]. Nearly every movement or gesture that Chaplin makes is either a mimed allusion or a demonstration of his technical skill, or both.
>
> (Rheuban 1983: 112)

In contrast, in Langdon's *Three's a Crowd* (1927b), the sequence where Harry defrosts a frozen nappy 'does not include a single joke based on a mimed metaphor or other double meaning' (Rheuban 1983: 112).

Chaplin's virtuosity is not just a function of his style of pantomime but is the way he places himself at the centre of his films. We saw how in *The Circus* (1928) Chaplin unwittingly gets an audition, and a job, as a clown with the circus. Although he appears to be unaware of what is happening to him or why, his success is in fact due to what we see as his superior skill compared with those around him. 'Charlie is a "sensation" and becomes the "hit of the show," as the titles assure us' (Rheuban 1983: 111). In *The Strong Man*, Langdon, when called upon to stand in for the drunken strongman, is a complete flop. In a similar situation, Chaplin gets an ovation and star status with his successfully improvised nonsense song in *Modern Times* (1936). And Keaton's performance, '[e]ven in situations [. . .] in which he is behaving like an inept boob [. . .] involves a feat of physical strength and coordination that is equal to or greater than that required by the proper response' (1983: 110), as in *College* (1927), where his attempts at sports are all wrong, but often still done with strength and facility, such as his two-footed jump and dive over a high-jump bar, landing in a head-stand with his head buried in the sand.

So, if we remove highly motivated problem-driven narrative (Keaton or Lloyd) and dense pantomimic virtuosity (Chaplin), what is left? The comic ineptitude of the 'boob', which in Langdon's case 'often extends to the complete physical debilitation of inertia or paralysis' (Rheuban 1983: 110). Rheuban characterises this as:

> Harry's voluntary actions appear to be governed by a disjunction between his perceptual and cognitive faculties and his motor responses.
>
> (1983: 59)

In simpler terms, he fails to achieve physical tasks. Langdon's means are in fact very simple. A large number of his physical errors consist of going too far or not far enough, either in space or in time. For example, he offers his hand to shake whilst standing too far away from the other person (*The Strong Man*). He bends his knees slightly in order to get a closer look at someone he is already very close to (*Tramp, Tramp, Tramp*). He runs for safety only after a falling tree has hit the ground (*Boobs in the Wood*). He throws a horseshoe extending his arm too far and leaving it in that position some time after letting it go (*Long Pants*). Some gestures never reach their end, as when a salute becomes a wave (*All Night Long*).

On the interpersonal and emotional level, Langdon is similarly a flop. He cannot be in love and eat at the same time. His attempts at aggression never hit the target, his fist never reaching the other man's face (*The Strong Man*). He reacts with utter understatement to a passionate kiss (*Long Pants*). He fails to respond to others' calls (*Tramp, Tramp, Tramp* and other films). Any communication he does undertake is either one-sided – talking to a headless mannequin – or goes on too long, continuing to talk to a cow when it has already become a steak (*Soldier Man*).

> The animate human antagonists to whom Harry addresses himself are, as often as not, either preoccupied and completely indifferent to Harry or are themselves unconscious and/or inert.
>
> (Rheuban 1983: 68)

Importantly for our understanding of clown, no attempt is made to justify these errors in the framework of the psychology of a character. This is more (or less) than a 'character'. Langdon gives an impression of absence, and it is the absence of a character.

> Langdon's comic character is described by this performance in such a way that the sort of interpretative speculation that is often practiced on and provoked by Chaplin's films is effectively discouraged in Langdon's films.
>
> (Rheuban 1983: 117)

Langdon is 'psychologically opaque' and

> provides the viewer with no nucleus in terms of characterisation from which to generate [...] presumptions.
>
> (Rheuban 1983: 117)

Rheuban links Langdon's comic non-character with the formal structure of his films:

> Narrative values were never significant in Langdon's comedies because of the barely coherent comic character that Langdon's performance defined.
>
> (Rheuban 1983: 47)

This is another case of clowns not driving narrative, as we saw with Sedita's Dumb One. Simon Louvish, in *Keystone – The Life and Clowns of Mack Sennett,* considers Langdon to be

> a throw-back, in some ways, to the halcyon age of the circus clown with his painted smile and melancholic interior.
>
> (2003: 225)

This situates Langdon squarely in the auguste rather than the eccentric camp, in contrast to Keaton, and of course, Avner the 'Eccentric', following Rémy's definition of the eccentric's means of operation as 'to accumulate obstacles in sufficient quantity to have the merit of triumphing over them for once' (Rémy 1945: 369).

Rheuban's analyses in particular thus give us a spectrum of clowns, ranging from the virtuosic/plot/action/obstacle-driven (Keaton), via the virtuosic/emotion-driven (Chaplin), to the non-virtuosic plot/action/character-less (Langdon). This also gives us another way of understanding to what extent a particular clown is, or seems to be, either inside or outside the fictional world or context. The more engaged in plot/action/narrative, the more 'in' the clown seems. In this way, a clown like Langdon appears to stand aside from the world he is in, whilst Keaton appears not just involved but hyper-involved.

Chapter

14 Clown Truth

INTRODUCTION

In this chapter I take a closer look at the ideology of 'truth'. I trace the development throughout the 20th century of the vision of clowns as revealers of truth, beginning with how Copeau's idolisation of the Fratellini is important in understanding contemporary clown's alliance with notions of authenticity, despite Copeau's subsequent disillusion with clowns. I show how Lecoq's later work brought to prominence the idea that clown is personal, and how parallel developments in stand-up comedy – the so-called sick comics – were functioning on the supposition that comedy reveals personal truths. I then demonstrate how the assumption that truth can be attained becomes problematic in clowning, looking at Gaulier's vision of theatre as pretence. This 'genealogy of contemporary clown' takes us finally to examine how the old and the new might draw together, moving beyond 'contemporary clowning' and towards a fusion of the 'personal clown' with pre-Lecoquian techniques.

COPEAU AND THE PURITY OF CLOWNS

With such a range of ways in which clown performers, teachers, biographers, theorists, anthropologists, historians, critics and others explain the 'how' and 'why' of clowning, the question is, can they be brought together? Most importantly, can we reconcile the view that clown is personal and in the moment with all of the knowledge about what clowns do and how they do it?

If we follow Eli Simon's aim of being 'deeply connected to truths rather than just gags' (2009: 6), then the answer is no. This opposition sets up 'gags' to be 'untrue'. In this scheme of thinking, anything which is pre-prepared, reproducible, non-individualised or not deemed to be spontaneously occurring in the moment cannot be 'true' and therefore cannot be used. This leaves 'truths', understood as having the opposite qualities to the above, taking full responsibility for everything that happens in clowning. This includes the moment of performance, as well as the material and content of that performance.

Without denying the usefulness of making a distinction between what appears to be happening now and what looks pre-prepared, it must be said that the complete elimination of the latter from the equation is a radical step. As we have already commented, with reference to the rise of realist theatre and Popov's realist clown, the radicalism of such moves often suggests that they are not merely aesthetic but also 'sociological events' (Shepherd and Womack 1996: 251).

Many commentators consider Jacques Copeau to be seminal in his influence on 20th-century ideas about what is good and bad in acting. Mark Evans credits him with being the forerunner of physical theatre, ensemble playing, mask-work, the revival of commedia dell'arte and clowning, game-playing and so on:

> The purity and simplicity of his purpose and his work, his belief in the moral and social power of theatre, and his passionate commitment to the training of the actor's body and mind as well as their voice, have shaped and inspired the work of so many of those who followed after him, both in France and further afield. Much that is now commonplace in contemporary theatre practice can be traced directly back to the work of Copeau and his small group of collaborators during the few decades between the two World Wars. If his influence is not so clearly evident at the start of the twenty-first century, then that is in part because it is so firmly embedded in the cultural framework of the British, European and American theatre industries that it has become taken for granted.
>
> (Evans 2006: 2)

For Copeau, artistic reform implied ethical reform, and he demanded 'moral integrity and artistic rigour from the critics' (Evans 2006: 7). This 'moral improvement' in the theatre necessitated the eradication of 'cabotinage' ('ham-acting', 'histrionics' or 'theatricality'). In a sense, this is simply a repetition of was being claimed on behalf of 'realist' acting some decades earlier. The emphasis is still on 'truth', which is placed in opposition to 'ham':

> What Copeau could not bear was the empty theatricality of the commercial theatres, where tricks, traditional stage 'business', hackneyed dialogue and over-simplified ideas of character and motivation brought popular success but revealed little of consequence about the nature of human existence.
>
> (Evans 2006: 7)

This desire for truth permeates Copeau's writing and those who comment on it. The vocabulary employed about the revolution to come suggests a cleansing of the past: purity, natural, unforced, simple, honest, unsullied, sincerity, wholeness, spontaneity. On the opposing team we have words like artificial, empty, theatricality, tricks, falseness, prostituting, vulgarity, lies, commercial, parasites, disease and debased.

Copeau never seems quite sure which camp to place clowns in:

> The Revue artistes, the Music Hall comedians – especially the popular Music Hall productions which communicate very closely with their public – and the circus clowns, all are more or less degenerated improvisers.
>
> (Copeau 1990: 153)

We have already seen how Copeau idolised the Fratellini, and yet he was clearly in two minds about them:

> I love these clowns. The gaiety of their faces, the delight they take in what they are doing
>
> [...]
>
> But, in spite of everything, there is a little of the routine in what they do, and one feels they could be even more extraordinary.
>
> (Copeau 1990: 162)

Consequently he restricted them to teaching his students acrobatics and juggling. The greater task of teaching improvisation, for which he had praised them, was denied them:

> When Copeau hired the Fratellini to teach at his theater school he had them instruct the young students in acrobatics and juggling, leaving such intellectual topics as form and structure in acting technique to his son-in-law Jean Dasté. With all his admiration for the skill of the Fratellini, Copeau's attitude toward them was essentially patronizing.
>
> (McManus 2003: 33)

But Copeau was not simply continuing the artistic demands of realist theatre. His focus on the training of the actor, and on ensemble performing, shifted the emphasis towards the actor as the prime creator in the theatrical event and away from the writer. The historic duality between writer and actor disappeared. The end of the 19th century had already re-situated the playwright as an 'artist' in their own right, often in the dual role of 'writer-director', whose will should be obeyed by the actors. In one way, Copeau can be seen as heralding a parallel counter-move on the part of the actor, claiming their rights to 'artist' status too. In another way, his notion of the ensemble brings about the possibility of actors, writers and directors working in equal partnership, not in rivalry as before but towards a unified artistic goal.

> The modern notion of the playwright-in-residence is a direct legacy of Copeau's practice, and whilst a true spirit of collaboration is still far from the norm within many company structures Copeau would certainly have approved of the integrated collaborative approaches of companies as Joint Stock/Out of Joint and Théâtre de Complicité, where the writer, the director, the designer and the performers come together towards the achievement of Copeau's 'single act'.
>
> (Evans 2006: 50)

This power-shift thus not only gives rise to collaborative companies but also leads the way to the actor-as-author. Although there are obviously historical examples of those who wrote as well as they performed, the notion that it is now an option for everybody is new. It is not difficult to see how this opportunity may wed itself to the mistrust of the 'pre-prepared' and the 'fake'. This new equation gives us the result that what the performer produces without preparing is, by definition, 'true'. And if it is 'true', then it is not only an option but also an obligation. The performer, consequently, *must* 'have something to say'. We now have the actor as a kind of 'super-artist', not the old singing-dancing-acting all-rounder, but a performer-writer-director all rolled into the same body.

LECOQ AND THE PERSONAL CLOWN

It is important to unravel how we got to Lecoq's 'body of the performer' which 'has something to say'. When Evans mentions, in relation to Copeau, that 'his legacy has become so pervasive that it is in danger of becoming invisible' (2006: 151), he is warning against an undervaluation of Copeau's work. But that influence has also led us up blind alleys, one of which says that clowns must necessarily produce their own material directly from their inner clown. This has left many stranded and incapable of fulfilling the demands of the *acteur-auteur*, as Lecoq terms it.

In Chamberlain and Yarrow's *Jacques Lecoq and the British Theatre* (2002), Simon Murray, quoting students' reflections on this method, attests to its limitations:

> I think the Lecoq set-up breeds the fallacy that everyone has the potential to be a 'writer'. The truth of the matter is that every actor has the potential to make an individual contribution to a show.
>
> (Murray 2002: 32)

> If you've done Lecoq, you can probably devise a quite funny and interesting five minutes around how to make a cup of tea, whereas another writer might pass over that as an unimportant incident. Of course, that may become something wonderful, surreal and dreamlike, but there might be some questions posed at the end about the value of the writing. It will always be a problem in theatre of what you are saying and why you are saying it.
>
> (Murray 2002: 34)

> We worked for about 10 months on a show which brought to light all the problems of working in a Lecoq style. As a group we had a strong resistance to having a director. It was very democratic which I now think is extremely hard – impossible, if everyone has an equal say if nobody has a final veto, and no-one has enough vision to see globally where the whole thing is going.
>
> (Murray 2002: 37)

And to its successes:

You are good when you find this *quelque chose à dire* (something to say). It's a phrase he uses which I think is very interesting, because coming from my background I had always connected hearing something to say with being political. But Lecoq's *quelque chose à dire* is a very personal thing. When you are communicating something effective about your world – or yourself then you are finding something to say. Everyone has something to say.

(Murray 2002: 39)

Ironically, the perception of theatre critics, at least in Britain, has been that Lecoq-inspired work is anything but personal. Murray cites Michael Billington's judgement of Theatre de Complicité, given on BBC2's *The Late Show* in 1992:

They have […] bred in me – and I think in some others as well – a kind of counter reaction which is whether the moral content of theatre is being subordinated to a display of technique … it was sometimes a feeling that technique was actually overlaying content.

(Murray 2002: 32)

Of course, the idea of the new as true and the old as false isn't new. And as everything that once was new becomes old one day, the heirs to the Copeau–Lecoq tradition may today be seen by some to indulge in 'empty technique'. This should be warning enough that the idea that clown or actor training is in some way embarked on an onward evolutionary march towards truth is a fallacy.

Historical examples of this assumption, that acting technique is in continuous positive evolution, are too numerous to mention. Nicholas Dromgoole devotes a whole book, *Performance Style and Gesture in Western Theatre* (2007), to unravelling his puzzlement:

The more interested I became in theatre history, the more puzzling I found it that nobody seemed to have noticed, much less tried to analyse, something distinctly odd about the development of British theatre. When the young actor David Garrick rose to fame on the eighteenth-century stage, he was hailed as being much more 'natural' than the previous generation. For close on forty years, I have been tucking into splendid lunches and dinners at the Garrick Club, surrounded by contemporary pictures by Zoffany and others of the great actor in his various roles, and one thing is very clear. To twenty-first-century eyes he was very far from being 'natural'. On the contrary, he looks incredibly mannered, exaggerated and stylised. What was even more puzzling was that as the 19th Century proceeded, each new star of the acting profession (Keats, Macready, Irving) was also hailed as being satisfyingly more 'natural' in comparison with the heavily old-fashioned and stylized manners of his immediate predecessors. What on earth, I wondered, was really going on? How was it possible? Could distinguished writers, critics and fellow actors have really been as misguided as they now seem to have been? Nor did it stop there. Sir Donald Wolfit, my first introduction to Shakespeare's leading roles, and indeed to Shakespeare's plays, was, I have been scornfully informed by people too young to have enjoyed his performances, inclined to 'ham it up' on stage, and my later demi-gods, Lord Olivier, Sir Ralph Richardson and Sir John Gielgud, have all been equally disparaged in their turn. This book is, in effect, an attempt to answer my puzzlement. Hopefully it involves much more than that.

(Dromgoole 2007: 7)

The simple answer about Garrick is that it was not for his gestures (as recorded in the painting) that he was deemed more 'naturalistic' but for his vocal delivery. Dromgoole also refers to pictorial evidence for his puzzlement over Edmund Kean being regarded as more 'natural'. Here the answer is more complex, and perhaps more interesting. In the age of Romanticism when emotion was a sign of 'nature' in a person, the expression of emotion signified something more 'human' and was therefore an indicator of being more 'natural'. The lesson is clear. Each age understands the sign of truth in its own way. The actor and the clown merely reflect that.

REVEALING PERSONAL TRUTHS: THE SICK COMICS

Whilst Lecoq's clowns had 'something to say', stand-up comedy's 'sick comics' told stories that revealed personal truths rather than jokes that could be bought and sold on the open market:

For comics who started before Mort Sahl and the rest of his generation introduced the idea that stand-up was about expressing the self, the idea that truth could be funny without being varnished by fictionalised jokework was unthinkable.

(Double 2005: 98)

Whilst Lecoq's clowns only retained the red nose from the clown's outlandish wardrobe, Mort Sahl, debuting in 1953 in San Francisco,

eschewed smart suits in favour of slacks, and a casual sweater worn over an open-necked shirt. His delivery was just as informal, and his subject matter was relevant to a young, hip, beatnik audience.

(Double 2005: 25)

In parallel with Lecoq's vulnerable clown, who makes us laugh by failing in front of us, the new comedian reveals their troubled inner truths in public. Even Bob Monkhouse, ostensibly more of a joke-machine than a truth-teller, acknowledges the debt:

[Lenny] Bruce showed me the trick of taking my worst moments and using them to amuse people, turning tears of despair into tears of laughter. It's a kind of therapy that's seen me get over a lot of woe by sharing it in the form of comedy.

(1998: 17)

Of all those who followed Sahl, Lenny Bruce took his mission more seriously than any other, persecuted by the law, his life and career shattered as a result. Despite the undeniable reality of his fate, Bruce's act also shows up how truth-telling, defined as speaking the unspeakable, is, in the end, just a game with the audience. Monkhouse recalls Bruce's debut in London in 1962, at the Establishment, the private club set up by Peter Cook and others to avoid the censorship of public performance in place at the time. Bruce toyed with his audience, first reeling off a list of swearwords, ignoring their supposed shock value or any potential they might have to make people laugh or giggle. The audience lapped it up, until:

> 'OK, you're all so hip, I think maybe you're ready for the big one. Here we go!'
>
> Bruce feigned blowing his nose into his hand and wiping the result on the back wall.
>
> 'Snot!'
>
> A stunned silence at first. Then a woman's cry of 'Shame!' And within a count of three, the crowd tuned into a lynch mob. Amid the angry outcry, someone threw a glass at Bruce and it smashed on the stage. A fist fight broke out near me and I saw Bruce being ushered from the stage as the mob began to demand their money back.
>
> Bruce had tested their brave new tolerance to destruction.
>
> (Monkhouse 1998: 16)

Speaking the truth in public is a game with conventions.

Just how far we as spectators can be taken in by these 'truth-effects' is indicated by the assumption that Edmund Kean was 'spontaneous':

Some of Kean's contemporary critics went too far and praised him for his 'spontaneity' on stage, as though he were intuitively reacting for the first time to events on stage, as if quite carried away by the emotion of the moment. Kean wrote to Garrick's widow:

> These people don't understand their business: they give me credit where I don't deserve it, and pass over passages on which I have bestowed the utmost care and attention. Because my style is easy and natural they think I don't study and they talk about the 'sudden impulse of genius'. There is no such thing as impulsive acting; all is premeditated and studied beforehand. A man may act better or worse on a particular night [...] but although the execution may not be so brilliant, the conception is the same.
>
> (Hawkins 1869: 208–209)

GAULIER AND THE THEATRE OF PRETENCE

If we abandon the search for truth, then, and take Gaulier's far subtler concept of 'pleasure', the 'true' versus 'fake' opposition disappears. 'Pleasure' is related as much to 'pretence' as gags are. Let us return for a moment to laughter in order to examine in practice how this might work.

If the performer's own laughter is an indicator of self-ridicule, of their own pleasure in clown, and a catalyst for more clowning to occur, then the audience's laughter can be seen not only as their own pleasure in witnessing the clown's self-ridicule but also as an indicator that the clown should continue. In other words, it is the signal that the audience gives permission to the clown to go on. This gives rise to another set of laughter-driven exercises, the most basic of which is the following. The clown must cross the space in front of the audience, but each step requires a real laugh from the audience. Audience laughs – clown steps – audience laughs – clown steps – and so on, until the space is crossed. In addition, if too much time passes without a laugh – let's say six seconds – then the clown must take a step back towards where they started. Interestingly, these steps back often stimulate the biggest laughs. Why? Because they are admissions of failure. Realising that the audience do not want to see more, the clown gives up and starts to leave. The flop gets the laugh. In fact, leaving the stage is one of the simplest ways of training yourself to accept the flop. Many clown students have problems in genuinely admitting when it isn't funny, but the physical act of leaving often unblocks this resistance. It is fitting that the clown should be 'better when they leave'. Once you have realised this, then you can turn it around and begin, rather than end, with this flop. You can enter in the same way as you left, admitting your failure from the outset. In this way, the clown is present from the first moment and the audience laughs at your entrance.

As with the mirror exercise, this exercise can be extended into generating more complex actions. Now, instead of actual steps, each step of an action will require a laugh from the audience in order for permission to be obtained to move on to the next step. Now it might be: audience laughs – enter to centre stage – audience laughs – sit on a chair – audience laughs – stand up – audience laughs – exit. This applies equally to speech, or 'verbal actions', if you prefer. Your actions may be improvised, or they may be scripted. It is irrelevant. The script may be simple, as above, or complex, as in a Hamlet soliloquy. In the latter case you must judge how big each 'step' is – it might be one line per laugh, for example.

The realisation that the point of the exercise does not depend on whether the material is improvised or scripted is vital. It clarifies one of the areas of confusion that has arisen from the clown-as-play model. The confusion results from the discovery that the flop cannot be scripted, that the clown's relationship with the audience must be created in the moment. It is often then assumed that everything the clown does must be somehow spontaneous, that the audience should see everything coming into creation in the present, as in the most radical type of improvisation, such as Ruth Zaporah here describes:

The job of [...] improvisers is to manifest their moment-to-moment experience – not just what they're doing but how they are experiencing what they're doing: either its meaning or how it feels or both.

(unreferenced citation of Zaporah in Johnston 2006: 76)

The problem here is that unless you want to specialise in improvisation, this is difficult to attain. This makes the preparation of performances that can be repeated successfully in front of different audiences extremely problematic. So the clown student finds themselves trapped. Hooked on clowning, their material disappoints them. But when we see clearly that it is only the relationship with the audience which must be improvised, then we are freed from the obligation to constantly freely improvise our material. As long as the audience is implicated in the performance itself, giving permission to the clown to continue with their act, then that act can be as planned as you want.

BEYOND CONTEMPORARY CLOWNING: FUSING OLD AND NEW, OUTER AND INNER

This insight offers us an opportunity to redress the imbalance that has been created in clown training over the last half-century. By re-visiting methods and techniques for scripting clown, we can provide a more complete clown training. If we were to combine Atkinson's categories and principles, Bouissac's analyses and insights, Tati/Bellos on gag types and Rheuban's analysis of Chaplin/Langdon/Keaton, and use them to sort out and simplify the thousands of examples of gags from Page, Denis, commedia lazzi and others, we would be well on the way to some kind of encyclopaedia of what clowns do, how they do it and how to generate it (Davison 2009b) – a dramaturgy of clown, if you like. The idea is an old one, as Simon Louvish tells:

In the authentic mode of the old vaudevillian, Roscoe left little to the ad lib. The *New York Sun* reported in 1917:

'Mr Arbuckle has probably the most complete joke library in the world. It is being scientifically indexed and edited under the personal direction of the screen's funniest fat man.... Every joke that appears in the weekly and monthly publications is clipped and placed on Mr. Arbuckle's desk and then classified in the library...

Arbuckle built himself up as an encyclopedia of comedy, with a mastery of gags and structure.

(2003: 84)

More recently, Bob Monkhouse can lay claim to being one of the great archivists of comedy. His personal collection of thousands of videotapes, radio recordings, films and memorabilia included many lost or deleted items and has only recently been sorted (see Coward and Perry's *Bob's Full House* 2009).

An even more ambitious project would then be to combine this encyclopaedic dramaturgy with a contemporary Gaulierian clown training. If it is more common nowadays to find clown teaching based on the 'personal clown', and rare to find training focused on the externals of clown, or 'gags', even rarer is a combination of the two. Most acting schools that teach clown either incorporate it into a mixed bag of methods, as we have seen, or place it within a Lecoquian system. Specialised clown training tends to be in single-teacher schools that teach a single method, such as Pochinko or Gaulier, with the teacher taking on a kind of whiteface clown role in opposition to the student's auguste. However, when they leave, students are supposed to be self-sufficient *acteurs-auteurs*. They become, in classical clown terminology, eccentrics: '[the eccentric] is at the same time the author and the actor of the comic poem that he composes and exposes' (Rémy 1945: 369).

New challenges arise when you combine both approaches in teaching. The immediate danger is that those parts of training which are open to logical, rational analysis (the dramaturgy part), and do not depend on a personal experience on the part of the student, can appear easier to understand. And logically so, as they are by definition understandable, just by thinking about them. One can comprehend how a gag works, for example, from an explanation of its dynamics. The student, understanding the rational explanation, then has the feeling that they have learned. Students often comment with regard to this kind of class that 'the teacher explained it very well' or 'I understand clearly'. The same student may then contrast this experience of learning with an exercise in the 'flop' where they are being constantly told they are not funny but, failing to accept their failure, they remain unfunny and conclude that 'I don't understand' or even that 'the teacher didn't explain what we were supposed to do'. But it is in the nature of this part of clown teaching that the student encounters the feeling of 'I don't know what to do' or 'I don't understand'. For this state is the clown state: not knowing what to do, the clown does it anyway. In terms of other modern educational models, the class on gags fits our expectations neatly. The teacher explains what the student is going to learn, the student understands, the teacher explains how it works, the student understands, the student tries for themselves, the teacher corrects the student, the student understands, the student does better, the teacher praises the student. But the class on the flop is a kind of anti-education, at least in modern terms. It is driven by a lack of understanding, stupidity and failure. For most students, this is new, as Clara Cenoz of the Escola de Clown de Barcelona explains:

Clown requires a destructuring of our usual way of learning things. Clown is learned through experience and observation. To do that you have to let go and not be asking questions all the time, not want to know things beforehand. We're not used to that. It implies being very active as a student, which we are not used to either. Students are asked to experience and to feel and then afterwards to extract their conclusions, as one should do in real life. We need to let ourselves be surprised by ourselves. And to draw positive conclusions, rather than negative ones like 'this is difficult'. Dealing with their resistance and saying yes to everything is a shock for some people.

(Cenoz 2011)

No amount of student's questions or teacher's feedback will make the learning easier. It cannot be spoon-fed. Perhaps that's why so many clown teachers draw on their own experience and practice as performers rather than on recycling the clown training they received as students:

We've taken many years to get to our understanding of clown. All those years of experiment, we've wanted to condense them in a short time, to share those discoveries, saving the students the pain! Anyone who says you shouldn't give away your secrets, that's not a real clown. I know clowns that do share everything they know and I believe strongly in that.

(Cenoz 2011)

That is another reason why, as mentioned earlier, it is not so easy to slot clowning into a conventional curriculum. On the one hand, clown training benefits from being undertaken in an environment completely dedicated to experiential learning:

The residential school, that's our proposal, which is quite a risky one for some people, as they have to leave everything. Having to live here in the middle of the countryside with total strangers is something daring. You have to leave your life behind for a while. You are not only the whole day in class but also have the experience of being surrounded by others who like you are focused on clown. As clown's objective is joy, being able to laugh at things, at yourself, then what happens is that the experience of living and working together changes people a lot, it usually changes their vision of things.

(Cenoz 2011)

On the other hand, that knowledge has to be integrated into one's 'real' life:

Many people see this as a paradise, an ideal society, though I think that's a mistake, as when you're a student here you don't have to worry about lots of things in real life, like paying bills and dealing with bureaucracy, daily worries and concerns. The ideal would be to attain that state that you find in here in the school in your life.

(Cenoz 2011)

The way we learn clown might even have something to teach us about how to learn in other disciplines, but the lessons might go so much against the grain of orthodox educational practice that it is debatable whether they would be heeded. Logic tells us that we should learn to walk before we can run. But why? A student once commented to me that he wished he had learned a particular, very simple, element of clowning before, and not after, he had to present a performance in public as it would have aided him in his performance. Maybe so. But I suggested that it might work the other way round. Perhaps learning a simple technique before realising its importance would be useless. Perhaps it is better to think, 'shit, I wish I'd known that before!' since this realisation would fix the experience in the memory and in the body.

So perhaps we learn better back-to-front. After all, we all learn to fall over before we can walk.

Conclusion: Clown Today

INTRODUCTION

In this concluding chapter I consider a range of practices today which use, apply or are guided by clowning, in order to gain an overview of the 'state of clowning today', particularly outside orthodox performance and training. I begin by looking at the marginalised condition of clowns working the streets and traffic-light junctions of Latin America, and how this reveals profound concepts about the social value or otherwise of clowning. Social value is reflected in a different way in the work of clowns who respond consciously in their work to the existence of fear and horror in society, here examined in Franki Anderson's approach to fooling and economic crisis, and in Peta Lily's concept of dark clown. A further manifestation of social clowning is that of humanitarian expeditions and hospital clowns, and here we discuss a range of views, from Patch Adams' radical stance through to the professionalisation of hospital clowning in many countries today. The attempt to apply clowning to develop new ways of thinking (stupidity as a form of intelligence) and making decisions on a global scale is examined with reference to the work of the World Parliament of Clowns. From clown forms of thought we move on to clown forms of spirituality, including those attached to organised religions, such as Christianity and Buddhism, as well as those which are not, as evidenced in the work of Jan Henderson or Clara Cenoz. Finally, we ask whether clowns can be everywhere and whether we can all be clowns or not, or whether clowns must remain misfits and outsiders in all fields, from performance to academia.

At the end of Part I, I looked at what clowns are doing today, via the work of some contemporary clown performers. But what about the 'how?' and 'why?' of clowning today?

What are clowns' responses to our own historical moment? What are our reasons for clowning? In what social contexts do clowns clown today? What does clown mean now at the beginning of the 21st century?

MARGINAL STATUS: TRAFFIC-LIGHT AND STREET CLOWNS IN LATIN AMERICA

In the 2009 general election campaign in Mexico, the Partido del Trabajo (Labour Party) put out a political broadcast on television which began with two motherly women gloomily chatting:

Woman 1: My son's going crazy, he couldn't find a place in high school, or a job either.
Woman 2: Good lord!
Youth: Mum ... I'm going to earn something, even if it's as a clown.

(Partido del Trabajo de México 2009)

We see the son off to juggle on the street, made-up as a clown, but with his mouth painted downturned so that he looks distinctly depressed. A politician appears on camera, expressing regrets for the lack of education or jobs, and ends with: 'we need to save Mexico. Vote for the Labour Party' (Partido del Trabajo de México 2009).

The broadcast played on the assumptions not just that clowning isn't a proper job but that it brings shame upon those who do it, their families and the whole nation, which provoked widespread complaints from the profession, demanding respect for clowns, as in this letter to the satirical magazine *El Chamuco*, which spoke of

true clown artists who are completely dedicated to their work and to their cultural contribution to the country. Let us not forget that street clowns are constantly sought out in public places by tourists, in Germany, in Spain, in Chile, in Argentina, in Colombia, in Canada and in Brazil.

(Balderas 2009)

But, despite her protest, Balderas draws a distinction between those who have chosen their profession and who 'work on their routines, invest in their costumes, in workshops, [...] even abroad' and those who out of necessity aim to 'get some quick money' as a 'payasito de semáforo' (the clowns and others who busk at traffic-lights, a common occurrence in Mexico and many other Latin American countries), which 'though not unworthy' are stigmatised by society.

In contrast, following an initiative in Bogotá, Colombia, 120 street mimes recently became government employees in Venezuela and are used to calm dangerous drivers at traffic-lights in Caracas:

Suarez frowned, thrust her hands forward in a 'stop' motion and then pointed to a red light as a motorcyclist raced toward a crosswalk filled with pedestrians.

(Christopher Toothaker for Associated Press, 8 October 2011)

This is a very different kind of street clown, sanctioned by officialdom and therefore imbued with formal dignity. The performers are more effective than the police at controlling anti-social behaviour, according to those who trained them:

Many times, the mimes can achieve what traffic police cannot achieve using warning and sanctions in their efforts to maintain control [...] Mimes, on the contrary, often achieve the same objective by employing artistic and peaceful actions.

(Toothaker 2011)

For the mayor of the district, this artistry goes further than traffic control, however, and would continue 'until the streets [...] are full of creativity and education' (Toothaker 2011).

Rubén Mendoza's film *La Sociedad del Semáforo* ('Traffic-Light Society'; 2010) presents a vision not of social engineering by or of clowns but the fantasy of one who dreams of being able to control the length of time the light stays red so that performers and street vendors in Bogotá have a chance of earning a better living.

If low-status street clowns are supposed to take advantage of waiting traffic and government-sponsored ones to maintain order, then those clowns who perform at well-respected and well-paid international festivals are expected to disrupt the traffic, from Kevin Brooking in the 1980s to today's Chilean duo, *Murmuyo y Metrayeta*. The latter even bring their own real car in which to race round the audience and create anarchy, which, although it takes place within the safe confines of the stewarded festival space, still has the capacity to step over spectators' boundaries, particularly in the way this duo surprise us with spraying liquids, which goes further than the average clown today.

SOCIAL CLOWNING AND THE RESPONSE TO FEAR AND HORROR: FRANKI ANDERSON AND PETA LILY

As is evident, clowns do not occupy a single position in relation to law and order, nor to the economy. Yet another perspective is one that consciously seeks to confront economic and social issues. The experience of Franki Anderson, who has taught and performed clowning and fooling since the 1970s, seems to show that clowns are heeded more in times of crisis. She reports that her show, *Fools Gold*, drew an indifferent response when it was first created two or three years previously: 'In the good times, comedy is crap, people don't want to know about failure' (Anderson 2011); but that the present economic crisis has sparked a lot of interest, as many are forced to face their fears they were previously unaware of:

On the one hand there are the facts about where money comes from, who controls through it, and how much it serves us. On the other hand there is how we feel about money or lack of it. This Fools show explores the archetypal human feelings, about money, that fear of experiencing drives people to do things they wouldn't rationally expect. Our ignorance of suppressed feelings keeps us unconscious about the real money story and makes us vulnerable to gross manipulation.

(Anderson 2009)

Anderson considers that today 'money feelings are more taboo than sex and politics', which means that 'people's stories are unprocessed, unspoken' (Anderson 2011). The business of clowns and fools is to visit these taboos:

> The art of the fool is to feel when you're on someone's boundary, hold it for a moment, then come back off as if to say 'oh but I'm just a poor fool, what do I know?'
>
> (Anderson 2011)

The willingness of clowns to address taboos without fear is what allows them to 'be representations of our vulnerability' (Anderson 2011). This insight – that clowning may be ideally placed to talk about those things which seem most dangerous to us – has been taken up in the field of 'social clowning'. Julie Salverson speaks of an

> investigation into clown and the absurd as an alternate vocabulary to what have become common methods for artists working in community with people's stories: popular-education-based scene development, theatre of the oppressed, story-telling, playback theatre. For years as a community-based playwright I have grappled with the problem of how to tell stories of violence [...] Above all, I've grown disturbed by what I call an aesthetic of injury, a tendency in socially motivated theatre to focus on pain.
>
> (Salverson 2008: 34)

Since clown starts from the acceptance that we inevitably fail, stories and experiences which seem impossible to express, and which we feel doomed never to succeed in overcoming, can be addressed:

> It is impossible to face the story of the atomic bomb and its consequences with comprehension. Clown offered a way to name this impossibility.
>
> (Salverson 2008: 35)

Despite failing, the clown continues:

> Her silliness, her grotesqueness, these are her humility, even her apology if you like. She admits that she has no right to be taken seriously in the face of this enormous event, and yet she is determined to be heard. This juxtaposition, paradoxically, lets us love her and take her seriously.
>
> (Salverson 2008: 38)

An alternative clown response to horror is what Peta Lily has termed 'dark clown', which seems to lie somewhere in between the terrain of clown and buffoon:

> When the Red Nose Clown falls over, we laugh and say, 'That's so stupid!' With the Dark Clown, [...] we laugh while thinking, 'I shouldn't be laughing at this.'
>
> (Lily 2011)

In dark clown, the audience's witnessing of, and laughing at, terrible things becomes what drives the performance, as in a scene from Lumiere & Son's *Circus Lumiere*:

> A tall and a small clown watch us apprehensively. We laugh at their discomfort. We notice a machine on stage. It has a dial. The tall clown picks up the attached cattle prod and begins to deliver electric shocks to the small clown, as we laugh. Aware that our laughter needs to keep coming, the dial is reset higher.
>
> (Lily 2011)

Dark clown creates a relationship between performers and audience where the latter seem to have the power but choose not to use it:

> That's the skill – to set up the conditions where the audience can notice themselves laughing at something awful, failing to call out 'stop!' before a cruel action is taken.
>
> (Lily 2011)

Dark clowns' performances are 'enforced' – they have no other option but to perform – enduring the laughter of the audience which signals that they should continue. Although this obligation to make us laugh is shared with red-nosed clowns, dark clowns experience this duty under duress whereas red-nosed clowns do so out of choice.

The point of this approach is not to mock suffering but to find a way to get nearer to the horror of events:

> In teaching the work I always make it clear that the intention is *not* to ridicule suffering or those who suffer, but rather to give the audience the experience of witnessing tiny moments of humanity (in Red Nose Clown the comedic glimpses of miffed feelings and shifting allegiances – in Dark Clown, the horror of stripped dignity and betrayals born of terror), that can make a large tragedy such as genocide more witnessed, more fully experienced (versus the understandable 'numb-out' these dreadful events can provoke).
>
> (Lily 2011)

HUMANITARIAN CLOWNS: PATCH ADAMS, HOSPITALS AND EXPEDITIONS

One of the pioneers of clowning in a variety of social contexts is Bataclown in France, the approach of which has been continued in Britain by the group Nose-to-Nose, founded by Vivian Gladwell, himself a graduate of the French group. Bataclown's 'clownanalysis' places clowns anywhere from business conferences to hospitals. In theory, clowns might intervene in any area of human society in order to bring a non-conventional perspective to creativity or solving problems. Again, it is the clown's ease in the face of failure and the resulting acceptance of vulnerability which expand the limits of our thinking and feeling, which are normally constrained by our obsessive drive for success and our fear of failure.

In the field of social clowning, hospital clowning is probably the aspect most familiar to a wider public, together with humanitarian expeditions, such as those carried out by Clowns Without Borders, founded in 1993 by Tortell Poltrona. Just as social clowning in the community is an attempt to refocus away from pain and tragedy without avoiding the real issues, so hospital and humanitarian clowning are partly founded on the ability of clowning to relieve pain and to refocus the sick or suffering person away from pain.

There have been extensive scientific studies made of the effects on the immune system of laughter:

> Although humor itself is difficult to evaluate, the response to humor– laughter – can be studied quite readily. Research has shown that laughter increases the secretion of the natural chemicals, catecholamines and endorphins, that make people feel so peppy and good. It also decreases cortisol secretion and lowers the sedimentation rate, which implies a stimulated immune response. Oxygenation of the blood increases, and residual air in the lungs decreases. Heart rate initially speeds up and blood pressure rises; then the arteries relax, causing heart rate and blood pressure to lower. Skin temperature rises as a result of increased peripheral circulation. Thus, laughter appears to have a positive effect on many cardiovascular and respiratory problems. In addition, laughter has superb muscle relaxant qualities. Muscle physiologists have shown that anxiety and muscle relaxation cannot occur at the same time and that the relaxation response after a hearty laugh can last up to forty-five minutes.
>
> (Adams 1993: 67)

Patch Adams' philosophy is not so much founded on the clown as a provoker of laughter and comedy, although that is an important part of his work. He places humour, within the practice of healthcare, alongside 'love, [...] wonder, curiosity, passion, forgiveness, giving, sharing, hope, enthusiasm, and joy' (Adams 1998: xi). For Adams, the priority is connection and friendship: 'As a physician, I have noticed that the most pain is associated with loneliness' (Adams 1998: 74). He continues:

> I would never agree laughter is the best medicine, I've never said it. Friendship is clearly the best medicine, friendship is the most important thing in life, our relationships with those we love. And so, unfortunately the media being the way it is, long before they meet me, they had the idea laughter is the best medicine and so when they write the article they just put this phrase in there because they are actually not thinking.
>
> (Adams 2007)

Adams extends his approach to include accompanying the dying, or 'mid-wifeing death', refocusing away from a fear of imminent death:

> Clowning in hospitals has convinced me that you can even take humor to a death bed. Imagine if you are the sick person and all your experience with your visitors is gloominess, even doom for your life. Is that the way you want to spend your hospital stay? Is that the way you want to die?
>
> (Adams 1998: 14)

And back towards the present, living moment:

> Whenever I spend time with a dying person I have, in fact, found a living person. The young who are dying have been most vocal about this. I remember an eleven-year-old girl who had a huge bony tumor of the face with one eye floating out in the mass. Most people found it difficult to be with her because of her appearance. Her pain was not in her dying but in the loneliness of being a person others could not bear to see. She and I played, joked, and enjoyed her life away. This is when I made a commitment to enjoy the profoundly ill and act normal around them.
>
> (Adams 1993: 81)

The consequences of Adams' vision of hospital clowning are more far-reaching than the picture painted by the Hollywood film *Patch Adams* (1998) starring Robin Williams, which is how most people are acquainted with his work:

> And so the movie gives the impression I'm about going into a sick child's room and being funny. And that's cute and good film, but it's not ... it doesn't make Brazil want to feed all of its hungry people and stop cutting down its Amazon river.
>
> (Adams 2007)

For Adams, if we are able to see a sick child's pain and have the impulse to do something about it, then we should also be concerned enough to speak up and act on all the other suffering there is in the world: 'And I am sorry that my name is to a movie that does not mention peace and justice' (Adams 2007). This radicalism bypasses the established structure of who owns healthcare: 'We have taken the most expensive service in America, medical care, and given it away for free (1993: 1).

In this sense, empathy is a radical act, as is happiness itself:

> The last weeks of medical school were soured by a dash with an assistant dean, who threatened that I wouldn't graduate. He criticized me in a memo as being 'excessively happy.'
>
> (Adams 1993: 14)

THE PROFESSIONALISATION OF CLOWNING IN HEALTH

Adams' vision of access for all applies both to those who are in need of receiving healthcare and to those who are willing to give: 'Experience is not required' (Adams 1993: 23). In contrast, others in hospital clowning see a need for professionalisation, which has led to the establishment of university-level study programmes, such as the BA at the University of Haifa, which began in 2006:

> The dual-major degree will focus on fields of knowledge related to therapy, such as nursing, developmental psychology and the history of medicine, as well as theatrical skills that are necessary for clowning, such as comedy acting, improvisation, street theatre and juggling.
>
> (Haifa 2006)

This placing of clowning studies on the same level as those related to medicine, a field whose high demands on its students is generally perceived as a marker of its professional seriousness and academic trustworthiness, has the effect of raising the status and recognition of clowning's value:

> the main goal of academically institutionalizing medical clowning is to make it a recognized profession, in the same league as physiotherapy, speech therapy and so forth. Academic recognition is one of the primary conditions necessary to make that happen.
>
> (Haifa 2006)

But it also has the purpose of restricting who can be a hospital clown:

> This academic training will contribute to setting standards that will determine who can provide therapy.
>
> (Haifa 2006)

Clearly there is a conflict of interests between professionalisation and access to volunteers. In response to the question 'do you accept volunteer clowns in hospitals?', Pallapupas, a group of hospital clowns in Barcelona, reply:

> No, *pallapupas* are all professional clowns. The main reason is that just as in hospitals there are no volunteer doctors so there are no volunteer clowns either.
>
> The craft of the clown is a profession which, like many others, requires many years of study. At *Pallapupas* we wish to dignify the profession of clowning and for that reason, after an audition and an interview, we employ professional performers knowing that they will do the best job possible. After that, we provide specific training for working in a health environment.
>
> (Pallapupas 2011)

This pro-professional stance is at times accompanied by a denigration of volunteer work:

This rapid expansion of clowns in health care settings has resulted in varying levels of professionalism and accountability. At their most professional, therapeutic clowns are respected complementary care providers who are able to articulate their role in the care of the patients as integral members of the health care team. At the other end of the spectrum, volunteer clowns, though well-intentioned, may be simply dressed-up people with little training and less understanding of the role and potential of the therapeutic clown.

(Koller and Gryski 2008)

Whilst most academic and scientific studies focus on the pro-professional approach, volunteer clowns do continue to work in health settings, despite marginalisation.

THE WORLD PARLIAMENT OF CLOWNS AND STUPIDITY AS A FORM OF INTELLIGENCE

Another social initiative which derives from that same insight – that clowns are in a unique position to deal with fear and can expand our capacity to behave, think and feel with greater freedom than we are accustomed to – is the World Parliament of Clowns. This was founded by Antoschka (Ekaterina Moshaeva) in 2006, who featured throughout the 1970s and 1980s with all the major circuses of the Soviet Union, in particular the Moscow State Circus, before establishing herself in Germany in the 1990s, where she continues to perform with her solo show.

The world is in a state of chaos. Yet clowns are not afraid: chaos is their element. Through creativity and spontaneity they can alter chaos and make it lose its destructive nature.
[...]
With wisdom and a smile, the World Parliament of Clowns – an initiative originated by some of the most celebrated clowns of our time – will try to re-stabilize our unbalanced ME-driven, business-oriented world, and bring it back to the solid grounds of reality, in harmony with the initial, spiritual WE-world.
[...]
The clowns of the world make up a unique species perfectly 'designed' to achieve this goal, [...] and they can persuade the inhabitants of this planet to think in new ways, and to take on a global responsibility.

(Moshaeva 2006)

The parliament's work is targeted at world decision-makers:

The World Parliament of Clowns will give scientists, politicians, managers and entrepreneurs, artists and religious leaders and also all people of the planet the Clowns Immunity to say all their thoughts and ideas and to give all their wisdom to the world without the fear of blame and humiliation. One of the rights of clowns is to fail.

(Moshaeva 2006)

The contribution to new thinking comes not only from the clown who, in McManus's words, is 'too smart' to believe in the conventional ways but also from the one who is 'too dumb' to understand reality. A panel discussion led by the World Parliament of Clowns at the World Culture Forum in Dresden in 2009 proposed a discussion of stupidity as a form of intelligence. Normally we define stupidity as a lack of intelligence, as a deficiency or defect. But since stupidity is also the opposite of wisdom, and since intelligence and wisdom do not always coincide, one can be intelligent and stupid (unwise) simultaneously:

> Professor Siegfried Seufert, one of the best known intelligence researchers of our time, prophesies: Stupidity has a great future ahead of it. He argues that it is precisely people who do not notice at all what is going on around them that enjoy the best chances in their personal and professional life. And elaborate testing allowed him to prove that:
>
> - In a stock exchange game played by students, the stupid ones accumulated all the money by the end, and the clever ones were all bankrupt.
> - The US army had a study of why there are so many idiots among high-ranking officers. The result: Most of the intelligent officers lost out when it came to the very first round of promotions. Those who heard and saw nothing, on the other hand, rose through the ranks steadily and unstoppably.
>
> (Riehn 2009)

Riehn claims that no-one wants to talk about stupidity:

> Politicians are afraid to discuss the manifestations of stupidity: vanity, egoism, ruthlessness, and forgetfulness.
>
> Managers avoid any discussions about stupidity, since it is the rock-solid foundation of their and their companies' success. Stupidity powers the economy.
>
> People do not want any discussion of their favorite quality.
>
> And stupidity is also taboo for the media, but equally essential since they profit greatly from it.
>
> That means that in debates it is left to the clowns, the fools of society, to expose stupidity, to cast light on it from all sides and to investigate how important stupidity is for our future.
>
> They hold a mirror in front of us in the hope that we recognize ourselves:
>
> Can a future be designed without stupidity?
>
> Does it have to be incorporated in every master plan as a 'specification'?
>
> Or will the members of the World Parliament of Clowns manage to play out stupidity ad absurdum and thus finally achieve a revolution in social thought, with the goal that every person on the plant assumes their responsibility for the whole world?
>
> (Riehn 2009)

Moshaeva and Riehn believe that

> the 21st century is the century of creativity, but it's difficult because managers now are unable to work with creativity, as they have their heads full of numbers and data.
>
> (Moshaeva 2011)

Clowns, on the other hand, deal with intuition rather than information. By definition, intuition is unbounded by rules or conventional ways of perceiving things, and thus also links to 'unintelligence', or 'doing things the wrong way'. For Moshaeva, these are the qualities which define human beings, and ultimately enable happiness:

> Foolishness defines humanity. The fool is not interested in possessions, but is glad just to look at the stars. Fools have joy, because you don't need a reason to be joyful.
>
> (Moshaeva 2011)

CLOWN SPIRITUALITY: JAN HENDERSON, ALAN CLAY AND ASTROLOGY

Broadly speaking, we can see that social clowning seeks to disseminate across a wide spectrum of society an appreciation of the value of what we could call 'clown philosophy', a value which lies in its potential to change individuals, situations and society in a positive direction. In a way, it offers an answer to the question 'why clown?', or even 'what is the meaning of clown?' But clowning based on such a philosophical foundation is not limited to those practices which seek to make use of clowning for some end, be that social, political or health. It is also widespread in clown teaching and consequently in clown performing, too.

Canadian clown teacher Jan Henderson considers that the clown is a path to meaning in life:

> In a lifelong search for meaning, I have found the clown to be the best, all-encompassing metaphor for the human condition – an uncompromising mirror to look into for glimpses of the truth. We look at the clown and see ourselves – our hopes, dreams, fears, and virtues, our flaws and our process.
> [...]
> With the best of intentions and no thought of failure, it leaps naively into danger – getting knocked down over and over – but never failing to get up and try again. It is an embodiment of hope in the face of hopelessness, and possibility in the face of the impossible. It blissfully ignores the obvious and somehow convinces us of the wisdom of folly, and if, as I suspect, we are here to bear witness to the universe, the clown aspect of ourselves provides the best color commentary.

Clowning is about the freedom that comes from a state of total, unconditional acceptance of our most authentic selves, warts and all. It offers us respite from our self-doubts and fears, and opens the door to joy.

(Henderson 2008)

Clown here is both a way to understand life and a way to live it. As such it has found correspondences with, and can claim to perform the same task as, spiritual teachings and practices, from astrology to established religions:

recently a new group of planetoids have been discovered in the solar system, called Centaurs, which are said to represent boundary crossing, interpenetrating energies, which sounds quite a bit like clown to me.

One of these has been named Pholus, and I suspect it relates to the Fool, because it links the orbits of Neptune, which represents illusions and dreams, with that of Saturn, which represents physical reality.
[...]
The boundaries of our personal world are to do with Saturn, and Chiron and Pholus link these personal limitations with the wider cosmic energies, the spiritual, intuitive, and imaginative.

Although we experience the world through a personal, and therefore limited point of view, the wash of everyone else's world is all about us, and the challenge is to mediate these energies so we can relate to one another without destroying one another because our worlds are so different, or alternatively, protecting ourselves with judgments and isolation.

(Clay 2005: 483–484)

CLOWNING AND THEOLOGY: CHRISTIANITY AND BUDDHISM

Two religions in particular have come to be associated with clowning: Christianity and Buddhism. Clown Ministry is principally a way of using clowning to communicate the meaning of religious parables, and is widespread in those parts of the world with a strong evangelical presence, particularly in parts of Latin and North America:

In the United States, this sharing of spiritual message became more widespread in the late 1970's. Rev. Floyd Shaffer and several others took the clown into the church to do skits and services and develop a new way to look at religious truths.

(World Clown Association 2011)

Some cite the New Testament as theological justification and see Christ as a clown or fool, one despised and mocked, standing for the victims of society:

We are fools for Christ's sake

(Bible, 1 Corinthians 4:10 King James Version)

For it is written, I will destroy the wisdom of the wise, and will bring to nothing the understanding of the prudent.

[...]

But God hath chosen the foolish things of the world to confound the wise; and God hath chosen the weak things of the world to confound the things which are mighty;

(Bible, 1 Corinthians 1: 19, 27; King James Version)

Moshe Cohen uses clowning with an awareness of the parallels and crossovers with Zen Buddhism, both in his clown teaching and in his performing practice at the Zen Center in Los Angeles.

One might say in general that the main similarity between clown and Zen is that if you are thinking, then you are not where you want to be. In metaphysical terms one might say that it is an activity led by heart and spirit rather than intellect.

(Cohen 2005)

In both clowning and Zen, intellect is abandoned by accepting that 'I don't know':

The practice of Not Knowing involves letting go of all preconceptions and knowledge, so as to bring full awareness to the situation at hand.

(Cohen 2007a)

Accepting 'not knowing' in clowning is the same as accepting failure, as discussed by Cohen in conversation with Bernie Glassman, a pioneer of socially engaged Buddhism:

Figure 16 Roly Bain, Anglican priest
Source: Roly Bain

Moshe: So did you say that the clown does not make mistakes?

Bernie: No, because if the clown trips somewhere, well that's not a mistake, they just tripped somewhere. But most people, if they trip somewhere where they are in the spotlight, they feel embarrassed like they made a mistake, whereas the clown – they tripped!

(Cohen 2007b)

Clara Cenoz identifies the ego as the obstacle to accepting failure:

The ego is a system of survival designed so that we can survive, constructed when we are young, and which doesn't work when we grow up, or is no longer necessary when we are adults. As the ego is based on the defence of our personality, our survival, it works based on a system of fears and desires. This construction is something with which we identify, but we are not this. That's the problem: identifying with a system of survival or defence which is often about illusory fears or problems.

In reality, there is no real danger for us, given that our essence is indestructible. In this way, the work of the ego in defending us is absurd. And that is what we have to realise. When one studies clown, what one is doing is reconnecting to one's essence, realising that no real danger exists out here for us. This construction for defence restricts our true essence, which we could say is beneath the ego, or behind it. The ego impedes our growth, our feeling, our evolution. The clown student has to identify the ego, recognise it, and realise that you are not your ego.

(Cenoz 2011)

The realisation that we need not fear failure is a major step in the process of clown training:

that's why people feel this liberation with clown – when we realise that really there's nothing to worry about, because there is no real danger, what do we obtain? A great joy, a great confidence, a great acceptance of ourselves, and thus of others too. There is an unconscious learning, that really all this which we have been defending since we were young, has no sense. The only 'danger' is that we have experiences which will help us to evolve. If one doesn't want to evolve, then one shouldn't do clown.

(Cenoz 2011)

And, since fear provokes suffering, clown is a way of overcoming or even eradicating it: 'suffering is something we have invented, it's a mental construct' (Cenoz 2011).

APPLIED CLOWN AND THE MISFIT: HILARY RAMSDEN

The extensive development of clown teaching at the end of the 20th century has led to ongoing explorations of the nature and dynamics of clowning, encouraging sustained reflection on the purpose and function of clown in wider society, and in turn enabling a range of applications of clown, in performance, health, philosophy, religion, politics and elsewhere.

This applicability or relevance of clowning is not new, however, as we have seen clowning's capacity for articulating a whole range of issues in a variety of contexts: Parisian post-war trauma in the 1870s, women's rights in Europe and North America around 1900, the expansion of London through immigration in the 1580s, or indeed the whole history of ideological change in the Soviet Union, from revolutionary optimism to perestroika in the 1980s, passing through Stalin's repression and Khrushchev's liberalisation.

What, arguably, may be new is a more conscious attempt to identify clown philosophies underpinning the practices of clowning, and clowning's capacity to explore and express our fears and hopes. It is perhaps clearer to us today, at the beginning of the 21st century, that clown can inhabit any field of human endeavour.

As Hilary Ramsden points out, 'clowning can pop up anywhere' (2011). She sees her role as bringing a clown perspective to the issues of the day, reflecting on how her clowning has changed since the early days of the Clandestine Insurgent Rebel Clown Army:

> My clown perspective on things, a clown logic of seeing and acting in the world, hasn't changed. But the world has changed, so the response to it is different. The applications change, we have different desires and responses, different hybrids between clown and people's issues.
>
> (Ramsden 2011)

Ramsden admits that her own problem is that

> I always want to get everyone to clown with me. In costume or make-up the audience knows you are the clown, you are different to them and they accept you will behave differently. Working without costume, you are like them, and they won't feel you are allowed to deviate. You can't be their peer and clown at the same time.
>
> (Ramsden 2011)

This can prove to be an obstacle to the introduction of clown logic and action into a wider environment, and it poses a dilemma: can society assume some of clown's insights and become more clown-like, or is the clown condemned, by definition, to remain an outsider, a misfit? Speaking of her own recent entry into the world of academia, Ramsden concludes:

> We don't fit. We've spent decades constructing our clown life, we don't fit others' worlds. What I enjoy about clowning is it's not about that at all. Clown shows us how we don't fit. How can you mark someone on their 'misfitness'? Our clown-ess is the polar opposite of the academy, and it's never going to get in there.
>
> (Ramsden 2011)

References

Abbott, Bud and Costello, Lou (1944) *Lost in a Harem* (Metro-Goldwyn-Meyer).
Adams, Patch (1993) *Gesundheit!* (Vermont: Healing Arts Press).
—— (1998) *House Calls* (San Francisco: Robert D. Reed).
—— (2007) Interview on *Roda Viva*, 9 April 2007 (TV Brasil), http://www.youtube.com/watch?v=9h0Zf9coyAo, date accessed 29 December 2011.
Allen, Tony (2002) *Attitude: Wanna Make Something of It?* (Glastonbury: Gothic Image).
Anderberg, Kirsten (2005) 'Women Street Performers and Sexual Safety', http://www.buskersadvocates.org/womenstreetperformers.html, date accessed 29 December 2011.
Anderson, Franki (2009) 'Fools Gold', http://www.playfool-theater.de/pageID_3240695.html, date accessed 29 December 2011.
—— (2011) Interview by telephone, 13 December 2011.
Angelo, Henry (1828) *Reminiscences* (London: Henry Colburn).
Armin, Robert (1972) *Collected Works*, ed. Feather, J. P. (London: Johnson Reprint Corporation).
Arratoon, Liz (2011) Review of *Slava's Snowshow*, *The Stage*, 19 December 2011, http://www.thestage.co.uk/reviews/review.php/34715/slavas-snowshow, date accessed 29 December 2011.
Aspa, Jordi (2009) 'La Integridad del Círculo', *Zirkolika, Revista Trimestral de les Arts Circenses* 21(Summer): 33.
Astruc, Gabriel (1929) *Le pavillon des fantômes* (Paris: Grasset).
Atkinson, Rowan (1992) *Visual Comedy, a Lecture by Rowan Atkinson M.Sc. (Oxon.)* (Tiger Television).
Auerbach, N. (1990) *Private Theatricals: The Lives of the Victorians* (Cambridge: Harvard University Press).
Balderas, Elizabeth (2009) Letter to *El Chamuco*, reproduced at http://clownplanet.blogspot.com/2009/06/spot-del-pt-partido-del-trabajo-de.html, date accessed 29 December 2011.
Ball, Lucille (1951) *I Love Lucy* pilot program, unaired episode (CBS).
—— (1952) *I Love Lucy* Season 1, Episode 52, 22 December 1952 (CBS).
Bandolier, Adolf (1890) *The Delight Makers* (New York: Dodd, Mead and Company).
Barker, Clive (1977) *Theatre Games* (London: Methuen).
Basch, Sophie (2002) *Romans de cirque* (Paris: Robert Laffont).
Baskervill, Charles Read (1929) *The Elizabethan Jig and Related Song Drama* (Chicago: Chicago University Press).
Baudelaire, Charles (1855) *On the Essence of Laughter*, in *The Mirror of Art* trans. and ed. Mayne, Jonathan (1955) (London: Phaidon Press).
Baugé, Isabelle (1995) *Pantomimes* (Cahors: Cicéro Éditions).
Beeman, William O. (1981) ' "Why Do They Laugh?" An Interactional Approach to Humor in Traditional Iranian Improvisatory Theatre: Performance and its Effects', *The Journal of American Folklore* 94(374), Folk Drama (October–December): 506–526.

Bellocq, Éric and Lavenère, Vincent de (2004) *Le chant des balles* (Vic-la-Gardiole: L'Entretemps).

Bellos, David (1999) *Jacques Tati* (London: The Harvill Press).

Billington, Michael (2008) Review of *Varekai* in *The Guardian*, 10 January 2008.

Boese, Carl (1931) *Grock (La vie d'un grand artiste)* (Universum Film AG).

Bogdanovich, Peter (1972) *Leo McCarthy Oral History* (Los Angeles: American Film Institute).

Bolton, Reg (1987) *New Circus* (Calouste Gulbenkian Foundation).

Bouissac, Paul (1972) 'Clown Performances as Meta-semiotic Texts', *Language Sciences* 19: 1–7.

––––––– (1997) 'The Profanation of the Sacred in Circus Clown Performances', in *By Means of Performance*, ed. Schechner, Richard and Appel, W. (Cambridge: CUP), 194–207.

Brecht, Bertolt (1955) *The Baden-Baden Lesson on Consent*, in *Collected Plays: Three*, trans. Kelton, Geoffrey (1998) (London: Methuen).

––––––– (1994) *Mann ist Mann*, in *Collected Plays: Two*, trans. Nellhaus, Gerhard (London: Methuen).

Brinn, David (2011) 'It's Not Just Clowning Around with Slava and his *Snowshow*', *The Jerusalem Post*, 13 August 2011, http://www.jpost.com/ArtsAndCulture/Entertainment/Article.aspx?id=233659, date accessed 29 December 2011.

Brown, Ismene (2011) Review of *Slava's Snowshow* in *theartsdesk*, 29 December 2011, http://www.theartsdesk.com/dance/slavas-snowshow-royal-festival-hall, date accessed 29 December 2011.

Brown, Maria Ward (1901) *The Life of Dan Rice* (New Jersey: Long Branch).

Bryant, Arthur (1952) *The Age of Elegance 1812–1822* (London: Collins).

Buten, Howard (2005) *Buffo* (Arles: Actes Sud).

Caillois, Roger (2001) *Man, Play and Games* (Chicago: University of Illinois Press).

Cairoli, Charlie (1966) *The Milk Number* at The London Hippodrome, http://www.youtube.com/user/escoladeclown, date accessed 29 December 2011.

––––––– (1973) *The Milk Number* at Cirque Bouglione, Paris, http://www.youtube.com/user/escoladeclown, date accessed 29 December 2011.

Calvi, Nuala (2011) 'Slava Polunin: Fool's Paradise', *The Stage*, 16 December 2011.

Cameron, Anne (1981) *Daughters of Copper Woman* (Vancouver: Press Gang Publishers).

Campardon, Émile (1880) *Les Comédiens du Roi de la troupe italienne* (Paris: Berger-Levrault et Cie).

Carlson, Marvin (2003) 'The Golden Age of the Boulevard', in *Popular Theater*, ed. Joel Schechter (London: Routledge), 22–31.

Carse, James P. (1986) *Finite and Infinite Games* (New York: Random House).

Cashin, Pat (2011) *Clownalley*, http://clownalley.blogspot.com, date accessed 29 December 2011.

Cazeneuve, Jean (1957) *Les dieux dansent à Cibola* (Paris: Gallimard).

Ceballos, Edgar (1999) *El Libro de Oro de los Payasos* (Mexico DF: Escenología).

Cenoz, Clara (2009) *Banana!*, http://www.youtube.com/watch?v=kxwciaUtS1o, date accessed 29 December 2011.

––––––– (2011) Interview at Escola de Clown de Barcelona, 20 November 2011.

Chai, Barbara (2011) 'The Red-Nosed Revolution', *Wall Street Journal*, 1 November 2011, http://online.wsj.com/article/SB100014240529702043948045770101802788814076.html, date accessed 29 December 2011.

Chamberlain, Franc and Yarrow, Ralph (eds) (2002) *Jacques Lecoq and the British Theatre* (Oxford: Routledge).

Champsaur, Félicien (1888) *Lulu, pantomime en un acte* (Paris: Dentu).

———— (1901) *Lulu, Roman clownesque* in *Romans de cirque*, ed. Basch, Sophie (2002) (Paris: Robert Laffont).

Chaplin, Charlie (1916) *The Pawnshop* (Mutual Film Corporation).

———— (1921) *The Kid* (First National).

———— (1928) *The Circus* (United Artists).

———— (1931) *City Lights* (United Artists).

———— (1936) *Modern Times* (United Artists).

———— (1964) *My Autobiography* (London: The Bodley Head).

Chekhov, Michael (1953) *To the Actor* (New York: Harper and Row).

CIRCA (2006–2011) http://www.clownarmy.org, date accessed 29 December 2011.

Claretie, Jules (1881) *La Vie a Paris* (Paris: Havard).

———— (1888) *Boum-Boum* (New York: William R. Jenkins).

Clay, Alan (2005) *Angels Can Fly, a Modern Clown User Guide* (Newtown, Australia: Artmedia Publishing).

Clowns of America International (2006) *20 Years of Laughter* (Nashville: Turner Publishing Company).

Cohen, Moshe (2005) 'A Short Look at Clown and Zen', http://www.clownzen.com/it/clownandzen2005.html, date accessed 29 December 2011.

———— (2007a) 'Conversations with Roshi Egyoku: The Three Tenets', http://www.clownzen.com/zenofit/threetenets.html, date accessed 29 December 2011.

———— (2007b) 'Conversation with Roshi Bernie Glassman', http://www.clownzen.com/zenofit/bernieglassman.html, date accessed 29 December 2011.

———— (2007c) 'Conversations with Egyoku: Joy and Zen', http://www.clownzen.com/zenofit/joyzen.html, date accessed 29 December 2011.

———— (2012) 'The Power of the (Clown) Nose', *Sacred Mischief*, http://yoowho.wordpress.com/2012/01/11/the-power-of-the-clown-nose, date accessed 11 January 2012.

Copeau, Jacques (1990) *Texts on Theatre*, ed. and trans. Rudlin, John and Paul, Norman H. (London: Routledge).

Cortés, Edouard (2007) *El Pallasso i el Fuhrer* ('The Clown and the Fuhrer') (Televisió de Catalunya).

Cosdon, Mark (2010) *The Hanlon Brothers: From Daredevil Acrobatics to Spectacle Pantomime, 1833–1931* (Illinois: Southern Illinois University Press).

Coward, Simon and Perry, Christopher Woodall (2009) *Bob's Full House* (Dudley: Kaleidoscope).

Crane, David and Kauffman, Marta (1994–2004) *Friends* (NBC).

Darwin, Charles (1859) *On the Origin of Species* (London: John Murray).

Dauven, L. R. and Garnier, Jacques (1971) 'Fellini's Clowns', in *Le Cirque dans l'Univers* #81 (Club du Cirque) trans. Goodman, Diane (1978) *Mask, Mime & Marionette* I(1), Spring: 41–44 (New York).

David, Larry (2000–2012) *Curb Your Enthusiasm* (HBO).

David, Larry and Seinfeld, Gerry (1989–1998) *Seinfeld* (NBC).

Davis, Janet M. (2005) 'Bearded Ladies, Dainty Amazons, Hindoo Fakirs, and Lady Savages: Circus Representations of Gender and Race in Victorian America', Lecture at the University of Virginia, 5–8 October 2005, http://www.circusinamerica.org/docs/janetdavislecture_rev.pdf, date accessed 29 December 2011.

Davison, Jon (2008) 'The Phenomenology of Clown', http://www.jondavison.net/theory.html, date accessed 29 December 2011.

—— (2009a) 'The Dramaturgy of Clown', http://www.jondavison.net/theory.html, date accessed 29 December 2011.

—— (2009b) 'An Encyclopaedia of Clown', http://www.jondavison.net/theory.html, date accessed 29 December 2011.

—— (2010) 'Clown Training Today', http://www.jondavison.net/theory.html, date accessed 29 December 2011.

Denis, Dominique (1985) *Le Livre du Clown* (Strasbourg: Éditions Techniques du Spectacle).

—— (1997) *1.000 gags de clowns* (Strasbourg: Magix Unlimited).

Dickens, Charles (1837) *The Post-Humourous Notes of the Pickwickian Club* (London: E. Lloyd).

Diercksen, Laurent (1999) *Grock: un destin hors norme* (Bet'vilard: Laurent Diercksen).

Dimitriev, Yuri (1967) *The Soviet Circus 1917–1941* (Moscow: Progress Publishers).

Disher, Maurice Willson (1925) *Clowns and Pantomimes* (London and New York: Benjamin Blom).

—— (1937) *Greatest Show on Earth* (London: G. Bell and Sons).

Double, Oliver (1997) *Stand-Up: On Being a Comedian* (London: Methuen).

—— (2005) *Getting the Joke* (London: Methuen).

Dromgoole, Nicholas (2007) *Performance Style and Gesture in Western Theatre* (London: Oberon Books).

Dryden, John (1811) *The Poetical Works of John Dryden*, vol. 2, ed. Warton, Joseph and Warton, John (London: Rivington).

Duranty, Louis-Edmond (1995) *Théâtre des Marionnettes – Répertoire Guignol du XIXe siècle* (Paris: Actes Sud).

Durwin, Joseph (2002) 'Coulrophobia and the Trickster', http://www.trinity.edu/org/tricksters/trixway/current/Vol%203/Vol3_1/Durwin.htm, date accessed 29 December 2011.

Eisenberg, Avner (c. 1980–2011) 'Exceptions to Gravity' (live one-man show).

—— (2005) 'Eccentric Principles', http://www.avnertheeccentric.com, date accessed 29 December 2011.

—— (2011) 'Interview with Christopher Lueck', 3 February 2011, www.clownsummit.com, date accessed 29 December 2011.

Evans, Mark (2006) *Jacques Copeau* (London: Routledge).

Feldberg, Robert (2010) 'Banana Shpeel is a Cirque du Soleil attempt at vaudeville', review of *Banana Shpeel* at The Beacon Theater, New York, *The Record*, 27 May 2010).

Feldman, Marty and Law, John (1966) *Class Sketch, The Frost Report*, 7 April 1966 (BBC).

Fellini, Federico (1970) *I Clowns* (Radiotelevisione italiana).

Findlater, Richard (1978) *Joe Grimaldi: His Life and Theatre* (Cambridge: CUP).

Fisher, John (2006) *Tommy Cooper – Always Leave Them Laughing* (London: Harper Collins).

Fleisher, Julian (1996) *The Drag Queens of York* (New York: Riverhead Books).

Franc-Nohain (1907) *Les mémoires de Footit et Chocolat* (Paris: Pierre Lafitte).

Franconi, Victor (1855) *Le cavalier, cour d'équitation pratique* (Paris: Michel Lévy).

Fratellini, Albert (1955) *Nous, Les Fratellini* (Paris: Éditions Bernard Grasset).

Fratellini, Annie (1989) *Destin de clown* (Lyon: Éditions La Manufacture).

—— (1997) 'L'enfant de la balle qui fit école', *L'Humanité*, 1 July 1997.

Fratellini, Valérie (2002) 'Ça mange quoi, un clown? Soliloque d'une dinosaure', *Jeu: revue de théâtre* 104(3): 109–115, http://www.erudit.org/culture/jeu1060667/jeu1109687/26410ac.pdf, date accessed 29 December 2011.

Frediani, Aristodemo (Beby) (1930) *Mémoires d'un clown* (Paris: La Liberté).

Frichet, Henri (1889) *Le Cirque et les Forains* (Tours: Alfred Mame et Fils).

Frost, Anthony and Yarrow, Ralph (1990) *Improvisation in Drama* (London: Palgrave Macmillan).

Fumagalli (2011) *Le Miel et la reine des abeilles* ('The Honey and the Queen Bee'), http://www.youtube.com/watch?v=YTBhsv4rA6o, date accessed 29 December 2011.

Gardner, Lyn (2009) 'Review of *Le Cirque Invisible* at the Queen Elizabeth Hall, London', *The Guardian*, 5 August 2009, http://www.guardian.co.uk/stage/2009/aug/05/le-cirque-invisible-review, date accessed 29 December 2011.

Gaulier, Philippe (2007a) *Le gégéneur/The Tormentor* (Paris: Éditions Filmiko).

—— (2007b) 'The King of My School', http://www.ecolephilippegaulier.com, date accessed 29 December 2011.

von Geldern, James and Stites, Richard (eds) (1995) *Mass Culture in Soviet Russia* (Indiana: Indiana University Press).

Gehring, Wes D. (1990) *Laurel & Hardy: A Bio-Bibliography* (Westport: Greenwood Publishing Group).

Gervais, Ricky (2006) *Ricky Gervais Meets . . . Larry David* (Channel 4).

Gervais, Ricky and Merchant, Stephen (2001–2003) *The Office* (BBC TV).

Gervais, Ricky, Merchant, Stephen and Davis, Warwick (2011) *Life's Too Short* (BBC TV).

Girolamo, Mercuriale (1569) *Arte Gymnastica Libri Sex* in Toole Scott, Robert (1958–1962) *Circus and Allied Arts: A World Bibliography* (Derby: Harpur & Sons).

Goffman, Erving (1990) *The Presentation of Self in Everyday Life* (London: Penguin).

Goncourt, Edmond and Jules de (2005) *Journal des Goncourt*, vol. 1: 1851–1857 (Paris: H. Champion).

Gordon, Mel (1983) *Lazzi* (New York: Performing Arts Journal Publications).

Goudard, Philippe (2005) *Anatomie d'un clown/Lire et Écrire le cirque* (Vic-la-Gardiole: L'Entretemps éditions).

Grantham, Barry (2000) *Playing Commedia – A Training Guide to Commedia Techniques* (London: Nick Hern Books).

—— (2006) *Commedia Plays – Scenarios, Scripts, Lazzi* (London: Nick Hern Books).

Grock (1931) *Life's a Lark* (London: William Heinemann Ltd).

—— (1957) *King of Clowns* (London: Methuen).

Halperson, Joseph (1926) *Das Buch von Zirkus* (Düsseldorf: Lintz A.-G.).

Hanna, William and Barbera, Joseph (1954) *Hic-Cup Pup* (Metro-Goldwyn-Meyer).

Harris, Paul (1996) *The Pantomime Book: The Only Known Collection of Pantomime Jokes and Sketches in Captivity* (London: Peter Owen).

Hawkins, Frederick W. (1869) *The Life of Edmund Kean*, vol. 2 (London: Tinsley Brothers).

Helm, Alex (1971) *Eight Mummers' Plays* (London: Ginn).

Henderson, Jan (2008) 'Philosophy of Clown', http://foolmoon.org/clownAndMask/clownPhilosophy, date accessed 29 December 2011.

Hicks, Bill (1989) 'What You Reading For?', *Sane Man* (Sacred Cow Productions).

Hornback, Robert (2009) *The English Clown Tradition From The Middle Ages To Shakespeare* (Woodbridge: D.S. Brewer).

Huizinga, Johan (1970) *Homo Ludens; a Study of the Play Element in Culture* (London: Paladin).

Hutter,   Gardi   (1981)   *Joan   of   ArPpo,*   http://www.youtube.com/watch?v= ZPdFJYK6fYY, date accessed 29 December 2011.

Jando, Dominique (2008) *The Circus: 1870–1950* (London: Taschen).

———— (2009) 'Behind the Scenes at the Circus', talk and panel discussion at the Baltimore Museum of Art, 31 March 2009, http://www.youtube.com/watch?v= 5FWPoqIp-bc&list= FLpcMgxiezNCvTR46FUxh46A&index= 29&feature= plpp_ video, date accessed 29 December 2011.

Jané, Jordi (1996) *Charlie Rivel* (Barcelona: Generalitat de Catalunya).

Jané, Jordi and Minguet, Joan M. (eds) (1998) *Sebastià Gasch, El Gust pel Circ* (Tarragona: El Medol).

Jara, Jesús (2004) *El Clown, un navegante de las emociones* (Sevilla: Proexdra).

Jigalov, Andrei and Csaba, Albert (2009) *The Sweets,* http://video.mail.ru/mail/baks-show/Jigalov/345.html, date accessed 29 December 2011.

Johnson, Bruce 'Charlie' (1993) *The Tramp Tradition* (Kenmore: Charlie's Creative Comedy).

———— (2000) 'Early Female Clowns', *The Clown In Times* 6(3).

———— (2010) 'History and Philosophy', *Clowning Around*, March/April 2010 (World Clown Association).

————   (2011)   'Historical   Asian   Clown   Characters',   http://www. charliethejugglingclown.com/asian.htm, date accessed 29 December 2011.

Johnston, Chris (2006) *The Improvisation Game* (London: Hern Books).

Jonson, Ben (1641) *Discoveries Made Upon Men and Matter,* ed. Schelling, F. E. (1892) (Bosotn: Ginn).

Kapoor, Raj (1970) *Meera Naam Joker* ('My Name is Joker') (R. K. Films).

Karandash (1987) *Karandash* (Moscow: Москва искусство).

Kaufman, Andy (1980) Appearance on *The Letterman Show,* 24 June 1980 (NBC).

Keaton, Buster (1920) *Neighbors* (Metro Pictures).

———— (1927) *College* (United Artists).

Kelly, Emmet and Kelly, Beverly (1996) *Clown* (New York: Buccaneer Books).

Kemp, Barry (1979) 'Bobby's Big Break', *Taxi* Season 1, Episode 18 (Paramount Television).

Kendrick, Lynne (2011) 'A Paidic Aesthetic: An Analysis of Games in Philippe Gaulier's Ludic Pedagogy', *Theatre, Dance and Performance Training* 2(1): 72–85 (London: Routledge).

Kerr, Walter (1975) *The Silent Clowns* (New York: Alfred A Knopf).

Koller, Donna and Gryski, Camilla (2008) 'The Life Threatened Child and the Life Enhancing Clown: Towards a Model of Therapeutic Clowning', *Evidence-Based Complementary and Alternative Medicine* 5(1): 17–25, http://www.hindawi.com/journals/ecam/2008/949505/cta/, date accessed 29 December 2011.

Kramer, Mimi (1998) 'Hot Ticket to Nowhere', *The New Yorker,* 21 November 1998.

Lane, Lupino (1945) *How to become a Comedian* (London: Frederick Muller).

Langdon, Harry (1924) *All Night Long* (Mack Sennett-Pathé).

———— (1925) *Boobs in the Wood* (Mack Sennett-Pathé).

———— (1926a) *Tramp, Tramp, Tramp* (First National Pictures).

———— (1926b) *The Strong Man* (First National Pictures).

———— (1927a) *Long Pants* (First National Pictures).

———— (1927b) *Three's a Crowd* (Harry Langdon Corporation).

Laurel, Stan and Hardy, Ollie (1929) *Unaccustomed As We Are* (Metro-Goldwyn-Meyer).

Lea, Kathleen Marguerite (1934) *Italian Popular Comedy Vol. 2: A Study in the Commedia dell'Arte, 1560–1620, with Special Reference to the English Stage* (Oxford: Clarendon Press).

Le Roux, Hughes (1890) *Acrobats and Mountebanks*, trans. Morton, A. P. (London: Chapman and Hall).

Levine, Josh (2010) *Pretty, Pretty, Pretty Good – Larry David and the Making of Seinfeld and Curb Your Enthusiasm* (Toronto: ECW Press).

Lily, Peta (2011) 'The Dark Clown – In pursuit of a different kind of laughter' (unpublished article).

Little, Kenneth (1981) 'Clown Performance in the European One Ring Circus', *Culture* 1(2): 67–72.

—— (1991) 'The Rhetoric of Romance and the Simulation of Tradition in Circus Clown Performance', *Semiotica* 85(3/4): 227–255.

—— (1993) 'Masochism, Spectacle, and the "Broken Mirror" Clown Entree: A Note on the Anthropology of Performance in Postmodern Culture', *Cultural Anthropology* 8(1): 117–129.

—— (2003) 'Pitu's Doubt: Entrée Clown Self-Fashioning in the Circus Tradition', in *Popular Theater*, ed. Schechter, Joel (London: Routledge), originally published in *The Drama Review* 112(1986): 182–186.

Louvish, Simon (2001) *Stan and Ollie: The Roots of Comedy* (London: Faber and Faber).

—— (2003) *Keystone – The Life and Clowns of Mack Sennett* (London: Faber and Faber).

Lowie, R. H. (1909) 'The Hero-Trickster Discussion', *Journal of American Folklore* 22: 431–432.

Makarius, Laura Levi (1974) *Le sacré et la violation des interdits* (Paris: Éditions Payot).

Mamet, David (1998) *True or False: Heresy and Common Sense for the Actor* (London: Faber and Faber).

Margueritte, Paul (1886) *Pierrot, Assassin of His Wife* in Gerould, Daniel (1979) 'Paul Margueritte and *Pierrot Assassin of His Wife*', *The Drama Review* XXIII (March): 103–119.

Mariel, Pierre (1923) *Histoire de trois clowns* (Paris: Société Anonyme d'Éditions).

Martin, Steve (2007) *Born Standing Up: A Comic's Life* (London: Pocket Books).

Marx, Harpo (1959) Appearance with Milton Berle on *The Kraft Music Hall*, 14 January 1959.

Marx Brothers, The Four (1933) *Duck Soup* (Paramount Productions Inc.) in (1972) *Monkey Business and Duck Soup* (New York: Simon and Schuster).

—— (1962) *Harpo Speaks!* (New York: Limelight Editions).

Mass, Vladimir (1930) 'Makhno's Men', in *Mass Culture in Soviet Russia*, ed. von Geldern, James and Stites, Richard (Indiana: Indiana University Press), 139–141.

McKerrow, R. B. (1910) *The Works of Thomas Nashe*, 3 vols. (London: Sidgwick & Jackson).

McKinven, John A. (1998) *The Hanlon Brothers* (Illinois: David Meyer Magic Books).

McManus, Donald (2003) *No Kidding!: Clown as Protagonist in Twentieth-Century Theater* (Newark: Delaware).

Meisner, Sanford (1987) *On Acting* (New York: Vintage Books).

Melville, Jean-Pierre (1946) *24 Heures de la vie d'un clown* ('24 Hours in the Life of a Clown') (Melville Productions).

Mendoza, Rubén (2010) *La Sociedad del Semáforo* ('Traffic-Light Society') (DíaFragma, Fábrica de Películas).

Metcalf, C. W. and Felible, Roma (1992) *Lighten Up – Survival Skills for People Under Pressure* (Massachusetts: Addison-Wesley).

Milazzo, Franco (2010) Review of *Le Cirque Invisible* at the Queen Elizabeth Hall, London, in *Londonist*, 10 August 2010, http://londonist.com/2010/08/circus_review_cirque_invisible_quee.php, date accessed 29 December 2011.

Monkhouse, Bob (1993) *Crying with Laughter* (London: Century).

—— (1998) *Over the Limit* (London: Century).

Moshaeva, Ekaterina (Antoschka) (2006) *World Parliament of Clowns*, http://worldparliament.org, date accessed 29 December 2011.

—— (2011) Interview by telephone, 20 August 2011.

Murray, D. L. (1930) *Candles and Crinolines* (London: Cape).

Murray, Simon (2002) ' "Tout Bouge": Jacques Lecoq, Modern Mime and The Zero Body: A Pedagogy for the Creative Actor', in *Jacques Lecoq and the British Theatre*, ed. Chamberlain, Franc and Yarrow, Ralph (Oxford: Routledge), 17–44.

—— (2003) *Jacques Lecoq* (London: Routledge).

Musson, Clettus (2003) *World's Best Clown Gags* (New York: D. Robbins and Co).

Nachmanovitch, Stephen (1990) *Free Play: Improvisation in Life and Art* (New York: Tarcher/Penguin).

Northbrooke, John (1577) *Treatise against Dicing, Dancing, Plays and Interludes* in Shakespeare Society (1843) *Early Treatises on the Stage* (London: Shakespeare Society), p. xvi.

Nose to Nose (2011) http://www.nosetonose.info, date accessed 29 December 2011.

Opie, Iona and Opie, Peter (1969) *Children's Games in Street and Playground* (Oxford: Oxford University Press).

Page, Patrick (1997) *150 Comedy Props* (London: Patrick Page).

—— (2005) *Book of Visual Comedy* (London: Patrick Page).

Pallapupas (2011) F.A.Q., http://www.pallapupas.org/es/pallapupas/faq.html, date accessed 29 December 2011.

Paret, Pierre (1959) 'Entrée de Grock', in *Le Cirque dans l'Univers* #34 (Club du Cirque), trans. Towsen, John (1978) *Mask, Mime & Marionette* I(1), Spring: 25–39 (New York).

Parson, Elsie Clews (1923) 'The Hopi Wöwöchim Ceremony in 1920', *American Anthropologist* 25: 156–187.

Partido del Trabajo de México (2009) *Party Political Broadcast*, http://www.youtube.com/watch?v=qZq9qBqT9Qk&NR=1, date accessed 29 December 2011.

Patkin, Max and Hochman, Stan (1994) *The Clown Prince of Baseball* (Texas: WSR).

Peacock, Louise (2009) *Serious Play – Modern Clown Performance* (Bristol: Intellect).

Pelling, Kate (2009) *Boo!*, http://www.katepelling.com/Equivocate/BOO.html, date accessed 29 December 2011.

—— (2011) Interview in London, 16 August 2011.

Perrodil, Edouard de (1889) *Monsieur Clown* (Paris: C. Dalou).

Petit, Lenard (2011) 'Clown Workshop for Actors', http://www.michaelchekhovactingstudio.com/clowning.htm, date accessed 29 December 2011.

Pierron, Agnès (2003) *Dictionnaire de la langue du cirque* (Paris: Editions Stock).

Pluvinel Antoine de (circa 1630) *L'instruction du Roy en l'art de monter à cheval* (Amsterdam: Jean Schipper).

Poliakoff, Nicolai (1941) *Coco the Clown: By Himself* (London: Dent and Sons Ltd).

Polunin, Slava (2001) Interview with Natalia Kazmina, trans. Delvaux, Julie, http://www.loscuadernosdejulia.com/2008/11/slava-polunin-monologue-of-clown-1.html, date accessed 29 December 2011.

—— (2011) Interview with Alexander Kan, Arts Editor of the BBC's Russian Service, 22 December 2011, BBC News online http://www.bbc.co.uk/news/entertainment-arts-16310653, date accessed 29 December 2011.

Popov, Oleg (1970) *Russian Clown* (London: Macdonald).

Ramsden, Hilary (2011) Interview by telephone, 16 December 2011.

Rémy, Tristan (1945) *Les Clowns* (Paris: Grasset).

—— (1954) *Jean-Gaspard Deburau* (Paris: L'Arche).

—— (1956) *Oleg Popov* in *France URSS* (April 1956, no. 127).

—— (1962) *Entrées Clownesques* (Paris: L'Arche).

Rheuban, Joyce (1983) *Harry Langdon: The Comedian as Metteur-en-Scène* (London and Toronto: AUP).

Riehn, Wolfgang (2009) 'Shaping the Future Intelligently or with Stupidity?', World Parliament of Clowns panel discussion at the World Culture Forum, Dresden, http://www.wcf-dresden.com/index.php?ILNK= Tag_Clowns&iL= 2&GalId= 10&PHPSESSID= 323d908588741fb957daf4b1b1b1b987, date accessed 29 December 2011.

Rivel, Charlie with J. C. Lauritzen, trans. Hoare, Ursula (1973) *Poor Clown* (London: Michael Joseph).

Robbins, Norman (2002) *Slapstick and Sausages, the Evolution of British Pantomime* (Devon: Trapdoor Publishing).

Robinson-Holden, Joey (2011) Interview with the author, London, 15 August 2011.

Romanushko, Marga (2008) *Leonid Yengibarov: Clown Eyes of a Poet* (*клоун глазамипоэма*) (Moscow: Москва Гео).

Rumyantseva, N. M. (1989) *Clown and Time* (*Клоун и Время*) (Moscow: Москва искусство).

Salverson, Julie (2008) 'Clown, Opera, the Atomic Bomb and the Classroom', in *The Applied Theatre Reader*, ed. Prentki, Tim and Preston, Sheila (London: Routledge), 33–40.

Sand, Maurice (1860) *Masques et Bouffons* (Paris: Michel Lévy).

Sangor, Michel (1892) 'Les Hanlons-Lees', *La Plume*, no. 82, 15 September 1892.

Schechter, Joel (1985) *Durov's Pig* (New York: Theater Communications Group).

—— (1998) *The Congress of Clowns and Other Russian Circus Acts* (San Francisco: Kropotkin Club of San Francisco).

Scheck, Frank (2010) 'Clown Flop lacks a-Peel', review of *Banana Shpeel* at The Beacon Theater, New York in the *New York Post*, 22 May 2010.

Sedita, Scott (2006) *The Eight Characters of Comedy* (Los Angeles: Atides Publishing).

Serafimovich, Alexander (1935) *The Iron Flood* (New York: International Publishers).

Shadyac, Tom (1998) *Patch Adams* (Blue Wolf).

Shepherd, Simon and Wallis, Mick (2004) *Drama/Theatre/Performance* (London: Routledge).

Shepherd, Simon and Womack, Peter (1996) *English Drama: A Cultural* History (London: Blackwell).

Simon, Eli (2009) *The Art of Clowning* (New York: Palgrave Macmillan)

Slavsky, R. (1980) *Vitaly Lazarenko* (Moscow: Москва искусство).

Smith, Winifred (1916) *The Commedia dell'Arte: A Study in Italian Popular Comedy* (New York: Columbia University Press).

Stephen, Alexander M. (1936) *Hopi Journal*, 2 vols. (New York: Columbia University Press).

Stoddart, Helen (2000) *Rings of Desire: Circus History and Representation* (Manchester: Manchester University Press).

Stott, Andrew McConnell (2009) *The Pantomime Life of Joseph Grimaldi* (Edinburgh: Canongate Books).

Strehly, Georges (1900) *L'Acrobatie et les Acrobates* (Paris: Delagrave).

Sylvander, Beril (1984) 'Looking for Your Clown … and Finding Yourself', first published in 1984 in *Art et Therapie* and reproduced at http://www.nosetonose.info/articles/bertilarticle.htm, date accessed 29 December 2011.

Tarlton, Richard (1884) *Tarlton's Jests*, ed. Halliwell, James Orchard (1973) (New York: AMS Press).

Tati, Jacques (1953) *Les Vacances de Monsieur Hulot* (Specta Films).

—— (1959) *Mon Oncle* (Specta Films).

—— (1967) *Cours du soir* (Specta Films).

Taylor, Millie (2007) *British Pantomime Performance* (Bristol: Intellect Books).

Taylor, Paul (2011) 'Slava's Snowshow at The Royal Festival Hall, London', *The Independent*, 23 December 2011.

Thayer, Stuart (1997) *Traveling Showmen* (Detroit: Astley & Ricketts).

Thorpe, Ashley (2007) *The Role of the Chou ('Clown') In Traditional Chinese Drama: Comedy, Criticism, and Cosmology on the Chinese Stage* (Lewiston, N.Y.: Edwin Mellen Press).

Ticketmaster (2011) Comments on *Slava's Snowshow*, http://reviews.ticketmaster.co.uk, date accessed 29 December 2011.

Toothaker, Christopher (2011) 'Shhh! Mimes tackle traffic chaos in Venezuela' for Associated Press, 8 October 2011, http://www.guardian.co.uk/world/feedarticle/9886059, date accessed 29 December 2011.

Toulmin, Vanessa (2007) Interview on *Making History*, 10 April 2007, BBC Radio 4, http://www.bbc.co.uk/radio4/history/making_history/making_history_20070410.shtml, date accessed 29 December 2011.

Towsen, John (1976) *Clowns* (New York: Hawthorne).

—— (2011) *All Fall Down, the Craft and Art of Physical Comedy*, http://physicalcomedy.blogspot.com, date accessed 21 November 2011.

University of Haifa (2006) 'Medical Clowning Studies', http://newmedia-eng.haifa.ac.il/?p=887, date accessed 29 December 2011.

Valentin, Karl (1976) *Der Reparierte Scheinwerfer* (Munich: Deutscher Taschenbuch Verlag).

Vàzquez, Gerard (2006) *Uuuuh!* (Barcelona: Proa).

Wallett, William F. (1870) *The Public Life of W F Wallett, the Queen's Jester* (Kondon: Benrose and Sons).

Webber, Kimberley (1996) *Circus!: The Jandaschewsky Story* (Sydney: Powerhouse Publishing).

Welsford, Enid (1935) *The Fool: His Social and Literary History* (London: Faber and Faber).

Wiles, David (1987) *Shakespeare's Clown* (Cambridge: CUP).

—— (2003) *A Short History of Western Performance Space* (Cambridge: Cambridge University Press).

Winnicott, D. W. (1971) *Playing and Reality* (London: Penguin).

World Clown Association (2011) Clown Ministry Department, http://worldclown. com/?page_id=10075, date accessed 29 December 2011.

Wright, Barton (1994) *Clowns of the Hopi* (Arizona: Northland).

Wright, John (2006) *Why Is That So Funny?* (London: Nick Herne Books).

Yengibarov, Leonid (1963) *Путь на арену* ('The Path to the Arena') (Armenfilm).

Zaporah, Ruth (1995) *Action Theatre: The Improvisation of Presence* (Berkeley: North Atlantic Books).

Zola, Émile (1881) 'La Pantomime', *Le Naturalisme au Théâtre* (Paris: G. Charpentier).

Index